Andrew Levine is Senior Scholar at the Institute for Policy Studies (Washington DC), and Research Professor in Philosophy at the University of Maryland, College Park. He is author of many books, most recently *Rethinking Liberal Equality: From A "Utopian" Point of View* (1998), *Engaging Political Philosophy: Hobbes to Rawls* (Blackwell, 2001), *A Future for Marxism?* (2003), and *The American Ideology* (2004).

To Marcus Raskin,
who suggested the idea

Political Keywords

A Guide for Students, Activists,
and Everyone Else

Andrew Levine

Blackwell
Publishing

BLACKWELL PUBLISHING

350 Main Street, Malden, MA 02148-5020, USA
9600 Garsington Road, Oxford OX4 2DQ, UK
550 Swanston Street, Carlton, Victoria 3053, Australia

First published 2007 by Blackwell Publishing Ltd

1   2007

Library of Congress Cataloging-in-Publication Data

Levine, Andrew, 1944–
Political keywords : a guide for students, activists, and everyone else / Andrew Levine.
    p. cm.
    Includes bibliographical references.
    ISBN-13: 978-1-4051-5064-4 (hardcover : alk. paper)
    ISBN-10: 1-4051-5064-5 (hardcover : alk. paper)
    ISBN-13: 978-1-4051-5065-1 (pbk. : alk. paper)
    ISBN-10: 1-4051-5065-3 (pbk. : alk. paper)   1. Political science—Dictionaries.
  I. Title.

  JA61.L48 2007
  320.03—dc22

                                                                2006025792

A catalogue record for this title is available from the British Library.

Set in 9.75/14pt Bell Gothic
by Graphicraft Limited, Hong Kong
Printed and bound in Great Britain
by TJ International Ltd, Padstow, Cornwall

The publisher's policy is to use permanent paper from mills that operate a sustainable forestry policy, and which has been manufactured from pulp processed using acid-free and elementary chlorine-free practices. Furthermore, the publisher ensures that the text paper and cover board used have met acceptable environmental accreditation standards.

For further information on
Blackwell Publishing, visit our website:
www.blackwellpublishing.com

Contents

Introduction

Most political keywords suffer from vagueness and ambiguity. Many are also contested – in part because their use is itself political. This is why all of us some of the time, and some of us all of the time use these words in confused and misleading ways. The problem is exacerbated by the fact that governments frequently deploy them deceitfully and hypocritically. It is made even worse when those who slavishly serve power – in the media, the schools and elsewhere – abet their government's deceits and hypocrisies. The predictable result is that political life is degraded – with consequences that are, at best, disabling, at worst, devastating. This is why efforts to explain and clarify the words that shape our political culture are always timely. However, at no point in recent history has the need been more acute. In the past quarter century, the political landscape has changed profoundly in ways that put formerly secure understandings in jeopardy. I believe that for politics generally, and for reflections on politics especially, these changes have been largely (but not entirely), for the worse. On the other hand, work in a number of academic disciplines in recent years has advanced understanding of politics and related areas of human activity – not dramatically, but nevertheless significantly. Unfortunately, these developments are not widely known even in academic circles. Thus to an unprecedented degree, there is lost knowledge to be recovered and new knowledge to be exposed.

To call this book *Political Keywords* is to imply that Raymond Williams' groundbreaking *Keywords* was a model for it.[1] It was, in part. But Williams' topic was "culture and society," not politics. His concerns were different too inasmuch as his focus was on the history or genealogy of the terms he discussed. The focus here is more analytical. I broach genealogical issues, but only insofar as doing so illuminates current usage. Investigating where current understandings came from can be an indispensable complement to philosophical analysis. But my aim is not to account for how political keywords came to have the meanings they do. It is to explain what they now mean.

Why these words rather than others?

Importance is one criterion; keywords are important words. But there is no uncontroversial way to measure importance, and therefore no good way to identify *the most important* words for inclusion. For the most part, therefore, it is not so much my sense of the comparative importance of the words I have chosen that guided my selection, but their pertinence to the project of restoring long-established and still timely understandings of political life that are at risk of becoming lost, and of spreading the word about new developments that ought to be more widely known than they presently are. Let me explain.

Restoring the old: the modern era was, in large part, a product of revolutionary upheavals – first in England, then in the Americas and France, and finally in Russia, China, Vietnam, Cuba and throughout the Third World. A widespread view nowadays is that after 1989, when the Berlin Wall fell, or after 1991, when the Soviet Union ceased to exist, this episode of human history has run its course. I am skeptical of this conclusion. But whether or not it is sound, there is no doubt that many of the basic understandings shaped by the revolutionary history of the last four centuries are at risk of becoming lost. For the Left, the consequences have been especially striking.[2] Remarkably, most people, including many who still identify with the Left, seem inclined to take these changes in their stride. Few lament the transformation of the framework within which politics has long been conceived; indeed, if they acknowledge this sea change at all, it is usually to applaud it. I believe instead that the constant and intensifying threat of devastating war, internal disorder and environmental catastrophe make the old understandings more, not less, timely. A prime consideration motivating the inclusion of entries in this volume was therefore my sense of the need to (re)familiarize readers with this cogent and still vital universe of discourse.

Spreading the word about the new: over the past quarter century, as political philosophy has become increasingly marginalized in our political culture, it and other academic disciplines have produced theoretical insights that people engaged in politics and in reflections on politics should find useful. Many of the entries in this volume were chosen with a view to making these developments accessible to a larger and more diverse audience than is presently the case.

There are also a few entries included mainly for the sake of their salience in current political affairs. The approach to many of the others is (partly) dictated by this consideration too. In general, I have tried to frame discussions in ways that are relevant to real world politics today.

There are many political words whose valence depends on when and where they are used. For example, it can matter whether someone is described as an *activist* or a *militant*, though these terms denote the same people. Or, among *activists/militants* who do more than occasionally protest, it can matter whether one is called a *patriot*, an *insurgent*, a *resistor*, a *rebel*, or a *revolutionary*; or, in an even more transparently rhetorical vein, whether one is called a *freedom fighter* or a *terrorist*. Charting the trajectories of these terms, and of many other political words, can be illuminating. But there is usually little of philosophical interest in what one is likely to find. Positive and pejorative connotations are therefore addressed here only insofar as they bear on issues of theoretical significance. Words like *activist* or *militant*, whose meanings are clear enough in context and whose (highly variable) rhetorical implications are philosophically inconsequential, are not discussed directly at all.

The entries

This volume comprises short essays on each of sixty-six keywords. It can be used as a dictionary inasmuch as the entries are freestanding and standard usages are treated as definitive wherever possible. But, unlike normal dictionaries, there is no pretense of reporting from a "neutral" or "objective" vantage point. In the political realm, that sort of perspective is generally elusive; where keywords are concerned, it is impossible. My accounts unashamedly reflect a certain view of political life. I accord the highest priority to the defining valuational commitments of the historical Left – liberty, equality, and "fraternity" (community); I believe that reports of socialism's demise are, to say the least, exaggerated; I support secularism and democracy; I am skeptical of nationalism and identity politics; I regard contemporary manifestations of imperialism as historical

Introduction

crimes; and (like many political philosophers several decades ago, but like very few today) I assume that the Marxist tradition remains overwhelmingly relevant for understanding political life. I also believe that the main theoretical advances of recent years have emanated mainly from sources whose political coloration is more liberal than socialist, and more mainstream than rebellious or "transgressive." The last of these convictions especially is not a majority view among academics who identify with the Left (or what they take to be its continuations) today. Some readers will find many of my contentions wrong-headed on this account. Others, whose views reflect more genuine affinities with the historical Left, will object to some of what I say on (still-lingering) sectarian grounds. They will find my occasional but unavoidable reflections on twentieth-century Communism too dismissive; or too forgiving. This is to be expected. I welcome such reactions; they show that our political culture is still alive. Were it possible consistently to explain and clarify political keywords in a way that pleases everyone, it would be a sure sign of an even-deeper malaise than the one that currently afflicts us.

Within the entries themselves, I seldom make direct reference to the literature that surrounds a keyword. I especially avoid contemporary sources. However, on occasion, I do refer to classics of Western political thought. Familiarity with this material can help orient readers. But it is not essential for grasping the main points.

I make extensive use of cross-referencing. My hope is that readers will follow the indicated leads. If they do, they will encounter a consistent perspective on political theory – developed through brief expositions of core concepts.

The entries are written, first of all, for general readers with no particular background in any of the academic disciplines that reflect on political life, and for students (undergraduate and graduate) making their way through these fields. They are also intended for political activists who, whether they know it or not, need to retrieve lost understandings and to assimilate new knowledge. Finally, because the positions set forth implicitly engage a number of ongoing controversies in political and social theory, this volume may also be of interest to specialists working in these fields.

Deliberately, in view of the volume's intended audiences, and inevitably, in view of the author's interests and experience, the entries assume a "First World" perspective, with particular emphasis on the United States. There is virtue in this necessity – if only because all politics is contextual. Nevertheless, First World and especially American readers should bear in mind the risks implicit in assuming this, or any other, vantage point. American imperialism menaces the entire world, not least the United States itself. But ironically, thanks to American hegemony, accounts that focus on American concerns can sometimes transcend the parochial limitations of a distinctively American point of view. Not always, however; and never entirely. I trust, even so, that readers encountering these keywords from different perspectives will find the ensuing discussions of them useful.

Each entry is followed by a list of other entries that are relevant to it, and by suggestions for *Further Reading*. There is also a Glossary at the end of the volume.

Suggestions for Further Reading: For the sake of accessibility, I have cited books, not journal articles, wherever possible; and I refer readers to editions currently in print. In a few cases, the same work is cited after more than one entry. Needless to say, each keyword is the subject of an enormous literature; the references indicated are in no way representative of the range or extent of it. My aim is only to lead readers to works that support claims made in the entries themselves and, in a few cases, to elaborate upon these contentions. To this end, I sometimes refer to writings of my own where the claims I make are developed at greater depth. I also comment briefly and in passing on some of the works cited. But the *Suggestions* are not rudimentary bibliographical essays. They are intended only to point readers to work they might instructively consult *next*. Often, this includes work with which I disagree.

Glossary. Unavoidably, the entries utilize terms of art in academic disciplines and other words that an informed general reader may need explained. Brief accounts of these terms are given in the Glossary. Where appropriate, some especially unfamiliar Glossary terms are also explained in the entries themselves. Most readers should be able to read some or all of the main entries without having to consult the Glossary at all.

Within each entry, the first use of terms referenced in the Glossary is indicated in **bold-face**. The same device is used in the Glossary itself, when Glossary entries reference other Glossary entries. When they reference entries on keywords, the first mention is indicated in SMALL CAPITAL letters. The Glossary entries do not provide exhaustive dictionary definitions – partly because they only address political uses of the terms in question. Exceptions are made only in rare instances where a word's non-political senses illuminate its political uses. Throughout the Glossary, as in the entries themselves, no attention is paid to whether a word is used as a noun, verb, adjective or adverb except, again in rare instances, where parts of speech affect shades of meaning.

Introduction

Notes

1 Raymond Williams, *Keywords: A Vocabulary of Culture and Society* (Oxford: Oxford University Press, 1985).

2 Thus Perry Anderson writes: "virtually the entire horizon of reference in which the generations of the sixties grew up has been wiped away – the landmarks of reformist and revolutionary socialism in equal measure. For most students, the roster of Bebel, Bernstein, Luxemburg, Kautsky, Jaurès, Lukács, Lenin, Trotsky, Gramsci have become names as remote as a list of Arian bishops." "Renewals," *New Left Review*, vol. 2, no. 1 (2000), p. 17.

Alienation

To *alienate* is to separate, to make foreign (or "other"). In late feudal and early modern Europe, law and custom restricted individuals' abilities to alienate (give away or sell) land, the principal means of production. Land that could not be alienated was *inalienable*. Towards the end of the seventeenth century, as rights claims were increasingly raised outside legal contexts, this usage carried over; thus some theorists – for example, John Locke (1632–704) – spoke of *inalienable rights*. Rights that are inalienable cannot be given up in a **social contract**. For this reason, *alienation* proved useful for articulating the defining liberal doctrine that sovereign power ought to be limited in principle. No one, not even a **sovereign**, can legitimately infringe an inalienable right.

The term also proved useful for giving theoretical expression to a certain sensibility that emerged as traditional social **solidarities** gave way to the **atomizing** social relations that the emerging capitalist organization of Europe brought into being. Leading *philosophes* of the French **Enlightenment** – most famously, Denis Diderot (1713–1784) – endeavored to articulate this condition. But the concept of alienation did not fully come into its own until the beginning of the nineteenth century, when the idea – and also the term – was taken up by German writers and poets and by post-**Kantian** German philosophers. By far the most important figure in shaping its contemporary meaning was G.W.F. Hegel (1770–1831). For Hegel, alienation was more than just a feeling or sensibility;

it was a state of being or, what came to the same thing in his philosophical system, a moment in the career of Spirit (*Geist*) in its movement towards self-awareness. Hegel's deeply **metaphysical** and highly idiosyncratic account of alienation found its way into political theory largely thanks to his dissident disciples, the so-called **Young** (or "Left") **Hegelians** of the late 1830s and early 1840s. Among them was Karl Marx (1818–1883). After Marx "settled accounts with his erstwhile philosophical conscience," as he put it in *The German Ideology* (1845), the Hegelian side of his thinking faded into the background. The term *alienation* never again appeared in his writings, though arguably the concept it designated remained a concern of his. However, in the mid-twentieth century, Marx's Young Hegelian writings assumed a special prominence in the work of anti-Stalinist Marxist philosophers. It is largely thanks to them that *alienation* is a key political concept today. In short order, the term was also taken up by both non-Marxist philosophers and social scientists. Today, it is a fixture of political discourse across the political spectrum. Contemporary understandings of the term typically have little to do with the metaphysical commitments that Marx and his fellow Young Hegelians developed in opposition to Hegel and his predecessors. Nevertheless, it is fair to say that current usage derives mainly from Marx's account.

That account is elaborated in the concluding section of the *Paris Manuscripts* (1844) where, for reasons that have mainly to do with the Young Hegelians' opposition to Hegel's **idealist ontology**, the root of alienation was held to be the worker's alienation from the product of his/her labor. The worker externalizes **essential** humanity onto an object of labor that then stands apart from him/her, as an estranged object. This core alienation then account for others – alienation from the labor process; from a consciousness of essential humanity ("species being" in Young Hegelian terminology) in oneself and others; and, finally, alienation from one's fellow workers. In Marx's view, as in Hegel's, alienation in its several senses is a metaphysical condition, not just a state of mind. But it does have experiential effects. It accounts for that sense of estrangement or otherness that the *philosophes* identified earlier and for an overall sense of the meaningless of work and, more generally, of life itself.

In the Hegelian and therefore Young Hegelian scheme, alienation is joined conceptually with a Kantian view of freedom. To be alienated is to be unfree or, more precisely, **heteronomously** determined (where heteronomy contrasts with **autonomy**). It is to be subject to the will of another. For reasons that Kant elaborated and that Hegel and his followers assumed, this is tantamount to saying that human beings, "ends in themselves" in Kant's account, become "means only" – in the thrall of the capitalist economic system. The obverse is also the case: what is ultimately only a **socially constructed** means, **capital**, becomes an end in itself. The economy rules us; not, as should be the case, the other way round. We are the slaves of our own creation. Today, the term is usually less metaphysically weighted, and its anti-capitalist implications are muted or excised. But the experiential aspect of Marx's account is retained. As was the case before Hegel, what the term nowadays suggests is a sense of estrangement from one's self and from other human beings, and of the meaninglessness of human endeavors. Marx sought to account for the psychological consequences of alienation by reference to the metaphysical condition he identified. This dimension of his reconstruction of the concept has proven less durable than the psychological side of his account, especially now that the development of an expressly Marxist anti-Stalinism is no longer an issue. But however the concept is understood, it is universally agreed that alienation is a condition and/or sensibility to combat.

Further Reading

French Enlightenment thinkers' treatments of the concept were mainly literary; the best known and most influential was Denis Diderot, *Rameau's Nephew* (London: Penguin, 1976; first published 1762). The entry on "alienation and estrangement" in Michael Inwood, *A Hegel Dictionary* (Oxford and Cambridge, MA: Blackwell Publishers, 1992) is a good place to turn for further elaboration of Hegel's use of the concept. Hegel's writings are notoriously difficult. For relatively accessible accounts of the larger context into which Hegel's concept fits, see Robert B. Pippin, *Hegel's Idealism: The Satisfactions of Self-Consciousness* (Cambridge: Cambridge University Press, 1989) and Charles Taylor, *Hegel and Modern Society* (Cambridge: Cambridge University Press, 1979). There are many collections of Marx's early writings that include the crucial *Economic and Philosophic Manuscripts*, the so-called *Paris Manuscripts* of 1844. See, for example, Eugene Kamenka (ed.), *The Portable Karl Marx* (London: Penguin, 1983) or Joseph O'Malley (ed.), *Marx: Early Political Writings* (Cambridge: Cambridge University Press, 1994). In the final decades of the twentieth century, academic interest in *alienation* waned along with a declining interest in Marx. In addition, setbacks to the broader labor movement jeopardized efforts to make work more meaningful and therefore less alienating. However, some of the studies produced decades ago remain timely. See, for example, Fritz Pappenheim, *The Alienation of Modern Man: An Interpretation Based on Marx and Tönnies* (New York: Monthly Review Press, 1964); Lewis Feuer, "What is Alienation? The Career of a Concept," *New Politics*, vol. 1, no. 3 (1962), pp. 116–34; and Istvan Meszaros, *Marx's Theory of Alienation* (London: Merlin Press, 1986). For more analytically focused studies, see, among others, Jon Elster, *An Introduction to Karl Marx* (Cambridge: Cambridge University Press, 1987), chapter 3; and Allen Wood, *Karl Marx* (London and Boston: Routledge and Kegan Paul, 1981), chapter 4. On the

Anarchism

connection between alienation and autonomy, see my *Engaging Political Philosophy: From Hobbes to Rawls* (Oxford and Malden, MA: Blackwell Publishers, 2002), chapter 6.

See also: CAPITALISM, FREEDOM/LIBERTY, LABOR, LEFT/RIGHT/CENTER, LEGITIMACY, LIBERALISM, MARXISM, RIGHTS, STALINISM

Anarchism

In ordinary speech, *anarchy* implies disorder or chaos, and *anarchists* are hooligans with a political veneer. *Anarchism*, then, is the ideology of anarchist practice. As with other stereotypes, there is a grain of truth in these descriptions, but only a grain. Some anarchists do advocate direct action that is provocative and violent. But there are also anarchists who are proponents of non-violence and who militate in thoroughly decorous ways. For more than a century, anarchists have thought of themselves as the most radical segment of the Left. Because this self-representation is generally correct, and because some anarchists very conspicuously do resort to violence, the word used to play the role that "terrorist" now does; it was used by ruling elites to scare the public. This usage has subsided in recent years, but it has not entirely disappeared. This is why anarchism remains a pole of attraction for persons with **progressive** and **secular** dispositions who are inclined towards symbolic forms of **rebellion**. However, most anarchists today are dedicated and peaceful militants, just as the vast majority of anarchists have always been.

Historically, *anarchism* was a philosophical concoction. Philosophers used the term long before the Left appropriated it, and therefore long before it entered into ordinary speech. For philosophers, *anarchism* is a (possible) position in a long-standing and ongoing debate about the legitimacy of political **authority**. Philosophical anarchism can take many forms. At its core, it is a negative doctrine; a claim about what cannot be done. In its most extreme version, philosophical anarchists maintain that political authority, the right to compel compliance through the use or threat of force, cannot be justified. Less extreme versions are directed only against the state form of political authority, not against political authority generally. Nowadays, this debate is largely confined to academic circles – because most anarchist militants are not interested in it and because most political philosophers are effectively apolitical. Nevertheless, there is some interaction between philosophical and political anarchism. It could hardly be otherwise inasmuch as political anarchists are generally reflective people and inasmuch as philosophical anarchists, being political philosophers, cannot entirely avoid reflecting on political arrangements. For the most part, though, the positive elaboration of institutional forms consistent with anarchist doctrine has fallen to the militants. For nearly two hundred years, they have conducted small-scale anarchist experiments in Europe, North America and elsewhere – with varying degrees of success. Perhaps the most important of these, in scope and longevity, are the Mondragon cooperatives in Spain.

One way to be a philosophical anarchist is to defend conditions that must be satisfied for political authority to be justified, and then to argue that no actual political institutions satisfy these conditions. A more radical way is to argue that no system of political authority can possibly satisfy defensible conditions. Defenders of these views should plainly be able to find common ground with political anarchists. If existing authorities are not or cannot be legitimate, then no one would be under any obligation to obey them. To be sure, individuals might sometimes or always find it in their interest to do what illegitimate authorities command. But their obedience would never be necessitated for reasons that transcend simple **prudence**. Therefore, anything goes – in the sense that no specifically political obligations constrain political behavior. The inference is sound, and it plainly has practical implications. That political and philosophical anarchism have gone separate ways to the extent that they have is therefore not theoretically necessitated. To explain it, one would have to turn instead to the sociological factors that shape anarchist politics and academic practice, respectively. A clear understanding might help to overcome the fissure that now exists. Then perhaps the ingenuity that philosophical anarchists expend on rebutting statist arguments and, more generally, claims for the defensibility of political authority could also be applied to the practical goal of elaborating institutional alternatives to existing ways of coordinating individuals' behaviors.

The separation of philosophical and political anarchism was not always as pronounced as it is today. Some of the major anarchist figures of the late nineteenth and early twentieth century – Mikhail Bakunin (1814–1876) and Prince Pëtr Kropotkin (1842–1921), among others – were, at once, political militants of the first order and penetrating thinkers. The strain of theory they produced engages the argument for states that Thomas Hobbes (1588–1679) pioneered. The connection is only implicit; neither Bakunin nor Kropotkin or any of the anarchist thinkers allied with them produced sustained discussions of Hobbes's work. But they did confront the kind of argument Hobbes produced, an argument that has become the basis for all subsequent justifications of coercive political institutions.

According to that argument, self-interested individuals find themselves unable to coordinate their activities in ways that accord with their interests, unless they are forced to do so by a power they all fear. Hobbes focused on security, but the problem he identified is more general. Many of the things people want, not just security, are obtainable in principle but inaccessible without **coercion** because individuals have insufficient incentives for producing these goods voluntarily. They want them, but not as much as they want others to contribute towards their production while they themselves **free ride**. Left to their own devices, then, rational individuals would withhold their contributions, and the good would not be produced. The only solution is to change the incentive structure by making the costs of free riding prohibitively high. Hobbesian statists maintain that there is only one way to do this: establish a common power that everyone fears enough to overcome free-riding preferences. They then identify that power with the state. The great anarchists avoided this conclusion by arguing that human beings are innately disposed to **cooperate** – that is, to defer from doing what is individually best in order to obtain a collective good. This is just what Hobbes and his followers deny. Anarchists would, of course, be obliged to concede that, in their depiction of real world men and women, Hobbesian statists are more right than they are. But they would maintain that cooperation is rare because it is quashed by the state itself, or by the state and the capitalist economic system it superintends. Remove these obstacles in the way of human freedom, the argument goes, and the natural disposition to cooperate will be expressed. In their view, the state is like an unnecessary but addictive drug. It does for people what they could have done as well or better for themselves before the addiction took hold, and without any loss of self-control. Like an addictive drug, the state enslaves us, even as it seduces us. Because this is an unhealthy situation, the need for a remedy is clear. Fortunately, one is at hand. Eliminate the source of the addiction and, after a period of (possibly turbulent) adjustment, people will be able to cooperate their way to realizing their ends.

This argument does not so much rebut the Hobbesian case for states as deny one of its premises, the claim that there is no natural disposition to cooperate. In this sense, anarchists and statists talk past one another. However, recent work at the intersection of evolutionary theory and the theory of games makes a case against Hobbesian statism directly – by accounting for the emergence of co-operative **norms**. It can be shown that, in certain contexts, cooperative strategies work better than non-cooperative strategies for winning games that are structurally similar to the situations individuals confront in their efforts to obtain the goods statists think can only be provided by states – provided that these games are played indefinitely many times. It therefore follows that if cooperative strategies emerge and become established within some subset of the general population, and if "players" interact repeatedly, those who cooperate will "win," thereby establishing cooperation as the norm – in much the way that randomly produced biological traits that enhance fitness will win out over those that do not, and therefore come to predominate in the biological populations in which they arise. Few proponents of this new departure in anarchist thinking believe that the state can be eliminated entirely. Their idea instead is just that much more of our behavior can be coordinated cooperatively than is generally supposed, and therefore that we can severely retract the realm of coerced coordination. If they are right, they will have defended something less than the full-scale anarchism of a Bakunin or a Kropotkin. But they do at least meet the statist argument head-on. In consequence of their work, it is now clear that even if we accept Hobbes's assumptions, cooperation is possible in many more aspects of our communal life than most people nowadays suppose. This is a foundation upon which to build. To date, however, this strain of anarchist thought is little known outside academic circles. Like more familiar forms of philosophical anarchism, it is almost entirely without real world political effects.

The Hobbesian argument is intended to justify the state form of political organization, the idea that all political power should be concentrated into a single institutional nexus. Strictly speaking, though, what it defends is political authority generally. Imaginable versions of philosophical anarchism could target the state only, leaving space for more diffused but still coercive institutional arrangements. Or the target could be political authority as such. In the modern world, some form of centralized administrative apparatus is indispensable, even if it operates in non-coercive ways. This is why Marx's collaborator Friedrich Engels (1820–1895), following the lead of the **utopian socialist** Pierre Proudhon (1809–1865), maintained that, in the end, "the governance of men" must give way to "the administration of things." Engels, along with other socialist and anarchist writers, left that idea unelaborated. There are, however, insights that can be gleaned from what he and others wrote. It would be well for defenders of cooperation at the societal level to take the indications they produced, along with the sparse but still revealing evidence provided by the (small-scale) anarchist experiments of the nineteenth and twentieth centuries, as points of departure for reflecting on the feasibility of anarchist or quasi-anarchist institutions.

Marxian communism and classical anarchism envision the same end: a co-operative society unburdened by public coercive mechanisms. The difference is in how they envision reaching that goal. For Marx and his followers, a radically democratized but still coercive state, a **proletarian** "class **dictatorship**" is indispensable for creating the conditions for the possibility of genuine statelessness. For anarchists, statelessness can only be achieved directly – by removing the burden of state power right away in order that a beneficent and self-sufficient human nature can be expressed. Given the current state of anarchist theory, it is impossible to determine definitively which side holds the more defensible view. It may even be, as most non-anarchists and non-Marxists believe, that there is no feasible way, as it were, to get from here to there. Anyone who finds merit in the common vision that sustained so many generations of Left militants cannot ignore these possibilities. At both a theoretical and practical level, there remains much work to be done.

Further Reading

On anarchism generally, see Daniel Guérin (Mary Klopper, trans.), *Anarchism: From Theory to Practice* (New York: Monthly Review Press, 1970) and George Woodcock, *Anarchism: A History of Libertarian Ideas and Movements* (Peterborough, ON: Broadview Press, 2004). For a concise and accessible account of philosophical anarchism, see Robert Paul Wolff, Jr., *In Defense of Anarchism* (Berkeley and Los Angeles: University of California Press, 1998). For a less radical, more libertarian, but more elaborated account of the issues philosophical anarchism engages, see A. John Simmons, *On the Edge of Anarchy: Locke, Consent and the Limits of Society* (Princeton, NJ: Princeton University Press, 1995). The writings of the great political anarchists are available in many editions, though some of the best collections are out of print. There are, however, new collections of key works by the two most important and philosophically penetrating of them: Peter Kropotkin, *Anarchism: A Collection of Revolutionary Writings* (Mineola, NY: Dover, 2002) and Sam Dolgoff (ed.), *Bakunin on Anarchism* (Montreal: Black Rose Press, 1980). Of particular interest to American readers will be Alexander Berkman, *What is Anarchism?* (Oakland, CA: AK Press, 2003) and Emma Goldman, *Anarchism and Other Essays* (Mineola, NY: Dover, 1969). As anarchism has become an increasingly marginal tendency on the Left, and as the Left itself has become increasingly marginalized, anarchist politics has all but dropped out of the purview of academic political philosophy. An important exception is David Schweickart, *After Capitalism* (Lanham, MD: Rowman and Littlefield, 2002). Schweickart provides insightful philosophical commentary on anarchist and quasi-anarchist real world experiments, with particular attention to Mondragon. Ironically, as interest in historical anarchism has declined, quasi-anarchist challenges to the Hobbesian case for states have flourished. A useful point of reference is Michael Taylor, *The Possibility of Cooperation* (Cambridge: Cambridge University Press, 1987). The findings that underlie this line of thought are set forth accessibly in Robert Axelrod, *The Evolution of Cooperation* (New York: Basic Books, 1984). The most sustained classical account of the Marxist case against anarchism (as a political program, not as an ultimate goal) is in Friedrich Engels, *Anti-Dühring: Herr Eugen Dühring's Revolution in Science* (New York: International Publishers, 1966), part 3, chapter 2.

See also: CAPITALISM, CLASS, COMMUNISM, COMMUNITY, IDEOLOGY, LEFT/RIGHT/CENTER, LEGITIMACY, MARXISM, PROGRESS, STATE, TERROR/TERRORISM, VIOLENCE/NON-VIOLENCE

C

Capitalism

The word *capitalism* is now used so widely that it is easy to forget that it is an invention of nineteenth-century social and economic theory, and easy to overlook how much of a breakthrough it was to identify an essential commonality in the array of heterogeneous economic practices and institutions we use the term to designate. It is also easy to ignore the Marxist pedigree of the concept behind the word, and Marxism's role in its adoption into contemporary political discourse.

By the end of the eighteenth century, a few prescient thinkers recognized that Western European societies were undergoing profound social and economic changes. But there was no agreement about how to conceptualize the relevant transformations. The efforts that led to the formation of the concept of capitalism can be seen, in retrospect, as interventions into this multifaceted discussion. The reality the term describes had already emerged by the fifteenth century in Italian city-states. Over the next few hundred years, capitalist institutions and practices grew, as Marx put it, "in the womb" of European feudalism, especially after the so-called Industrial Revolution began. But it was not until the middle of the nineteenth century that the term itself appeared in European languages. It first use is attributed to the English novelist William Makepeace Thackeray (1811–1863). In short order, it was taken up by the French socialist thinker Pierre-Joseph Proudhon (1809–1865), and then by Karl Marx (1818–1883) and his collaborator, Friedrich Engels (1820–1895). In the second half of the

16

nineteenth century, its currency grew. As the twentieth century dawned, the term was very nearly as widely used as it is today.

For Marx, the term denotes, in the first instance, an economic system, and only secondarily forms of civilization based on this type of economy. This understanding has been assumed from the outset by everyone who uses the word. Marx's principal concern, from the 1850s on, was to discover what he called "the laws of motion" of capitalist societies. These laws have mainly to do with the appropriation of **surplus value** – that is, with capitalists' **exploitation** of workers. But, despite what is often maintained, the processes Marx identified are not what defines capitalism for him. It is to his theory of history, historical materialism, that we must turn for a definition, rather than to Marx's economic analyses.

Historical materialism divides human history into discrete economic structures, distinguished by the forms of **property** they support. Capitalism is the penultimate structure. As such, its mission, as it were, is to create the material conditions that make communism, the final structure, and, more immediately, socialism, communism's first stage, possible. This capitalism does, once a certain level of economic surplus is attained, by facilitating a massive development of what Marx called **forces of material production**. To this end, the private ownership of other persons, a feature of all pre-capitalist economic structures, ends under capitalism; though, arguably, persons do own themselves in the sense that they have control and revenue rights over their own bodies and powers. Ownership of external things or, more exactly, of those things that count as productive resources, is in private hands. It is not until capitalism is superseded by socialism that this form of ownership is **deprivatized**.

Once the term and the idea behind it became established, there were influential writers, Max Weber (1864–1920) among them, who conceived capitalism's essential properties differently. For Weber, what distinguishes capitalism is less the forms of property it supports than the preeminence it accords to rational economic calculation. Capitalism, in Weber's view, renders methodical accumulation the supreme good of human life. Weber's characterization is not so much at odds with Marx's as orthogonal to it. Indeed, his account resonates with aspects of Marx's theory of alienation. But Weber's concern, and the concern of most of his successors in the sociological tradition, was not, like Marx's, to ascertain capitalism's place in the trajectory of human history, or to reflect on its role in making a qualitatively different and unequivocally better form of human life, communism, possible. Weber's aim instead was to understand capitalism's "spirit" and its implications for individuals' mentalities and societal practices.

Capitalism

In Marxist circles, it is customary to speak of "late" (as distinct from "classical") capitalism. Late capitalism is capitalism that has survived beyond the point where productive forces are sufficiently developed to permit its transcendence. The logic of late capitalism differs from that of the capitalism Marx investigated. When the conditions that make socialism possible already exist, but capitalism is still firmly entrenched, it is possible to prevent systemic crises by promoting **effective demand** – typically through wasteful military spending, and by fostering consumption through the inculcation of false needs. Thus, late capitalism suffers from irrationalities that its ancestor form did not. For all the evils classical capitalism engendered, immiseration and alienation among them, it was, for its time, a rational economic system in the sense that it was indispensable for developing productive forces in accord with compelling human needs. Marx insisted too that it was a stage humanity had to pass through on the way to communism. Late capitalism lacks these redeeming features. Paradoxically, though, its tenancy seems more secure than was that of its predecessor. Classical capitalism was often contested; late capitalism seldom is.

For most of the twentieth century, capitalism had few enthusiastic defenders. Its proponents defended it because they believed that the only feasible alternative to it was socialism, and because they thought that socialism would be even worse. It was not uncommon too for capitalism's defenders also grudgingly to accept the socialist argument that capitalism was ultimately doomed. However, with corporate **globalization** on the rise, along with **neo-liberalism**, its justifying theory, the situation has changed. Nowadays, capitalism has many enthusiasts, just as it did in the early nineteenth century. The first pro-capitalists never quite named the system they defended. Today's pro-capitalists do. But it is far from clear that they have anything to add to arguments that were long ago discredited, in both theory and practice. What sustains their prestige is just the apparent success of the system they defend, and the comparative weakness of the forces opposed to it. Should circumstances change as globalization's economic and social consequences become increasingly burdensome, one can be sure that the intellectual bankruptcy of capitalism's defenders will again be widely understood.

Further Reading

The main source for Marx's account of capitalism is, of course, his masterwork, *Capital* (Moscow: Progress Publishers, 1965). It consists of three massive volumes – the first published in 1867; the last two edited by Engels and published posthumously in 1893 and 1894, respectively. Weber's some-what different view is developed in Max Weber (Guenther Ross and Clauss Wittich, eds.) *Economy and Society*, 2 vols. (Berkeley and Los Angeles: University of California Press, 1978). There are many general accounts of Marxian and Weberian social and economic theory, and libraries full of more focused studies on aspects of their thought. However, there is nothing that focuses directly on similarities and differences between Marx's and Weber's conceptions of *capitalism*. Readers inter-ested in exploring this topic on their own would do well to turn to G.A. Cohen's seminal reconstruction of historical materialism, *Karl Marx's Theory of History: A Defence* (Oxford and Princeton: Oxford University Press and Princeton University Press, 1978), and to Jon Elster's overview of Weber's social theory in "Rationality, Economy and Society" in Stephen Turner (ed.), *The Cambridge Companion to Weber* (Cambridge: Cambridge University Press, 2000). Just as the literature on Marx and Weber is enormous, in recent years there have been many celebrations of modern capitalism. Still, the most cogent defenses of capitalism remain those written in the middle decades of the twentieth century, before the present period of capitalist triumphalism began. Two "classics" are Milton Friedman, *Capitalism and Freedom* (Chicago: University of Chicago Press, 2002), and Friedrich A. Hayek, *The Constitution of Liberty* (Chicago: University of Chicago Press, 1978).

See also: ALIENATION, COMMUNISM, HISTORICAL MATERIALISM, LABOR, MARXISM, REVOLUTION, RIGHTS, SOCIALISM

Civil religion

A *civil religion* is a common faith that binds the members of a society together. The word entered mainstream political discourse during the French Revolution, and its contemporary uses derive mainly from early twentieth-century social theory. However, the idea is of ancient lineage. Within the philosophical tradi-tion that runs from Plato (427?–347?BC) through Jean-Jacques Rousseau (1712–1778) and beyond, it is acknowledged that common myths and rituals are indispensable for communal well-being. There is also widespread recogni-tion of the fact that actual religions ill serve this purpose – especially when they compete with one another or when their representatives seek political influence. Thus, the idea emerged that there is a need for distinctively *civil* rituals and myths. Rousseau expressly formulated this thought in *The Social Contract* (1762). During the most radical phase of the French Revolution, Maximilien Robespierre (1758–1794) derived inspiration from this source in establishing a Cult of Reason. Emile Durkheim (1857–1917), whose *Elementary Forms of Religious Life* (1912) developed the modern sociological understanding of religion as the institutional nexus that holds societies together, also acknow-ledged a debt to Rousseau.

Civil religion

For Durkheim, a religion is a system of practices and beliefs, institutionally sustained, that recognizes a **categorical** distinction between the *sacred* and the *profane*. Within the sociological tradition Durkheim inaugurated, it is therefore not the content of beliefs or practices that constitute religions, but the fact that there are beliefs and practices that fit into these categorical divisions. The profane is the workaday world of ordinary life and the forms of being and acting associated with it. The sacred is a realm apart – not, of course, in a physical sense, but in the "collective consciousness" of the population. Durkheim claimed that the function of religion, so conceived, is to cement societies together, and that there is no other effective means for doing so. Thus, he inferred that societies must have religions, on pain of dissolution. He argued, inconclusively, that ethnographic and historical evidence supports this inference.

On Durkheim's account, religions need not be **theistic**. The aboriginal Australian religions that Durkheim studied in *The Elementary Forms* were pre-theistic in the sense that they had no notion of a God or gods, but only anticipations of these concepts. Without quite saying so expressly, Durkheim supposed that, in the **secular** societies of the modern era, theistic religions had already become largely disassociated from prevailing civil religions. They survive even so, but for extra-social (psychological) reasons.

For the just state of *The Social Contract*, Rousseau proposed a civil religion that was theistic, but neither Catholic nor Protestant nor anything else contentious (and therefore potentially disruptive). Modern social theorists, in line with Durkheim's **positivist** bent, are loathe to advocate anything directly, but they are prepared to countenance categorical distinctions between the sacred and profane, and myths and rituals built upon them, that are secular in content. Implicit in their view, and therefore in contemporary uses of the term, is the conviction that, in principle, a civil religion can dispense with the key elements of theistic religious forms.

No human society has reached this point yet, though the Communist countries tried. Even so, it is well to consider the civil religions of contemporary Western European countries and of Japan with this thought in mind. These countries still acknowledge the myths and practices of the religions that helped to shape their collective identities. Some of them even have established churches. But the social (as distinct from the psychological) meaning of these theistic expressions of religiosity is no longer what it was formerly. Their civil religions have little, if anything, to do with belief in God. Thanks to its religious diversity and its liberal origins, this is also true of the United States. But, despite the official separation of church and state that the founders of the American republic made constitutional, the American civil religion, to the extent it exists, does seem to have a more entrenched theistic component than is evident in other liberal democracies.

The Rousseauean–Durkheimean notion of civil religion has become part of the common sense of our time. Nevertheless, it is worth questioning both its descriptive and **normative** aspects. Like Rousseau, Durkheim assumed that well-integrated and largely homogeneous societies are the norm. The diverse, hetero-geneous societies of the United States, Canada, Australia and, increasingly, much of Western Europe belie this supposition. The United States, in particular, has long been less socially integrated than Durkheim's model, early-twentieth-century France, a fact that is often invoked to explain the comparative feeble-ness of American welfare state institutions. By the end of the twentieth century, however, most developed countries, including those with more developed welfare states, were, as noted, becoming increasingly like the United States. Whether or not this trend should be applauded is debatable. But even if Durkheim and his followers are right in thinking that a weak civil religion augers societal dissolution, it is far from clear that it is wise to try to *invent* shared understandings at the level of existing states. It is worth recalling that Robespierre's attempt turned out poorly, and that he didn't have to contend with the complications **ethnic** and racial heterogeneity introduce. Even if we accept that religion in Durkheim's sense is an inexorable fact of human collective exist-ence, it would be foolish to make a virtue of this necessity, especially in polit-ical communities comprised of many distinct and overlapping sub-communities. Relations of **solidarity** across ethnic and national lines offer more hope for establishing worthwhile communal values than any putative religion based on common citizenship. Many people nowadays assume reflexively that this prospect is dangerously **utopian**. But it is not far-fetched to expect that, in forg-ing new communal forms on solidaristic bases, what is estimable in the idea of a civil religion will reassert itself in a new, more decentralized way – as a by-product of collective existence in a freer and more egalitarian social order.

Further Reading

Rousseau's views on *civil religion* are concisely delivered in Book IV, chapter 8 of *The Social Contract*. See Jean-Jacques Rousseau (Victor Gourevitch, ed.), "*The Social Contract" and Other Later*

Political Writings (Cambridge: Cambridge University Press, 1997). A good recent account of Robespierre's relation to Rousseau and his appropriation of the concept of civil religion can be found in David P. Jordan, *The Revolutionary Career of Maximilien Robespierre* (Chicago: University of Chicago Press, 1989). On the social function of religion, see Emile Durkheim (Karen E. Fields, trans.), *Elementary Forms of Religious Life* (New York: Free Press, 1995). Durkheim reflects on his intellectual debt to Rousseau in Emile Durkheim, *Montesquieu and Rousseau: Forerunners of Sociology* (Ann Arbor, MI: University of Michigan Press, 1960). For a more contemporary perspective, see Robert N. Bellah and Phillip E. Hammond, *Varieties of Civil Religion* (New York: Harper, 1982). There is an enormous literature on Durkheimian and alternative understandings of social order and therefore, implicitly, civil religion. For an insightful and concise overview of the main positions, see Jon Elster, *The Cement of Society* (Cambridge: Cambridge University Press, 1989). For a perspective friendlier to the Durkheimian view, see the essays in Jeffrey Alexander (ed.), *Durkheimian Sociology: Cultural Studies* (Cambridge: Cambridge University Press, 1990). On the notion of a "common faith" and its political consequences, John Dewey's *A Common Faith* (New Haven, CT: Yale University Press, 1960) is an indispensable point of reference.

See also: COMMUNISM, DEMOCRACY, EQUALITY/EGALITARIANISM, FREEDOM/LIBERTY, IDENTITY POLITICS, INTERNATIONALISM, LEFT/RIGHT/CENTER, LIBERALISM, NATION/NATIONALISM, RACE/ RACISM, REVOLUTION, STATE, WELFARE/WELFARE STATE

Civil rights/civil liberties

In some contexts, *civil rights* designates roughly what **human rights** does. The difference is that, conceptually, civil rights are grounded in the positive laws of political communities, while human rights conceptually precede positive laws and therefore exist even when they are not legally implemented. Human rights are ascribed to persons just in consequence of membership in the human race; civil rights exist in consequence of membership in particular political communities. Similarly, *civil liberties* are basic freedoms authorized and protected by laws.

In the United States, these terms are often used in a narrower way. From the end of the Reconstruction period until the 1960s and beyond, the civil rights of former **slaves** and their descendants were denied by law in the South and in practice everywhere else in the United States. Thus, the struggles of African-American people and, by extension, of other persons of color, became a civil rights struggle – in both name and fact. Accordingly, African-American and other political movements for social and political inclusion came to be called "*civil rights* movements." This usage persists. In its narrowest sense, "civil rights movement" designates the constellation of political forces that struggled to end the legal and **de facto** segregation that blighted American politics after Reconstruction.

The term is also used to denote contemporary continuations of those struggles and, more generally, any organized political effort undertaken by systematically **oppressed** persons for full incorporation into the mainstream society.

Because the elimination of legal or customary impediments to full citizenship is necessary but not sufficient for genuine political equality to obtain, the term can also designate political struggles that look beyond the horizons of positive law – to fundamental institutional structures, including those that generate economic inequalities, and to norms and attitudes. In partial disregard of the original and strict meaning(s) of the term, the struggle for civil rights today can therefore be a way of designating struggles of oppressed groups, racial or otherwise, for full equality. It is sometimes said that, with the legal gains of the past several decades, the need for civil rights movements of this sort has passed. However, the continuing existence of oppression based on race and other ascriptive properties belies this conclusion.

In the United States, defenders of liberties specifically identified in the US constitution or in its canonical interpretations are commonly designated *civil libertarians,* particularly when their support for these liberties is undertaken mainly in judicial arenas. The liberties in question are, for the most part, those that many believe should be enjoyed by all human beings. American civil libertarians are also concerned to protect rights that are peculiar to the American constitutional regime – particular **due process** rights, for example, and the separation of church and state. Elsewhere in the world, persons concerned to defend these and similar rights also sometimes call themselves *civil libertarians.*

The liberties civil libertarians in the United States defend are, for the most part, similar to those that exist elsewhere. But their way of defending these rights is idiosyncratic. It is a curious feature of American political life, a consequence of America's historical origins and its Protestant culture, that the Constitution is regarded across the political spectrum as Holy Writ, awaiting literal implementation (for the Right) or liberal interpretation (for the Left). Instead of debating, say, the question of free speech directly, discussions of free speech in the United States typically take the form of commentaries on the First Amendment to the US Constitution. This attitude carries over to general defenses of liberty. This is why civil libertarianism in the United States, and in other countries influenced by the American model, is articulated in a constitutionalist idiom. In practice, this constraint is usually innocuous. But it would nevertheless seem wise, so far as possible, not to contribute to the prevailing fetishization of constitutionalist thinking, and instead to encourage public policy debates that proceed in a more direct fashion.

Just as the persistence of racism and the enduring legacy of slavery makes a civil rights movement, in the American sense, indispensable in the United States, even now that legal impediments to civil incorporation have been removed, the constant temptation of political elites to restrict liberties – made palpably evident in the United States during the so-called War on Terror – makes political mobilization around civil liberties as necessary as it ever has been. As the great abolitionist and civil libertarian Wendell Phillips (1811–1884) famously said "eternal vigilance is the price of liberty."

Further Reading

The literature on the civil rights movement in the United States is enormous, but accessible scholarly studies that provide a general overview are rare. An exception is Mark Newman, *The Civil Rights Movement* (Westport, CO: Praeger, 2004); another is Aldon D. Morris, *Origins of the Civil Rights Movement* (New York: Free Press, 1986). For judicial rulings concerning American constitutional protections for civil liberties, see Lucius J. Barker, Twiley Barker, Michael W. Combs, Kevin L. Lyles, H.W. Perry, *Civil Liberties and the Constitution: Cases and Commentaries*, 8th edition (Upper Saddle River, NJ: Prentice Hall, 1999).

See also: EQUALITY/EGALITARIANISM, FREEDOM/LIBERTY, FREEDOM OF EXPRESSION, LEFT/RIGHT/CENTER, RACE/RACISM, RIGHTS, STATE, TERROR/TERRORISM

Class

Throughout history, *class* divisions have existed in societies where productive capacities are sufficiently developed for people to live beyond subsistence levels. Individuals and (usually) households have occupied distinct spaces in hierarchically structured social orders. Class membership has profound and salient cultural effects. At the psychological level, it helps to shape persons' conceptions of themselves. Class also figures in the explanations of many social phenomena.

Theories of class fall into two broad categories: Marxist and Weberian. For Karl Marx (1818–1883) and those influenced by him, class membership is a consequence of individuals' relations to **means of production**. The idea, central to historical materialism, is that wherever an economic surplus exists, there is a struggle for its appropriation. The **property** relations peculiar to the **modes** of production in place determine the parties to that struggle. Property relations are decomposable into rights to benefit from and to control productive assets. If societies are viewed statically (at discrete moments), these rights determine class structures. Viewed dynamically (over time), the explanatory import of class is even greater. Wherever there are classes, there is class struggle. The course of history is in part shaped by these struggles; indeed, in *The Communist Manifesto* (1848), Marx and Friedrich Engels (1820–1895) famously proclaimed that human history just is the history of class struggles. Alternatively, class divisions can be conceived independently of claims about history's structure and direction. Following the lead of Max Weber (1864–1920), classes can be thought of as status divisions only. On some accounts, income and wealth are proxies for status; for others, gradations of income and wealth constitute relevant status divisions in their own right. For Marx and his followers, in capitalist societies, the relevant classes are capitalists and workers (and various intermediate positions), along with vestiges of the classes distinctive of superseded modes of production. On Weberian conceptions, the relevant differences are those of rich and poor. Thus we have upper, lower and middle classes – along with pertinent sub-divisions, especially of the so-called middle class. In both ordinary and academic discussions, *class* is often used loosely – in ways that straddle these distinct conceptions.

From the Marxist perspective, capitalist societies sustain class divisions specific to capitalist property relations. In Europe, these divisions were superimposed on class structures derived from earlier social formations. Thus, in addition to capitalists and workers, there were also **aristocrats** and, of course, **peasants**. Where European colonists established capitalist societies in the Americas and in Australasia, these older social divisions were generally not reproduced (though, of course, vestiges of them lingered in peoples' minds and, to some degree, in their social interactions). Inasmuch as native populations, when not literally decimated, were unfailingly subordinated, social divisions characteristic of their societies never took their place. This is why, in the United States, class divisions proper to capitalism prevail almost exclusively.

Class distinctions everywhere interact with systematic differences based on **gender**. In most New World **postcolonial** societies, they also interact with divisions arising out of the social, political, and psychological legacies of **slavery**, and the racially weighted politics that followed slavery's abolition. The American case is illustrative. Slavery was pervasive in the American South during the early decades of the republic. Being property, slaves had no rights to own external things or to control or benefit from their own powers. They nevertheless comprised a class (of servants and direct producers), dominated by masters. The class system slavery sustained was ultimately inimical to capitalism. Therefore the two could not long survive together; a condition that ultimately led to Civil War in the United States and everywhere to slavery's demise. Once slavery ended, former slaves and their descendants were incorporated into the expanding capitalist order. But slavery's cultural and economic effects continued to resonate. In the post-Civil War period, these effects were sometimes deliberately, sometimes implicitly, reinforced by social and political elites. Class relations in the United States have been profoundly affected – to the point that awareness of racial differences has often superseded **consciousness** of class.

It is sometimes said that, in contrast to most of the rest of the world, class divisions do not matter in the United States. From a cultural point of view, this is a plausible contention. Arguably, there is comparatively little class consciousness, at least at the lower rungs of American society. From an analytical point of view, however, American society is as class divided as any other. The perception that class is of only minimal importance in the United States is epitomized in the notion of the "American dream," according to which anyone, native born or foreign, can rise to the top of the class structure regardless of social background. For descendants of slaves, native or immigrant Spanish-speaking populations, and other **oppressed** groups (including native Americans) that dream is notoriously elusive. But it is true that American society has been unusually welcoming of European immigrants. Within a generation or two, many immigrant communities have become fully assimilated. Nevertheless, the idea that there is more class mobility in the United States than in other developed capitalist countries is largely a myth. Because there are no vestiges of **feudal** social structures in the United States, social origin probably does count for less in the overall status hierarchy than it does in many European or Asian societies. But the class into which one is born is as important a determinant of where in the class structure one is likely to end up in the United States as anywhere else.

Where distinctively Marxist understandings of class give way to status-based conceptions, and where class consciousness is muted, it is natural to depict class oppression as only one form of subordination among many. Thus, in the United States, race, gender and class are often grouped together as co-equal sites of oppression – as evils to be removed, rather than defining features of economic or social structures. Classical Marxists were inclined to focus exclusively on class divisions. Today, however, it is universally acknowledged that racial and

gender oppression, like oppressions based on sexual preference or physical disabilities, are irreducible to oppression based on class – though, of course, they
intersect. But class is not on a par with the rest. In contrast to the others, class
divisions play a pivotal structuring role in accounting for the nature of social
orders, and class struggle governs the prospects for their transformation.

Further Reading

The literature on class and, more generally, on social stratification is enormous. However, because
most of this work is empirically focused, it is often difficult to tease out conceptions of class. For
an account of the general contours of the concept, Ralph Dahrendorf's *Class and Class Conflict in
Industrial Society* (Stanford, CA.: Stanford University Press, 1959) remains unsurpassed. Another
venerable point of reference is Anthony Giddens, *The Class Structure of Advanced Societies* (New
York: Harper and Row, 1979). Giddens' conceptual orientation is largely Weberian. A Marxist position is elaborated in Erik Olin Wright, *Classes* (London: Verso, 1985). Wright's reconstruction of
the Marxist position is debated in Erik Olin Wright et al., *The Debate on Classes* (London: Verso,
1989). On questions pertaining, among other things, to class mobility and class/gender interactions,
as conceived within this conceptual framework, see Erik Olin Wright, *Class Counts: Comparative
Studies in Class Analysis* (Cambridge: Cambridge University Press, 1997). On the subtle connections between racial and class oppressions in the United States, see Ira Katznelson, *When Affirmative Action Was White: An Untold History of Racial Inequality in Twentieth Century America* (New
York: W.W. Norton and Company, 2005). As remarked, it has become unfortunately commonplace
in academic circles to deny the central role that classical social theory, Marxist or Weberian, accords
to class divisions – even by those who continue to acknowledge the explanatory importance of class
oppression. A representative collection of writings in this vein is Margaret L. Andersen, Patricia
Hill Collins, *Race, Class and Gender: An Anthology* (Santa Rosa, CA: Wordsworth, 2003).

See also: CAPITALISM, CULTURE, HISTORICAL MATERIALISM, MARXISM, RACE/RACISM, RIGHTS

Communism

The word *communism* has been in use since the 1840s, when it was taken up
by radical socialists intent on emphasizing a commitment to equality and social
solidarity. It entered into the general political lexicon with the publication by
Karl Marx (1818–1883) and Friedrich Engels (1820–1895) of *The Communist
Manifesto* (1848). In the decades that followed, the term became increasingly
associated with Marx and his followers, though non-Marxist socialists used it too.
After the publication of *The Communist Manifesto*, *communism*, not *socialism*,

Communism

was the name Marxists commonly used to designate what they aimed ultimately to establish. By the end of the 1850s, this usage was underwritten by Marx's theory of history, historical materialism, where *communism* designates the final economic structure, the one that will usher in a realm of freedom.

Marx and his followers had little to say about what they thought communism would be like. Marx insisted that its institutional forms could not be specified in advance, but instead had to emerge in the course of their (democratic) construction. Once the reign of **capital** ends, communism, Marx maintained, will be a work in progress. But even if he was opposed in principle to specifying communism's institutional forms, he did set out a few general indications. In his view, under communism, there is no private ownership of productive assets; instead, all resources employed in generating wealth are socially owned. Marx also maintained that because communism presupposes material **abundance**, questions of distributive justice would lose their urgency. It would no more matter who owns what or how much they own than it matters to us now how much air people breathe. For this reason too, there would be no struggle for the control of productive resources or for the surplus wealth they generate. Communist societies would therefore be free of class divisions. More generally, they would be without systematic social divisions of any kind. Because they are classless, and because the state, in Marx's view, is ultimately the means through which ruling classes **coercively** sustain their domination of subordinate classes, communist societies would also be stateless. Under communism, "the administration of things" would replace "the governance of men." Communism also makes human emancipation real; it is a world in which, as *The Communist Manifesto* proclaimed, "the condition for the free development of each . . . [is] the free development of all." Finally, as Marx wrote in *The Critique of the Gotha Program* (1875), under full-fledged communism, there would no longer be differential remunerative rewards for productive contributions, as there would still be under socialism, communism's initial (and therefore transitional) stage. The reigning distributional principle would be "from each according to ability, to each according to need."

In Marx's early writings, especially *The German Ideology* (1845), communism is described in **utopian** ways. For reasons that derive from his **philosophical anthropology**, Marx maintained that, under communism, individuals would be free to develop all of their potentialities; that they would, as he famously said, "hunt in the morning, fish in the afternoon, and **criticize** at night," without becoming hunters, fishermen or "critical critics." For bucolic and contemplative pursuits, this might be a feasible picture. But, in general, given limited time and the fact that most potentialities require long and painstaking effort to actualize, Marx's vision of polymorphous human self-actualization cannot be maintained. No matter how free people might become from the domination of capital, it is unlikely that very many individuals would be able, say, to play the piano (at a professional level) in the morning, perform surgery in the afternoon, and solve complicated mathematical problems at night.

In the aftermath of the Paris Commune (1871), *communist* came to designate the revolutionary side of the socialist movement. As Social Democrats became increasingly integrated into the political systems of their various countries, they therefore refrained from adopting the designation. Still, it was only after the majority of Social Democratic parties voted to support their respective governments in World War I that a hard distinction between socialism and communism came into general use. In 1918, the "Russian Social Democratic Labor Party," dominated by **Bolsheviks**, changed its name to the "All-Russian Communist Party (Bolshevik)." Then, with the founding in 1919 of the Third International, under **de facto** Russian leadership, formerly Social Democrat parties that placed themselves under the leadership of the Russian party assumed the name *Communist*. Modern usage follows from this name change.

From 1919 on, (capital-C) *Communist* in its narrowest sense referred to political parties or movements aligned with the Soviet Union. In a slightly broader sense, the term referred to all political groupings that identified with Bolshevism, in contrast to other socialist currents, especially Social Democracy. In this broader sense, Trotskyists and Maoists are Communists. In the latter half of the twentieth century, in order to distinguish themselves from official Communists, Trotskyists typically modified *Communism* with the adjective "revolutionary." For a similar reason, Maoists identified themselves as "Marxist Leninists." In each case, the contention was that their Communism was the authentic version. But Trotskyists, Maoists, and others who identified with Bolshevism were of one mind with official Communists in distinguishing their own political orientation from that of post-World War I Social Democracy.

With the collapse of the Soviet Union in 1991 and the transformation of the Chinese Communist Party into an agent of capitalist restoration, the Communist movement that began with the formation of the Bolshevik party and that played such an important historical role throughout the twentieth century is effectively defunct, though traces of it survive in Cuba and elsewhere in the **Third World**. It is far too soon for anyone now to offer a definitive assessment of the Communist episode in world history. Nevertheless, the prevailing view in most, though of course not all, quarters is negative. This perception is likely to last for some time. Thus it is unlikely that the (big-C) Communist movement will ever revive. But (small-c) communism remains a potentially viable ideal. Future Left political currents may well come to believe that official and dissident twentieth-century Communism were deviations from a tradition of thought and action that they would again make their own.

Further Reading

For Marx's own view of communism, Karl Marx and Friedrich Engels, *The Communist Manifesto* (1848; available in many editions) is the best source. It is also worthwhile to consult the five volumes of Hal Draper's *Karl Marx's Theory of Revolution*; vol. 4, subtitled *Critique of Other Socialisms* (New York: Monthly Review Press, 1989) is especially pertinent. For a more skeptical view, see Jon Elster, *Making Sense of Marx* (Cambridge: Cambridge University Press, 1985), chapter 9. A comprehensive account of the political economy of official Communism in its declining years is János Kornai, *The Socialist System: The Political Economy of Capitalism* (Princeton: Princeton University Press, 1992). I elaborate on the claims made here for the timeliness of (small-c) communism in *The General Will: Rousseau, Marx, Communism* (Cambridge: Cambridge University Press, 1993), chapters 8–9; and in *Rethinking Liberal Equality: From a "Utopian" Point of View* (Ithaca, NY: Cornell University Press, 1998), chapter 5.

See also: CAPITALISM, CLASS, DEMOCRACY, EQUALITY/EGALITARIANISM, FREEDOM/LIBERTY, HISTORICAL MATERIALISM, JUSTICE, LEFT/RIGHT/CENTER, MAOISM, MARXISM, REVOLUTION, SOCIAL DEMOCRACY, SOCIALISM, STATE, TROTSKYISM

Community/communitarianism

Familial ties aside, modern political philosophy depicts social, political, and economic institutions as contrivances of individuals who are, metaphorically, like atoms: fundamental constituents (of social facts), radically independent of one another, and joined together only by **external relations**. This **individualistic** way of thinking is epitomized in **contractarian** political philosophy. It reflects the actual situation wherever markets organize social life. In contrast, traditional societies are constituted by bonds that embed individuals into integral social wholes, *communities*. Communal norms and practices then structure individuals' lives. In modern times, the individual and his or her interests are the point of departure for thinking philosophically about social, political, and economic life. In more traditional societies, communities are. Perhaps in the future, under very different conditions, this will again become the case.

Traditional communities accord individuals a place where they are, so to speak, at home. They therefore protect against alienation (estrangement), the distinctively modern form of human bondage. However, because they also severely constrain individuals' life prospects and opportunities, they are, if anything, even more inimical to freedom than are market societies. It was capitalism that vanquished traditionalism, installing in its stead an **atomized** social order. So far-reaching was this transformation that it has become part of the common sense of our time to think of atomization as our "natural" condition, and to regard social groups as artificial constructs. In traditional societies, this commonsense view would be as counter-intuitive as it has become intuitive for us.

By the end of the eighteenth century, the atomization of traditional (specifically, **feudal**) **solidarities** was well underway in Western Europe. This process was widely recognized and generally endorsed. But it was also criticized – both by traditionalist opponents of modernity on the Right, and by their archenemies on the revolutionary Left. Thus, the French revolutionaries battled not only for liberty and equality, but also for **fraternity** – for communities composed of free (autonomous) persons linked together by affective ties like those that join brothers. The Right yearned for a restoration of a pre-capitalist Golden Age. On the Left, the idea instead was to install new forms of human solidarity based on an awareness of common humanity. The socialist movement took up this understanding. Along with liberty and equality, socialists have always stood for new and free communal connections – at least in theory.

Unfortunately, socialists' dedication to this goal, much as to the others, has often been more rhetorical than real. As Social Democracy became increasingly domesticated in the decades preceding World War I, and then as the establishment of the Soviet Union transformed the entire socialist movement, making Leninism and then Stalinism a point of reference (pro or con) for all socialists, community, even more than liberty or equality, became an orphan ideal. Experiments in forging new communal forms did not die out entirely. But they were increasingly marginalized. Thus, some nineteenth-century **utopian socialist** projects survived into the twentieth century, and some new ones were begun. In addition, in the Soviet Union and China, and in their respective spheres of influence, agricultural production was collectivized, partly following utopian socialist models. For the most part, however, collectivization in the Communist world was accomplished **coercively** and at great human cost. Thus, Soviet and Chinese collectivization did little to renew interest in efforts to transform atomized market societies into communities of free and equal persons. On the other hand, in the kibbutz movement in Palestine and later Israel, collective agricultural and industrial enterprises were established and maintained voluntarily. This is why, despite their role in what has always been an essentially colonial enterprise, they helped, in the years that they flourished, to revive the communal side of socialist thought. Also in Spain, before the fascist victory in the Civil War, anarchists struggled to create new kinds of productive communities. These examples notwithstanding, efforts to form post-capitalist communities have not been high priorities on the Left. *Community* has become a vague, mainly rhetorical aspiration; not, as the early socialists anticipated, a well-defined policy objective.

In academic circles associated with the political Center, there has been a renewed interest in community – giving rise to two fairly distinct intellectual tendencies, both of which take the name *communitarianism*. Philosophical communitarianism arose in reaction to the work of John Rawls (1921–2002). In the 1980s, *communitarians* faulted Rawls's theory of justice, and, by extension, his version of liberalism for the way it appeared to abstract individuals away from the communal affiliations that constitute their identities, and not unrelatedly for its apparent disregard of **socially constructed** meanings. Implicitly, responses to some of these criticisms found their way into subsequent reformulations of Rawls's theory of justice. Nowadays, however, it is generally conceded that the communitarian critique of Rawls, when it was not simply mistaken, pertained more to some of the ways Rawls argued for his theory than to the theory itself. It is worth noting that this line of criticism has subsided in recent years.

Communitarianism also designates contemporary continuations of early and mid-twentieth-century sociological critiques of mass society and totalitarianism. So conceived, it celebrates the civilizing mission of the non-political institutions and practices that constitute **civil society**. It encourages their reinforcement as an antidote to the ills of modern life. Hardly anyone faults this conviction; and the vast majority of those who are in a position to promote public policy today would probably also agree, if pressed, with communitarian policy prescriptions. But, for as long as communitarianism has existed as a discernible intellectual tendency, communitarians have had to compete with free-marketeers. As the political culture of the past several decades has drifted ever more towards the Right, and as the Right has increasingly embraced free market doctrine, communitarians have found themselves marginalized too, despite their centrist orientation and the nearly universal acceptance of the principles underlying their policy prescriptions. To the degree that communitarian thinking has had an impact on real world politics, it has been mainly in the formerly Communist world. There, the need for communitarian remedies was more palpable than in the West, inasmuch as independent (non-state) societal institutions generally fared poorly under Communist regimes.

Despite obvious affinities, neither philosophical nor sociological communitarians have made common cause with proponents of identity politics. They too seek to install a sense of rootedness based on membership in communities. But the identity politics movement would do so by encouraging group differences, especially those based on the ascriptive (that is, non-voluntary) properties that they consider constitutive of individuals' identities. Communitarians are more disposed to support the (**uncoerced**) obliteration of differences than their indefinite continuation. In their view, for community to be achieved in pluralistic societies, the "melting pot" must first do its work.

Even those who would forge new kinds of communities based on ties of universal human solidarity must concede that there is more than a grain of truth in communitarian doctrine. But insofar as it tends to cast a nostalgic eye on "the good old days" (that never were), communitarianism can also distract from this effort.

Further Reading

A seminal study of the rise of atomistic ways of thinking is C.B. Macpherson, *The Political Theory of Possessive Individualism: Hobbes to Locke* (Oxford: Oxford University Press, 1962). A rather different account of the origins of modern individualism is provided in J.G.A. Pocock, *The Macchiavellian Moment: Florentine Political Thought and the Atlantic Republican Tradition* (Princeton, NJ: Princeton University Press, 2003). I elaborate on individualism and the metaphor of atomization in connection with Hobbes's theory of sovereignty in *Engaging Political Philosophy: From Hobbes to Rawls* (Malden, MA: Blackwell Publishers, 2002), chapter 1. Rawls' account of justice is set out in John Rawls, *A Theory of Justice* (Cambridge, MA: Harvard University Press (Belknap Press), 1971) and *Justice as Fairness: A Restatement* (Cambridge, MA: Harvard University Press (Belknap Press), 2001). The most influential communitarian critique of Rawlsian justice is Michael J. Sandel's *Liberalism and the Limits of Justice*, 2nd edition (Cambridge: Cambridge University Press, 1998). Focusing on the importance of socially constructed meanings in theories of justice, a related charge is leveled against Rawls in Michael Walzer's *Spheres of Justice:*

A Defense of Pluralism and Equality (New York: Basic Books, 1984). An insightful guide through this literature can be found in Will Kymlicka, *Liberalism, Community, and Culture* (Oxford: Clarendon Press, 1989). On sociological communitarianism, see Amitai Etzioni, *The Essential Communitarian Reader* (Lanham, MD: Rowman and Littlefield, 1998). For an empirically focused communitarian critique of contemporary American society, see Robert D. Putnam, *Bowling Alone: The Collapse and Revival of American Community* (New York: Simon and Schuster, 2001).

See also: ALIENATION, ANARCHISM, CAPITALISM, COMMUNISM, EQUALITY, FASCISM, FREEDOM/ LIBERTY, IDENTITY POLITICS, JUSTICE, LEFT/RIGHT/CENTER, LENINISM, LIBERALISM, MARKETS, REVOLUTION, SOCIAL DEMOCRACY, SOCIALISM, STALINISM, TOTALITARIANISM, ZIONISM

Conservatism

Conservative is often used as a synonym for "right-wing." This usage can be misleading, inasmuch as there are right-wing ideologies, like fascism, that are anything but conservative. Nevertheless, there is seldom risk of confusion. Conservatives are generally ill-disposed to changing the status quo while, in existing circumstances, the Left, including the liberal left, is intent on changing it. Thus, conservatives oppose the Left. When they are the main opponents of left-wing politics, as is almost always the case, they comprise the political Right.

Conservatives are not against change altogether. They are for it when it is necessary to accommodate new circumstances or conditions. What they abhor are abrupt or radical transformations. In a word, conservatives are gradualists. Philosophically, what conservative positions have in common is a sense of the inability of human beings, through the exercise of rational capacities alone, to govern wisely or, at the extreme, to maintain governing structures at all. This is why, when changes are necessary, conservatives favor gradual modifications of traditional ways. Conservatives typically extend this way of thinking to extra-political forms of social control like the family and the Church, and to extra-institutional **mores** and customs.

In the modern West, conservatism developed into a full-fledged political ideology at odds with socialism and liberalism. This ideology is sustained by two distinct, but generally compatible, rationales – one of Christian origin, the other arising out of reactions to the French Revolution. In consequence of Western imperial domination of the rest of the world, conservatism in the Western sense has taken root nearly everywhere, often abetted by indigenous political traditions that, for other (usually religious) reasons, also favor traditional structures of social control.

The Christian strain of conservative ideology, evident today particularly in traditionally Catholic countries in southern Europe and Latin America, derives from the distinctively Christian doctrine of Original Sin. The idea is that, in consequence of our Fallen nature, we human beings are incapable of doing well for ourselves in matters of fundamental concern. What matters to us fundamentally is our own salvation. But, in consequence of Original Sin, no one deserves to be saved, and no one can do anything to become worthy. A few, however, are elected for salvation through unmerited grace. In the view of Augustinians, Calvinists, and other orthodox Christian thinkers (though perhaps not of most Christian believers or promulgators of Christian doctrine), the vast majority are not; their destiny is the one all sinful beings deserve. With so many locked into a Fallen condition, wisdom requires that we regard human beings generally as so depraved that they cannot insure civil order – what St. Augustine (354–430) called "the peace of Babylon" – through their own efforts. Were we left free to do what our nature inclines, we would therefore find ourselves locked into a devastating war of all against all. This is why we need powerful political and extra-political institutions to save us from ourselves and from each other. In modern, **secular** versions of this doctrine – the argument Thomas Hobbes (1588–1679) set out in *Leviathan* (1651) is an example – individuals contrive a sovereign who, by coercive means, keeps their natures in check, as their interests require. In earlier Christian versions, they are incapable even of this. The institutions that repress the free expression of Fallen human nature are divinely imposed.

On this view, in both its theological and secular versions, order is the pre-eminent political value. But order is always problematic because human beings are incapable of realizing it, at least directly. Whenever it is attained, it is therefore a fragile achievement. It is perilous to put it at risk by doing anything potentially destabilizing. The more far-reaching changes are, the more destabilizing they can be. Hence, gradualism is advised.

The strain of conservatism that developed in the early nineteenth century in reaction to the specter of revolution, was, at first, mainly an English concoction. It is indifferent to Original Sin or functionally equivalent theories of human nature. This strain of conservative theory is based instead on a view of the nature of governance. The guiding idea is that governing people is an activity that, by its very nature, is not susceptible to radical reconstitution; in other words, that it resembles cooking or carpentry more than mathematics. It is an activity in which a reservoir of accumulated wisdom and good sense, built up over generations and materialized in techniques and traditions, matters more than rational insight or deductive acuity. From this vantage point, the French revolutionaries were, as later conservative thinkers would put it, **rationalists** in politics – intent on building a new world on the ashes of the old, just as Euclid built a new geometry on the basis of rationally accessible first principles, regardless of traditional ways of thinking about spatial entities. This, conservatives maintain, is deeply mistaken. Wise governance requires adherence to traditional ways, modified gradually and artfully – when, but only insofar as, changes are required. This rationale is derived, in part, from English common law, according to which, wherever possible, legal disputes are to be settled by finding precedents under which new cases can be subsumed. The thought is that, by doing so, we are less likely to go dangerously wrong than we would were we to deploy principles in a rationalist spirit. To the extent that we are able to deal with the future in ways that we have already developed to deal with the past, we will end up no worse off than we already are. Were we instead to rethink everything through from the beginning, we risk going disastrously astray. Conservatives of this stamp are therefore generally also intent on sustaining traditional, extra-political forms of social control. But they are motivated to do so not because they fear the consequences of untrammeled human nature, but because they believe that public affairs go better when, instead of attempting to contrive alternatives, we nurture institutions that have already done well enough for us to get us to where we now are.

The tradition established at the founding of the United States was commercial and liberal. This sets American conservatism somewhat apart from European (and even British) conservatisms. It is why American conservatism is unusually business-friendly. Private enterprise, however, is an unlikely target for conservative concern because it disrupts traditional ways of life. As Karl Marx (1818–1883) and Friedrich Engels (1820–1895) observed in *The Communist Manifesto* (1848), and as the majority of conservatives outside the United States realize, capitalism causes "all things solid to melt into air." But where capitalism is the tradition, it is what conservatives would conserve. American conservatives therefore find themselves in a paradoxical situation. On the one hand, they value a capitalist ethos at odds with traditional forms of social **solidarity** and social control; on the other hand, they are drawn, temperamentally and by conviction, to support what capitalism effectively subverts. It is worth noting that it was precisely to sustain these structures that conservatives in Germany and elsewhere introduced forms of positive state assistance that, in the second half of the twentieth century, in conjunction with the efforts of differently motivated political actors, developed into the institutional arrangements that constitute the welfare state. This is why many conservatives outside the United States normally favor measures that most American conservatives abhor, and vice versa. What contemporary conservatives throughout the world have in common, then, is not exactly a commitment to particular policies or institutions, though there are notable convergences – on traditional "family values," for example. Instead, the common core of modern conservatism is a commitment to gradualism and, more importantly, a general opposition to the Left – motivated, in part, by philosophical orientations that Left thinkers reject. However, conservatism's **skepticism** about human perfectibility and its related abhorrence of rationalism in politics evince a certain humility and wisdom that partisans of liberty, equality, and fraternity ignore at their peril.

Further Reading

On Augustinian (Christian) conservatism, Herbert Deane's *The Political and Social Ideas of Saint Augustine* (New York: Columbia University Press, 1966) remains unsurpassed. For Hobbes's secular restatement of the Augustinian view, see Thomas Hobbes (C.B. Macpherson, ed.), *Leviathan* (Harmondsworth, UK: Penguin, 1980; originally published 1651), chapters 13–16. I discuss the Hobbesian argument and its relation to Christian political thought in *Engaging Political Philosophy: From Hobbes to Rawls* (Malden, MA: Blackwell Publishers, 2002), chapter 1. The anti-rationalist case for conservatism is made most trenchantly in Michael Oakeshott, *Rationalism in Politics and Other Essays* (Indianapolis, IN: Liberty Press, 1991). Oakeshott's position develops themes implicit in, for example, Edmund Burke's *Reflections on the Revolution in France* (Oxford: Oxford University Press, 1999) and Alexis de Tocqueville (Stuart Gilbert, trans.), *The Old Regime and the French Revolution* (Garden City, NY: Anchor, 1955). I elaborate on the idea of a rapprochement between conservative and traditional Left ideas in *The End of the State* (London: Verso, 1987), chapter 4.

See also: CAPITALISM, COMMUNITY, EQUALITY, EGALITARIANISM, FASCISM, FREEDOM/LIBERTY, IDEOLOGY, IMPERIALISM, LEFT/RIGHT/CENTER, LIBERALISM, REVOLUTION, SOCIALISM, STATE, WELFARE/WELFARE STATE

Cosmopolitanism

In ordinary speech, *cosmopolitanism* suggests worldly sophistication. In the Stalin era, the term was used by Communists in Eastern Europe and the Soviet Union in a derogatory way to suggest "rootlessness." In their (barely veiled) **anti-Semitic** campaigns, *cosmopolitan* was a euphemism for "Jew." The literal meaning of the term is "citizen of the world." That idea arose in classical antiquity, and was revived in Western Europe during the **Enlightenment**. It was subsequently taken over by socialists. Thus, by the middle of the nineteenth century, it entered into the thinking of the nascent labor movement, where it helped to shape workers' and **intellectuals'** notions of nationalism and internationalism.

A citizen of the world is ipso facto not a citizen of any particular state. However, it is impossible literally to be a citizen of the world, because the world, not being a political entity, has no citizens. In the world today, it is seldom possible not to be a citizen of any state. Even where it is possible, few become stateless voluntarily. Perhaps more would, if it were easier to renounce one's actual citizenship without taking up citizenship elsewhere. But the main reason why so few try is that *cosmopolitan* more nearly designates a sensibility or attitude than a legal status.

Cosmopolitanism gives expression to a sense of universal human **solidarity**. This is not to say that, in the cosmopolitan view, differences between human beings are of no **ethical** significance. Cosmopolitans can and typically do countenance special obligations and duties – for family and friends. But they would have persons accord no special ethical status to those with whom they only share citizenship, except perhaps for **strategic** or **pragmatic** reasons.

The cosmopolitan idea bears a deep affinity to the moral point of view, according to which in deciding what we ought to do, we deliberate from an **agent-neutral** standpoint, rather than from the standpoint of any particular agent. No doubt, it was this fact that made cosmopolitanism appealing to Enlightenment thinkers. This is why too, in a world of growing inequality and in an age of permanent war, a cosmopolitan sensibility is something to foster and protect. Because it grows from the same soil as the modern (egalitarian) sense of justice, and because it expresses solidaristic aspirations, Left thinkers have generally been especially receptive to cosmopolitan ways of thinking. Hardly anyone, Left or Right, has seriously promoted the establishment of a world state. But the majority of Left thinkers, both liberal and socialist, have supposed that in a more just world, cosmopolitan sensibilities would be sustained spontaneously everywhere.

Further Reading

For a classical statement of the nature of cosmopolitanism and its connections to morality, see Immanuel Kant, "Idea for a Universal History With a Cosmopolitan Purpose" and "On the Common Saying:

'This May Be True in Theory, But It Does Not Apply in Practice'," in H.S. Reiss (ed.), *Kant: Political Writings* (Cambridge: Cambridge University Press, 1991). For more recent accounts of these issues, see Kwame Anthony Appiah, *Cosmopolitanism: Ethics in a World of Strangers* (New York: W.W. Norton and Company, 2006) and Steven Vertovec and Robin Cohen (eds.), *Conceiving Cosmopolitanism: Theory, Context and Practice* (Oxford: Oxford University Press, 2003). The political implications of cosmopolitan sensibilities are debated in Daniele Archibugi, *Debating Cosmopolitics* (London: Verso, 2003). A collection of timely, philosophically oriented essays is Gillian Brock and Harry Brighouse (eds.), *The Political Philosophy of Cosmopolitanism* (Cambridge: Cambridge University Press, 2005).

See also: COMMUNISM, EQUALITY/EGALITARIANISM, INTERNATIONALISM, JUSTICE, LABOR MOVEMENT, LEFT/RIGHT/CENTER, LIBERALISM, MORALITY, NATION/NATIONALISM, SOCIALISM, STALINISM, STATE

Culture

The word *culture* has a long and complex genealogy. It therefore has had and continues to have many meanings. Centuries ago, the majority of these meanings clustered around notions of *cultivation*. Some of these uses survive. Thus to culture, say, bacteria is to grow bacteria under controlled conditions. We also still speak of ag*riculture*. In recent centuries, *culture* has also been used to refer to a society's music, literature, painting, and sculpture, and to its scientific, philosophical, historical, and scholarly achievements. Until the middle of the twentieth century, *culture* in this sense designated what some critics then began to call "highbrow culture." It was contrasted with "lowbrow culture" and sometimes with "middle-level culture" too. Thus, the designation of the term expanded. There were also contemporaneous analyses of "mass culture" by critics of fascism and totalitarianism. Following the lead of these investigators, the term has come to be used to refer to aspects of life that have nothing directly to do with the arts and sciences. Thus, we have the new academic field of "cultural studies."

In politics, the term is used to designate a variety of phenomena, but it usually has only one, rather abstract meaning. A *culture* is a set of **norms** that affect the functionings of social groups. These groups may be organizations of any size (except nuclear families or other intimate associations) – firms, institutions, political parties, social movements, and the like. Or they may be entire political communities or sub-sections of political communities. Or the group in question may be a collection of political communities. Sometimes too, *culture* is used more or less interchangeably with *civilization*. Thus, "Western culture" and "Western civilization" are often synonymous. Recent invocations of "a clash of civilizations" between the Christian and post-Christian (secular) West and the Muslim world could as well be described as a conflict of cultures.

Group cultures are seldom monolithic or uncontested. Within groups joined together by a common culture, so-called conflicts over cultural matters will periodically erupt. In the late 1980s and early 1990s, and continuing on into the present, universities and other "cultural institutions" were riven by so-called "culture wars." In this instance, **political correctness** was the ostensible point of contention. Within academic disciplines, there are divisions too that could be described as cultural struggles. For example, for much of the twentieth century, academic philosophy had **analytical** and "continental" wings. Inasmuch as the difference has more to do with how philosophy is done than with doctrines or beliefs, it reflects the existence of different (intellectual) cultures within the (academic) sub-community of professional philosophers.

How constraining the norms that constitute cultures are in particular circumstances is always an open question. All that can be said in general is that the answers, as best they can be ascertained, will vary from case to case. There is also no general rule that describes the malleability of cultural constraints. Presumably, the more constraining cultures are, the more difficult they are to transform. This presumption often carries the day. But not always. Even deeply entrenched cultures sometimes undergo abrupt transformations – either in consequence of radically changed circumstances or thanks to deliberate efforts to institute changes.

Culture and politics are interconnected. To be sure, many factors, not just political practices and institutions, shape cultures. Custom and tradition loom large in their formation and sustenance. But, intentionally or not, politics affects social norms as much as social norms affect politics. Thus, the transformation of culture can become an express objective of political actors. This was the official rationale behind, for example, the Chinese **Cultural Revolution** of the 1960s and 1970s. Many of the great political philosophers of the modern era – including Jean-Jacques Rousseau (1712–1778), Karl Marx (1818–1883), and John Dewey (1859–1952) – acknowledged the political importance of cultural struggles; that is, of struggles in and over societal norms. It is also very nearly the consensus view among legal scholars and political theorists that, in constitution writing, it is not just a society's basic laws that are at stake, but also the foundation for the political culture that will eventually develop.

Since the nineteenth century, nationalists have used the term to refer to what is distinctive within national communities. A national culture typically involves

Culture

a common language, a set of (generally practiced) customs, shared traditions, and a general sense of intergenerational continuity. Like nations, national cultures are, at least partly, imagined. Therefore, they are always, to some degree, deliberately contrived. But once they exist in the popular imagination, they become factors in real world politics. The construction of a national culture is especially important in state building, particularly when the state is a nation state or a multi-ethnic state on the way to becoming a nation-state. Contemporary theories of multiculturalism effectively assume the nationalist's understanding of culture. For multiculturalists, policies should be pursued within political communities comprised of distinct national or ethnic groups that have the effect of sustaining national or ethnic differences, causing them to flourish (within the framework of a single state).

The idea that Western culture (or civilization) is at odds with Muslim culture (and perhaps with other cultures too) is, in its present incarnation, a contrivance of neo-conservative ideologues. But the idea that Western civilization is under threat was a feature of a good deal of twentieth-century thought. At first, the idea was taken up as much by liberals and socialists as by conservatives. For them, the threat to civilization came not from non-European civilizations – Japan apart, they were too weak to threaten the imperial centers of Europe and North America – but from social movements of European origin. Thus, fascism and especially Nazism were widely portrayed as threats to Western civilization. In time, some came to view Communism in a similar way. In retrospect, these contentions seem grotesquely exaggerated. Unless civilization becomes significantly derailed through their machinations, the latest neo-conservative variation on this well-worn theme will no doubt some day seem similarly outlandish.

It is important not to ignore connections between politics and culture, as academic political philosophers are wont to do. Institutional arrangements, public policies and political strategies, on the one hand, and norms governing social organizations, on the other, are intimately related; and all genuinely transformative political ventures have an irreducibly cultural dimension.

Further Reading

All the classics of political thought engage the question of culture in one way or another; and culture is Topic A for social and anthropological theory. Raymond Williams endeavored to draw pertinent aspects of these diverse literatures together. His work became seminal for the subsequent development of cultural studies. The most systematic account of it is Raymond Williams, *The Sociology of Culture* (Chicago: University of Chicago Press, 1995). Recent claims for a culture clash between the West and the Muslim world are epitomized in Samuel Huntington's *The Clash of Civilizations and the Remaking of the Modern World Order* (New York: Simon and Schuster, 1998). Huntington's book has often been rebutted, though it continues to have its (mainly neo-conservative) defenders. A collection of essays that effectively sets contemporary discussions of culture on a more productive trajectory is Richard A. Falk (ed.), *ReFraming International: Law, Culture, Politics* (New York: Routledge, 2002). Some of the essays in it address Huntington's thesis in passing.

See also: CONSERVATISM, COMMUNISM, COMMUNITY, FASCISM, IDEOLOGY, IDENTITY POLITICS, IMPERIALISM, LIBERALISM, MAOISM, MARXISM, MULTICULTURALISM, NATION/NATIONALISM, NEO-CONSERVATISM, SOCIALISM, STATE, TOTALITARIANISM

D

Democracy

Etymologically, *democracy* means "rule of the *demos*," the people, where "people" designates the popular masses (in contrast to social or economic elites). Until the eighteenth century, democracy, much like *anarchy* today, was widely regarded as a theoretical possibility that no right-thinking person would favor. However, since the beginning of the nineteenth century, the term has taken on increasingly positive connotations. After World War II, following the historic defeat of fascism, the last officially anti-democratic ideology, all significant political tendencies have sought to enlist the word on their own behalf. But they have not all had the same notion in mind. Thus, the **peoples' democracies** of the Soviet era and many of the putatively democratic regimes established in the **Third World** differed substantially from American democracy and, more generally, from the varieties of democracy developed in the West. In none of these self-identified democracies, though, does the *demos* rule, except in the most attenuated of senses. This fact on the ground nowadays resonates at the theoretical level. The term has become so shorn of class content that we commonly call systems of elite rule *democratic*, so long as they institutionalize competitive elections or other iconic practices associated with more philosophically grounded notions of democracy.

Perhaps, in time, islamist and other theocratic movements will come again to eschew the label *democratic*. This has not happened yet – but it is not inconceivable, if, as alternative models disappear, *democracy* comes to mean only Western democracy. Then it would be understandable if proponents of intrinsically undemocratic ideologies who are also the victims of Western democracies decide that they want nothing to do with the political system glorified in the West. But this has not yet happened. It is worth noting that theocratic regimes can and sometimes do claim to be democratic (according to what used to be one of the term's familiar senses), inasmuch as they depend for their legitimacy on popular support. For the same reason, a similar prerogative was open to fascist governments. Indeed, it is fair to say that the entry of the *demos* into the political arena worldwide is a singular, and probably irreversible, triumph of modernity. So too, however, is the development of institutional means for neutralizing demotic aspirations. This is very evident in Western democracies, where ostensibly democratic institutions, like periodic elections, operate more to legitimate elite ruling structures than to implement what Abraham Lincoln (1809–1865) aptly called "government of, by and for the people."

Contemporary philosophical accounts of Western democracy fall broadly into two categories: one identifies *democracy* with democratic procedures, emphasizing affinities between markets and democratic collective choice; the other, by emphasizing deliberation, rather than collective choice, revives the ideal of the Athenian forum and, along with it, the notion of a political community joined together in search of collective ends. In both cases, the class perspective the term once implied is effectively missing.

Accounts of democracy that invoke considerations used in defenses of market arrangements come in individualistic and non-individualistic versions. In the former, it is assumed that individuals chose among alternative outcomes in contention. The objective is to combine their choices democratically – that is, in such a way that the collective choice is solely a function of individuals' choices. Normally, this is done through voting. If all votes are counted equally, if everyone votes, and if a decision procedure such as the method of majority rule is employed, then, intuitively, the collective choice will correctly reflect the choices of the electorate. Of course, none of these conditions hold strictly in most real world situations. Even allowing that elections are free and fair (in the sense that the right to vote is not unduly restricted and that the rules governing the electoral process are acknowledged as legitimate and are generally observed), it is seldom the case that all votes count equally. In American presidential elections, the situation is particularly egregious. Because that electoral contest is indirect, with voters selecting electors pledged to candidates on a state-by-state basis, the winning candidate in each state getting all that state's electors, and because the number of state electors is equal to the number of a state's representatives in Congress plus two (since each state, large or small, has two Senators), a single vote in a small state, especially where the contest is close, counts for more than a vote in a large state, especially if the outcome there is predictable. It is also the case that many individuals do not vote – either because they are legally ineligible (often for reasons that are arbitrary from a democratic point of view) or because they freely choose not to participate. In addition, the theory is silent on how the alternatives voters choose among come into being and, more generally, on how the agenda is set. For insuring outcomes that accord with elite interests, controlling the agenda is often more important than winning or losing on particular votes. It is also relevant that, in most circumstances, voters do not rule on measures directly. Instead, they select representatives to rule for them. At best, then, they control the outcomes of collective choices only to the extent that their representatives represent the choices of their constituents. With winner-take-all, infrequently held, periodic elections – where all that is at stake is the selection of two very similar candidates – there is very little that compels them to do so.

In addition, it can be demonstrated that formal models of majority rule voting, and of many other ostensibly democratic collective choice rules, exhibit incoherencies that put into question their ability to generate collective choices that properly aggregate individuals' choices. Thus, it has been known for some time that any method for combining individuals' choices into a social choice that satisfies a few apparently innocuous, but uncontroversially democratic conditions (such as that no single individual is able to dictate an outcome, that an alternative that is unanimously preferred is socially preferred, and that no individuals' choices are excluded) is "impossible." The method of majority rule satisfies these conditions. The incoherence of majority rule voting is evident in the fact that it is susceptible to generating cyclical outcomes. Suppose, for example, that in the three-way 2000 presidential election in the United States, someone (a mainstream Democrat, say, who was intent on maintaining the existing party duopoly) would choose Gore over Bush and Bush over Nader (and therefore Gore over Nader). Suppose too that someone (with more left-wing sensibilities) preferred Nader to Gore and Gore to Bush (and therefore Nader to Bush). Suppose, finally, that someone else (a right-winger) preferred Bush to Gore and Gore to Nader (and therefore Bush to Nader). If these three comprised the voting population, the method of majority rule would not produce a unique outcome.

Assuming that these individuals vote in accordance with their preferences, if we compare Nader to Bush, and then pair the winner against Gore, Gore will win. If we begin by comparing Gore and Bush, Nader will win. And if we first compare Nader and Gore, Bush will win. Thus, every alternative is preferred to every other alternative. Needless to say, in real world cases, this problem will only arise if each of the candidates has an equal number of supporters or in other, generally improbable, circumstances. But it is a theoretical possibility; a fact that arguably damages any democratic justifying theory that relies on the coherence of majority rule voting. In the case just given, the so-called voting paradox, this situation manifests itself in the fact that, if the alternatives are compared pairwise, with the winner of each contest paired against the remaining alternative, the remaining alternative will always win. What this observation suggests is that majority rule voting is not the neutral aggregating procedure it appears to be.

Political scientists have long recognized that the individualism of the market model, where individuals stand in a direct and unmediated relation to the state, is unrealistic. Decades ago, they proposed that **interest groups**, not individuals, are the principal political actors, where an interest group is a voluntary association. In recent political science, with the rise of identity politics, group identifications not based on voluntary associations have been added to the picture. However, the basic idea remains: political actors make choices that democratic collective choice rules aggregate. Outcomes are democratic to the extent that they accurately reflect the distribution of choices among the voters. This idea, that democracy is essentially a procedure for generating collective choices, is put forth both as a descriptive account of what is the case and as a **normative** vision of what ought to be. Reduced to its core, the normative claim is just that democratic procedures are justified because, in ideal cases, they represent all relevant interests fairly.

The rival view, modeled on the public forum, in contrast to the market, aims not so much at securing a fair outcome as a correct result. In the extreme case, epitomized in *The Social Contract* (1762) of Jean-Jacques Rousseau (1712–1778), it is maintained that there is a "general will" that aims at what is best for the whole community. Then, according to Rousseau, when individuals genuinely seek to discover what the general will is – when they deliberate with this objective in mind – the majority will discover this matter of fact. As Rousseau's example attests, the deliberative model presupposes that, in some politically pertinent sense, there is a genuine collective interest that is not just a combination of the discrete interests of the voting public. On this view, majority rule voting is not at all like bargaining or negotiating in market transactions; it is a truth-discovery procedure – as it plainly is, for example, in jury deliberations. Those who, like Karl Marx (1818–1883), believe that real world societies are riddled by social divisions deny that genuinely collective interests can exist, so long as these divisions persist. They therefore hold that there are no facts for ostensibly disinterested deliberators to discover. For them, the general will is more nearly an aspiration than a metaphysical fact. In any case, since no one can seriously maintain that the search for a general will takes place in actual Western democracies, the deliberative account of democratic governance operates strictly at a normative level. Its descriptive adequacy is nil. Nevertheless, deliberative democracy has today become the dominant philosophical stance in liberal egalitarian circles. Thus, there is, at the heart of this generally **progressive** philosophical tendency, a major disconnect between democratic theory and the real world of ostensibly democratic politics.

The fact that reality falls so far short of the deliberative ideal, and that the procedural model fares only slightly better, has led many to acquiesce to the actual situation. Without quite abandoning the normative theories that comprise the philosophical tradition, they maintain, sometimes expressly, sometimes only by implication, that we should reserve the term *democracy* for political systems relevantly like the one in the United States and other Western democracies. This is the understanding implicit in the mainstream political culture too. The traditional understandings remain in the background, legitimating ongoing practices by confounding the actual with the ideal.

Western democracies are *liberal democracies*, amalgams of liberal and democratic components. Without exception, they are more liberal than democratic. Liberal protections from state interferences have long been a hallmark of political life in the West, especially in the United States – notwithstanding periodic efforts to curtail them severely, as in anti-Communist witch hunts of the 1950s and in the Bush Administration's "war on terror." But with respect to "government of, by and for the people," liberal democracies offer, at best, only pale approximations. In the United States, the democratic aspect of the regime is unusually slight, even by the standards of other Western democracies – thanks largely to the weakness of the boundaries separating economic from political power in American society. In consequence, there are two entrenched parties, the Democrats and Republicans, which, though differing in the constituencies from which they draw votes, differ hardly at all on matters of basic policy.

Democracy

Those who genuinely do believe in government of, by, and for the people find themselves obliged not only to defend the gains already made, but also to go on the offensive against those who would, wittingly or unwittingly, impede the process of democratization. They must therefore become advocates of institutional changes designed to make democratic practice conform more to democratic theory. Ultimately, they may also find that they must militate for the democratization of the underlying economic system, the root cause of democracy's ills. Capitalism has been a boon for democracy in many ways. But, in the final analysis, it is an obstacle to its full realization and a permanent threat to its proper functioning. The fact that ours is a democratic age – that, officially, everyone supports government of, by and for the people is a two-edged sword. It can and does impede democratization, as ways of speaking and acting, derived from democratic theory, are deployed in anti-democratic ways. But it is also a foundation on which to build.

Further Reading

A clear and accessible account of contemporary philosophical theories of democracy can be found in Jon Elster, "The Market and the Forum: Three Varieties of Political Theory," in J. Elster and A. Hylland (eds.), *Foundations of Social Choice Theory* (Cambridge: Cambridge University Press, 1986). For a more extended discussion, see the first two chapters of John S. Dryzek, *Deliberative Democracy and Beyond: Liberals, Critics, Contestations* (Oxford: Oxford University Press, 2000). The economist Kenneth Arrow discovered the "impossibility" of majority rule voting in the early 1950s. His treatment of the subject, though technical, remains indispensable – see Kenneth Arrow, *Social Choice and Individual Values* (New Haven, CT: Yale University Press, 1970). A less technical account is available in Kenneth Arrow, "Public and Private Values," in Sidney Hook (ed.), *Human Values and Economic Policy* (New York: New York University Press, 1967). An earlier study of voting that anticipated Arrow's discovery and some of the theoretical departures it launched is Duncan Black, *The Theory of Committees and Elections* (Norwell, MA: Kluwer Academic Publishers, 1987). On Arrow's and Black's work and related issues, Amartya K. Sen, *Collective Choice and Social Welfare* (San Francisco: Holden Day, 1970), though technical in parts and difficult to find nowadays, is extremely lucid and comprehensive. A classic statement of interest group theory is David Truman, *The Governmental Process: Public Interests and Public Opinion* (Berkeley and Los Angeles: University of California Press, 1993). An anthology of recent writings on democracy, focused on deliberative democratic theory, is David Estlund (ed.), *Democracy* (Malden, MA: Blackwell Publishers, 2002). A venerable and influential proposal for identifying *democracy* with *liberal democracy* is Joseph Schumpeter, *Capitalism, Socialism, and Democracy* (New York: Harper, 1962). For further elaboration of the claims made here about connections, or the lack of them, between *democracy* and the *demos*, and about the disconnectedness of contemporary democratic theory see my *The General Will:*

Rousseau, Marx, Communism (Cambridge: Cambridge University Press, 1993), chapter 4, and *The American Ideology: A Critique* (New York: Routledge, 2004), chapter 7.

See also: ANARCHISM, CAPITALISM, CLASS, COMMUNISM, EQUALITY/EGALITARIANISM, FASCISM, FUNDAMENTALISM, IDENTITY POLITICS, IDEOLOGY, IMPERIALISM, LEFT/RIGHT/CENTER, LEGITIMACY, LIBERALISM, MARKETS, POLITICAL ISLAM, TERROR/TERRORISM, THEOCRACY, WAR

E

Environmentalism

For as long as our species has existed, we human beings, like other living things, have transformed the environment in which we live. Because we act intentionally, the changes our activities bring about are sometimes deliberate. More often, they are by-products of activities undertaken for other purposes. Our consciousness and volition indirectly account for the fact that our species' environmental impact is especially consequential; it is in virtue of these capacities that we can and do contrive technologies that literally change the world. It would be difficult to exaggerate the environmental impact of the tool-aided hunting and gathering of our distant ancestors or of the settled agriculture that superseded it. But what human beings did in the remote past pales before what we do now. With the emergence of modern industry, the effect of human activity on the non-human world has increased by orders of magnitude.

Some indigenous peoples in Africa, the Americas, and Australasia appear to have endeavored to minimize the deleterious effects of their own activities. However, from time immemorial, the vast majority of the world's inhabitants either didn't notice or didn't care. If the phenomenon was referenced at all in religious or philosophical doctrines, it was only to justify it. Thus, in the Book of Genesis (I: 28), God commanded Man (*sic*) to take control of the earth and to rule over the animals. This injunction reflects popular understandings the world over. It marks the so-called Abrahamic religions (Judaism, Christianity, Islam), but it is by no means exclusive to them.

Until recently, **progressive** thinkers had no argument with this nearly universal assumption. In fact, the idea that there are limits to growth arose in pro-capitalist conservative circles; it was promoted principally by thinkers hostile to the aspirations of workers and impoverished people. Thomas Malthus's (1766–1834) *Essay on Population* (1798) is the best-known expression of this point of view. Malthus maintained that economic growth was rapidly approaching a limit beyond which it would unleash population growth, which would, in turn, drain natural resources, stifling further growth, leaving workers worse off than before. Progressive thinkers, both socialist and liberal, were scornful of such claims. They maintained that technological advances would solve the problems growth itself might cause. In this respect, their position reflected what was generally, if unreflectively, assumed throughout the political culture. Because the world's resources are finite, thoughtful people, Left or Right, would have had to concede that there must be some point beyond which growth that depends on the **exploitation** of natural resources would be impeded by resource depletion. But, by nearly universal assent, it was thought that that limit lies beyond the reach of human endeavor in even the most distant imaginable future.

Nevertheless, by the latter half of the twentieth century, it had become evident that the consensus view was problematic. Communist societies had devastated the natural environment in their relentless struggle to industrialize. The developed capitalist world despoiled the environment even more, if only because its level of economic activity was greater. As the post-World War II economic expansion neared its apogee, the fact that environmental problems existed and were in need of redress dawned on many prescient thinkers. Not long afterwards an environmental movement was born. Almost immediately, it took hold around the world.

Modern environmentalism draws on many sources. **Enlightenment** thinkers emphasized the influence of physical surroundings and other environmental factors on human development. This has been, for the most part, a salutary development. But it has also had its downside. It bears notice that, for many years, the term *environmentalism* was associated with the biological theories of Jean-Baptiste Lamarck (1744–1829). Lamarck argued, plausibly but incorrectly, for "the inheritance of acquired characteristics," an implicitly anti-Darwinian view of biological evolution that Joseph Stalin's (1879–1953) official geneticist, Trofim Lysenko (1898–1976) carried to extreme conclusions, much to the detriment of Soviet biology and agronomy. However, the modern environmental movement's most important sources are recent. From the beginning of the twentieth century, conservationists sought to protect biodiversity for scientific, aesthetic, and spiritual reasons. Modern environmentalism continues their efforts. From the 1950s on, awareness of the deleterious effects of environmental degradation on human health became increasingly widespread. These worries too helped to fuel modern environmentalism. Also, around that time, a so-called New Age spirituality that claimed to draw on the traditions of ancient and indigenous peoples took hold of some sectors of the **New Left** and the larger "counter-culture." By the late 1960s, these and other sources crystallized into the environmental movement. From that time on, a variety of new theories and practices emerged and flourished.

Environmentalists today are less inclined than earlier generations of conservationists were to view the natural world as a treasure to be preserved. They tend instead to look to entire ecological systems, and to the place of human beings within them. For most environmentalists, "nature" includes human beings. So far from being masters of all that is non-human, we are, in the environmentalist's view, integral parts of a single system that includes the human and non-human alike. Conservationists wanted to turn what remains unspoiled into living museums of nature; modern environmentalists aim for a dissolution of the distinction between the human and natural worlds. Their goal is to reconstruct the connections between these parts of nature on a sounder basis than God's proclamations in Genesis imply. This is one reason why religious fundamentalists are usually hostile to environmentalism.

Contemporary environmentalism is a complex and multifaceted phenomenon. Much like feminism, its core concerns have seeped into the mainstream culture across the political spectrum. But environmentalist ideals, like feminist ones, are more honored in name than in practice. Often they are directly subverted, even as they are nominally upheld. This is why the environmental movement continues to grow; and why, like the feminist movement, it is urgently needed. It has an expressly political component. It also has an academic side. "Environmental Studies" has become an academic subject in its own right, and environmental concerns have registered in many fields in the arts and the sciences. In addition, journalists, public intellectuals, and even professional politicians nowadays write on environmental topics and sometimes even militate in favor of environmental causes.

Whether or not there really are practical limits to growth remains an open question. But it is beyond dispute that the traditional Left, like every other political tendency, was shortsighted with respect to the concerns that contemporary environmentalism has brought to the fore. Socialist and liberals, along with their opponents, thought of politics as an activity of, by, and for human beings. But even if we only aim to make life better *for people*, regardless of the consequences for animals and other living things or for nature generally, environmental concerns cannot be ignored or set aside in the way that they traditionally have been. Economic development affects natural environments; until now, its effects have been devastating. Nostalgia for pre-industrial ways of living is therefore a temptation. Some environmentalists have succumbed. But development is essential – if not morally, then politically. It is indispensable for maintaining the levels of consumption that we in the global North have come to assume, and it is crucial if the lives of people in the global South are to improve. But it is still necessary to look beyond consumption levels, and to focus too on the quality of life. Environmental concerns are of central importance in this regard.

Nevertheless, there is by now a dawning awareness that it is indefensible to remain as **anthropocentric** as we have been for millennia. Many environmentalists would accord rights to animals and other parts of nature. Others seek to advance the interests of non-human things in other idioms. In recent decades, political militants of the socialist and liberal Left have begun to take these ways of thinking increasingly seriously. Despite their historical neglect of them, there is no theoretical obstacle blocking the way. At the same time, environmentalist movements have increasingly taken on a Left coloration. As traditional social democratic and revolutionary socialist parties have taken a rightward turn or disappeared altogether, political environmentalism has, to some degree, filled the void. Green parties now exist in many developed countries. A Green Party is active in the United States; it has already won small, but significant, victories. In parts of Western Europe, the Greens are a significant political force. In Germany especially, even as descendant political formations of traditional Left parties remain powerful, the Greens occupy a position to the left of them.

Further Reading

Since the 1960s, academic and popular writing on environmental issues has become a growth industry. Much of this literature is worth reading, but hardly anything stands out as indispensable. Even the handful of books that inspired the (re-)emergence of environmentalism several decades ago – for example, Rachel Carson's *Silent Spring* (Boston: Mariner Books, 2002) or Aldo Leopold's *A Sand County Almanac* (Oxford: Oxford University Press, 1966) – now seem dated and of mainly historical interest. Readers interested in a clear and comprehensive overview of the history of modern environmentalism and of ways of thinking that anticipated it would do well to consult Ramachandra Guha, *Environmentalism: A Global History* (New York: Longman, 1999) or David Pepper, *Modern Environmentalism: An Introduction* (New York and London: Routledge, 1996). On Green politics today, see Jeffrey St. Clair, *Been Brown So Long, It Looked Like Green to Me: The Politics of Nature* (Monroe, ME: Common Courage Press, 2003).

See also: CAPITALISM, COMMUNISM, CONSERVATISM, CULTURE, FEMINISM, FUNDAMENTALISM, LEFT/RIGHT/CENTER, LIBERALISM, PROGRESS, REVOLUTION, RIGHTS, SOCIALISM, STALINISM

Equality/egalitarianism

In mathematics, *equality* and cognate terms like *equivalence* are basic in the sense that they cannot be defined using more fundamental concepts. We can only say that quantities, shapes, and other mathematical structures are equal or equivalent when, for mathematical purposes, they are effectively the same. This idea has been imported into the physical sciences where, for example, forces can be equal (say, in magnitude), and into other domains where mathematical representation is appropriate. This usage has passed into non-mathematical areas too. Thus it is sometimes said that synonyms are equivalent in meaning or that particular moral or aesthetic values are of equal importance. In politics, however, *equality* usually carries a **normative**, rather than a descriptive, connotation, and it almost never implies sameness or identity. When equality is proclaimed, the idea is that all individuals (or groups) that fall into the same (politically relevant) category ought to be treated in the same way (in relevant respects). For example, if equality is claimed for men and women, the idea is that public institutions (and perhaps also private organizations) ought to treat men and women in the same manner. When equality is demanded between races, the contention is that racial differences ought to be similarly irrelevant. Equality in a normative sense is compatible with empirical differences among members of groups comprised of equal members, and between groups that are deemed equal. This is why it does not embarrass the normative claim that "all men (*sic*) are created equal" to point out that in many respects, including some that bear on individual conduct and public policy, people differ from one another significantly.

What joins the political use of the term to its original mathematical meaning is a core philosophical conviction that has become pervasive wherever morality is recognized as an appropriate normative standard. The moral point of view, impartiality, requires that persons be thought of as morally equal agents. If they are not so regarded, the perspective that defines the moral point of view, **agent-neutrality**, would make no sense. That perspective is implicit in the Golden Rule. Why "do unto others as others as you would others do unto you," if differences from others, rather than commonalities, were what mattered? The so-called Abrahamic religions, Judaism, Christianity and Islam, advanced an ancestor notion when they proclaimed the equal value of "souls" to God. But, for them, equality "in the mind of God" had few, if any, worldly implications. This understanding changed radically when, with the onset of modernity and **secularism**, moral equality replaced theological equality as the paramount public concern. Then it came to be assumed that the moral equality of persons creates a presumption in favor of equal treatment by basic political, social, and economic institutions.

This presumption can, of course, be overridden – there need only be compelling reasons that trump the presumption for equality. In capitalist economies, the presumption of equal treatment, especially in the economic sphere, is typically and systematically overridden. But, even there, because the burden of proof attaches to whoever would defend inequalities, reasons for deviating from equal outcomes – or, more specifically, for endorsing institutional arrangements that inevitably generate inequalities – must be provided; not the other way round. Wherever it is believed that there are moral dimensions to the evaluation of basic institutional arrangements, the conclusion is inescapable – there is always a case, though not necessarily a decisive one, favoring equal treatment.

Egalitarianism can be used to designate any doctrine that endorses equality in this moralized sense. Thus, there is a sense in which all moral theories are egalitarian. In order to give substance to their commitment to the moral equality of persons, they all endorse equality along *some* dimension. Utilitarianism, for example, counts persons equally as bearers of utility. Moral philosophies that regard **property** rights as inviolable, like John Locke's (1632–1704) or the neo-Lockean philosophies that some contemporary libertarians advance, consider persons equal as rights holders. **Kantians**, more straightforwardly than proponents of other moral theories, base accounts of right action on the idea that persons are equal as (rational) agents.

In ordinary political discourse, *egalitarianism* has a narrower meaning. Egalitarians are proponents of income and wealth equality – or, more commonly, of economic and social policies that diminish inequalities of income and wealth.

In this narrower sense, neo-Lockean libertarians are not egalitarians; the economic system their position implies – a capitalist market economy with a "night watchman state" that never deliberately redistributes market-generated shares – gives rise to enormous inequalities of income and wealth. Neither, necessarily, are proponents of other major moral philosophical doctrines, though the positions held by, for example, utilitarians or Kantians, are susceptible to being enlisted in the egalitarian cause. However, in consequence of the presumption for equal treatment, no side is overtly inegalitarian. Because this presumption obtains, inequalities must be justified. Thus, neo-Lockeans maintain that property rights outweigh the presumption for equal income and wealth distribution; utilitarians, if they are not also egalitarians, would have to argue that overall utility is increased if distributions of income and wealth conform to some non-egalitarian pattern; and Kantians who are not egalitarians would have to maintain that respect for "humanity as an end in itself" implies that persons reap the benefits and bear the costs of what they freely choose to do with the resources they (privately) own.

Egalitarianism in this narrow sense should be distinguished from a superficially similar position according to which everyone should be accorded a minimal sufficiency of income and wealth beyond which it doesn't matter what the distribution of income and wealth is. It might be thought that the demand for sufficiency is motivated by a concern for the poorly off which is motivated, in turn, by a sense of the moral equality of persons. Perhaps it is, in some instances. But it is fair to say that, more usually, what motivates positions of this kind is the ancient, pre-moral idea that there is a duty to help others in (desperate) need. That there is such a duty is, of course, compatible with moral theory; indeed, on nearly all accounts, its recognition is morally required. But it is one thing to defend a duty to help, and something else to maintain that justice requires that the presumption for equal income and wealth distribution should prevail. The latter conviction leads to egalitarianism in the narrower sense; the former does not.

In the modern world, there is only a presumption for equal income and wealth distribution, but there is a consensus on other normative equalities. Everyone favors political equality – equality of citizenship. To be sure, equality in this domain is often denied systematically and institutionally, as was blatantly the case for African-Americans in the United States in the days of segregation and exclusion from the electoral process. Similar, though less blatant, phenomena are still common. In the United States and elsewhere, full equality of citizenship is more nearly a goal to aspire towards than a description of present-day life. But the ideal is universally endorsed. This is why it is comparatively easy to garner support for efforts to end legal or customary Apartheid, and to diminish the effects of subtler forms of second-class citizenship, wherever its existence is exposed.

There is also a consensus around the idea of equal opportunity – at least to the extent that no one expressly defends inequality of opportunity. But there is considerable disagreement about what support for equal opportunity implies. At one extreme are those who think that equal opportunity exists whenever legal (or perhaps legal and customary) impedances to competitions for scarce powers or offices or resources are removed. Others maintain that "affirmative" efforts must be made to "level the playing field" when, as is often the case, background inequalities of condition or the legacies of past inequalities put some individuals or groups at a disadvantage. Egalitarians of the kind who favor income and wealth equality typically favor robust, affirmative conceptions of equal opportunity.

As remarked, the demand for material equality typically devolves into a demand for income and wealth equality. Income and wealth are obvious targets for political contestation. But it is hard to imagine a reason why a particular distribution of income and wealth, equal or not, would matter for its own sake. For one thing, they comprise only a subset of the resources individuals (or groups) control. There is no reason to single them out except that they are good proxies for the others; especially inasmuch as other resources – talents, for example – are more difficult to redistribute directly or indirectly (by redistributing the income they generate). One might also wonder why egalitarians should be concerned directly at all with the distribution of resources, inasmuch as resources are only means for what matters intrinsically, rather than ends in themselves. The issue is clouded by the fact that the only way available, technologically and **ethically**, to distribute what might be thought to matter intrinsically – welfare or well-being is the most obvious and certainly the most discussed candidate – is through a particular distribution of resources.

In recent years, these considerations have led liberal egalitarian philosophers to investigate precisely what egalitarians want; in other words, what it is that they think should be equally distributed. The problem, very generally, is that inasmuch as distributional outcomes can only be achieved, directly or indirectly, by distributing resources, and inasmuch as individuals "process" resources into welfare at different rates, equal resource distributions will inevitably lead to unequal welfare distributions and vice versa. People with expensive tastes require a larger resource share than people with inexpensive tastes to be brought to an equal level of well-being. But it is hard to see why an egalitarian in the narrow sense of the term should favor distributions that give more than an equal share to those who need more than an equal share to be as well-off as, say, the average person. There are related problems pertaining to people with handicaps or other special needs resulting from unusually low levels of well-being. Considerations such as these make some form of resource egalitarianism attractive, even if resources only matter instrumentally. On the other hand, resource equality can leave persons (and perhaps also groups) very unequally well off with respect to what matters. This consideration militates against resource egalitarianism.

Liberals are inclined to be resource, not welfare, egalitarians. The reason has to do with their commitment to a broadly Kantian notion of freedom. The guiding thought is that individuals ought to be held accountable for the distributional consequences of what they freely choose to do. Therefore, liberal theories of justice ought to aim only for a fair distribution of the resources with which persons can then set out to realize their particular aims. Their subsequent successes or failures in achieving these goals are not in themselves matters for public concern. Exactly how to specify what form of resource equality liberal egalitarians advance is problematic; and it is not beyond dispute in liberal circles that egalitarians should worry directly about resources at all or that they should do so to the exclusion of all else. The idea that egalitarians should concern themselves directly with what matters intrinsically is too compelling. For these reasons, philosophers have contrived other candidates for distribution that aim to incorporate what seems right about welfare and resource egalitarianism, while eschewing what is apparently indefensible. Some of their suggestions take an **Aristotelian** turn. Thus, it has been argued that what matters is doings (functionings, capabilities) more than being in certain conditions (for example, being well-off). This has been, on the whole, a fruitful area for philosophical investigation. But at a policy level, the differences in the positions that have been put forward fade away, at least insofar as the discussion assumes a capitalist economic structure and a Kantian liberal view of individual responsibility. Then income and wealth distribution remain the best, indeed the only feasible, proxies for whatever ultimately egalitarians want. In this sense, income and wealth egalitarianism wins the intra-liberal debate by default, though only on a policy level.

There are, however, strains of socialist theory, Marxist and otherwise, that advance a more radically egalitarian vision – upholding the desirability of equal distributions of what matters intrinsically, while denying that peoples' distributional shares should depend on what they freely do with what they privately own.

Distributional arrangements within families or among close friends anticipate the kinds of principles that might shape egalitarian theory once the conceptual horizons of liberal egalitarianism are surpassed. The Aristotelian turn in recent liberal egalitarianism flows naturally into this more radical construal of what egalitarians want. But philosophers still have much work to do in elaborating precisely what equality entails.

By all appearances, egalitarianism would seem to have won the day. Disagreements remain about what equality means, but hardly anyone stands opposed to the ideal. Moreover, at a policy level, many of the theoretical differences that divide egalitarians effectively converge. Nevertheless, inequality rages. In recent years, a constellation of related phenomena – **globalization**, the resurgence of **neo-liberal** economic doctrines, the decline of welfare state institutions, the weakness of the labor movement – have combined to exacerbate material inequalities in almost all countries, and at a global level. Remarkably too, the struggle for racial and **gender** equality, and for equal treatment of persons generally, is far from won – even where there is nearly universal support for equal citizenship and for one or another form of equal opportunity. There is plainly an enormous divide between theory and practice. Notwithstanding recent advances in understanding equality philosophically, this phenomenon is not well understood. Egalitarians ignore it at their peril.

Further Reading

Recent philosophical discussions of equality that focus on what egalitarians want equally distributed – the so-called "equality of what?" debate – address concerns raised perspicaciously in Amartya K. Sen, *Inequality Reexamined* (New York: Russell Sage Foundation and Cambridge, MA: Harvard University Press, 1992). Ronald Dworkin contributed substantially to this debate in a series of articles available in the first part of Ronald Dworkin, *Sovereign Virtue* (Cambridge, MA: Harvard University Press, 2002). See also Richard Arneson, "Equality and Equal Opportunity for Welfare," *Philosophical Studies*, vol. 56 (1989), pp. 77–93. This essay is reprinted, along with a variety of other important writings on equality, in Louis Pojman and Robert Westmoreland (eds.), *Equality: Selected Readings* (Oxford: Oxford University Press, 1997). That collection includes the most influential case for sufficiency (in contrast to equality), Harry Frankfurt's essay "Equality as a Moral Ideal." Of prime importance too in the "equality of what?" debate is G.A. Cohen, "On the Currency of Egalitarian Justice," *Ethics*, vol. 99 (1989), pp. 906–44. The Aristotelian turn in recent philosophical accounts of equality is particularly evident in some of the contributions to Martha C. Nussbaum and Amartya K. Sen, *The Quality of Life* (Oxford: Oxford University Press, 1993). See also my *Rethinking Liberal Equality: From a "Utopian" Point of View* (Ithaca, NY: Cornell University Press,

Equality/egalitarianism

1998), where the main themes set forth here are elaborated at greater length. The main influence motivating recent philosophical discussions of equality is John Rawls, *A Theory of Justice* (Cambridge, MA: Harvard University Press (Belknap), 1971). Somewhat different aspects of the idea are investigated in Larry S. Temkin, *Inequality* (Oxford: Oxford University Press, 1996). A witty and engaging discussion of the topic, orthogonal to contemporary philosophical treatments but germane to them, is George Bernard Shaw, *The Intelligent Woman's Guide to Socialism and Capitalism* (New York: Brentano, 1928).

See also: CAPITALISM, COMMUNITY/COMMUNITARIANISM, FREEDOM/LIBERTY, JUSTICE, LABOR MOVEMENT, LEFT/RIGHT/CENTER, LIBERALISM, MARKETS, MARXISM, MORALITY, RACE/RACISM, RIGHTS, SOCIALISM, UTILITARIANISM, WELFARE/WELFARE STATE

F

Fascism

For liberals and socialists and, since World War II, for conservatives too, *fascist* is a term of reproach. The word conjures up images of paramilitary organizations in the thrall of a supreme Leader, and of violent mobs that threaten the achievements of civilization itself. Anything illiberal or anti-democratic, racist or rabidly nationalistic, **authoritarian** or totalitarian – in short, anything inimical to political decency or civility – is liable to be labeled *fascist*. Strictly speaking, however, the term refers to a political tendency that came to fruition in Europe in a historical context shaped by World War I, the **Bolshevik** Revolution, and, above all, by the failure of revolutionary socialist revolutions in Eastern and Central Europe in the aftermath of the war. Fascism came to power in Italy in the 1920s and in Germany and the Iberian peninsula in the 1930s. In the course of World War II, fascist movements emerged in many of the territories occupied by the German army. In a few instances, they briefly ruled their countries of origin. But then, with the allied victory, the fascist upsurge quickly subsided. It is fair to say that fascism suffered a historic defeat. After the war, it survived only marginally – in Spain and Portugal (until the 1970s) and, more tenuously, in some Latin American and Middle Eastern countries where political entrepreneurs launched mostly unsuccessful, but still significant, political movements based on the European model. Currently, Latin American fascism has been marginalized too, and "classical" fascism has all but vanished from the Middle East. With the collapse of Communism, a few remnants of Eastern European fascism reemerged in the Balkans and elsewhere. This phenomenon too is of only marginal importance in Europe today.

The world of the early twenty-first century is very different from the world in which fascism emerged and briefly flourished. However, political styles reminiscent of fascism have not disappeared. Neither have popular mentalities developed to a point where the temptations of the fascist style of political engagement are extinguished. Fascistic elements survive everywhere even if fascism itself, as a distinctive political ideology, is now effectively defunct. Nowadays, these elements manifest themselves in subtle ways, but not always. In recent decades, religious movements of many kinds – not only those associated with political Islam – have taken on a distinctly fascistic aspect. Classical fascism was hostile to religion. But, from its inception in the 1920s, the Roman Catholic Church and its counterparts in Eastern Europe sustained a **clerical fascist** component. In the Christian world, clerical fascism never quite caught on as a mass movement. It remains to be seen whether blowback from Western, especially American, imperialism will fuel the success of what some contemporary writers, insensitive to social and historical differences, represent as Muslim clerical fascism. The phenomenon is real, but the description is inaccurate. Fascism was a creature of a particular moment in world, especially European, history. The rhetorical gain in confounding it with phenomena that are superficially similar in some respects, and then in tarnishing them all with the same brush, is more than offset by the loss of analytical clarity.

At the dawn of the twentieth century, as Social Democracy became increasingly integrated into the political cultures of European states, some erstwhile socialists in France and Italy effectively abandoned their commitment to socialism at the same time that they exalted socialism's revolutionary traditions. They came to value revolution for its own sake, seeing revolutionary violence as redemptive. These thinkers, along with other social and political theorists from the same milieu – Georges Sorel (1847–1922), Wilfredo Pareto (1848–1923), Charles Peguy (1873–1914), Gaetano Mosca (1858–1941) and others, were not themselves fascists, strictly speaking. But their thinking helped to shape fascist ideology.

The name *fascist* was taken up during World War I by the followers of Benito Mussolini (1883–1945), dictator of Italy from 1922 until his overthrow in 1943. Giovanni Gentile (1875–1944), a philosopher associated with Hegelian **idealism**, was described by both himself and Mussolini as fascism's quasi-official philosopher.

For Gentile, under fascism the people would express their spirit and find their strength in the direction of a supreme Leader. Then the class struggle would give way to a **corporatist** organization of society in which labor, **capital**, and the state collaborate to govern all aspects of political and social life. Corporatist rule would supersede parliamentary forms of governance. Multi-party systems would therefore be abolished; only one *fascist* party would rule – in the interests of the entire nation, rather than any particular class. Above all, fascist states would renew themselves continually through the discharge of revolutionary violence. By this means, they would purify the body politic and mobilize its collective expression.

In both theory and practice, fascism was committed to leaving intact the power of capital. In principle, the state can rightfully interfere with the operation of capitalist markets if it is necessary to fulfill its national mission – especially in times of war. But, in normal circumstances, capitalists should be free to do as they please. Thus, in the fascist creed, the targets of revolutionary violence were not the **exploiters** of labor, as revolutionary socialists and anarchists maintained. Rather, violence would be exercised against elements within the political community who are, for whatever reason, at odds with the spirit of the nation. Foreigners generally – and, in the historical context within which fascism emerged, Jews in particular – are likely candidates for such attention. But, strictly speaking, fascism need not be **anti-Semitic** or racist. In contrast to the German case, Italian fascism was generally tolerant of racial differences and it did not become overtly anti-Semitic until Mussolini's alliance with Hitler's Germany forced compliance with **Nazi** racial policies.

Fascist societies are therefore capitalist societies, and fascism is a pro-capitalist ideology. But, because fascist states accord exceptional power to the state, capitalists' freedom of action is less secure under fascism than it is under liberal forms of governance. This is why fascism is generally not optimal for capitalist development. Classical fascism arose in extraordinary circumstances; its appeal to capitalists, in the time and place of its inception, depends on this fact. As a theory and practice, fascism is beneficial for capitalists in circumstances in which a potentially revolutionary labor movement has suffered a major setback, but still remains strong enough to pose a threat to capitalists' privileges. Then, despite the risks to their own power and independence, capitalists have an interest in supporting the system from which they benefit by supporting fascist movements – both in and out of power. This configuration of circumstances is decisive. For capitalists, especially those with much to lose, fascism is desirable and arguably even necessary when the working class, though weakened, is still a danger to its most fundamental interests. This pattern obtained throughout fascism's classical period. It explains fascism's success in Germany as much as it does in Italy. It also explains why fascist movements were able to win and retain power in Spain and Portugal, and why they have been a pole of attraction in Latin America and elsewhere.

As a mass revolutionary movement of the Right, fascism was in competition with revolutionary socialism for the hearts and minds of workers and other popular constituencies. It is worth noting that, at a rhetorical level, fascists were less hostile towards socialism (but not Communism!) than towards liberalism and parliamentary democracy. The Nazis even called their movement "National Socialism." But, of course, the resemblances are superficial. Socialism aims to install the rule of Reason in society; fascism draws on repressed atavistic sentiments and attitudes. It empowers irrationality. But the collective insanity that marks fascist societies does not erupt spontaneously. For its profoundly anti-social and destructive spirit to take hold of the political scene, it must be unleashed by determined political forces, moved by real material interests. This is what happened in the time and place of fascism's ascendance.

In the 1930s, when fascist movements threatened liberal democracy, many liberal and socialist intellectuals believed that the world stood, as it were, at a crossroads between socialism and "barbarism." It was a contest between Reason and Unreason. Fascism encouraged the expression of the darkest side of human nature. It was literally *anti*-**progressive**. Despite their different histories and social contexts, contemporary manifestations of fascistic political styles merit a similar assessment, especially insofar as they meld with religious fanaticism. In an imaginable but unlikely future, neo-fascist remnants of classical fascist movements could again pose dangers. In actual circumstances, a far greater danger is posed by theocratic movements – both in their own right and because the fear of them is so easily exploitable by political elites in the West. But this menace should not be confused with fascism. Fascism is not just, or even primarily, a political style. It is a form of class struggle – waged by capitalists, particularly those with the most to lose, to crush working-class movements that threaten their dominant position. It is always wise to name the enemy correctly. This is what happened in the anti-fascist movements of the past – in the American **New Deal** and in contemporaneous **Popular Front** initiatives in Europe and elsewhere. To avoid the barbarism that threatens many decades later, we owe ourselves no less.

Further Reading

A useful anthology of writings on fascism is Roger Griffin (ed.), *Fascism* (Oxford: Oxford University Press, 1995). Another is Aristotle A. Kallis, *Fascism Reader* (New York: Routledge, 2002). The latter contains important contemporaneous discussions as well as more recent accounts, and provides examples of liberal, Marxist, and post-modern analyses. For an accessible and comprehensive history of the movement, see Stanley G. Payne, *A History of Fascism: 1914–1945* (Madison, WI: University of Wisconsin Press, 1995). On fascism's precursors, Zeev Sternhell, *The Birth of Fascist Ideology* (Princeton, NJ: Princeton University Press, 1995) is indispensable. Useful insights are conveyed too in George L. Mosse, *The Fascist Revolution: Toward a General Theory of Fascism* (New York: Howard Fertig, 2000). At a psychological level, the temptations of fascism are conveyed in an illuminating way by the writer Umberto Eco in his essay "Ur-Fascism," in Umberto Eco (Alastair McEwan, trans.), *Five Moral Pieces* (New York and San Diego, CA: Harvest, 2002).

See also: ANARCHISM, CAPITALISM, CLASS, COMMUNISM, CONSERVATISM, DEMOCRACY, IDEOLOGY, IMPERIALISM, LABOR, LABOR MOVEMENT, LEFT/RIGHT/CENTER, LIBERALISM, MARKETS, NATION/ NATIONALISM, POLITICAL ISLAM, PROGRESS, RACE/RACISM, SOCIAL DEMOCRACY, SOCIALISM, STATE, THEOCRACY, TOTALITARIANISM, VIOLENCE/NON-VIOLENCE, WAR

Feminism

Feminism denotes a wide range of social, political, and cultural theories. The term is also used more vaguely to refer to ways of thinking and acting that privilege women's concerns. Some versions of feminism are sufficiently comprehensive to count as ideologies. **Progressive** women's movements are guided by feminist ideologies, and there is a feminist component to progressive ideologies generally. In part for historical reasons, and in part because feminist and Left values overlap, feminism is usually associated with the political Left. However, there are feminists positioned across the political spectrum. Though most feminists are women, many men are feminists too. Though most cultural and intellectual feminists are, to some extent, committed to feminist politics, some are apolitical or content to confine their politics to **consciousness raising**. In view of this diversity, it is tempting to say that there is no common core uniting all the diverse expressions of feminist theory and practice; that, at most, there are only "family resemblances" joining some feminisms to others. Nevertheless, at a very general level, all feminists are united in their opposition to **patriarchy** or, more specifically, to patriarchal attitudes and their institutional implementations. Feminists see the world – or at least the social world – from the perspective of women, and feminist political programs are in one way or another dedicated to advancing women's interests. Some feminists see the feminist project as an effort to achieve women's liberation; others seek to promote equality between women and men; others just want to improve women's position in society. Although there are many divisions within the feminist movement, these self-representations are, for the most part, complementary; the differences are mainly ones of emphasis.

Patriarchy has existed since the dawn of civilization. Whether any societies anywhere were **matriarchal** or egalitarian with respect to women and men is a matter of dispute. There is no doubt, however, that the world's major religions have encouraged patriarchal attitudes and practices – notwithstanding recent efforts to the contrary among some practitioners of a few of them. Thus, feminism arose and developed in the course of the long struggle to **secularize** human societies. It first emerged as a distinctively political and cultural tendency in advanced intellectual circles in Western Europe in the eighteenth century. A number of important **Enlightenment** figures, including the Marquis de Condorcet (1743–1794), championed women's interests, especially in education. Mary Wollstonecraft's *A Vindication of the Rights of Women* (1792), an unambiguously feminist work, brought together many strains of nascent Dutch, French and especially British proto-feminism. However, it was not until the early nineteenth century that a full-fledged feminist movement emerged. In the aftermath of the French Revolution, some French **radicals** and socialists became feminists more or less instinctively. In Britain, feminism was a component of the larger movement for social **reform**. John Stuart Mill's (1807–1873) *Subjection of Women* (1869) is perhaps the best-known and most cogent expression of this genre of feminist thought. Pre-Civil War feminism in the United States was of a piece with British feminism, and was closely associated with the struggle against **slavery**. Still, at first, the US lagged behind the British and French. The first women's rights convention in the United States was held in Seneca Falls, New York in 1848. Thereafter, Americans have been at the forefront of feminist struggles, though a few other countries – New Zealand and Canada, among them – precede the US in granting women the vote.

From the latter half of the nineteenth century until the 1920s and beyond, women's suffrage was the principal goal of organized feminist movements throughout the world. Other concerns included women's education and access to the professions. Militants in these movements are nowadays called "first wave feminists." With voting rights secure, "second wave feminism" emerged in the

1960s and 1970s. Second wave feminists were concerned mainly with economic equality between men and women, and with reproductive rights. They led the struggle for workplace equality and for the legalization of abortion. Despite tensions that persist to this day, second wave feminists were also the first to accord prominence to lesbians within the women's movement.

Second wave feminists popularized a distinction between **gender** and sex, where gender is a social category, and sex is a biological one. Feminist theorists emphasized how internalized notions of gender affect all aspects of women's lives, including expressions of sexuality. They also maintained that, because gender categorizations are social (or, as is often said, **socially constructed**), they are susceptible to being changed. They can therefore become objects of political struggle. Second wave feminists engaged this struggle – for, as they said at first, "women's liberation." Of course, it is an open question how biological and social factors interact in particular instances. Feminists generally, and radical feminists in particular, are inclined to discount the importance of biological constraints on women's lives. It is plain, though, that biology cannot be discounted altogether. As long as women bear children and men do not, biology is, to some degree, destiny. This is not to say that there are inexorable biological reasons why the burdens of childcare must fall inordinately upon women, or that women's traditional roles are as they are in consequence of an unchangeable women's nature. It is to say, however, that the consequences of sex for gender cannot be entirely denied.

Although the feminist analogue to "racist" is "sexist," rather than "genderist," "gender" nowadays often substitutes for "sex" in mainstream political discourse. In part, the influence of feminist ideology from the time of the emergence of the second wave accounts for this usage. However, it is also plain that, to some extent, "gender" is employed as a euphemism for "sex." This usage reflects a long-standing puritanical streak in American culture. It also reflects a characteristic disequilibrium in the American popular psyche. Contemporary American puritanism coexists with (and nourishes) an omnipresent sexualization of daily life. This tension is pervasive and debilitating. Although feminism is ostensibly a subversive ideology, a challenge to mainstream beliefs, a similar ambivalence is also evident in feminist thinking.

Second wave feminism was born in the political cauldron of the **New Left**. It was self-consciously part of the "sexual revolution" of the 1960s. Sexual emancipation has remained a tenet of some strains of feminist theory and practice, and few feminists reject the idea outright. But it was not long before the liberation of desire gave way, in many feminists' minds, to a countervailing concern with freedom from power imbalances in sexual relationships – and, more generally, with **politically correct** sex. These concerns reinforce the puritanical side of the political culture. Because American feminists played a vanguard role in feminism's second wave and thanks also to American cultural imperialism, this sensibility soon radiated out to feminist circles throughout the world. The politicization of sex has had some salutary consequences. The feminist conviction epitomized in the slogan "the personal is political" has raised everyone's consciousness. But intrusions into the realm of intimacy can also be inimical to the goal of sexual liberation and also to human emancipatory interests more generally. Whether feminists have struck the right balance remains an open question.

For the sake of equality in sexual relations, some second wave feminists were disposed to disparage heterosexual relations altogether, seeing lesbianism as the only feasible way to implement feminist ideals. However, as the influence of second wave feminist theory and practice increasingly permeated into the larger political culture, this extreme position, along with others in a similar vein, diminished in importance. Debates about hetero- and homosexuality – and, more generally, about **separatism** – came to be increasingly confined to the movement's radical, mainly academic, fringes. Nowadays, on matters of intimacy, the views of the vast majority of feminists are indistinguishable from those of the general population. Specifically, most feminists are liberals with respect to male/female relations. Their main concerns involve public, not intimate, matters; their goal is to secure equal rights. This objective fits easily into the framework of contemporary politics; hardly anyone officially disagrees. In practice, however, the ideal of gender equality is far from realized and opposition to its implementation remains fierce, especially in non-liberal religious circles. Thus, liberal feminists still have much to do – to promote more equal distributions of home labor and childcare, and to insure equality in the paid economy. Contrary to what is nowadays widely believed, this is not a time for liberal feminists to declare victory and then disappear.

It is common in feminist circles to contrast liberal feminism, which seeks the full integration of women into the social and political life of liberal states and a more equal distribution of household labor, with radical feminism, which continues some of the original themes of second wave feminism – in separatist (if not always expressly homosexual) directions. Radical feminism also comes in many varieties, but all radical feminists believe that women should create their own institutions to some extent. Radical feminism has a strong presence in the academy, where, as noted, it often has an apolitical character. When socialism was still a vital presence on the political landscape, there were also socialist feminists, intent on integrating feminist perspectives into socialist and Marxist theories and programs. Socialist feminists, Marxist or otherwise, are heavily outnumbered in today's feminist movement. But, to this day, some of the most active and lucid socialists are socialist feminists, as are some of the major figures of contemporary feminism. There are other varieties of feminism as well. Most of them are more theoretical than political, even when they link up self-consciously with political movements. Thus, for example, *ecofeminists* address environmental concerns from a feminist perspective, although it is far from clear that there is a distinctive ecofeminist practice or that ecofeminism represents a distinct tendency within the environmental movement. In any case, the boundaries between feminisms are, in nearly all cases, fluid.

"Third wave feminism" emerged in the late 1980s. The difference between it and second wave feminism is more generational than ideological. Third wave feminists have only a theoretical knowledge of the oppressions second wave feminists helped to banish. Third wave feminists are also less likely than second wave feminists to have been involved with Left politics. The issues have also changed. Having come of age at a time when the right to an abortion seemed secure, third wave feminists are less concerned with reproductive rights than second wave feminists were. Also, with improved job prospects for professional women, they are less inclined to emphasize the inclusion of women in male-dominated professions. But third wave feminists are intent on expanding received understandings of gender and sexuality, and also, at least at a theoretical level, in connecting with women of color and other non-traditional constituencies. Third wave feminism is, if anything, even more of an academic phenomenon than was second wave feminism. Ironically, though, it is generally less constrained by rigorous intellectual norms. Many third wave feminists are practitioners of fashionable, but shallow and confused, **post-modernist** modes of thought.

First and second wave feminism were largely movements run by and, to some degree, for educated, middle- and upper-class women in developed countries. The social background of third wave feminists is no different. But they have deliberately focused on the situations of working-class women and women of color, and of women around the world. In addition, in the decades since second wave feminism emerged, many women throughout the world, especially in **postcolonial** societies, have, in one way or other, taken up the feminist banner. Thus, feminism has become a more ecumenical and cosmopolitan movement than it used to be. Ironically, this change has stirred up conflicts between feminists and multiculturalists, their erstwhile and presumptive allies. The problem is straightforward and apparently unavoidable because many of the cultures multiculturalists would celebrate are profoundly and irreducibly patriarchal. Now that Western, and especially American, imperialism has stimulated an upsurge in theocratic politics of a fundamentalist kind, the tension has become acute. It has become increasingly clear to many feminist theorists and activists that unalloyed multiculturalism may not be good for women.

Some second and third wave feminists were inclined to disparage liberal rights in favor of "an ethic of care." Their idea was that women are especially disposed to virtues consistent with their (biological?) role as nurturers, and that these virtues hold out more promise for making the world better than can any rights-centered doctrine. For several decades, debates have raged in feminist circles about these contentions. By now, many feminists would agree with what has always been the predominant view of non-feminist moral philosophers: that the very idea of an ethics of care is empirically and conceptually flawed. But even more than the problems inherent in what was once promoted as a new and distinctively feminist ethics, the resurgence of patriarchal attitudes and practices among "the wretched of the earth" is bound to focus feminists' attention on the merits of an "ethic of rights." If feminist thinking adapts to this situation, the feminism of the future is likely to meld into other, more comprehensive, progressive ideologies that privilege notions of universal **human rights.**

In the academy, the feminist turn in social science, historiography, literary and cultural criticism, legal theory, political theory, and philosophy (including ethics and the history and philosophy of science) has had a salutary effect in incorporating women's concerns into ongoing discussions. However, the jury is still out on the importance of this development for theory construction and revision. It appears, as of now, that more has been promised than delivered. The problem is especially evident in the more theoretical academic disciplines. Historians are mostly atheoretical; they construct narratives, rather than theories, and they do so subject to few, if any, theoretical constraints. Accordingly, feminist historiography has contributed significantly to our understanding of the past. The feminist turn has yielded fruitful results in literary and cultural domains too, notwithstanding the occasional intrusion of overblown theoretical pretensions. It is debatable, though, whether feminist legal and political theory or feminist philosophy and social science have been similarly successful. In these disciplines (more than the others), feminist work, though tolerated and even encouraged, is effectively ghettoized – thanks partly to separatist inclinations among feminists themselves. Focusing on problems of concern to women, and introducing women's perspectives, has been useful in these fields too. But the main theoretical traditions of political and legal theory, philosophy, and the social sciences have so far been little affected.

Further Reading

Nearly every academic discipline in the humanities and social sciences today has a feminist component, and feminist thinking has permeated into the wider academic and political culture. Consequently, the literature on feminism is enormous. For a general historical perspective, Estelle B. Freedman's *No Turning Back: The History of Feminism and the Future of Women* (New York: Ballantine Books, 2002) is useful.

Key texts that anticipate the modern feminist movement are collected in Miriam Schneir, *Feminism: The Essential Historical Writings* (New York: Vintage, 1994). For some of the most important second wave feminist literature, see Miriam Schneir, *Feminism in Our Time: The Essential Writings, World War II to the Present* (New York: Vintage, 1994). By common consensus, an important impetus for second wave feminism was Simone de Beauvoir, *The Second Sex* (New York: Vintage, 1989). Of almost equal importance in the United States was Betty Friedan, *The Feminine Mystique* (New York: W.W. Norton and Company, 2001). The obscurantist character of many third wave feminist writings is on display in Judith Butler and Sarah Salih (eds.), *The Judith Butler Reader* (Malden, MA: Blackwell Publishers, 2004). Tensions between feminism and multiculturalism are discussed in Susan M. Okin (Joshua Cohen, Matthew Howard, Martha C. Nussbaum, eds.) *Is Multiculturalism Bad for Women?* (Princeton, NJ: Princeton University Press, 1999). The claim that women and men are disposed to adapt different views on caring and on rights and other universal, abstract principles comes from the (much-disputed) research of Carol Gilligan – see *In a Different Voice: Psychological Theory and Women's Development* (Cambridge, MA: Harvard University Press, 1993). Gilligan's research is applied expressly to moral philosophical questions in Nel Noddings, *Caring: A Feminist Approach to Ethics and Moral Education* (Berkeley and Los Angeles: University of California Press, 2003). For a critical, but generally sympathetic assessment of feminist political philosophy, see Jonathan Wolff, *An Introduction to Political Philosophy* (Oxford: Oxford University Press, 1996), chapter 6. Examples of the genre include Catherine MacKinnon, *Feminism Unmodified* (Cambridge, MA: Harvard University Press, 1987) and Carole Pateman, *The Sexual Contract* (Stanford, CA: Stanford University Press, 1988). Feminist contributions to other areas of philosophy are included in Nancy Tuana and Rosemarie Tong (eds.), *Feminism and Philosophy* (Boulder, CO: Westview Press, 1995), and Janet A. Kourany, James P. Sterba, and Rosemarie Tong (eds.), *Feminist Philosophies: Problems, Theories and Applications*, 2nd edition (Upper Saddle River, NJ: Prentice Hall, 1998).

See also: COSMOPILATISM, CULTURE, EQUALITY/EGALITARIANISM, ENVIRONMENTALISM, FREEDOM/ LIBERTY, FUNDAMENTALISM, IDENTITY POLITICS, IDEOLOGY, IMPERIALISM, LEFT/RIGHT/CENTER,

Freedom of expression

LIBERALISM, MARXISM, MULTICULTURALISM, PROGRESS, RACE/RACISM, RIGHTS, SOCIALISM, STATE, THEOCRACY

Freedom of expression

In the "culture wars" of the 1990s, speech codes proscribing speech offensive to particular identity groups were debated on many college campuses in the United States. One might therefore suppose that the issue of free speech is still unresolved in our political culture. Perhaps this is so around the edges. In the main, however, support for tolerance generally, and for freedom of expression in particular, have won the day. Even in the debates over speech codes, the burden of proof fell on those who proposed restricting expression. More tellingly, the arguments defenders of speech codes offered were tailored to accord with liberal justifications for tolerance.

John Stuart Mill (1806–1873) provided a clear statement of the liberal view in *On Liberty* (1859), a work which, with the exception of *The Communist Manifesto* (1848), is still the most widely read tract of nineteenth-century political thought. In Mill's formulation, **coercive** interference with individuals' lives and behaviors, whether undertaken by the state through legal penalties or by **civil society**, through "the moral coercion of public opinion," is always wrong – except to prevent (serious) harm to (identifiable) others. Along with religious toleration, tolerance of speech and other forms of expression have always been paramount liberal concerns. Liberals are therefore of one mind in extending the benefits of tolerance to expression. But since the notion of (significant) harm to (identifiable) others is amenable to a (small but not insignificant) range of interpretations, general adherence to the liberal view does not automatically settle policy questions. This is why debates about speech codes are possible within a liberal framework.

In the United States, debates about free speech are typically cast in a constitutionalist guise. The question often becomes – what does the First Amendment to the US Constitution imply? The constitutionalization of policy disputes is a long-standing feature of political life in the United States. However, in this case more than most, the constitutional question is a proxy for a question that needs no constitutional carapace. The real question is – what ought social policy to be with respect to freedom of expression? There may be good political reasons to pose policy questions like this one in a legalistic framework. Doing so may enhance public order and social stability. However, for purposes of philosophical understanding, there is no reason to take on legalistic constraints, no reason not to ask the real question directly.

Mill argued for freedom of thought and expression on utilitarian grounds. He maintained that, of all possible social policies with respect to speech and other forms of expression, the one that produces the best outcomes in a utilitarian sense is tolerance. As with other utilitarian justifications for public policies, Mill's case rests on contestable empirical speculations. But, as Mill's example shows, a plausible case can be made, even so. Like many other nineteenth-century thinkers, Mill assumed that the growth of knowledge is utility enhancing. He then argued that tolerance leads to the discovery of new truths and therefore to the growth of knowledge better than would any less tolerant policy. Tolerance also improves outcomes indirectly by making individuals better "consumers" in what we would nowadays call "the marketplace of ideas" – thereby enhancing the efficacy of tolerance in the discovery of new truths. In a word, tolerance is an improver. Even if, in some times and places, intolerance of some forms of expression might plausibly lead to better outcomes, the long-run consequence of maximally tolerant public policies is, on the whole, more beneficial than any alternative policies would be.

Because it depends ultimately on how the world works, the utilitarian defense of free speech is too precarious for some liberal philosophers. Also, some liberals, probably a majority of them, are opposed to utilitarianism on other grounds. They therefore defend free expression in other ways. For the most part, these defenses fall into two broad categories – one libertarian, the other **Kantian**. The libertarian defense is typical of the strain of libertarian thought that takes its inspiration from the work of John Locke (1632–1704). The core idea is that there are rights, including free speech rights, that are morally primary, and that public policies must therefore accommodate. This justification is structurally similar to the constitutionalist justifications that predominate in the United States. The difference is that, for liberal constitutionalists, there is no mystery as to how free speech rights derive. They are grounded in a constitution that articulates the basic rules of the political order. Libertarians, however, merely assert the existence of the morally primary rights that justify the policy prescriptions they favor. There is typically nothing that they do or can say in their defense. The Kantian justification, on the other hand, appeals to the moral equality of persons. Very generally, the idea is that suppressions of free expression fail to accord the respect due to moral personality. It is fair to say that the most philosophically cogent and subtle defenses of free speech take this contention as their point of departure.

The philosophical consensus holds that, in ideal conditions (or close approximations of the ideal), tolerance should rule the day. Those who challenge the wisdom of tolerance in all instances – defenders of speech codes, for example – maintain that the reason to deviate from the policy prescriptions directly implied by the philosophical consensus is that real world conditions fall sufficiently short of the ideal. As remarked, the arguments advanced by those who press this position are usually couched in liberal terms. Thus, it is sometimes held that, given background conditions of racial or **gender oppression**, hate speech and other forms of expression that give offense constitute genuine harms. Or it is argued that speech that derogates particular individuals or groups fails to accord persons equal respect.

An argument associated with the **New Left** pushes the boundaries of liberal discourse more decisively. This is not surprising, inasmuch as the argument grows out of the **critical theory** tradition and is therefore ultimately derived from Marxism. Its best-known exponent was Herbert Marcuse (1898–1979). In an essay called "Repressive Tolerance" (1965) that was widely read at the time, Marcuse argued that "pure tolerance," tolerance regardless of content, is, as liberals suppose, warranted in ideal conditions – not exactly for the usual liberal reasons, but because, as liberals also believe, it enhances human freedom. But thanks to background (economic) inequalities and also to the narcotizing effects of new media and other technological means for shaping opinion – or, as critical theorists would say, for "controlling **consciousness**" – pure tolerance, far from serving emancipatory interests, has become a mechanism through which dissenting voices are effectively quashed. Metaphorically put, Marcuse's contention was that free expression lets off steam, thereby neutralizing the subversive power of dissenting ideas. In this way, it functions "repressively" – not by suppressing ideas directly, as literal repression would, but by establishing a rationally indefensible conformity in a comparatively benign, but nevertheless insidious, way.

The only remedy, on this view, is for insurgent groups to create conditions that force the victims of the existing order to "take consciousness" of their situation. To this end, New Left proponents of Marcuse's position advocated a dramatic and conspicuous break with the rules of the game – in disregard of the requirements of civility and decorum. Marcuse's essay, unlike Mill's tract, was addressed to insurgents, not political elites. But it is obvious, even so, that were liberal constraints on public policy to break down, it would be the victims of the existing order, rather than its leaders, who would suffer most. It therefore became clear, in short order, that if it ever makes sense to act in ways that put liberal tolerance in jeopardy, it can only be when liberal protections are secure. But since tolerance is generally not secure, even in countries where it is officially promoted, Marcuse's argument is politically irrelevant in most imaginable circumstances.

Nevertheless, it is of considerable theoretical interest. For one thing, it calls attention to the problems severe social and economic inequalities pose for theories of freedom of expression. The problem is not just that individuals with ample resources are better positioned than others to make themselves heard in "the marketplace of ideas." It is also that the powerful establish the framework within which discussion proceeds. Thus, they are able to marginalize ideas detrimental to their interests, without actually proscribing them. It was a conviction of Marcuse's that much of what lies beyond the pale in political cultures like ours is, in fact, true; and therefore that its **de facto** exclusion is not a consequence of a rational consensus but of a deliberate or, more often, unwitting exercise of power.

Marcuse's argument also calls attention to the general problem of what morality requires in a world that is recalcitrant to its demands. Consider **pacifism**. Many, probably most, non-pacifists would agree that, in ideal conditions, resorts to violence are wrong. But, in their view, existing conditions are so far from ideal that abstentions from violence can lead to outcomes that actually increase the overall level of violence or otherwise make existing situations worse. Pacifists maintain, on the other hand, that the way to move towards an ideal non-violent world is to act now as if the ideal already existed. This is a dispute that can never be settled definitively; the consequences of resorts to violence and abstentions from it are too context-dependent for there to be only one right answer. But there is a general lesson to be learned — that what is best when Reason is in control is not necessarily best in real world conditions. Then there is often no substitute for careful, case-by-case evaluations. Defenders of pure tolerance are like pacifists in the sense that they advise acting here and now as if ideal conditions obtained. But there is an important difference. In our world, there are comparatively few pacifists, but a great many advocates of pure tolerance. Because this is the case, those who deviate from the path of strict tolerance, no matter how circumspect or judicious they may be, and no matter how well intentioned, almost always end up making intolerance itself the issue, rather than the conditions they seek to rectify. Thus, from a **strategic** point of view, intolerance is almost always unwise, even if it is not strictly proscribed by the requirements of political morality. In general, there is no universally correct way to apply ideal theory to real world cases. Pacifism is not always indisputably the best policy. But where matters of speech are involved, the way forward is clear enough: we can and should act now as if we were where we ultimately want to be.

Further Reading

Classical liberal cases for free expression are set forth in John Stuart Mill, *On Liberty* (London: Penguin, 1975) and in John Locke, *A Letter Concerning Toleration: Humbly Submitted* (Indianapolis, IN: Hackett, 1983). A useful guide through the thicket of American constitutional treatments of free expression issues is Daniel A. Farber, *The First Amendment: Concepts and Insights* (New York: Foundation Press, 2002). See also Cass Sunstein, *Democracy and the Problem of Free Speech* (New York: Simon and Schuster, 1995). An original and insightful critique of free speech can be found in John Durham Peters, *Courting the Abyss: Free Speech and the Liberal Tradition* (Chicago: University of Chicago Press, 2005). A sophisticated non-utilitarian, non-constitutionalist treatment of free speech issues that draws on Kantian themes in moral philosophy is T.M. Scanlon, "A Theory of Freedom of Expression," in T.M. Scanlon, *The Difficulty of Tolerance: Essays in Political Philosophy* (Cambridge: Cambridge University Press, 2003). Marcuse's essay "Repressive Tolerance" can be found in Robert Paul Wolff, Jr., Barrington Moore, Jr. and Herbert Marcuse, *A Critique of Pure Tolerance* (Boston: Beacon Press, 1965). I discuss Mill and Marcuse at greater length in *Engaging Political Philosophy: From Hobbes to Rawls* (Malden, MA: Blackwell Publishers, 2002), chapter 4.

See also: CULTURE, EQUALITY/EGALITARIANISM, FREEDOM/LIBERTY, IDENTITY POLITICS, LIBERALISM, LIBERTARIANISM, MARKETS, MARXISM, MORALITY, POWER, RACE/RACISM, RIGHTS, STATE, UTILITARIANISM, WAR

Freedom/liberty

No word in the political lexicon carries more positive connotations than *freedom*. It is therefore not surprising that none is more susceptible to abuse. In the United States, for example, those who do America's bidding in **Third World** countries or, previously, in the Soviet and Chinese spheres of influence are called "freedom fighters" in government **propaganda** – even, indeed especially, when they are anything but. Sometimes too the word is used to stand for quite different notions that also carry positive connotations. Thus, *freedom* and *democracy* are sometimes conflated. To add to the confusion, people sometimes talk as if *freedom* and *liberty* designate distinct concepts. In fact, they are synonyms. That they might not appear to be so is a consequence of the Norman conquest of Anglo-Saxon England a thousand years ago. Because the English language thereafter drew on both German and Latin sources, there are sometimes two words for the same thing. *Swine* and *pork* are examples; so are *freedom* and *liberty*.

The origins of *freedom* can be found in ancient legal systems. *Free* was a legal status that contrasted with *slave*. Thus, the idea arose that to be free is to be independent or, what comes to the same thing, to be undominated by others. This usage persists when we speak of "national liberation" or of "free states." Recent revivals of republican political theory recover this understanding.

As liberal political ideas developed, freedom came to be conceived differently – as *negative liberty*. Thomas Hobbes (1588–1679) epitomized this way of thinking when he called freedom "the absence of external Impediments." One is free, Hobbes thought, to the extent that one is free from interferences. Classical liberalism made this understanding its own. It also imposed an austere view of what counts as an interference. It is uncontroversial that simple inabilities do not restrict liberty; no one would claim that we are unfree to walk through walls simply because we are unable to do so. On the other hand, deliberate interventions by others – the state, above all – plainly are freedom restricting. For classical liberals, these are the only "external Impediments" there are. Many latter-day liberals are inclined to view this understanding as indefensibly restrictive. This is why, in addition to deliberate interferences, they would count non- or extra-political institutional impediments as among the means by which freedom can be diminished. Institutional impediments result from the (often deliberate) activities of others, but they do not expressly aim at preventing anyone from doing anything. Thus, on the classical liberal view, unemployed workers would be unfree, say, to buy the factory that fired them if there were laws prohibiting the purchase. But if they are unable to buy the factory only because, given prevailing economic and social practices, the factory costs more than they can afford, they are free to buy the factory, albeit unable to do so. In short, classical liberalism assimilates institutional impediments to simple disabilities. In contrast, modern liberals – unlike libertarians – regard institutional impediments as freedom restricting in roughly the way that deliberate interferences are. They take seriously the intuition that, even in the absence of restrictive laws, unemployed workers are not free to buy their own factories.

Freedom/liberty

In standard accounts, negative liberty contrasts with *positive liberty*. Positive liberty pertains to the range of things agents are able to do. So conceived, the contrast may not be quite as clear as is widely believed. Put metaphorically, for proponents of negative liberty, the larger the area of non-interference, the freer one is; for proponents of positive liberty, the more one is able to do what one wants, the freer one becomes. But it is plain that expanding the area of non-interference often increases individuals' capacities to do what they want. Still, the two notions are not the same. For proponents of positive liberty, enhancing abilities ipso facto enhances freedom. Not so, for those who value negative liberty only; for them, what matters is expanding the area of non-interference.

These (related) concepts cry out for philosophical elaboration if only because negative and positive liberties vary widely in their importance to individuals' freedom. Imposing some new restrictions – say, by adding laws restricting parking at rush hour – diminishes overall (negative) liberty only trivially. On the other hand, a law prohibiting freedom of expression would be devastating to overall (negative) liberty. This would be true even for those who care little about free speech and deeply about parking regulations. Thus, philosophers must somehow rank freedoms by their overall importance, and they must do so on grounds other than their actual importance to some (or all) individuals. Similarly, it would be a hollow notion of positive liberty if all abilities were regarded on an equal footing. An individual's positive liberty is enhanced little by opening up a few new parking spaces. On the other hand, positive liberty would be much enhanced if new means for enhancing public expression came into being. It is not enough just to count abilities to ascertain how free persons are. Different degrees of urgency attach to different positive liberties, just as they do to negative liberties. Any satisfactory account of human freedom would have to take these differences into account, and to justify them.

In general, proponents of positive liberty are inclined to focus on the *source* of control, and therefore to suppose that we are free to the extent that we are the authors of our own actions. In the most refined philosophical formulation of this idea, freedom is **autonomy**, subordination to laws one has legislated oneself. It was this idea that Jean-Jacques Rousseau (1712–1778) introduced into political thought and that Immanuel Kant (1724–1804) went on to make the basis of the most powerful and influential moral philosophy of our era. Autonomy and non-domination, the republican ideal, plainly have much in common. But the Rousseauean–**Kantian** notion is more demanding. It requires that persons act on principles of their own legislation; the republican concept makes no corresponding demand. The Rousseauean–Kantian idea also became the basis for the Hegelian–Marxian notion of alienation. In their sense, to be alienated is to have one's autonomy violated, and to apprehend this violation experientially.

It is an open question whether freedom, in any of its senses, is a historically conditioned value, or whether a yearning for freedom is, as it were, hard wired into human nature. The fact that a yearning for freedom does seem indispensable for explaining the struggles of oppressed peoples throughout history supports the view that there is a trans-historical and causally efficacious desire for freedom built into human beings' psychological constitutions. Ultimately, however, this is an empirical question that cannot be decided on speculative grounds alone.

It has long been a mainstay of **progressive** thought that the struggle for freedom or, as some would say, for human emancipation is the guiding principle of human history. The French revolutionaries overthrew the Old Regime for the sake of liberty – and, of course, for equality and **fraternity** too. It is telling, though, that liberty came first. The idea that freedom is of preeminent importance received its decisive philosophical formulation in Kantian moral philosophy and then in G.W.F. Hegel's (1770–1831) philosophy of history, according to which human history is simply the **dialectical** unfolding of the Idea of Freedom. Virtually all Left thinking agrees with Hegel in according freedom pride of place, even if, in other respects, the philosophical convictions of progressive thinkers sometimes differ profoundly from those of Hegel. As the name implies, liberals make freedom – usually but not necessarily in the sense of negative liberty – the highest value. Their practice, however, often belies this theoretical commitment. Tragically, the socialist Left, especially its Communist wing, has also been disposed, when in power, to honor freedom in words only. This is why it is urgent to expose uses of the term that, wittingly or not, work to the detriment of the value that freedom's self-declared defenders officially espouse.

Further Reading

The most influential account of the distinction between positive and negative liberty is Isaiah Berlin's essay "Two Concepts of Liberty," in Isaiah Berlin, *Liberty* (Oxford: Oxford University Press, 2002). Berlin's distinction has somehow survived, despite decisive challenges in, among others, Gerald C. MacCallum, "Negative and Positive Freedom," *Philosophical Review*, vol. 74 (1967), pp. 312–34; and C.B. Macpherson, *Democratic Theory: Essays in Retrieval* (Oxford: Oxford University Press, 1973), chapter 5. My views on these matters are elaborated in *Liberal Democracy: A Critique of*

Fundamentalism

Its Theory (New York: Columbia University Press, 1981) and *Arguing for Socialism: Theoretical Considerations* (Boston: Routledge and Kegan Paul, 1984; 2nd edition London: Verso, 1988), chapters 1 and 9. On the concept of negative liberty, see Quentin Skinner, *Liberty Before Liberalism* (Cambridge: Cambridge University Press, 1997). On the importance of different freedoms, see Charles Taylor, "What's Wrong With Negative Liberty?," in Alan Ryan (ed.), *The Idea of Freedom* (Oxford: Oxford University Press, 1979); and T.M. Scanlon, "The Significance of Choice," in Stephen L. Darwall (ed.), *Equal Freedom*: *Selected Tanner Lectures in Human Values* (Ann Arbor, MI: University of Michigan Press, 1995). An insightful and comprehensive account of what freedom entails is developed in Philippe Van Parijs, *Real Freedom for All: What (If Anything) Can Justify Capitalism?* (Oxford: Oxford University Press, 1995). On connections between freedom and human nature, see Joshua Cohen, "The Arc of the Moral Universe" in *Philosophy and Public Affairs*, vol. 26 (1997), pp. 91–134. The Hegelian notion of freedom is explained lucidly in Allen W. Wood, *Hegel's Ethical Thought* (Cambridge: Cambridge University Press, 1990), chapter 2; and in Charles Taylor, *Hegel and Modern Society* (Cambridge: Cambridge University Press, 1979).

See also: ALIENATION, COMMUNISM, DEMOCRACY, EQUALITY/EGALITARIANISM, FREEDOM OF EXPRESSION, LEFT/RIGHT/CENTER, LIBERALISM, LIBERTARIANISM, MARXISM, NATION, NATIONALISM, PROGRESS, REPUBLICANISM, SOCIALISM, STATE

Fundamentalism

Fundamentalism is a comparatively new entry in the political lexicon. Its conceptual boundaries are therefore fluid. But the usefulness of the term is becoming increasingly evident, as the (superficially disparate) phenomena it describes become increasingly prevalent.

In its strictest sense, *fundamentalism* designates a tendency within evangelical Protestantism that adheres to literal interpretations of Biblical texts and to non-ritualistic, charismatic forms of worship. In the United States, fundamentalism arose largely in reaction to modernizing trends within Protestant churches and in American society more generally. The Darwinian theory of evolution by natural selection, the cornerstone of modern biology, has always been an object of animosity for fundamentalists, presumably because it contradicts elements of the creation story set out in the Book of Genesis.

Fundamentalism is generally hostile to modern science and, along with it, to modern civilization. However, fundamentalists are seldom averse to taking advantage of technological advances. This is not the only respect in which their position verges on inconsistency. Of greater moment is the fact that literal interpretations of Biblical texts are seldom possible, thanks to equivocations, anachronisms, and outright contradictions between various passages. Moreover, because fundamentalists are Christians, and because Christianity is based on the claim that the New Testament supersedes the Old, many biblical passages that could be interpreted literally – the legal prescriptions and prohibitions in the first five books of the Old Testament (the Torah), for example – are discounted or else accommodated in a highly selective (and therefore highly interpreted) manner. For this reason, it is pointless to try to spell out precisely what fundamentalists believe. They differ too much among themselves, at the same time that particular fundamentalist positions totter on the edge of incoherence. Therefore, from a political point of view, fundamentalism is more a social than a theological phenomenon. It is a reaction to modernity expressed in a religious form.

In recent decades, the term has been extended to non-Christian religious movements that resemble Protestant fundamentalism in their rejection of aspects of modernity. Thus, we speak of Islamic fundamentalists and we identify fundamentalist currents in all the world's major religions. Since many of these movements acknowledge multiple authorities – some of which are not, strictly speaking, texts at all – the pretense of literal textual interpretation is not a constant feature of fundamentalism in this broader sense. What is constant, though, is opposition to changes in religious practices and doctrines – motivated largely by nostalgia for older, pre-modern forms of life. Inasmuch as technological progress and other aspects of modernity are very likely irreversible, non-Christian fundamentalists find it as difficult to act on this nostalgia consistently as Protestant fundamentalists do. Efforts to restore traditional ways of living therefore select some facets of pre-modernity and reject others.

Religious fundamentalists seem to be most attracted to aspects of pre-modern life that involve the subjugation of women. Most fundamentalists are also puritanical with respect to sexual morality. Protestant fundamentalism emphasizes conversion experiences – being "born again." In this respect, it represents, in an exaggerated form, the long-standing Protestant concern with inwardness. Other religious traditions are more concerned with practice than with belief or its inward manifestations. This fact underscores a need for caution in applying the term outside its original area of application. There is a danger inherent in these broader uses of *fundamentalism* of assuming that what is distinctive of Christianity holds universally. For as long as it has been a world religion – since, roughly, the fourth century AD – Christianity has emphasized doctrinal conformity over legalistic practice. What other basis could there be for joining together the Roman Empire's diverse collection of peoples? With the worldwide dominance of Christian countries in the past several centuries, this understanding has migrated over to other religious traditions too. But, at their heart, these traditions – including some, like Judaism and Islam, that are historically related to Christianity – are relatively undemanding in matters of belief. Instead, emphasis is placed on adherence to ritual, and strict obedience to religious law. Their focus is on ways of life more than on systems of belief.

Because fundamentalists are steadfast adherents of their beliefs and practices, the term has come to be used to describe political currents that are similarly doctrinaire, even when the principles they endorse are **secular**. Thus, critics of **neo-liberal** economic policies speak of "free market fundamentalism," and the Green movement in Germany used to have a self-described *fundamentalist* wing. The first of these descriptions is pejorative; the second ironic. The term lends itself to these uses. But it can also be used non-pejoratively and without irony – to illuminate the character of a number of political movements in the world today. Thus, the Cambodian Khmer Rouge under Pol Pot are sometimes described as Marxist (or Maoist) fundamentalists. So long as the term is not reserved for religious movements, the description is apt. Though militantly **atheist**, the Khmer Rouge were as ruthless and doctrinaire as any theologically minded counterpart, Afghanistan's Taliban included.

The first fundamentalists saw themselves as victims of a world in transition, at the same time that they envisioned no earthly solutions to their discontents. They took refuge in **illusory** expectations of a better world beyond the horizons of human existence. With the Left in retreat, a similar sense of the futility of any more **enlightened** hope has become a factor in the thinking of desperate and humiliated people everywhere. *The Communist Manifesto* (1848) famously proclaimed that, under capitalism, "all that is solid melts into air." This is the signal experience of modernity. It is hardly surprising, therefore, that, when more rational alternatives seem foreclosed, some of the victims of changes underway should seize upon their "old time religions" – placing their faith usually, but not necessarily, in the supernatural or divine. Thus, what began in the American hinterland among evangelical Protestants has morphed into a worldwide phenomenon that transcends the horizons not just of Protestantism, but also of religion generally. Superseding fascism, fundamentalism has become the predominant form of **reactionary** politics in our time.

Further Reading

An excellent book, which illustrates the usefulness of the concept beyond its traditional historical context, is Tariq Ali, *The Clash of Fundamentalisms: Crusades, Jihads and Modernity* (London: Verso, 2003). A comprehensive history of the fundamentalist movement in the United States is George M. Marsden, *Understanding Fundamentalism and Evangelicalism* (Grand Rapids, MI: William B. Eerdmans, 1991). Informative essays on Islamic fundamentalism are collected in Abdel Salam Sidahmed and Anoushiravan Ehteshami (eds.), *Islamic Fundamentalism* (Boulder, CO: Westview Press, 1996). On the complexities of using the fundamentalist label for self-identified Marxist (or Maoist) movements, see Philip Short's biography *Pol Pot: Anatomy of a Nightmare* (New York: Henry Holt and Company, 2005).

See also: ENVIRONMENTALISM, FASCISM, FEMINISM, LEFT/RIGHT/CENTER, MAOISM, MARXISM, POLITICAL ISLAM, PROGRESS, TECHNOLOGY

H

Historical materialism

Historical materialism is the traditional name for Karl Marx's (1818–1883) theory of history. This theory was a cornerstone of the Marxist synthesis during Marxism's classical period – from the time of the founding of the Second International in 1881 until the outbreak of World War I. It was also a component of official Communist doctrine after the **Bolshevik** Revolution. From the 1920s on, most non-Communist Western Marxists were inclined to oppose historical materialism, though they seldom acknowledged doing so explicitly. However, the reconstruction and defense of Marx's theory of history played a seminal role in the development of **analytical Marxism** from the 1970s on.

Historical materialism divides history into discrete epochs, conceived as economic structures or **modes of production**; and it identifies an **endogenous** dynamic that moves humanity along from one epoch to another – or, more precisely, that would do so in the absence of intervening **exogenous** causes. In this way, historical materialism provides an account of history's structure and direction, in much the same way as Hegel (1770–1831) and earlier philosophers of history. Their philosophies, however, relied on a notion of causality, derived from Aristotle (384?–322?BC) and endemic throughout medieval science, according to which entities realize determinant purposes or ends. The major figures in the rise of modern science in the seventeenth and eighteenth centuries rejected this way of thinking. So too did Marx, implicitly. Historical materialism also provides an account of the connection between forms of **consciousness** and legal and political **superstructures**, on the one hand, and the underlying economic structure or "base," on the other.

Although historical materialism can have implications for the work of practicing historians, it does not offer explanations of the kind that historians normally produce. It does not explain particular events. Instead, it accounts for trends – not as accidental by-products of the changes historians record, but as consequences of the endogenous dynamic process it identifies. Historical materialism's core claim is that the level of development of **productive forces** explains social relations of **production**. The former term denotes means of production, but also the organization of the production process and even knowledge insofar as it plays a role in transforming nature in accord with human designs. Social relations of production are real (as distinct from merely juridical) **property** relations that govern control of economic resources and the distribution of the economic surplus (that is, of what direct producers produce in excess of what is required to reproduce their labor power). A set of production relations constitutes a mode of production. Thus, in the historical materialist view, the level of (technological) development explains why the economic base is as it is and not otherwise. The theory then goes on to maintain, somewhat independently, that this economic base explains forms of consciousness and legal and political superstructures.

There have been "vulgar Marxists" for whom everything non-economic is merely **epiphenomenal**. But this is not what historical materialism claims. Historical materialism admits causal interactions between forces and relations of production, and between the economic base and superstructural phenomena. But in each case, there is an explanatory (as distinct from a causal) asymmetry because in each case the former explains the latter, but not vice versa. Thus, Marx's theory of history, like evolutionary biology, makes use of **functional explanations**. This idea can be illustrated by a thermostat – essentially, a thermometer and a switch for turning a furnace off and on. When such a mechanism regulates the firing of the furnace, there is a two-way causal connection between the ambient temperature of a room heated by the furnace and the firing of the furnace – when the temperature falls below the level set on the thermostat, it causes the furnace to go on; when the furnace fires, it causes the room temperature to rise, turning off the furnace. However, we would say that the function of the furnace is to heat the room, not that the function of the room temperature is to cause the furnace to go on or off. In this sense, the operation of the furnace explains the ambient temperature, but not vice versa. Similarly, in the historical materialist view, the relations of production are as they are because, at particular levels of development, their being that way is functional for developing productive forces. Then, as forces develop, the production relations come increasingly to "fetter" further development – and "an era of social revolution" ensues. If there is a class agent capable of sustaining new social relations of production, and if it rises to its historical mission, it will install a new economic base – one that is **optimal** for developing productive forces to the next stage. In like manner, forms of consciousness and legal and political superstructures are as they are because their being that way is functional for reproducing the economic base.

Historical materialism explains actual epochal transformations only to the extent that the endogenous process it identifies is the predominant cause of the changes in question. Thus, it is possible that the underlying dynamic Marx identified is real, but that it is sometimes or always swamped by other factors. Similarly, biologists might be right in identifying, say, a genetic program in all living organisms that, if left to work its course, will lead to the death of these organisms – even if, in fact, some other factor (say, mortal encounters with predators) accounts for all the deaths in a given population. If factors other than the historical materialist dynamic explain some or all real world epochal transformations, then Marx's theory would explain less than many of its proponents assumed. It might not explain, for example, how capitalism arose in European **feudal** societies. But it would explain how capitalism became a **materially** possible future for those societies. In other words, historical materialism would, at the very least, provide a map of historical possibilities, an account of ways that societies can be organized. It may, in addition, provide reasons for thinking that, in the absence of overwhelming countervailing exogenous causes, there is only one way to move along this map; that having reached a particular designation, there is no turning back. However, it may not, in some or all cases, explain actual movement forward. If not, the theory's explanatory power would be less than many Marxists supposed. But it would still be considerable.

Orthodox historical materialists seemed to believe too that Marx's theory explains everything pertaining to forms of consciousness and legal and political superstructures. However, it is obviously false that there is an economic explanation (of the historical materialist kind) for everything. It is entirely plausible, however, that the functional requirements of the economic base do explain forms of consciousness and superstructural phenomena to the extent they impinge on the underlying historical materialist dynamic. Thus, there may be no economic explanation, only a theological one, for why some religious dogma is precisely as it is. But if, as is widely thought, there are aspects of theology that are genuinely functional for reproducing prevailing social relations, then their predominance and role should be explicable on those grounds.

Suitably modified and with its explanatory pretensions accordingly reduced, historical materialism seems to withstand even the most severe analytical scrutiny. This is important because the theory underwrites the central explanatory role that Marxism has always accorded to class analysis; and, more importantly, the central political role that it assigns to class agency. It is also the theory that vindicates the long-standing Marxist conviction that communism is the end of human history – not in the medieval-Hegelian sense, but because it is comprised of relations of production that, once established, no longer fetter further development or, more precisely, since communism presupposes **abundance**, no longer fetter the rational deployment of the resources humanity will, by then, have at its disposal.

Further Reading

Marx's most direct account of the main theses of historical materialism can be found in his 1859 Preface to *The Critique of Political Economy*. It is available in many editions including Eugene Kamenka (ed.), *The Portable Karl Marx* (London: Penguin, 1984). The seminal work for recent, analytical reconstructions of Marx's theory of history is G.A. Cohen, *Karl Marx's Theory of History: A Defence* (Oxford and Princeton: Oxford University Press and Princeton University Press, 1978). Cohen clarifies and modifies aspects of his reconstruction in G.A. Cohen, *History, Labour and Freedom: Themes from Marx* (Oxford: Oxford University Press, 1988). The account of historical materialism presented here is elaborated in Erik Olin Wright, Andrew Levine, and Elliott Sober, *Reconstructing Marxism* (London: Verso, 1992), part 1. See also Allen Wood, *Karl Marx* (London and Boston: Routledge and Kegan Paul, 1981), part 2.

See also: CAPITALISM, CLASS, COMMUNISM, LABOR, LEFT/RIGHT/CENTER, MARXISM, REVOLUTION, TECHNOLOGY

I

Identity politics

Despite the name, *identity politics* designates a range of views most of which are only tenuously political. Identity politics aims to celebrate and thereby reinforce differences that are socially (and sometimes also politically) salient. The relevant categorizations can be voluntarily assumed; more often, individuals are born into them. Thus, the relevant identities are usually ascribed, rather than chosen. The distinction is not always clear-cut, however, inasmuch as individuals or groups can deliberately undertake to cultivate ascribed identities.

Identity politics opposes assimilation. In many European countries – France, most famously – assimilation of non-native populations has always been the goal of the state. Because the United States has welcomed European immigrants since its inception, and because it imported African slaves, subordinated indigenous peoples, and incorporated large swathes of what had been settled Mexican territory, the dominant culture was saturated with potential entrants; absorption through direct assimilation was therefore never a very feasible solution. Thus, throughout the twentieth century, the United States was described as a "melting pot" in which diverse populations did not just assimilate into the traditional (Anglo-Protestant) culture, but also changed it by adding their own distinctive contributions, much like ingredients in a stew. Identity politics arose in the United States in reaction to the melting pot model because, in the circumstances that prevailed several decades ago, the melting pot seemed to have worked too well for European immigrants, obliterating cultural legacies in just a few generations; and not nearly well enough for people of color, who remained **de facto** second-class citizens. The civil rights struggles of African-Americans were particularly important in the emergence of identity politics, as were the cognate social movements that followed in their wake. The goal of civil rights struggles, especially at first, was equality. But, as the movement developed in the 1960s and thereafter, elements within it came to oppose assimilationist objectives – particularly as it became clear that attitudinal and institutional racism made the melting pot uncongenial for persons of African descent. The civil rights struggles of latinos and other **ethnic** minorities, and of women, replicated this development.

Insofar as proponents of identity politics dwell on social, cultural, and religious differences, they veer in an apolitical direction. However, there is and always has been a more expressly political tendency within the larger identity politics movement. It is associated with the Left or, more precisely, with those who view themselves as proponents of some (but not all) Left objectives. This (minority) current warrants attention because of what it reveals about the traditional Left and current prospects for orienting political **strategies** around its goals.

Historically, the Left sided with the **exploited** and **oppressed**. Just as adamantly, it upheld a vision of universal human **solidarity**. Thus, when socialists and anarchists made the interests of the working class their own, it was not only because workers were victims of the capitalist order. Of at least equal importance was the belief that workers' **material** interests coincided with the interests of humanity in general. However, in principle, a commitment to workers and oppressed peoples and to humankind in general can diverge. In the more politicized segments of the identity politics movement, this theoretical possibility finds a real world example.

In these quarters, it is claimed that the Left, including the **New Left**, with which many proponents of identity politics were once associated, is now either defunct or discredited, and that identity politics represents a continuation of what remains living in that superseded tradition. To the degree that this characterization is plausible, it is because a commitment to the oppressed defines this political tendency. It bears mention, however, that many of the persons and groups whose salient characteristics fall within the identity politics purview are materially well off and therefore hardly among those who, in the words of the *Internationale*, the great anthem of the working-class movement, comprise "the wretched of the earth." The oppression that concerns proponents of identity politics is more cultural than material; more psychological than economic.

A signal achievement of the New Left was the recognition that working-class emancipation would not automatically eliminate racial or **gender** oppression. This awareness underwrote the rise of new social movements dedicated to the relief of non-class forms of oppression. At the same time, spurred on by capitalism's relentless demand for cheap labor, the developed world imported people from **Third World** countries at unprecedented levels. In consequence, capitalist societies became more pluralistic than they had been – making ethnic and other differences central to the political cultures of many developed countries. In addition, feminism focused attention on human diversity generally. Thus, homosexuals and transsexuals constituted themselves into politically engaged social groups, as did disabled people. Because these changes coincided with the eclipse of traditional socialist aspirations and with the relentless homogenizing cultural effects of late capitalism, group identifications have come effectively to prevail in many circles that had once been unequivocally committed to universal human solidarity. Thus, today, even where the traditional Left has all but disappeared, identity politics survives. It is sometimes said, by its proponents, that the celebration of group differences is itself a means to a more universal human solidarity – in much the same way that traditional Leftists saw participation in the labor movement as a means for advancing human ends generally. This contention would be more plausible if proponents of identity politics envisioned an eventual withering away of what is distinctive in the groups they celebrate. Instead, they envision these groups enduring in perpetuity. This is what one would expect inasmuch as most of the characteristics that define the relevant identities cannot be transformed away (though their importance can be made to diminish).

For those who uphold the ideal of universal human solidarity, *identity politics* therefore has a pejorative connotation. On the other hand, its proponents embrace the description. They insist that because they see the world from the bottom up – from the perspective of victims, not of social, political or economic elites – they continue what is still living in the remains of the Left. The plausibility of their view is likely to remain an open question for some time. In the final analysis, only a revival of genuinely Left politics can prove the position of the identity politics side wrong.

Like communitarianism, identity politics advances a vision of the good society according to which individuals are rooted in historically situated communities. However, these communities are usually not based on the voluntary associations communitarians defend. The identities identity politics celebrates are more imposed than chosen. An individual hardly has a choice whether or not to be African-American, for example, or Jewish or gay or deaf. However, free choice does intrude at a different level. So long as political equality, equality of citizenship, is maintained, one can choose whether or not to make ascriptive properties the main structuring features of one's cultural and political identity. Thus, in contemporary liberal societies, like the United States, members of some groups – for example, those like homosexuals that are not easily identifiable or those that are broadly accepted in the larger society, as all "white" ethnic or religious groups nowadays are – can, to varying degrees, opt out of their respective ascriptive designations. Whether or to what extent they should do so is, again, a question about which reasonable people can disagree. Even traditional Leftists must concede that proponents of identity politics have a point. As capitalism homogenizes cultural forms, the assumption of a group identity can be a way of resisting the dominant culture or of forging a special niche within it. For example, Jewish immigrants to the United States in the decades before World War I were hardly in a position to decide to identify as Jews. That identity was thrust upon them by their own acculturation and by the dominant culture; they could not have forsaken it, even had they wanted to. This is much less true of their grandchildren and great-grandchildren. For them, to espouse a Jewish identification is as much a political statement as an acknowledgment of an unavoidable fact. Whether or to what extent it is a good thing that such statements be made is, for now, a profoundly unsettled issue.

Like nationalism, identity politics is not a full-fledged ideology. It is more nearly a pole of attraction towards which individuals and groups gravitate. Nevertheless, as with nationalism, it is possible to identify philosophical antecedents and anticipations. With its emphasis on community, identity politics draws on the tradition in social theory that sees in **civil society** an antidote to mass culture and its totalitarian temptations. Defenders of identity politics also appeal to Hegelian philosophy – with its emphasis on "recognition." In the first part of the nineteenth century, nationalists seized on this element of Hegel's thinking. But, for Hegel, recognition was more an aspiration of individuals than of groups. Thus, the appropriation of Hegel's views – first by nationalists, then by proponents of identity politics – represents an extension of Hegelian thought, not a literal application of it.

Because it recognizes and responds to the fact of pluralism and to the variety of systematic oppressions, there is plainly something to learn from identity

Ideology

politics. It would, therefore, be unwise to adopt a purely dismissive attitude. But, in this case more than most, proponents of universal human solidarity should be wary of the teacher.

Further Reading

The neo-Hegelian underpinnings of philosophical justifications of identity politics are laid out accessibly in Axel Honneth, *The Struggle for Recognition: The Moral Grammar of Social Conflicts* (Cambridge, MA: MIT Press, 1996). Political and philosophical implications of this line of thought are developed in Iris M. Young, *Justice and the Politics of Difference* (Princeton, NJ: Princeton University Press, 1990) and *Inclusion and Democracy* (Oxford: Oxford University Press, 2002). A more critical, but still sympathetic purchase on identity politics is evident in Seyla Benhabib, *The Claims of Culture: Equality and Diversity in the Global Era* (Princeton, NJ: Princeton University Press, 2002). See also Nancy Fraser and Axel Honneth, *Redistribution or Recognition: A Political-Philosophical Exchange* (London: Verso, 2003). Issues pertinent to identity politics arise prominently in philosophical discussions of multiculturalism. These issues are explored, from a liberal point of view, in Will Kymlicka, *Multicultural Citizenship: A Liberal Theory of Minority Rights* (Oxford: Oxford University Press, 1996), and *Politics in the Vernacular: Nationalism, Multiculturalism and Citizenship* (Oxford: Oxford University Press, 2001). Positions that trade on identity concerns are subjected to incisive critiques in Brian Barry, *Culture and Equality: An Egalitarian Critique of Multiculturalism* (Cambridge, MA: Harvard University Press, 2002).

See also: ANARCHISM, CAPITALISM, CIVIL RIGHTS, COMMUNITY/COMMUNITARIANISM, CULTURE, EQUALITY/EGALITARIANISM, FEMINISM, FREEDOM, IDEOLOGY, LABOR MOVEMENT, LEFT/RIGHT/CENTER, LIBERALISM, NATION/NATIONALISM, RACE/RACISM, SOCIALISM, STATE, TOTALITARIANISM

Ideology

Thanks to the term's contested history, *ideology* has a number of fairly distinct senses. The word was introduced in 1796 by the French philosopher Destutt de Tracy (1754–1836) to stand for what we would today call "the philosophy of mind." His aim was to distinguish a "science of ideas," consonant with **enlightenment rationalism**, from traditional **metaphysics**. This usage has not survived. Over the next several decades, *ideology* came to be used to describe more or less coherent bodies of (mainly) political doctrine. This meaning has survived. In the early nineteenth century conservatives used the term (in roughly this sense) disparagingly, applying it to the democratic or socialist ideologies they disapproved of, but not to positions they favored. "Ideologues," conservatives argued, deliberately apply (or misapply) social theories to public policy questions, in disregard of the pitfalls of rationalism in politics. Before long, the term was used on the Left as well. By the time Karl Marx (1818–1883) and Friedrich Engels (1820–1895) took it up in the mid-1840s, it still had a pejorative connotation. But its meaning had become sufficiently fluid that they were able to give it a new sense. For them, an ideology was an account of ideas abstracted from real historical processes. Thus, in *The German Ideology* (1845), Marx and Engels faulted German philosophy generally, and their **Young Hegelian** colleagues in particular, for a general failure to ground ideas in **material** realities. On this understanding, ideologies are, in the final analysis, false, though, as the Young Hegelians maintained, they can be susceptible to interpretations that yield genuine knowledge. This is because ideologies, like everything with political effects, are rooted in underlying social realities that **criticism** can uncover. But even when they "reflect" the real, they misrepresent it. These positions follow from an antecedent claim that Marx and Engels were the first to advance: that material interests drive ideological formulations. Not just *any* interests, however. The ruling ideas of any epoch, Marx and Engels maintained, are the ideas of its ruling class or, as they might better have said, they are expressions of its interests. Thus, ideologies, so conceived, help to maintain existing systems of domination – not deliberately in most cases, but nevertheless "objectively."

A decade later, Marx effectively introduced a slightly different sense of *ideology* – one that accords with the historical materialist account of history's structure and direction. A central tenet of that theory is that **social relations of production functionally explain** legal and political **superstructures** and forms of **consciousness.** Following Marx's lead, Marxists came to use *ideology* to stand for forms of consciousness generally. On orthodox interpretations of historical materialism, this would mean that everything aesthetic, religious, or cultural is ideological, regardless of the material interests it serves. One would expect that science would count as ideological too; it is, after all, a form of consciousness. However, most proponents of historical materialism, and certainly Marx himself, excluded (genuine) science. Not to do so would court incoherence, inasmuch as Marx thought that it was science, his own science of history, that discovered the connection between forms of consciousness and social relations of production. Thus, in even the most orthodox currents of the Marxist tradition, *ideology* contrasts with science. The term in the historical materialist sense therefore designates everything pertaining to consciousness that is not genuinely scientific. Contemporary reconstructions of historical materialism, motivated by criticisms of the orthodox theory, diminish historical materialism's explanatory pretensions by limiting its scope to only those aspects of superstructural phenomena and forms of consciousness that affect the underlying historical dynamic the theory identifies. On this non-orthodox account, not all forms of consciousness, science excepted, would count as ideological; whatever does not impinge on the historical materialist dynamic would be excluded as well. This usage brings the historical materialist sense of the term closer to the understanding implicit in *The German Ideology*.

In the 1960s and 1970s, Louis Althusser (1918–1990) and other **structuralist** Marxists endeavored to reconstruct Marxist theory as an account of fundamental structural determinations of social formations. Human agency, Althusser insisted, "supports" social structures, but has no independent determinative role in affecting outcomes. In this recasting of Marxist doctrine, Althusser transformed the historical materialist understanding of ideology and, not unrelatedly, of the state. He used *state* to designate all those institutional practices that coordinate human behaviors, not just the **coercive** ones. Thus, he depicted family and religious institutions as "state apparatuses" – indeed as "ideological state apparatuses" insofar as they fashion consciousness of subjectivity by "interpellating" subjects – that is, by "calling [persons] to account." Imagine a police officer walking down the street, seeing someone suspicious, and calling out for him to stop. The officer "hails" or calls the suspect to account for himself. Althusser focused on the process by which the person being hailed recognizes himself as the subject of the interpellation, and how he then learns to respond. What shapes this knowledge is the nature of the state apparatus (construed broadly enough to include all institutional mechanisms of social control). In this way, our concept of who we are is determined by the social structures we "support." Through their interpellations of us, we identify ourselves as subjects. Althusser went on to maintain that different **modes of production** interpellate subjects in different ways. In his view, orthodox Marxists were right to insist that **bourgeois** ideology designates forms of consciousness that are functional for the reproduction of bourgeois society. But, because their concept of ideology was unduly constricted, they failed to see how, more generally, ideological state apparatuses inculcate the entire form of consciousness proper to the mode of production in which the bourgeoisie is a ruling class, the capitalist mode of production. It follows that there is also (potentially) a **proletarian** ideology – a way of interpellating subjects that would consolidate the power of the proletariat as a ruling class. Thus, in contrast to traditional understandings, this use of *ideology* is not necessarily pejorative.

Marxists contributed substantially to the development of the concept and to establishing its centrality in modern social and political thought, but they did not invent the concept of ideology, and neither did they make it exclusively their own. This is why it is not surprising that, even as interest in Marxism has waned, there is as much talk of ideology as there ever was. In academic circles, the sociology of knowledge has long been a thriving enterprise. It has generally not assumed a Marxist mantle. Even so, Marxist understandings have always played an important role in it. This is particularly evident where *ideological* is used to mean "beneficial to particular social interests." For the most part, though, understandings of ideology have taken a backwards step in recent years. Especially in non-academic contexts, senses of the term that emerged in the nineteenth century, before there was any distinctively Marxist contribution to the topic, predominate. As it did a century and a half ago, *ideology* nowadays often just denotes comprehensive political doctrines.

Insofar as interests, not evidence, govern forms of consciousness, it follows that ideological claims need not be false. Their ideological aspect consists in their social function, not their truth-value. This is why the concept of ideology is susceptible to appropriation by **post-modern relativists** for whom the very idea of truth is problematic. For them, it is natural to say that all claims are only ideological; that they express power relations, but not relations between assertions and what is the case. Needless to say, this was not Marx's understanding, nor is it the prevailing view in the sociology of knowledge traditions that draw on Marx's thought. For them, ideological claims usually are false, but it is not in virtue of their falsity that they are ideological. Since it is their social function, not their relation to evidence, that makes them ideological, they could as well be true. In other words, though their falseness can generally be assumed, it is not logically necessitated.

There is no harm and often much benefit in using the term in non-Marxist ways. But there is also much to gain by returning to developments within the Marxist tradition – especially for those who seek to understand the ideological dimensions of political struggles. The Marxist writer who contributed most to this topic was Antonio Gramsci (1891–1937). Gramsci's work was an inspiration for Althusser's. Their common line of thought is a resource to mine.

Further Reading

The main contours of the subject are laid out in Terry Eagleton, *Ideology: An Introduction* (London: Verso, 1991). For a critical assessment of the view that the ruling ideas of an epoch are those of its ruling class, see Nicholas Abercrombie, Bryan S. Turner, and Stephen Hill, *The Dominant Ideology Thesis* (New York: Routledge, 1984). A founding text of the academic discipline still called the sociology of knowledge is Karl Mannheim, *Ideology and Utopia: An Introduction to the Sociology of Knowledge* (New York and San Diego, CA: Harvest, 1955). Althusser's account of ideology can be found in his essay "Ideology and Ideological State Apparatuses," in *Lenin and Philosophy and Other Essays* (New York: Monthly Review Press, 2001). To tease out Gramsci's contributions, see Antonio Gramsci, *Selections From the Prison Notebooks* (New York: International Publishers, 1971). I discuss Althusser and the Gramscian bases of his thought in *A Future for Marxism?* (London: Pluto Press, 2003), chapters 3–4.

See also: CAPITALISM, CLASS, CONSERVATISM, CULTURE, DEMOCRACY, HISTORICAL MATERIALISM, LEFT/RIGHT/CENTER, LIBERALISM, MARXISM, SOCIALISM, STATE

Imperialism

The modern use of *imperialism* to mean the direct or indirect domination of lands and peoples by more economically developed or militarily powerful states is of late nineteenth-century origin. Originally, the term designated the rule of an emperor, a **sovereign** who controlled numerous territories. Personal rule was central to early conceptions of imperialism. The idea that imperialism involves the acquisition by states of foreign dependencies outside their borders, usually by force and contrary to the wishes of their populations, is recent. Even more recent is the idea that imperialism need not involve formal political incorporation – in other words, that ostensibly independent countries, not just colonies, can be in the thrall of imperial powers.

The contemporary understanding of imperialism was shaped by European power politics. Like the populations they ruled, many mid-to-late-nineteenth-century political leaders in Western European countries were influenced by nationalistic passions. The quest for national glory was a spur to imperialist projects. However, modern theories of imperialism focus on the state, not the nation, and are right to do so. For imperialists in the modern sense of the term, imperialism is mainly a means for the extension of state power. However virulent its nationalist or racist components, modern imperialism is driven by the idea that capitalist economies require expansion beyond national boundaries to flourish or even to survive. It was not just the socialist – especially Marxist – Left that advanced this view. Many liberals did too. Anticipations of it can even be found in early-nineteenth-century German philosophy – for example, in G.W.F. Hegel's (1770–1831) *Philosophy of Right* (1821).

Nineteenth-century liberals, like their counterparts today, were inclined to favor "free trade" over **coercive** means of subordination. This was not a benign preference. Then, like now, the existence of severe economic inequalities, with their attendant differences in bargaining power, made ostensibly voluntary transactions more beneficial to the rich than the poor, who were often more harmed than benefited by the practice. Thus, throughout the nineteenth century, free trade policies worked to the advantage of Great Britain and, to a lesser degree, other maritime powers. However, late in the nineteenth century, Germany and other industrializing European countries began to erect protective tariffs. Other countries, Britain included, were obliged to follow suit. With tariffs in place, it became increasingly attractive, from an economic standpoint, to dominate dependent areas directly – in part to have markets for produced goods, in part to have access to raw materials. It was largely for this reason that, by the turn of the century, liberal thought generally was won over to imperialist policies. Historians are nearly unanimous in maintaining that, in fact, imperialism was not generally good for business. But the contrary belief had become part of the common sense of the time.

There were important liberal writers who took an opposing view. John Hobson (1858–1940) was among the most influential of them – for the cogency of his arguments, but also because Hobson's statistical analyses (many of which were flawed) influenced V.I. Lenin's (1870–1924) thinking, and because his account of imperialism anticipated the views of John Maynard Keynes (1883–1946) on the problems of underconsumption (in the home market). Hobson maintained that imperialism drained the British economy. He also argued that egalitarian redistribution within a capitalist framework could expand the purchasing power of the working masses enough to render misguided imperialist ventures unnecessary. Hobson sought to save liberalism from imperialist temptations and, in doing so, to pave the way for progressive social reforms. He was also an ardent critic of **jingoism** and related manifestations of nationalistic fervor. His thinking on these matters was taken up and developed by social theorists after World War II – among them, Hannah Arendt (1906–1975), who, using some of Hobson's ideas, identified connections between imperialism and fascism, maintaining that they both result from similar departures from the principles of a genuinely liberal order. Thus, Hobson's influence on other thinkers was considerable. However, his political recommendations went generally unheeded.

Max Weber (1864–1920) attacked imperialism for its role in strengthening the prestige of undemocratic rulers and the position of capitalists seeking **monopoly** profits. He derided this form of "predatory capitalism" as parasitic on a system of production and exchange based on rational calculation. He also faulted **intellectuals** intent on seeing their national culture and therefore their own influence enhanced by promoting imperialist ventures. Joseph Schumpeter's (1883–1950) important 1919 essay "The Sociology of Imperialisms" expanded on Weber's and Hobson's positions. He argued that imperialism is not a product of capitalism, as Marxist writers maintained, but an "atavistic" survival from pre-industrial times that generates "warlike" passions serving no rational purpose. In Schumpeter's view, imperialism, like nationalism, derived from social traditions surviving from the age of **absolutist** rule. Capitalism, he maintained, was inherently anti-imperialist. But even Schumpeter conceded that "monopoly capitalism," as it existed prior to the outbreak of World War I, did turn capitalists' interests in an imperialist direction. This fusion of rational and atavistic interests was, in his view, a departure from the path of true capitalism. He also thought it a transitory phenomenon. Schumpeter's work is helpful for understanding the late nineteenth- and early twentieth-century rush for colonies in Africa and elsewhere. But its shortcomings are also evident. Among other things, Schumpeter sharply distinguished imperialism from free trade. Thus, he was unable to account for American "free trade imperialism" in the decades prior to World War I. For much the same reason, his work is of limited usefulness for explaining contemporary imperialist forms.

Marxist theories of imperialism are grounded in Marx's account of "the laws of motion" of capitalist development, from which it follows that industrial capitalism is bound to founder on a falling rate of profit and a tendency to generate ever more acute economic crises. Marxists then argued that the collapse of the system could be averted temporarily by imperialist expansion. This contention was an innovation. The importance of imperialism for the analysis of capitalism did not become apparent to Marxists until the waning years of the nineteenth century. Marx, who died in 1883, did argue that external markets can help to cushion the effects of economic crises, but he insisted that what went on in peripheral areas was of only marginal importance to the internal dynamic of capitalist development. Engels' writings of the 1890s advanced a similar view. In that decade, August Bebel (1840–1913) became the first Marxist writer to maintain that imperialism is an inevitable by-product of capitalism. But it was events around the turn of the century and then in the years leading to the outbreak of World War I that forced imperialism into the forefront of Marxist thought.

In *Finance Capital* (1910), Rudolph Hilferding (1877–1941) advanced the first full-fledged Marxist theory of imperialism. In Hilferding's view, imperialism is not a marginal phenomenon, but a necessary accompaniment of capitalism as it matures and finance **capital** becomes increasingly important. Nationalist and racist ideologies may be used to justify imperialist expansion, but its underlying causes are intrinsic to the logic of capitalism itself. Rosa Luxemburg (1871–1919) developed this line of thought in *The Accumulation of Capital* (1913). Luxemburg's work joined the classical Marxist case for communism's inevitability with a remarkably flexible and even voluntaristic politics. Accordingly, her account of imperialism attempts to explain both the apparently indefinite postponement of capitalist breakdown and the centrality of revolutionary struggle. Following Hilferding's lead, Luxemburg maintained that, by the dawn of the twentieth century, continued capital accumulation depended on the existence of areas that were not yet extensively exploited by capitalists. But since there is only so much "virgin" territory to incorporate, and since the rush to acquire it was proceeding at full throttle, imperialism is only a temporary palliative for an inevitable breakdown of the capitalist order. Just as Marx maintained (though not quite in the way he envisioned it), capitalist development itself will, in short order, undermine the conditions for its own possibility. Because she assumed that capitalists would realize all the gains from imperialism and therefore did not foresee spillover benefits to workers in imperialist countries, Luxemburg saw imperialist fervor in developed countries as superficial and transitory. She thought that, as capitalism's inevitable structural crisis came due, workers would shed their imperialist enthusiasms and rise to their historical mission. Thus, the overthrow of imperialism would be largely the work of revolutionary workers in the imperialist centers.

Lenin's *Imperialism: The Highest Stage of Capitalism* (1916) took issue with Luxemburg's and Hilferding's contention that capitalism cannot survive without imperialism. But his general account was largely consistent with theirs. For Lenin, imperialism is capitalism in its "monopolistic stage." In this period, the concentration of capital is so far advanced that monopolies, not small independent firms, play a decisive role in economic life. In addition, as Hilferding stressed, bank capital and industrial capital have largely merged. In these conditions, the export of capital becomes more important than the export of commodities or even the search for raw materials. It is mainly for this reason that the larger imperial powers carve out their own spheres of influence. Contrary to Luxemburg's view, Lenin emphasized that imperialism could well divide the working class internationally and also within national economies, by creating privileged strata funded in part from the wealth generated by imperialism. Like Luxemburg, but unlike most other Marxists of the time, Lenin maintained that the battle against capitalism (and therefore imperialism) had to be fought out mainly on the political plane. But, unlike Luxemburg, he saw an opportunity for joining forces with colonial peoples. An ossified version of Lenin's doctrine survived into the official Communism of the Stalin era and beyond.

Anti-imperialism became the hallmark of Asian Communism after the Sino-Soviet split. For Maoists, the term came to subsume every form of economic or political influence of Western nations in **Third World** countries. Maoists viewed the revolt of Third World peoples against imperialism as the principal form of revolutionary struggle in our time. Much as earlier generations of Marxists foresaw the inevitability of a **proletarian** revolution in the home countries, Maoists maintained that a definitive victory against imperialism was inevitable, despite the obvious strategic imbalances between peasant insurgents and the militaries of the imperial powers. That victory was a necessary stage for the triumph of socialism worldwide, including the imperialist centers themselves.

During the last half of the twentieth century, especially during periods of intense turmoil in Third World countries, new theories of imperialism were developed. Most of them emphasize the geopolitical aspects of imperialism in a **postcolonial** age. Because they maintain that the true sources of imperialism lie with the political interests of elites, not with the internal logic of monopoly capitalism, their stance is closer to Schumpeter's than to Lenin's. In the 1950s and 1960s, theories of imperialism merged with theories of "development." For some neo-Marxist writers, this fusion led to a critique of mainstream development theory. Mainstream development theorists, on the other hand, came to look with favor on at least some of what earlier critics of imperialism and their contemporary followers abhorred. In any case, the term, along with many of the core understandings of classical and more recent theories, was increasingly relegated to marginalized left-wing academic circles. In the political mainstream, even to use the word was considered a provocation. Thus, as insights about the phenomenon accumulated, talk of imperialism declined. It is only with the ascendance of neo-conservatism in Washington and elsewhere that the term has been revived, this time with a positive connotation.

There are therefore influential voices today who urge the United States to assume an explicitly imperialist stance. Their idea is that the West, especially the United States, has a "civilizing mission" to discharge – and that it can do so best by asserting its presence throughout the world, by military means if necessary. For contemporary neo-conservatives, the civilizing mission of the West today may not be quite what nineteenth-century thinkers proposed. Their discourse is not overtly racist. Thus, they call for the installation in the Middle East and elsewhere of what, with breathtaking hypocrisy, they call "freedom and democracy." But, in the end, their thinking is of a piece with those who, more than a century ago, assumed "the white man's burden." They think that the capitalist West knows best. Not incidentally, they find it easy to make common cause with "predatory capitalists" who (usually) do know better.

For understanding the present world system, classical and contemporary theories of imperialism are indispensable tools. The work of Immanuel Wallerstein (1930–) and his colleagues, "world systems theory," is especially illuminating. It provides insight into the economic exigencies that have led to the domination of peripheral areas by a handful of more developed states. On the world systems view, the division of the world into metropolitan centers and dominated territories emerged at the very dawn of the capitalist era, and has changed very little since. Other contemporary theories advance understanding of the social and political factors that cause some nations to dominate others.

Throughout their history, theories of imperialism developed to accommodate ever-changing manifestations of the phenomenon. General theories have been proposed, but none has emerged unscathed as circumstances have changed. Perhaps this is inevitable; perhaps, as the classical Marxists maintained, a general theory of imperialism is tantamount to a theory of capitalism itself. In any case, a renewal of interest in theories of imperialism would be welcome. The phenomenon exists, and its virulence is on the rise. Imperialism today is a major source of world instability, and a cause of savage injustices. Efforts to understand the phenomenon are, if anything, more timely now than they have ever been.

Further Reading

An extremely clear and comprehensive account of the literature on imperialism is Wolfgang J. Mommsen (P.S. Falla, trans.), *Theories of Imperialism* (Chicago: University of Chicago Press, 1980). On the pervasiveness of the phenomenon, see Harry Magdoff, *Imperialism Without Colonies* (New York: Monthly Review, 2003). The classics of the pre-World War I period remain of interest – especially, J.A. Hobson, *Imperialism: A Study* (Ann Arbor, MI: University of Michigan Press, 1965); Max Weber, *Economy and Society: An Outline of Interpretive Sociology* (Berkeley and Los Angeles: University of California Press, 1978); Joseph Schumpeter, *Imperialism* (New Haven, CT: Meridian Books, 1958); and V.I. Lenin, *Imperialism: The Highest Stage of Capitalism* (London: Pluto Press, 1996). Also still of great interest are the theoretical departures in Marxist theory that underwrite Marxist accounts of imperialism – especially Rudolph Hilferding, *Finance Capital: A Study of the Latest Phase of Capitalist Development* (London and Boston: Routledge and Kegan Paul, 1981), and Rosa Luxemburg, *Accumulation of Capital*, 2nd edition (New York: Routledge, 2003). A more recent theory of imperialism that pioneered the analysis of the development of "underdevelopment" is André Gunder Frank, *Capitalism and Underdevelopment in Latin America* (New York: Monthly Review, 1969). A classic analysis of neo-colonialism is Kwame Nkrumah, *Neo-Colonialism: The Last Stage of Imperialism* (New York: International Publishers, 1966). See also Maurice Zeitlin, *Capitalism and Imperialism: An Introduction to Neo-Marxian Concepts* (Chicago: Markham, 1972). A good introduction to "world systems theory" is Immanuel Wallerstein, *World-Systems Analysis: An Introduction* (Durham, NC: Duke University Press, 2004). Contemporary calls for an imperialist revival, when they are not neo-conservative screeds, come in the form of thinly veiled glorifications of the overtly imperial past. An interesting example is Niall Ferguson, *Empire: the Rise and Demise of the British World Order and the Lessons for Global Power* (New York: Basic Books, 2004). Justifications for so-called "humanitarian interventions" can also be vehicles for justifications of imperialist policies. A none-too-subtle example is Michael Ignatieff, *The Lesser Evil: Political Ethics in an Age of Terror* (Princeton, NJ: Princeton University Press, 2004). For an incisive rejoinder to these lines of thought and the policies they justify, see Chalmers Johnson, *The Sorrows of Empire: Militarism, Secrecy and the End of the Republic* (New York: Metropolitan Books, 2004), and Noam Chomsky, *Hegemony or Survival: America's Quest for Global Dominance* (New York: Metropolitan Books, 2001).

See also: CAPITALISM, CULTURE, DEMOCRACY, EQUALITY/EGALITARIANISM, FASCISM, FREEDOM, IDEOLOGY, JUSTICE, LABOR MOVEMENT, LEFT/RIGHT/CENTER, LENINISM, LIBERALISM, MAOISM, MARXISM, NATION/NATIONALISM, NEO-CONSERVATISM, POWER, PROGRESS, RACE/RACISM, REVOLUTION, SOCIALISM. STALINISM, STATE

Internationalism

The "national" in *international* means "state." "International relations" are relations between states; and "international law" designates law at a global, not state, level. The term is therefore misleading, because states are not nations. It is nevertheless in general use across the political spectrum.

In recent decades, internationalists have worked to build global institutions, like the United Nations, and regional institutions that, to some degree, assume state functions with respect to cultural, economic, and military affairs. Because these institutions impinge implicitly on national (state) **sovereignty**, states have been reluctant to cede power to them, except when it is clearly in their interests to do so. In general, the more powerful the state, the less likely it is to accord standing to international **authorities** it does not control. The United States, in particular, uses international institutions as instruments of its own state interests; when it is unable to do so, it either ignores them or impugns their authority outright. For this reason, it has proven difficult, though not impossible, to extend the scope of international law and otherwise to address regional and global problems through regional and global institutions. Nevertheless, the ideas, if not the reality, of genuinely international systems of administration and law have taken root in the political culture. Documents like the *Universal Declaration of Human Rights*, proclaimed in 1948 in the General Assembly of the United Nations, articulate "a common standard of achievement" that, in theory if not in practice, "all peoples and all nations" seek to implement.

On the Left, *internationalism* sometimes takes on a different meaning. By the time the International Workingmen's Association, the First International, was founded in 1864, *internationalism* designated a commitment to the interests of workers (and **oppressed** peoples more generally), regardless of country and irrespective of national or sectional interests. Internationalism in this sense, **proletarian** internationalism, promises allegiance to the workers of the world, not to the interests of workers' respective states, which, on this view, largely reduce to the interests of their states' ruling classes. Despite the *-ism* suffix, this idea is hardly a basis for a full-fledged ideology. But it does indicate a clear political orientation.

In practice, internationalists have always believed that they ought to work mainly on behalf of the interests of workers and oppressed peoples in their own countries. In theory, this conviction does not follow from any special identification with fellow citizens. It is based instead on the idea that, in a world divided into states, the struggle against capital has to proceed on a state-by-state basis. Internationalists recognize that to be effective, they must involve themselves in the political life of their own countries. Ostensibly, this is why internationalists, even when thinking globally, nevertheless act locally or, at least, nationally. However, the actual focus of declared internationalists may well be more than just a **pragmatic** adaptation to circumstances. Internationalist identifications seldom run deep. Experience has shown countless times that patriotic or nationalist passions easily trump them. Thus, unlike nationalism, which is a genuine pole of attraction for many people, internationalism is more often honored in theory than in fact.

For much of the twentieth century, the implications of proletarian internationalism were clouded by circumstances. The "revolutionary defeatism" of the leaders of the **Bolshevik** Revolution, their acceptance and even encouragement of Russia's defeat in World War I, evinced a traditionally internationalist perspective. But as Soviet power consolidated in the aftermath of the revolution, and as revolutionary ventures elsewhere in the world failed, Communists and their co-thinkers came to promote the idea that internationalists were obliged, above all, to rally to the defense of the national (state) interests of the Soviet Union. They maintained that the interests of the world proletariat were identical to the interests of the Soviet state. Decades later, Maoists in the West advanced a similar position with respect to China. Nowadays, views that identify the interests of the world's workers with those of a particular state are plainly anachronisms, however plausible they may have seemed when first proposed.

There is an evident affinity between internationalism and cosmopolitanism, an ancient idea, rediscovered and given new life in the **Enlightenment**. Cosmopolitans see themselves as citizens of the world, not of any one country. Through this conviction, they express a sense of universal human **solidarity** according to which all persons stand in the same relation to one other – except perhaps insofar as they are joined together by special ties of family or friendship. For cosmopolitans, citizenship confers no special standing; it is a morally arbitrary political status. When cosmopolitan sensibilities combined with the belief that, in this historical period, working-class interests reduce ultimately to general human interests, and when this belief was supplemented by the conviction that these interests must be addressed nationally (state by state), cosmopolitanism effectively turns into proletarian internationalism.

Further Reading

For accounts of post-World War II efforts to extend notions of human rights and international law, see Richard A. Falk, *Human Rights Horizons: The Pursuit of Justice in a Globalizing World* (New York: Routledge, 2000), and Philippe Sands, *Lawless World: America and the Making and Breaking of Global Rules from FDR's Atlantic Charter to George W. Bush's Illegal War* (New York: Viking, 2005). The nature and perils of de facto American control of the United Nations is documented in Phyllis Bennis, *Calling the Shots: How Washington Dominates Today's UN* (Northampton, MA: Interlink Publishing, 2000). There is an enormous literature on facets of proletarian internationalism, as it has developed over the past 200 years. But there are no comprehensive accounts. A useful introduction to an important strain of this literature is John Bellamy Foster, "Marx and Internationalism," *Monthly Review*, vol. 52, no. 3 (2000), pp 11–22. The Bolshevik version of the ideal, later taken over and corrupted in the Stalin era, is described in R. Craig Nation, *War on War: Lenin, the Zimmerwald Left, and the Origins of Communist Internationalism* (Durham, NC: Duke University Press, 1989).

See also: CAPITALISM, CLASS, COMMUNISM, COSMOPOLITANISM, CULTURE, IDEOLOGY, LEFT/RIGHT/ CENTER, MAOISM, MORALITY, NATION/NATIONALISM, PATRIOTISM, POWER, REVOLUTION, RIGHTS, SOCIALISM, STATE

J

Justice

The core intuition underlying the idea of *justice* is that like cases should be treated alike. However, this is only a formal principle; it leaves open what counts as a like case and what equal treatment involves. Examples of substantive principles that give content to it include "to each according to need" and "to each according to productive contribution." Debates about what substantive principles are appropriate in particular situations and about what they imply have raged since ancient times.

For Plato (427?–347?BC), all **normative** questions pertaining to **ethics** involve justice. Thus, he used "justice" and derivative terms in ways that we would not today – to indicate what might better be described as "rightful" or "legitimate." It is in this sense that we still speak of "just states." In the main, though, following Aristotle's (384?–322?BC) lead, the term is used more narrowly – to give theoretical expression to intuitions about fairness (as distinct from goodness). Aristotle distinguished *retributive justice*, which deals with punishment, from *distributive justice*, which deals with the distribution of benefits and burdens. Distributive justice has become the principal normative concern of modern political life – from the revolutionary upheavals of the seventeenth century to the present day.

In practice, accounts of distributive justice often deal with more than just the distribution of benefits and burdens. Questions of justice (or, as is sometimes said, **equity**) arise in nearly all contemporary normative accounts of public life. Even so, the Aristotelian distinction between the just and the good remains in force. That distinction is especially evident in the liberal tradition, where it is almost always assumed in reflections on public policy. To cite one conspicuous example: since the notion of **efficiency** is connected conceptually and historically to a welfarist account of the good, so-called equity/efficiency trade-offs, a mainstay of contemporary policy debates, frequently arise. It has also become standard to think of rights that constrain state activities as requirements of justice. It is in this sense that neo-Lockean libertarians deem state intrusions into what they regard as morally primary **property** rights as offenses to justice.

The most important and influential liberal theorist of justice in recent decades was John Rawls (1921–2002). Rawls maintained that justice is "the first virtue" of social institutions, in the way that truth is of scientific theories. In *A Theory of Justice* (1971), he set out an account of what justice requires for a society's fundamental, social, political, and economic institutions. Justice, as Rawls conceived it, regulates the distribution of **primary goods**, goods that are instrumental for the realization of a wide range of (possible) conceptions of the good. The primary goods include basic rights and liberties, powers and offices, income and wealth, the bases of self-respect and perhaps also leisure. Rawls maintained that the distribution of these goods is regulated by two principles, the first of which must be satisfied before the second applies. The first principle holds that basic rights and liberties are to be distributed equally and to the greatest extent possible. The second holds that, once opportunities are distributed in a suitably fair way, income and wealth and the rest should be distributed equally unless an unequal distribution would increase the share going to the least well off. Thus, Rawlsian justice is non-utilitarian, since utilitarianism would demand distributions that maximize aggregate well-being, regardless of the impact on the least well off. It is also egalitarian – not literally, but in the sense that it licenses deviations from strictly equal distributions of income and wealth only for the sake of bringing the bottom up. From the 1970s on, nearly all academic social, political, and moral philosophy in the English-speaking world has engaged Rawls's arguments in one way or another. Contemporary communitarianism developed in reaction to Rawls's theory of justice; so too have neo-Lockean rights theories of justice, according to which justice obtains whenever morally primary rights are respected, and injustice consists only in the violation of these rights. One would expect that Marxist philosophers would be the exceptions to the rule. In the strict historical materialist view, questions of

Justice

justice are relative to underlying **modes of production**; they therefore have no applicability across history's epochal structures. In recent decades, however, this conviction has been largely abandoned. Partly thanks to the cogency of Rawls's arguments and the influence they exercise, even self-identified Marxists nowadays are inclined to concede that the concept of justice has trans-historical applicability.

It has long been understood that questions of justice are central to political life. It could hardly be otherwise inasmuch as modern politics is largely a struggle within and between social groups for control of resources. It has become apparent in recent years that other aspects of social and political life also involve questions of justice. This is plainly true of issues pertaining to the environment. In a sense that is uncontroversial, policies concerning the use of natural resources raise issues of fairness between living persons and future generations. Somewhat more controversially, questions can be raised about relations between human beings and other parts of nature. It is also plain that, in an increasingly interdependent world, questions of justice arise not only within political communities but also between them. In the years ahead, working towards a more just distribution of resources between rich and poor countries is bound to become a paramount political concern.

People also speak of injustices that are, so to speak, cosmic, in the sense that they are beyond human control. Sadly, it is our fate as human beings to suffer injustices of this kind; in the final analysis, life is unfair. But injustices that are consequences of what human beings do are within our power to correct. Indeed, morality requires that we seek to eliminate these injustices whenever and wherever we can. Motivated by this objective, the Left has always gravitated towards a vision of egalitarian justice of the sort that Rawls and his followers have clarified and developed. Proponents of Right ideologies that are hostile to or indifferent towards equality are therefore obliged to develop rival accounts. Only neo-Lockean libertarians have risen to the challenge, but with questionable degrees of success. The close connection Rawlsians and utilitarians and others identify between justice and equality is as close to certain as any philosophical position can be.

Further Reading

Although it is pre-Rawlsian and therefore dated, the best general overview of the concept is still Chaim Perelman (John Petrie, trans.), *The Idea of Justice and the Problem of Argument* (New York: Humanities Press, 1963), chapters 1–3. Rawls's theory is set out in John Rawls, *A Theory of Justice,* revised edition (Cambridge, MA: Harvard University Press (Belknap), 1999). A briefer account is John Rawls, *Justice as Fairness: A Restatement* (Cambridge, MA: Harvard University Press (Belknap), 2001). The literature on Rawlsian justice and its implications is enormous. Of particular interest is Brian Barry, *Justice as Impartiality* (Oxford: Oxford University Press, 1996). I discuss Rawls at greater length in *Engaging Political Philosophy: from Hobbes to Rawls* (Malden, MA: Blackwell Publishers, 2002), chapter 5. In contemporary discussions of justice, utilitarianism is more a foil than a contending position. But there are exceptions. A technical, but generally accessible and highly illuminating utilitarian account of distributive justice that anticipates one of the main arguments Rawls adduces in support of his own non-utilitarian theory is John C. Harsanyi, "Cardinal Utility in Welfare Economics and in the Theory of Risk-Taking," *Journal of Political Economy*, vol. 61 (1953). The main source for the contemporary libertarian revival of Lockean accounts of justice is Robert Nozick, *Anarchy, State, and Utopia* (New York: Basic Books, 1977). The main source for contemporary communitarian critiques of Rawlsian justice is Michael Sandel, *Liberalism and the Limits of Justice* (Cambridge: Cambridge University Press, 1998). For Marx's views on justice, see Allen Wood, *Karl Marx* (London and Boston: Routledge and Kegan Paul, 1981), chapters 9–10. An incisive and comprehensive account of the problem of justice and morality generally in Marx's thought is provided in Steven Lukes, *Marxism and Morality* (Oxford: Oxford University Press, 1985).

See also: COMMUNITY/COMMUNITARIANISM, EQUALITY/EGALITARIANISM, ENVIRONMENTALISM, FREEDOM/LIBERTY, HISTORICAL MATERIALISM, IDEOLOGY, INTERNATIONALISM, LEFT/RIGHT/CENTER, LEGITIMACY, LIBERALISM, LIBERTARIANISM, MARXISM, MORALITY, POWER, REVOLUTION, RIGHTS, STATE, UTILITARIANISM, WELFARE/WELFARE STATE

L

Labor

To *labor* is to work or to toil. In ancient Greece, laborers were **slaves**. The low esteem in which they were held was reflected in Greek philosophy and in classical thought generally. This attitude dominated Western philosophy until the nineteenth century when, with the pace of industrialization quickening, progressive thinkers began to assert the dignity of labor. Marx and his followers were especially conspicuous in pressing this view. In Marx's **philosophical anthropology**, labor is human "generic activity"; human beings are **essentially** productive animals. However, the labor of real world workers, the direct producers in the new capitalist order, is alienated labor. As such, it is metaphorically the inverse of what is **essentially** human. Generic activity is unalienated labor; labor that is meaningful, free, and creative.

Aristotle (384?–322? BC) famously disparaged labor. It is therefore ironic that Marx's account of unalienated labor draws substantially on Aristotle's notion of **praxis**. Aristotle contrasted praxis, purposeful activity guided by an ideal, with "poesis," making or doing. All animals, not just human beings, make or do things; poesis is therefore not a distinctively human activity. Praxis is. Of course, poesis is purposeful too. But praxis involves second-order purposes – purposes about purposes. A second-order mental life is what defines Reason. Praxis is therefore possible for human beings because human beings, alone in the animal kingdom, have rational capacities. This is what Aristotle intended when he declared that "man is a rational animal"; in other words, that rationality (and, in Aristotle's view, nothing else) is essential for being human. But inasmuch as Reason has practical as well as theoretical applicability, Marx realized that, severed from its unwarranted (but typical) disparagement of practical endeavors, this position, if sound, implies that (creative) productive activity is essentially human too. Thus, the idea that human beings are essentially productive is not so much an alternative to Aristotle's account of the human essence as an extension – or, more accurately, a correction – of it.

In unalienated labor, second-order purposes are freely (**autonomously**) chosen. Artistic, especially literary, activity is a model. There is an important difference, however: the purposefulness of literary objects is internal to the objects themselves. As **Kantian** aestheticians maintained, art exhibits "purposefulness without a purpose." Unalienated labor is not similarly self-contained; it connects individual workers with their fellow workers and with human beings generally. It forms a community of free and equal moral agents. In short, it exhibits purposefulness with a purpose. It aims, to use another formulation of Kant's, to establish a "republic of ends" (of human beings regarded as ends-in-themselves) that instantiates the ideal of a harmonious, internally coordinated association of rational beings.

Marx's **Young Hegelian** writings on alienation have a counterpart in his account of history's structure and direction, historical materialism. In the historical materialist view, as productive forces develop under capitalism's aegis, **abundance** comes within reach. Thus, the need for burdensome toil diminishes. However, because capitalism increasingly "fetters" the rational deployment of **productive forces**, this potentially liberating transformation of the human condition remains unrealized. Burdensome toil becomes more, not less, pervasive; alienation intensifies. This is why Marx maintained that alienated labor will be a fact of human life for as long as capitalism survives. It is only with the installation of (socialist and eventually communist) **production relations** – or, what comes to the same thing, only when the praxis of free and equal persons manifests what Reason requires, and therefore when Reason controls social life – that essential humanity can be actualized. Then human beings will finally become, as Aristotelians might say, what they implicitly are.

Further Reading

Historical understandings of labor and leisure are reviewed and assessed in Sebastian de Grazia, *Of Time, Work and Leisure* (New York: Vintage, 1994). Contemporary perspectives are discussed in John T. Haworth and A.J. Veal (eds.), *Work and Leisure* (New York: Routledge, 2005). On Marx's philosophical anthropology, see Jon Elster, *Making Sense of Marx* (Cambridge: Cambridge University Press, 1985), chapter 2.

See also: ALIENATION, CAPITALISM, COMMUNISM, COMMUNITY/COMMUNITARIANISM, EQUALITY/ EGALITARIANISM, FREEDOM/LIBERTY, HISTORICAL MATERIALISM, MARXISM, MORALITY, SOCIALISM

Labor movement

The socialist movement that coalesced in the aftermath of the French Revolution sided, from the beginning, with workers and therefore with the incipient labor movement. This bond links **utopian socialism** with Marxism and later with anarchism and twentieth-century Social Democracy. Many liberals evinced similar sympathies. In some cases, the links were theoretical as well as political. Thus, for Marx and his followers, ties to the labor movement were underwritten by the conviction that the working class would be the agent of a socialist revolution, and that it would lead the transition from socialism to communism. For other **progressive** thinkers, the connections were less weighted theoretically. This was especially true for liberals and for "laborite" and other non-Marxist socialists in the twentieth century. For them, the idea was only that justice requires more egalitarian distributions of income and wealth than a capitalist state, without a strong and organized labor presence, is capable of providing.

In the nineteenth century, some working-class organizations were expressly revolutionary. However, by the beginning of the twentieth century, a more **economistic** "trade union consciousness," as V.I. Lenin (1870–1924) called it, had become pervasive. This is why Lenin insisted that "revolutionary consciousness" had to be introduced by a revolutionary **vanguard**, comprised mainly of **intellectuals** (most of whom, inevitably, would come from non-working-class sectors of society). Otherwise, workers would only fight to defend their immediate interests, not to advance the cause of general human emancipation.

Vanguardist thinkers like Lenin were not alone in noticing that, with the passage of time, the labor movement, as it grew, lost its revolutionary zeal. A variety of sociological explanations for this phenomenon were proposed. It was argued, for example, that trade unions were especially appealing to the "labor **aristocracy**" – that is, to the most skilled and best-paid strata of the working class. These workers had more to lose than their chains; for them, therefore, trade unions were more like trade associations than revolutionary organizations.

But there is a difference. In capitalist economies, workers can never be just one interest group among others because the system itself depends on their **exploitation**. Thus workers occupy a strategic and unique position in the economic structure. This is why a labor movement, whatever else it may do for workers, is indispensable for protecting them against capitalists who are, as it were, compelled by the economic structure itself to seize opportunities to take advantage of them. As the labor movement evolved, this understanding shaped efforts to organize the growing ranks of unskilled workers. For a while, their inclusion into the organized labor movement revived labor's militancy. In recent decades, however, thanks in part to the loss of manufacturing jobs in developed countries, these sectors of the working class have also become increasingly incorporated. It is a downward spiral: the less militant and visionary workers' organizations become, the less successful they are, and therefore the less able they are to attract new adherents.

In a world of growing economic insecurity, where the mainstream culture endeavors ceaselessly to quash **solidaristic** impulses and collective struggles, it has become a commonplace that the labor movement, whatever its accomplishments, has become irrelevant; that it is a victim of its own success. This is a curious claim inasmuch as it trades both on the increasing weakness of the working class and its organizations, and on the (supposed) fact that workers are now sufficiently well off not to need unions. It is hard to see how these contentions can both be true, and harder still to see how anyone can claim that workers today are better off than in decades past. But, as with so much else in our political culture, arguments count for less than repeated assertions by those who have the power to make themselves heard.

In the not too remote past, anti-union positions were couched in different terms. Then the usual way to attack the labor movement was by invoking the specter of revolution. This strategy was very nearly as disingenuous as the one that replaced it, inasmuch as organized labor's revolutionary socialist origins had all but faded into historical memory well before the end of the nineteenth century. Only a handful of revolutionary labor unions survived into the twentieth century. The Industrial Workers of the World (the IWW) is an important American example; there were others elsewhere. They left their mark on the popular imagination, but their political influence was negligible.

Throughout the twentieth century, the trend was in the other direction – the labor movement became a player in established political institutions, and developed a stake in their continuation. This happened in different countries in different ways. After World War I in Europe and elsewhere, trade unions won a measure of political representation. The labor movement became the backbone of Social Democracy. In some countries after World War II – Italy and France are examples – increasingly conservative Communist parties became the **de facto** political representatives of important segments of organized labor. In the United States, however, trade unions were content to throw in their lot with the Democratic Party, an unabashedly capitalist party with other constituencies (including, for a time, segregationists in the South) to appease. Organized labor in the United States therefore never had the political clout of its European counterparts.

Even so, for as long as the American labor movement was strong enough to compel Democratic Party leaders to address its concerns, advances were made. To be sure, welfare state institutions remained less developed in the United States than elsewhere. Nevertheless, a liberal–labor alliance in the Democratic Party and even in some quarters of the Republican Party did encourage the adoption of social policies that led to improvements in workers' standards of living. But in consequence of the American labor movement's feeble attempts at organizing new workers and its capitulation to **Cold War** anti-Communism, the trade union movement in the United States ossified. In conjunction with the indifference of its political allies and, in recent decades, the vicissitudes of world capitalism, the balance of class power has therefore changed to the detriment of the working class. In consequence, capitalists have gone back on the offensive. At the political level, the Thatcher government in Great Britain led the way; in the United States, the Reagan administration followed suit. In other developed capitalist countries, anti-labor offensives unfolded too, though usually in more benign forms. Thus the tacit, post-World War II **social contract**, according to which the labor movement would not intrude on capitalists' fundamental interests so long as wages and working conditions improved, gave way to the more antagonistic forms of capital–labor relations which had characterized earlier periods.

In the United States, this phenomenon has been especially marked. But the power of the trade unions has declined everywhere. The result is that the gains of the past century are increasingly in jeopardy, and that workers have become more disempowered than ever. It is fair to say that the rightward drift of world and especially American politics is largely attributable to organized labor's decline. Consequently, perhaps the most urgent task the Left faces today is to revitalize the labor movement. In the United States, awareness is dawning that this is a task that is too important to be left to existing union leaderships or to their (supposed) allies in the Democratic Party.

Further Reading

There is an enormous literature on the history of the labor movement and its vicissitudes in the United States and throughout the world. For an accessible account of American labor history, see Joseph G. Rayback, *History of American Labor* (New York: Free Press, 1966). A more contemporary and global perspective is provided in Ellen Meiksins Wood, Peter Meiksins, and Michael Yates (eds.), *Rising from the Ashes: Labor in the Age of Global Capitalism* (New York: Monthly Review Press, 1999).

See also: ANARCHISM, CAPITALISM, CLASS, COMMUNISM, CONSERVATISM, CULTURE, EQUALITY/ EGALITARIANISM, FREEDOM/LIBERTY, HISTORICAL MATERIALISM, JUSTICE, LABOR, LEFT/RIGHT/ CENTER, LENINISM, LIBERALISM, MARXISM, PROGRESS, REVOLUTION, SOCIAL DEMOCRACY, SOCIALISM, WELFARE/WELFARE STATE

Left/right/center

From the time of the French Revolution, when the more **radical** delegates to the National Assembly seated themselves to the left of the presiding officer, *Left* has designated a relatively stable, though evolving and multifaceted, political orientation. Thereafter too, *Right* took on a corresponding, contrary meaning. These polar points constitute a spectrum along which policies, programs, and political parities can be arrayed. In recent years, the usefulness of this spatial metaphor has been called into question – not only by partisans of so-called **third ways**, but also by those who think the left/right spectrum is historically superseded. Nevertheless, the distinction remains an indispensable reference point, not just for historical reasons but because, despite what some may think, it continues to be useful and timely.

What *left* and *right* signify is impossible to explain precisely, though the difference is well understood throughout the political culture. This is because an idealized or notional left/right spectrum has been recognized, more or less explicitly, by nearly everyone for more than two hundred years. Very generally, the Left is dedicated to continuing the French Revolutionaries' commitment to "liberty, equality, and **fraternity** (community)." Tradition, **authority** and order are core values for the Right. For the most part, left parties are indifferent to

115

or hostile towards the core values of the Right; right-wing parties, on the other hand, sometimes militate for liberty, equality, and community. But the Right's purchase on these objectives often has little to do with Left understandings. In general, conceptions of freedom, equality, and community differ across the political spectrum. Socialists of all types, anarchists and some liberals are on the Left; conservatives are usually, though perhaps not necessarily, on the Right.

The terms *left* and *right* introduce a useful ambiguity into descriptions of political orientations. They are ambiguous because *left* and *right*, being spatial metaphors, are relational notions; *left* is defined in contrast to *right*, and vice versa. This is why, except in the most general sense, they have no fixed meaning. Political parties and social movements that everyone understands to be on the Left have left and right wings, as do movements and parties of the Right. As with any continuum, there are also finer gradations. How many there are, and how they should be described, depends on the context.

In keeping with the spatial metaphor that has defined the political universe for so long, there is a *center* too. But the political center is almost never a figurative midpoint between the Left and the Right. Neither is it an **Aristotelian** "intermediary" or "mean." Those terms denote positions that are appropriate to prevailing circumstances. There is no reason to think that centrist positions are always or, for that matter, ever appropriate in this sense. Rather, what counts as centrist is whatever is proper to the political mainstream at particular times and places. *Center* is therefore even less amenable to a general characterization than are *left* and *right*. Typically, the Center leans towards one or another pole on the spectrum. However, it is almost always at some remove from each of them. The Center is also where most individuals and parties gravitate.

In liberal democracies, where periodic elections help to maintain political legitimacy, there is a particularly strong tendency for left- and right-wing parties to cluster around the center. They do so in order to garner as many votes to their left or their right as they can. More generally, there is a tendency to pitch policies towards the median voter. In this way, the natural weight of the center is reinforced by the institutional structure of the regime. Political parties intent on rallying their own constituencies may nominally endorse more extreme positions. But they seldom actively promote them. This is why radical aspirations are frequently stifled in the political arena, even when support for them runs strong in the general population.

Nevertheless, in periods of profound upheaval, the center can fail to hold. Then centrist parties, along with the constituencies they represent, radicalize –

siding usually with the tendency that wins the day. This is the exception that proves the rule. The Center is where it is in consequence of the balance of forces between the Left and the Right. In "normal" times, especially when the Left and the Right are roughly equal in strength, a large and accommodating Center helps to maintain an equilibrium between them. But in situations in which the regime itself is in question, the Center is often rapidly depleted of its former occupants, rendering it, for a time, politically insignificant. As the crisis is resolved and a new mainstream is constituted, a reconstructed center will again become the point on the (notional) left/right continuum where the majority of positions and policies in play at that time and place cluster.

Further Reading

I elaborate on the left/right/center metaphor, with special attention to the American scene, in *The American Ideology: A Critique* (New York: Routledge, 2004). On the tendency of left-wing parties to move towards the center in liberal democracies, see Adam Przeworski, *Capitalism and Social Democracy* (Cambridge: Cambridge University Press, 1986).

See also: ANARCHISM, COMMUNITY/COMMUNITARIANISM, CONSERVATISM, CULTURE, DEMOCRACY, EQUALITY/EGALITARIANISM, FREEDOM/LIBERTY, LEGITIMACY, LIBERALISM, REVOLUTION, SOCIALISM

Legitimacy

For as long as the state form of political organization has existed, the consensus view among political philosophers has been that state power rests ultimately on force. Thus, since at least the seventeenth century, the most fundamental problem political philosophers have confronted has been to justify the right of states to compel compliance; it being assumed that **coercion** exercised by any other agency (except perhaps a few non-state institutions, like the family) or by individuals is unjustifiable. But, inasmuch as the force states rely upon can only derive from its citizenry, it follows, as David Hume (1711–1776) pointed out, that "opinion" is the real foundation of the state. The state's coercers cannot be everywhere; and even if they could, who would coerce them? Thus, the argument goes, most people must, in varying degrees, acknowledge the legitimacy of the institutions that (sometimes) force them to do what they do not want to do; they must believe, in other words, that these institutions coerce them rightfully. This

117

is why no state – indeed, no political entity at all – can exist for long if its legitimacy is in doubt, and why a robust sense of the legitimacy of existing institutions is indispensable for their proper functioning.

It is useful to distinguish **de jure** legitimacy, legitimacy in right, from **de facto** legitimacy, legitimacy in fact. For those who think that "might makes right," the distinction collapses. But hardly anyone does think that might makes right. For everyone else, it is plain that de jure and de facto legitimacy have little, if anything, to do with one another. Consider this analogy: some people believe that "God exists." But this fact leaves open the question of whether God really does exist. Similarly, all of us some of the time (thoroughgoing anarchists excepted), and some of us all of the time, believe that political authorities, when they command us, do so rightfully. But this fact, the undeniable reality of de facto legitimacy, leaves the question of de jure legitimacy open. Political philosophers are concerned with this latter question, just as philosophers of religion are concerned to investigate the existence of God. But in just the way that the religious life of communities depends more on what people believe about God than on whether or not their beliefs are true, political life depends more on de facto than de jure legitimacy. Struggles to change political institutions fundamentally are always, in large part, struggles to delegitimize the old regime and to legitimize a new one. In "normal" politics too, questions of de facto legitimacy often arise because what political actors are able to do depends, in part, on what people believe they are able to do rightfully.

What establishes de facto legitimacy? The answer varies according to time and place. In the modern world – because the demos is everywhere an actor in the political arena and because the rule of law is everywhere esteemed (if not always honored) – there appear to be two main factors. There must, first of all, be some way of indicating that the people consent to the regime that governs them. Almost everywhere, elections are the preferred means. And the rulers must not overstep their constitutionally prescribed roles. They must adhere, in other words, to the rules of the game by obeying publicly promulgated and generally understood laws.

In liberal democracies, periodic and competitive elections, accompanied by the appearance of conformity to legal **norms**, almost always suffice to assure de facto legitimacy. In other kinds of states – for example, in the former Soviet Union and the countries that followed its example – legitimacy is more precarious. There, direct force was more important for assuring stability than is usually the case in liberal democracies.

118

It is fair to say that one reason why it takes so little to establish de facto legitimacy in liberal democracies is the dominance of the liberal over the democratic component in liberal democratic regimes. By retracting the public sphere and situating most of what people care about in an ostensibly apolitical civil society, liberalism effectively depoliticizes issues that would otherwise be politically contentious. Then, because the state has − or seems to have − little impact on daily life, people are inclined to accept its institutional arrangements, even if they work against their deeper interests. They are therefore inclined to acquiesce when legally established governments do things with which they disagree. This is why, so long as liberal democracies do not impose burdensome requirements on their citizens, their de facto legitimacy is assured, and why they are remarkably stable.

In normal times, the only question of political moment that arises for most citizens of liberal democracies, and then only at intervals of several years, is which of a few (usually two) like-minded individuals they will vote for. Even that question is one that many citizens either don't bother to answer or else with which they deliberately refuse to engage. A higher level of politicization would almost certainly increase democratic participation, enhancing the prospects for a deeper democratization of the social order. It would also raise more momentous questions than whether to vote for Tweedledum or Tweedledee − giving rise to unprecedented opportunities for improving the social and political side of human life qualitatively and perhaps even for changing its nature fundamentally. In such circumstances, theories of de jure legitimacy, currently of only academic interest, might again become politically relevant.

Further Reading

The distinction between de facto and de jure legitimacy is implicit in the opening chapters of Jean-Jacques Rousseau, *The Social Contract* (1762), available in many editions, including Jean-Jacques Rousseau (Peter Gay, ed.), *The Basic Political Writings* (Indianapolis, IN: Hackett, 1987). The best sociological account of how de facto legitimacy comes into being and is sustained is still Max Weber's in ``Politics as a Vocation,'' available in Hans Gerth and C. Wright Mills, *From Max Weber: Essays in Sociology* (Oxford: Oxford University Press, 1958). A more recent, but still classic account of the role of legitimation crises in political struggles is Jürgen Habermas (Thomas McCarthy, trans.), *Legitimation Crisis* (Boston: Beacon, 1975). I elaborate on positions sketched here in *The Politics of Autonomy: A ``Kantian'' Reading of Rousseau's ``Social Contract''* (Amherst, MA: University of Massachusetts Press, 1976); *The General Will: Rousseau, Marx, Communism* (Cambridge:

Cambridge University Press, 1993); and *Engaging Political Philosophy: From Hobbes to Rawls* (Oxford and Malden, MA: Blackwell Publishers, 2002).

See also: ANARCHISM, COMMUNITY/COMMUNITARIANISM, DEMOCRACY, EQUALITY/EGALITARIANISM, FREE-
DOM/LIBERTY, LEFT/RIGHT/CENTER, LIBERALISM, STATE

Leninism

Leninism designates a form of Marxist political theory and practice, based on the work of Vladimir Ilyich Lenin (1870–1924), the leader of the 1917 **Bolshevik** Revolution and the founder of the Soviet state. The word entered the Marxist lexicon in the first decade and a half of the twentieth century. What it stood for was, at first, a minority current; even in Russia, Lenin and his followers had many opponents. However, after the Revolution, everything changed. For many decades, Leninism became the dominant political tendency of self-identified Marxists and a point of reference for all the rest. Both Stalinists and Trotskyists vied for the title – the latter claiming, with some plausibility, to be "classical" Leninists. Even Maoists claimed to be Leninists, despite their insistence that Mao Zedong (1893–1976) had moved beyond Lenin in much the way that, in Stalin's and Trotsky's view, Lenin had moved beyond Marx. Official Communists, during the Stalin era and for some time thereafter, called themselves "Marxist-Leninist." By the mid-1960s, that description had been taken over by the Maoists. Most distinctively **New Left** political formations implicitly rejected Leninism. But they nevertheless held Lenin in high regard. Nowadays, the pendulum has swung back. Leninism is in disrepute in most sectors of the Left.

Leninists are, above all, **vanguardists**. In their view, the leading role in promoting socialist revolutions and in constructing socialist regimes falls to a vanguard party of class-**conscious** workers – and, secondarily, **peasants** and other subordinate strata – along with professional revolutionaries drawn from all classes. The revolutionary party Lenin envisioned is a quasi-military organization run according to the principles of "democratic centralism": tactical leadership emanates from the top down, party cadres executing the party's orders faithfully and (in public, at least) unquestioningly, while general **strategy** is determined from the base up by party militants through democratic deliberation and collective choice. However, as one would expect of a hierarchically structured practice, the reality often belies the theory. In Leninist parties, there is typically very little effective activity at the base.

The theoretical standpoint of the party Lenin constructed derives from Marxism, as Leninists understand it. Lenin argued that, because workers and other oppressed peoples lack access to educational and cultural resources, they are, with few exceptions, capable spontaneously only of "trade union consciousness." They can grasp what they need to do to defend themselves against the predations of capital, but they are unable, without guidance, to realize what must be done to undo the root causes of those predations. "Revolutionary consciousness" must therefore be introduced from the outside – by professional revolutionaries capable of turning Marxism into a practicable revolutionary theory.

Lenin's views on party organization were formed in Czarist Russia in the face of pervasive police repression. For him and his co-thinkers, constitutionally protected forms of political struggle were out of the question. Following Lenin's lead, Leninist political formations have a clandestine structure, with militants organized into cells and branches. The idea was that, even where Communist parties can operate openly, they should be capable of going underground at a moment's notice. Leninists were not the first revolutionaries to adopt organizational forms of this kind. They were preceded by so-called populists in Russia and elsewhere who developed similar structures to enable the execution of military operations or terrorist acts. Lenin and his followers inveighed against these tactics, declaring them to be counter-revolutionary in effect, if not in intention. In their view, a party organized on democratic centralist principles is indispensable for directing the working masses and bringing them to power. Rival strategies, Lenin argued, only provide vehicles for acting out revolutionary fantasies. Thus, Lenin derided what he called "infantile leftism."

In Communist countries, with Communist (and therefore Leninist) parties in power, party membership was indispensable for personal success in most fields. Even in these conditions, however, party structures continued to reflect their clandestine origins. Party membership was seldom kept secret. But organizational forms concocted in pre-revolutionary times, when Communists were repressed, remained intact. Leninists, especially Communists, out of power were less forthcoming. Even when their political activities were constitutionally protected, Leninists were inclined to be secretive about their political affiliations, doing their public political work in front organizations.

Lenin was not only a political strategist and leader. He also advanced distinctive positions in a variety of areas, including political theory and political economy. He was one of a number of late-nineteenth- and early-twentieth-century thinkers, not all of them Marxists, who developed theories of

121

imperialism and its relation to capitalism. Lenin sided with other Marxist writers – among them, August Bebel (1840–1913), Rudolph Hilferding (1877–1941) and Rosa Luxemburg (1871–1919) – in insisting on imperialism's inevitability as the logic of capitalist development unfolds. Lenin differed from the others in emphasizing the revolutionary implications of anti-imperialist struggles not just in the home countries but also in the territories dominated by imperial powers. It was Lenin's work, more than that of any other Marxist of his time, that laid the groundwork for the **Third Worldist** turn that Marxism would take in the second half of the twentieth century.

Lenin was also the author of a philosophical treatise, *Materialism and Empirio-Criticism* (1909), and of commentaries on the writings of Hegel and other philosophers. In the Stalin era and subsequently, his philosophical positions ossified into **dialectical materialism**, the official doctrine of Soviet philosophy. Partly for this reason, and partly because Lenin wrote in a hectoring, non-academic style, his contributions to philosophy have been largely ignored in the West. This is unfortunate, since Lenin made a number of insightful contributions to ongoing philosophical debates – especially to the venerable conflict between **idealism** and **materialism**. His work on Hegel is of particular interest. Lenin also had much to say *about* philosophy, as well as *within* it. He was a "meta-philosopher" of some moment.

Leninism is unlikely ever to revive. Too many of Lenin's distinctive ideas were peculiar to his time and place. His theory of political organization was appropriate, if at all, to a world very different from the one we now live in, and events have proven many of his positions wrong. Whether the evils of Stalinism (and Maoism) are inevitable extensions of Leninist theory and practice – or whether they were betrayals of it – remains in dispute. The connections between these political tendencies are, in any case, complex. Thus, even if a convincing case could be made for the continuity of Leninism and Stalinism, it still would not follow that Leninism should be rejected along with its offshoot. Lenin was a brilliant thinker and strategist. When the historical context of his work is taken into account, there is much still to learn from him.

After his death in 1924, Lenin's reputation grew. He assumed an almost godlike status in the Soviet Union and wherever else Communism (or Maoism and, despite its more urbane cast, even Trotskyism) appealed. Fortunately, he is no longer the object of a thoroughly un-Marxist tradition of veneration. If anything, the opposite is now the case. This is also unfortunate, inasmuch as there is much in Lenin's work that remains valuable. But the disregard into which Leninism has fallen is not an entirely bad thing. Since there is now very little political contestation over *Leninism*, the time is propitious for a critical and potentially useful reassessment of his work.

Further Reading

The best way to acquire a sense of the nature and rationale for Leninist theory and practice is through Lenin's own writings. They are available in many editions, and in his *Collected Works* (*CW*) published in the 1960s and 1970s by Progress Publishers, Moscow. "What is to be Done?" (1902; *CW*, vol. 5) sets forth Lenin's views about the vanguard party. "Left-Wing Communism: An Infantile Disorder" (1920; *CW*, vol. 31), written when the Bolsheviks were already in power, amplifies many of the themes of that earlier work. For Lenin's views on the state, see *The State and Revolution* (1917; *CW*, vol. 25). His study of imperialism is *Imperialism: The Highest Stage of Capitalism* (1916; *CW*, vol. 22). His main philosophical and metaphilosophical work is *Materialism and Empirio-Criticism* (1909; *CW*, vol. 14). Rosa Luxemburg's critical but sympathetic contemporaneous writings on Leninism remain timely: see *The Russian Revolution and Leninism or Marxism?* (Ann Arbor, MI: University of Michigan Press, 1961). Among twentieth-century Marxist philosophers who have reflected on Lenin's contributions to political theory and philosophy, two especially stand out: Georg Lukács, *Lenin: A Study in the Unity of His Thought* (London: Verso, 1997); and Louis Althusser, "Lenin and Philosophy," in *Lenin and Philosophy and Other Essays* (New York: Monthly Review Press, 2001). I reflect on Althusser's account of Lenin in *A Future for Marxism?* (London: Pluto Press, 2003), chapters 3–4.

See also: CLASS, COMMUNISM, DEMOCRACY, IMPERIALISM, LEFT/RIGHT/CENTER, MAOISM, MARXISM, POPULISM, REVOLUTION, SOCIALISM, STALINISM, TERROR/TERRORISM, TROTSKYISM

Liberalism

Liberal theory and practice emerged in the early modern period in Western Europe in the aftermath of the Protestant Reformation and the ensuing wars of religion. Having fought to exhaustion, the competing sides were inclined to tolerate each other's religious convictions. In time, a virtue was made of what had begun as grudging acceptance. Then, during the English revolutions of the seventeenth century, with the **absolutist** state in question, liberal defenses of religious toleration developed into principled theories of limited **sovereignty**. The guiding idea was that there are areas of individuals' lives and behaviors that states cannot rightfully infringe. From the beginning, liberal ideas were also invoked in defense of **laissez-faire** economic arrangements and private **property**.

Liberals also defended free expression. Thus, from its inception, liberalism marked out a private sphere, **civil society**, apart from the state. Economic institutions belonged to civil society. So too did religion, which, for the first time in human history, came to be thought of as a matter of private conscience and therefore not a matter of political significance. Because liberals accorded pride of place to liberty, which they understood as freedom from **coercive** institutions, liberalism was disposed, from the outset, to minimize the role of the state and to expand the sphere of civil society. However, liberals were not anarchists; like their absolutist rivals, they believed that states were indispensable for insuring order and for providing other public goods. More generally, the role of the state, in the liberal view, is to provide the conditions under which civil society can flourish.

In the aftermath of the French Revolution, what began as a defense of limited sovereignty developed into a full-fledged ideology, friendly to many of the goals and achievements of the revolutionaries, but hostile to revolutionary politics. Thus, whatever liberals thought about private property and markets or about the role of the state, liberalism became part of the nascent Left. Unlike more **radical** Left currents, however, liberalism was a doctrine of permanent **reform**, of change – sometimes substantial, more usually incremental – imposed from above. Post-Revolutionary liberals were as dedicated as other leftists were to changing the world in **progressive** ways. But they were determined to do so within the framework of existing legal institutions and **norms**. Desirable transformations, in their view, should be the work of **enlightened** elites, rather than insurrectionary masses. This ostensibly "middle of the road" position was an amalgam of two implicitly contradictory impulses. On the one hand, liberalism was disposed to accept the basic claim of conservatives – that change is best pursued in piece-meal fashion, without taking on the system in its totality. Like conservatives, liberals resisted the temptations of a **rationalist** politics. On the other hand, liberals were themselves rationalists in the sense that they sought to engineer a better world. In this way, they differed from the revolutionary wing of the Left only in not regarding insurgent masses as agents of Reason in history. That role they assigned to themselves as enlightened reformers, latter-day philosopher kings.

Since the early nineteenth century, liberalism has coalesced into a number of distinct configurations of which the most pertinent, for American politics today, is the one achieved in the **New Deal** and continued, in fits and starts, through the collapse of the **Great Society**. Inasmuch as these configurations differ substantially, especially on the role of the state in economic affairs, it could be argued that liberalisms share, at most, a family resemblance, and that the connections between them are more historical than philosophical. Or, more plausibly, it could be held that, despite their differences, there is a common core. Proponents of the latter view maintain that what all liberalisms share is the idea, implicit in early liberal defenses of religious toleration, that political institutions should be "neutral" with respect to competing "conceptions of the good." Most liberals would agree that the good life is one that maximizes human freedom. But, strictly speaking, liberalism is not committed to any particular view of the good life, or at least to no view that is in any serious way contentious. Rather, what liberals are committed to is the idea that the political community should neither favor nor impede particular conceptions – except perhaps those that are inimical to the continuation of liberal institutions themselves. Instead, the state should provide a framework in which various conceptions can fairly compete. Thus, New Deal/Great Society liberalism, which advocated an active role for the state in regulating economic life, in promoting civil rights, and in advancing a social agenda similar to that of European social democracy was of one mind with the various laissez-faire liberal settlements of other times and places in *not* using state power in ways that contravene individuals' own determinations of what is good for themselves. A state that tolerates different religious denominations by making faith a matter of private conscience, that collapses religious differences into a common citizenship, implements neutrality in this one historically crucial domain. A full-fledged liberal state generalizes this practice.

The Great Society effectively stretched the limits of liberal neutrality. Because Great Society liberals were also (small-d) democrats, drawn to proceduralist understandings of what democracy requires, they were inclined to reduce social problems – poverty especially, but also racial injustice – to interests of adversely affected individuals and groups. Justice (fairness), in their view, required that these interests be represented proportionally in voting to their actual distribution in the society at large. But since poverty and racism disable individuals from participating in political processes in ways that permit their interests to register, it devolved to an affirmative state to rectify this situation – by empowering disenfranchised groups. On the surface, policies of this sort appear to implement particular conceptions of the good – ones in which poverty and racism have no place. But it was not to implement these conceptions that the more radical Great Society planners proposed these policies. It was to achieve conditions in which all conceptions would compete fairly. This may seem like a distinction with only an abstract philosophical difference. Perhaps it is. But it is an extension of ideas that have been implicit all along in the New Deal/Great Society configuration of liberal positions. It is what draws this last great age of American liberalism closer to social democracy than had been the case before. And it is this understanding that underlies uses of the term according to which *liberal* designates the left of the mainstream political spectrum.

As a political orientation and, more dramatically, as a word describing that position, *liberalism* has fallen into disfavor in recent years, even as liberal philosophical positions flourish in academic circles. The Great Society foundered on the Vietnam War, though some of its proponents fought on in ensuing decades. With the revival of **neo-liberalism** in the 1980s, New Deal/Great Society liberalism went almost entirely on the defensive. Thus, a remarkable transformation has occurred. Not long ago in the United States nearly everyone in the political mainstream, Republican and Democrat alike, called themselves *liberals*. In most cases, the designation was at least somewhat appropriate. Nowadays, self-described liberals have very nearly become an endangered species. Because the Vietnam War, and the larger **Cold War** in which it was embedded, were largely fashioned by liberals, the hard Left came to reject the term. The resurgent Right treated it with derision. Disparaged by all sides, only a few stalwarts retained the name. This is why nowadays many who would count as *liberals* in the New Deal/Great Society sense prefer to be called "progressives."

At one level, this is a harmless change; what, after all, is in a name? But it can have unfortunate consequences. New Deal/Great Society liberalism, and the Progressive era liberalism out of which it grew, drew on a distinctively American tradition of liberal thought – born out of nineteenth-century **Transcendentalism** and culminating in the work of John Dewey (1859–1952). This is a tradition that was once prominent in universities and in journals of opinion, as well as in public life. It no longer is. But it still has much to teach us. It would be regrettable if its insights become lost and, more importantly, if the political practices that tradition underwrote become forgotten because of associations that currently attach to the term that describes them.

Further Reading

There are useful discussions of liberalism in Will Kymlicka, *Contemporary Political Philosophy: An Introduction* (Oxford: Oxford University Press, 1990), chapter 3; and Jonathan Wolff, *An*

Introduction to Political Philosophy (Oxford: Oxford University Press, 1996), chapter 4. The idea that liberal tolerance should be construed as neutrality owes everything to the recasting of liberal theory in John Rawls, *A Theory of Justice*, revised edition (Cambridge, MA: Harvard University Press (Belknap Press), 1999), and John Rawls, *Political Liberalism* (New York: Columbia University Press, 1995). However, Rawls himself was dubious of the term. Thus, "neutrality" entered mainstream academic discourse largely thanks to the work of Ronald Dworkin. See, especially, Ronald Dworkin, "Liberalism," in Stuart Hampshire (ed.), *Public and Private Morality* (Cambridge: Cambridge University Press, 1978). Dworkin's account of the New Deal liberal "settlement" is illuminating. On the idea of neutrality, see also Charles E. Larmore, *Patterns of Moral Complexity* (Cambridge: Cambridge University Press, 1987), chapter 3. I elaborate on these issues in *The American Ideology: A Critique* (New York: Routledge, 2004), chapter 6; and in *Engaging Political Philosophy: From Hobbes to Rawls* (Oxford and Malden, MA: Blackwell Publishers, 2002), chapter 5. A classic of the distinctively American strain of liberal theory and practice that has, unfortunately, faded from popular awareness is John Dewey, *Liberalism and Social Action* (Amherst, NY: Prometheus Books, 1999).

See also: ANARCHISM, CIVIL RIGHTS, CONSERVATISM, DEMOCRACY, FREEDOM/LIBERTY, FREEDOM OF EXPRESSION, IDEOLOGY, JUSTICE, LEFT/RIGHT/CENTER, LEGITIMACY, MARKETS, PROGRESS, PUBLIC GOODS, RACE/RACISM, REVOLUTION, SOCIAL DEMOCRACY, STATE

Libertarianism

This term designates a form of liberalism developed in the nineteenth century and revived by the pro-capitalist Right in recent years. In contemporary politics, libertarians are the main defenders of economic liberties – above all, the right to accumulate **property** privately and without limitation, and the right to engage in market transactions without government interference. Libertarians therefore believe that individuals are entitled to their market-generated shares – provided, of course, that they are acquired legitimately. Accordingly, they oppose state-sponsored redistributions of individuals' holdings and, more generally, non-voluntary transferals of property. Libertarians, like other liberals, are not anarchists. They believe that states are necessary for providing public goods, and they understand that states need resources to do so. They are therefore not opposed to taxation per se. They also realize that public goods provision can have unintended redistributive consequences. What they oppose is taxation that is deliberately redistributive – whether undertaken for the sake of some (for them, false) conception of justice, for welfare enhancement, or for any other reason. Most libertarians also believe that the economic liberties they uphold and the civil liberties all liberals defend comprise a seamless web. Libertarians are therefore often at the forefront of efforts to defend civil liberties.

Libertarian positions can be supported in a variety of ways. One influential strategy, following John Locke's (1632–1704) example, supposes that in principle individuals can justly acquire unowned things (by "mixing" their labor with them) and can then justly transfer what they own in market transactions or gifts. The outcome of these processes is then deemed just. On this view, a just outcome is any consequence of just procedures. How equal the outcome is – or how well it conforms to any pattern of distribution one might think justice requires – is irrelevant. Locke endeavored to defend his claims about rightful acquisition and justice preserving transfers. However, his arguments were, by common consensus, flawed. Nevertheless, they were and continue to be influential. Ironically, Locke's "labor theory of property" helped to shape the labor theories of value of classical political economy. Thus, his account is part of the ancestry of Marxian economics.

Unlike Locke himself, contemporary neo-Lockeans seldom try to defend their faith in rights that trump other considerations. Instead, they simply assert the existence of rights that ground libertarian positions and then insist on their inviolability. Their arguments are therefore unlikely to convince anyone who does not already accept their premises. It is also obvious that, in a world where most wealth was initially acquired through plunder and theft and in which real world markets fall short of the ideal, it requires an enormous leap to hold that what Locke and his contemporary followers deem rightful in principle applies in actual cases. Neo-Lockean libertarians make this leap. They think that their case for an ideal capitalism justifies the distributions we find in existing capitalist societies.

Nineteenth-century libertarians were more likely to be utilitarians than Lockeans. Many of contemporary libertarians, especially if they are economists or legal theorists, follow their lead. Insofar as they do, their guiding idea is that, among all the feasible ways to organize social and economic life, libertarian arrangements have the best utility consequences overall. Most defenders of this view are not strict utilitarians, however. In part because they harbor doubts about the cogency of interpersonal utility comparisons, a prerequisite for utility maximization, they seldom appeal to that standard as such. Instead, they would maximize efficiency, a notion that retrieves what they find sustainable in traditional utilitarian doctrine. When they defend libertarian policies, therefore, it is because, in their view, these policies serve efficiency better than any feasible alternative. In arguing their case, they characteristically deploy the concepts and explanatory strategies of neo-classical economics. Their arguments are often ingenious. But they are hardly compelling. Therefore they too are unlikely to convince those who are not already on board.

In the 1980s and 1990s, a few egalitarian liberals, persuaded by the neo-Lockean thesis of "self-ownership," according to which individuals have property rights in their own persons and powers, but also convinced, as egalitarian liberals are, that morally arbitrary factors do not generate entitlements to external things, developed a left (egalitarian) version of libertarianism. Like other liberal egalitarians, left libertarians took seriously the morally arbitrary nature of the factors that generate market shares in real world capitalist economies. These include, among other things, wealth (including **human capital**) acquired by the usual means through which wealth is acquired in the real world, and internal resources (talents). Left libertarians believe that, in right, these income-generating factors are owned by everyone collectively and therefore that the revenues that accrue from their use should be equally distributed. Individuals, then, have entitlements only to that portion of their market-generated holdings that can be attributed to their own freely undertaken efforts. Left libertarian principles would lead to distributional outcomes far more equal than those envisioned by even the most **radical New Deal** liberals. However, the appeal of this line of thought is mitigated by the fact that, like its neo-Lockean rival, it rests on dubious claims – not least the thesis of self-ownership itself. In recent years, interest in left libertarian theory has waned, along with interest in neo-Lockean justifying theories in general. With the rightward drift of the political culture, libertarianism has become so deeply entrenched that its proponents feel little need to defend it. At the same time, its theoretical bases have been so often discredited, that, for many of its opponents, there is no need to add yet another voice to the chorus.

In the United States especially, spontaneous or reflexive libertarianism is pervasive. This is what makes possible, for example, the argumentative strategy used by politicians of both major parties to justify cutting taxes. Their real purpose may be to redistribute from the poor to the rich and, not unrelatedly, to generate **fiscal** crises that render efforts to revive or even maintain welfare state programs otiose. But, rhetorically, the trope is that individuals have entitlements to their market-generated shares, and therefore that governments should leave them with as much of "their own money" as is consistent with the provision of national defense and perhaps a few other public goods. Of course, the reality is that market-generated shares, so far from preceding fiscal policies and laws in both fact and right, are instead consequences of these policies and laws. This is a case where clear-headed philosophical analysis can dispel a dangerous intuition that resonates throughout the political culture.

Further Reading

The Lockean positions that underlie some contemporary versions of libertarian theory are set forth in John Locke (C.B. Macpherson, ed.), *The Second Treatise of Government* (Indianapolis, IN: Hackett, 1980; originally published 1690). The founding text for contemporary neo-Lockean thought is Robert Nozick, *Anarchy, State, and Utopia* (New York: Basic Books, 1977). I discuss Locke and Nozick in *Engaging Political Philosophy: from Hobbes to Rawls* (Malden, MA: Blackwell Publishers, 2002), chapter 3. A classic quasi-utilitarian defense of libertarian policies is Milton Friedman, *Capitalism and Freedom* (Chicago: University of Chicago Press, 2002). For examples of more recent versions, any of the many books published over the past several decades by Richard A. Posner provide good illustrations. Among the most interesting is *Sex and Reason* (Cambridge, MA: Harvard University Press, 1994). Perhaps the most influential is *Economic Analysis of Law*, 2nd edition (Boston: Little Brown, 1977). Contemporary interest in the doctrine of self-ownership owes much to the work of G.A. Cohen. See G.A. Cohen, *Self-Ownership, Freedom, and Equality* (Cambridge: Cambridge University Press, 1995). Left libertarianism is debated in Peter Vallentyne and Hillel Steiner (eds.), *Left Libertarianism and Its Critics: The Contemporary Debate* (New York and London: Palgrave Macmillan, 2001). A rather different sort of left libertarianism that aims to maximize "real freedom for all" is defended in Philippe Van Parijs, *Real Freedom for All: What (If Anything) Can Justify Capitalism?* (Oxford: Oxford University Press, 1995). On the fallacies of spontaneous libertarianism and its policy consequences, see Liam B. Murphy and Thomas Nagel, *The Myth of Ownership: Taxes and Justice* (Oxford: Oxford University Press, 2002).

See also: ANARCHISM, CAPITALISM, CIVIL RIGHTS/CIVIL LIBERTIES, EQUALITY/EGALITARIANISM, FREEDOM/LIBERTY, JUSTICE, LABOR, LEFT/RIGHT/CENTER, LEGITIMACY, LIBERALISM, MARKETS, MARXISM, MORALITY, PUBLIC GOODS, STATE, UTILITARIANISM, WELFARE/WELFARE STATE

M

Maoism

After Joseph Stalin's (1879–1953) death, serious rifts emerged between the Soviet Union and Communist China. By the late 1950s, it was plain to everyone, except fanatical **Cold Warriors** obsessed with "monolithic" Communism, that there was a division in the world Communist movement. Then, during the 1960s, even the most extreme anti-Communists came to recognize the reality of the Sino-Soviet split. The Chinese side was named for the chairman of the Chinese Communist Party, Mao Zedong (formerly written "Mao Tse-tung") (1893–1976). Mao was a leading theoretician of Chinese Communism. But, like Stalin, Mao was also the object of a "personality cult." Therefore, like Stalin, he was credited as the author of almost every new idea that bore official approval. Much like the Trotskyists (whom Mao and his lieutenants opposed), Maoists thought of themselves as the legitimate continuators of the **Bolshevik** Revolution. To mark this claim, they appropriated the name "Marxist Leninist" which, by the 1960s, came to mean *Maoist*.

In the 1960s and thereafter, without benefit of any formal "International" or other organizational structure, Maoism developed into a worldwide movement. All Maoists expressed fidelity to "the thought of Mao Zedong." But at a practical level, self-identified Maoist political formations differed considerably. In parts of Asia, where conditions were similar to those that prevailed in China before the Chinese Revolution (1949), Maoism was largely a **peasant** movement.

Maoism

Based in the countryside, Maoists engaged in guerilla warfare, seizing and administering vast tracts of land. Their goal was eventually to surround the towns and then, aided by workers' insurrections in the cities, to seize state power, just as the Chinese Communists had done. Once in power, the Chinese Communists proceeded to reorganize political, social, and economic institutions along the lines pioneered in the Soviet Union. Most Maoists in Asia proposed to do the same. Elsewhere in the **Third World**, especially in Latin America, self-identified Maoists, facing very different conditions, had to modify classical Maoist forms of revolutionary struggle. They would sometimes even ally themselves with **Castroists** and therefore, indirectly, with mainstream Communists. In addition, Latin American and African Maoists were generally less fixated on replicating the institutions the Chinese Communists established. Their fidelity to the Chinese model was more rhetorical than substantive.

In the developed capitalist countries, where the peasantry had all but disappeared or where it had never existed at all, and where the state was more than capable of suppressing armed insurgencies, *Maoism* meant something very different. For some, it was a way of continuing a fundamentally Stalinist and **workerist** political practice, as official Communist Parties began to "de-Stalinize." For others, especially as the "Great **Proletarian Cultural Revolution**" that began in the mid-1960s developed in China, it was a way of expressing a kind of anti-imperialist purity, joined with a generally Third Worldist political orientation. This strain of Western Maoism was particularly attractive to young people of middle- and upper-class origins, partly for its ostensible purity, partly because it provideda way to be "communist" without being Communist. Needless to say, their Maoism had little in common with the Maoism that reigned in China.

In retrospect, it is fair to remark that all Western Maoists and many Third World Maoists too were united by a profound ignorance of the facts on the ground. It could hardly have been otherwise. Unrecognized by the United States and other Western countries, and pursuing a largely autochthonous strategy of economic development, China was cut off from the rest of the world. For a time, therefore, China functioned like a Rorschach test for the extreme Left. Militants saw in it what they wanted to see.

In Western countries like Italy or France, where Communist parties had large working-class constituencies, *Maoism* took on an additional significance. To be a Maoist there was to be a Communist outside the ambit of the increasingly conservative and bureaucratized Communist parties. Trotskyism had a similar appeal. But that identification implied disassociation from the Communist-led workers' movement of the preceding decades. Nevertheless, like Trotskyism, Maoism attracted few workers. This condition was partly self-inflicted. Thanks to the Third Worldist orientation of many Maoist groups, traditional working-class organizing often gave way to political work in immigrant communities (in Europe) and in Third World and African-American communities (in the United States).

After Mao's death, as China opened up to the outside world, Maoism quickly lost its appeal. By the early 1980s, it had all but vanished as a pole of attraction. Today, Maoist remnants survive only in remote areas of desperately poor countries in South and South East Asia and Latin America. Even there, self-identified Maoists are more likely to engage in banditry and drug trafficking than in struggles to advance the programs and goals of the Russian and Chinese Revolutions. They are more likely to terrorize peasant populations and to exploit them than to "serve the people" as Mao proclaimed, or to fight for their liberation.

A key Maoist theoretical innovation was the idea that political transformations of the sort necessary to lead to communism (in Marx's sense) can and should be undertaken even before the "**material** conditions" for communism have fully matured. Despite Maoism's official allegiance to Communism's Stalinist past, this conviction implicitly opposed the Stalinist insistence on postponing **radical** social and political transformations indefinitely, while attention is paid to developing industrial capacity. It was this idea – that politics should be "in command" even over economic affairs – that led Mao to launch a far-reaching effort to collectivize agriculture in the so-called "Great Leap Forward" of the 1950s, and then to the Cultural Revolution itself. In theory, that revolution targeted bureaucratized sectors of the Communist Party and the Chinese state apparatus. In the West, it was perceived as a program of de-Stalinization from the left. Historical evidence nowadays suggests that Mao had more self-serving motives – that the Cultural Revolution was launched mainly as an intra-bureaucratic initiative. However that may be, the Cultural Revolution's human costs were enormous, and its economic impact disastrous. Measured against its professed goals, it was also counter-productive. In its aftermath, the once-despised "capitalist road," with its attendant inequalities and discontents, is now enthusiastically endorsed by large segments of the Chinese population and by their still-reigning Communist rulers.

There is, of course, another side to the story. The Chinese Revolution decisively overthrew age-old, profoundly stultifying economic and social structures. It transformed the lives of many Chinese people for the better. Therefore, even more than with other world-transforming revolutionary upheavals, it is too soon to make a balanced historical assessment. But awareness of Chinese Communism's excesses, particularly in its most radical phases (the Great Leap Forward, the Great Proletarian Cultural Revolution), has tarnished perceptions of Maoism, perhaps irrevocably. Nevertheless, it would be a mistake to conclude that Maoism's theoretical innovations cannot bear scrutiny, especially the one that, more than any other, defined Maoism in the West – the idea that cultural revolutions are indispensable for building the kinds of societies the Left has always envisioned.

Much like China itself in the days when information about it was hard to come by, that concept can mean almost anything one wants it to mean. For some self-identified Maoists in Europe several decades ago, it was of a piece with Antonio Gramsci's (1891–1937) writings on the need for socialists to struggle for cultural hegemony. Despite the antipathy Maoists and Trotskyists have always evinced towards each other, there are also obvious affinities to Trotsky's doctrine of **permanent revolution**. And, ever since the expression entered the political lexicon in the 1960s, artistic radicalism and oppositional ways of life that identify with the Left are sometimes held to constitute an ongoing cultural revolution. It is impossible to say what "cultural revolution" means strictly speaking – because the expression never had a strict sense. But the idea and the practices it inspires have an evident appeal, especially for those intent on correcting the shortcomings of Communist theory and practice. It is therefore worth investigating the episode of Chinese and world history in which the notion arose. There is much to learn from doing so.

Further Reading

An insightful and sympathetic account of Maoism is Maurice J. Meisner, *Marxism, Maoism and Utopianism: Eight Essays* (Madison, WI: University of Wisconsin Press, 1982). A scholarly and comprehensive reference work on Third World Maoist movements is Robert J. Alexander, *International Maoism in the Developing World* (Westport, CT: Praeger, 1999). On Western Maoism, see Daniel Singer, *Prelude to Revolution: France in May 1968*, updated edition (Cambridge, MA: South End Press, 2002). Western notions of cultural revolution and their connection to the work of Antonio Gramsci are discussed in Carl Boggs, *The Two Revolutions: Gramsci and the Dilemmas of Western Marxism* (Cambridge, MA: South End Press, 1985). See also my *A Future for Marxism? Althusser, the Analytical Turn, and the Revival of Socialist Theory* (London: Pluto Press, 2003), chapter 2. Mainstream Western perceptions of Mao and Maoism have varied over the years. Before the Sino-Soviet split was universally acknowledged, Mao was seen as a pawn of the Soviet Union. Immediately afterwards, he was depicted as evil incarnate. This changed abruptly after Richard Nixon's 1972 visit to China. Partly because the Nixon Administration and other Western elites then had an interest in promoting his stature, Mao began to be recognized as an important and relatively independent Marxist thinker, and a brilliant political strategist. Now the pendulum is swinging back. Once again, Mao is a monster, as he is described, for example, in Jung Chang and Jon Halliday, *Mao: The Unknown Story* (New York; Alfred A. Knopf, 2005). Their unrelentingly negative assessment should be balanced against the positive assessments published several decades ago, as the defining moments of Chinese Communism unfolded. Two works that continue to merit close attention are William Hinton, *Fanshen: A Documentary of Revolution in a Chinese Village* (Berkeley and Los Angeles: University of California Press, 1997) and Maria-Antoinetta Macchiocchi, *Daily Life in Revolutionary China* (New York: Monthly Review Press, 1973).

See also: CAPITALISM, COMMUNISM, CONSERVATISM, CULTURE, EQUALITY/EGALITARIANISM, IMPERIALISM, INTERNATIONALISM, LEFT/RIGHT/CENTER, LENINISM, MARXISM, POWER, REVOLUTION, STALINISM, STATE, TROTSKYISM, WAR

Markets

A *market* transaction is a voluntary exchange between a buyer and a seller. From time immemorial, *markets* were places where people went to make market transactions. For the past several centuries, the term has taken on an additional meaning. We now say that markets coordinate the allocation and distribution of resources when these tasks are accomplished through (multiple) market transactions. Market economies contrast with economies in which political **authorities (coercively)** allocate and perhaps also distribute resources. In modern times, the contrast is with **central planning**. However, markets and plans are not mutually exclusive. Many market economies rely on planning mechanisms to some extent; and all of them employ governmental regulation, which is a kind of planning. A market economy, then, is one in which markets are the predominant coordinating mechanism.

Market transactions are voluntary (not coerced). But unless we take freedom to be the absence of *deliberate* coercion, voluntary exchanges are not necessarily free. The wage bargain is a case in point. Unlike serfs or **slaves** who are forced to labor, workers voluntarily exchange labor for a wage. In principle, they could choose not to do so. But if the alternatives to working for a wage are dire – if, to take an extreme but apt example, starving for want of any other source of income is the alternative – then, critics contend, the exchange, though voluntary is unfree.

135

Even those who insist that only the deliberate actions of others (including the state) can restrict freedom still challenge the legitimacy of at least one kind of ostensibly voluntary transaction. Exchanges based on the deliberate provision of false information, fraud, are everywhere deemed illegitimate. In the usual view, fraud is a form of coercion, albeit one that does not rely on the use or threat of force. Exchanges based on fraud therefore only seem voluntary. For this reason, fraudulent exchanges are ruled out for the same reason that exchanges based directly on force are: not because they offend a notion of freedom that accommodates the idea that circumstances can render individuals unfree, but because, appearances notwithstanding, they are not voluntary at all.

Where market arrangements prevail, no one makes allocation decisions at the level of the whole economy. What happens in the aggregate is an unintended consequence of individual-level choices. The contrast with central planning is clear. Where economic life is coordinated (mainly) through planning, the objective is precisely to implement societal goals by implementing economic policies at the societal level.

Insofar as individuals are (means–ends) rational, they will do what is best for themselves in market transactions – given the choices they confront, the means at their disposal and their preferences or tastes. In *The Wealth of Nations* (1776), Adam Smith (1723–1790) famously conjectured that if individuals do act to advance their own interests, then, as if an "invisible hand" guided the allocation of resources, the outcome at the societal level will be the best possible. To the extent he was right, then greed, a private vice, works for the good of society as a whole, and is therefore, paradoxically, a public virtue. Smith was vague about how to understand the societal good. If it is understood in the way that modern economists have come to understand it – as **efficiency (Pareto optimality)**, a state of affairs in which everyone is as well-off as can be in the sense that any improvement to one individual's welfare would diminish someone else's – then Smith conjectured correctly. This was formally demonstrated in the 1950s by the economists Kenneth Arrow (b. 1921) and Gerard Debreu (1921–2004). They proved that, if we take individuals' preferences or tastes and their budget constraints as given, and if we assume that no new productive technologies are introduced, then at equilibrium – when all markets clear because there are no further potential gains from trade – the outcome will be efficient (Pareto optimal). This result holds, however, only if, among other things, there are no economies of scale (no savings in the cost of production of an item as the quantity of items produced increases), no **externalities** (costs or benefits to parties who do not directly transact with one another), no costs involved in moving resources from one allocation to another, perfect information on the part of economic actors, a complete absence of **monopolies**, and so on. It assumes, in other words, that a host of impossible to implement conditions obtain.

The proof of Smith's conjecture grounds what has come to be known as "neo-classical" economic theory, the basis of most academic economics in the twentieth century. Inasmuch as economists have recently learned how to deal formally with the (patently unrealistic) neo-classical treatment of information, the (unmodified) neo-classical paradigm is no longer as dominant as it formerly was. The best contemporary economic theory takes account of real world information deficits and asymmetries in its formal modeling, forcing a rethinking of some of the neo-classical paradigm's central tenets. From a strictly theoretical vantage point, therefore, there is no longer any reason to think that an invisible hand will guarantee the best of all possible worlds, if only markets are kept free of governmental interference. But even apart from advances in economic theory, it has always been obvious that it requires a leap of faith to suppose that what holds for the Arrow–Debreu model holds for real world market economies, where there plainly are economies of scale, transfer costs, externalities, monopolies, and the rest. In short, the case for the efficiency advantages of markets, especially unregulated markets, is and always has been an ideologically motivated **illusion**.

There are prima facie arguments to be made for markets over plans that appeal to values other than efficiency – specifically, to freedom, welfare, and justice. To the extent that it is fair to identify the voluntary with the free, then restricting markets renders persons less free than they would be if markets were unrestricted. Similarly, if market transactions are genuinely motivated by self-interest, and if we assume that self-interested individuals are generally able to act in accord with their interests (and therefore to maximize their own welfare), welfare is best served by allowing market transactions to take place, inasmuch as they leave both buyers and sellers better off. Finally, if to say that ownership entails a right to exchange what one owns, then restricting market transactions offends justice by violating the rights of individuals. These arguments raise complex questions. But they are all vulnerable to the same charge – that they fail to take into account the inevitable effects of market transactions on individuals who are neither the buyers nor the sellers in particular transactions. Thus, it could be argued that, in some or all cases, restricting market transactions enhances freedom and/or welfare overall; or that proscribing markets is indispensable for attaining just distributions of benefits and burdens at the societal level.

In the end, therefore, the case for markets over plans comes down to their efficiency advantages. Ideological invocations of Smith's conjecture aside, the consensus view nowadays is that, on this score, markets are indeed superior to plans. The reason is that central planning apparently generates more disabling inefficiencies than do markets. The problem, in brief, is that in any modern economy, where economic choices reverberate throughout the entire system because everything depends on everything else, there is too much information for the center to process. This was certainly the case in the early days of Soviet economic planning; it is likely to remain true no matter how much computer technology advances. Planners might decide, for example, to produce 100,000 automobiles in a given year. But this decision affects how much of all the components of automobiles there must be, how much fuel is needed to run them, how much infrastructure is necessary and so on. And each of these choices radiate out in a similar way. Thus, there are too many simultaneous equations demanding real time solutions. There is also the problem, identified by Friedrich Hayek (1899–1992), that some relevant information is necessarily *local* and therefore inaccessible to planners. In some instances, only people on the scene, with an intimate knowledge of actual conditions, are able to ascertain what efficiency requires. Local knowledge, Hayek insisted, is so extensive that there is no reliable way to convey to the center the information it would need to process, even if it were able to do so.

Where markets coordinate economic activities, these difficulties are avoided – not perfectly, but adequately in most cases – by decomposing economic choices into a host of individual-level optimizing problems that economic agents, motivated by self-interest, can solve on their own. They need only determine what is best for themselves, given their interests and circumstances. What emerges at the societal level may not be optimal in the neo-classical sense, but it will usually be good enough, especially if it is supplemented with limited planning and targeted regulation. In any case, it will be better than the alternative. It is this sort of consideration that has led contemporary socialists to rethink their long-standing opposition to market economies, and to seek to incorporate market arrangements into the institutional structures they propose. Thus, the best case for markets rests not on any of their purported virtues, but on the belief that, compared to central planning, they are less bad. This consideration leaves intact all the old complaints against market arrangements – especially the idea that markets are "anarchic," as Marx and other socialists maintained, and alienating. Also unaffected is the observation that markets replace communal connections, based on affect and **solidarity**, with "mechanical" (instrumental) links based on self-interest. This is why if, despite its traditions, the (socialist) Left must in the end embrace markets after all, it is a consequence to regret.

Everyone who is not a doctrinaire anarchist recognizes that markets cannot exist outside the protection of states. By establishing order, states provide a necessary condition for markets to operate and flourish. Political institutions are also indispensable for providing public goods that markets cannot supply. Even the most ardent free-marketeers would agree. But there is no reason to draw the line where the free-marketeers do. They are in the thrall of the ideologically driven conviction that it is desirable, wherever possible, to enlarge the scope of market arrangements and to diminish or even eliminate the economic role of the state. But insofar as the case for markets rests on efficiency considerations alone, it is always an open question what kinds of state interventions, if any, best serve efficiency objectives. The idea that the invisible hand of the market is always preferable to the visible hand of the state is plainly indefensible. But because it speaks to the perceived interests of the most myopic sectors of the capitalist class, it has become remarkably influential, especially in the United States.

Further Reading

A comprehensive and accessible account of the virtues and shortcomings of market arrangements is Charles E. Lindblom, *The Market System: What It Is, How It Works, and What to Make of It* (New Haven, CT: Yale University Press, 2002). See also my *Arguing for Socialism: Theoretical Considerations*, revised edition (London: Verso, 1988), chapter 3. Hayek's case for the importance of local knowledge is explicit in Friedrich Hayek, *The Fatal Conceit: The Errors of Socialism (The Collected Works of F.A. Hayek)* (Chicago: University of Chicago Press, 1991). On information asymmetries and their relevance for the neo-classical model and therefore, ironically, for the prospects for market socialism, see Joseph E. Stiglitz, *Whither Socialism? (Wicksell Lectures)* (Cambridge, MA: MIT Press, 1994). A version of market socialism that can withstand the kind of criticism Stiglitz launches is defended in John E. Roemer, *A Future for Socialism* (Cambridge, MA: Harvard University Press, 1994). This book also usefully recounts the history of the market socialist idea. Despite the failures of central planning, not all contemporary socialists are won over to the idea of market socialism. The idea is debated in James Lawler, Hillel Ticktin, and Bertell Ollman (eds.), *Market Socialism: The Debate Among Socialists* (New York: Routledge, 1998).

Marxism

See also: ALIENATION, ANARCHISM, CAPITALISM, CLASS, COMMUNITY/COMMUNITARIANISM, FREEDOM/
LIBERTY, IDEOLOGY, JUSTICE, LEFT/RIGHT/CENTER, LEGITIMACY, LIBERALISM, MARXISM, PUBLIC GOODS,
RIGHTS, SOCIALISM, STATE, WELFARE/WELFARE STATE

Marxism

What *Marxism* is has been contested for as long as the term has been in use.
By the 1870s, a self-identified Marxist current had already emerged among
European socialists. With the founding of the Second International in 1881,
Marxism became the official doctrine of much of the socialist movement, and
a point of reference for all socialists. Over the next hundred years, as distinct
and sometimes opposing tendencies developed within that movement, and as socialist aspirations came to animate political struggles throughout the world, different kinds of socialists sought to represent themselves as Marxists. Then abruptly,
in the final decade of the twentieth century, self-identified Marxists all but
disappeared. What had only recently been a living presence on the world scene
came to seem a relic of a lost past. But reports of Marxism's demise are exaggerated. Many of the ideas that Marxists embraced remain viable, and the
conditions that sustained the Marxist movement for so long continue very much
in force.

With Marxism no longer an object of contestation, it has become easier than
it used to be to reflect on what the term signifies. All Marxists identify their
theory and practice with the work of Karl Marx (1818–1883). Marxists also
share a common, though complex history. This is why, however much they may
differ among themselves, Marxist currents, like Christian denominations, are joined
by family resemblances. What might be called "classical Marxism," the
Marxism of the decades preceding the **Bolshevik** Revolution, amalgamated
three distinct, but related, bodies of theory. There is, first of all, a theory of
human emancipation and, along with it, a vision (deliberately unelaborated)
of ideal social, political, and economic arrangements. Then there is a theory of
history, historical materialism, an account of how the capitalist present under
which humanity suffers arose, and of capitalism's (possible) futures. Finally, there
is a commitment to the working class as the agent of the desired epochal
transformations. In line with these principal elements are a number of subsidiary
bodies of theory. Of greatest importance, historically and conceptually, is the
one that Marx himself devoted most of his life to elaborating: an economic

theory or, as Marx would put it, an account of "the laws of motion" of capitalist societies. There is also a distinct purchase on cultural and historical studies that was of particular concern to later generations of Marxists. These strands of theory are largely freestanding. By the late twentieth century, the connections between them had become increasingly strained. This is why, even before Marxism's eclipse as a political presence, it was already problematic to think of *Marxism* as a distinct and coherent ideology.

The most vulnerable component of Marxist theory is the one that joined the others into an integral whole: its account of the **proletariat**, the (mainly industrial) working class, as the agent of universal human emancipation. Marx first ascribed this mission to the working class in the 1840s, at a time when modern industry barely existed in his native Germany or anywhere else apart from a few cities in England. But Marx had already envisioned a developed capitalist order as his and other societies' future; and, in such an economic structure, it was the workers, Marx reasoned, whose labor is indispensable and whose stake in maintaining the system that **exploits** them is nil. Thus, as Marx and Friedrich Engels (1820–1895) wrote in *The Communist Manifesto* (1848), the workers of the world, the agents of the coming communist revolution, have "nothing to lose but their chains." In the days of Marxism's (pre-World War I) Golden Age, the labor movement was, if not quite a classical proletariat (with nothing to lose and a world to win), then a close approximation. But it was already evident that the proletariat of Marxist theory was becoming increasingly integrated into the capitalist system. This process has continued. As "the laws of motion" of modern capitalism have unfolded, the working class has become more integrated and less strategically situated; it has become less of a proletariat. The Marxist vision of an emancipated humanity may remain intact and so too its account of historical possibilities. But in the absence of a genuine proletariat, there seems to be no easy transition – and certainly no automatic passage – from where we now are to the communist future Marx envisioned.

The Leninist notion of a **vanguard** party was, in part, a response to this situation. Following V.I. Lenin's (1870–1924) lead, many Marxists believed that professional revolutionaries, fighting on behalf of the working class, were indispensable for inculcating the class **consciousness** that Marx thought circumstances would impress directly upon the workers. With this modification, some feasible approximation of the original synthesis arguably did remain intact. But the Leninist reconstruction of the classical Marxist view lost much of its appeal as **Bolshevism** gave way to Stalinism. As vanguard parties of Bolshevik origin increasingly promoted the idea that class consciousness required support for the Soviet Union even at the expense of workers' interests domestically, the idea that a revolutionary vanguard could effectively forge the class consciousness assumed in the classical Marxist notion of the proletariat became increasingly strained.

Not all Marxist **intellectuals** identified with Leninism, and fewer still sided unambivalently with official Communism. Thus, a number of Marxists in Europe – some within, some outside, the official Communist movement – developed dissident strains of Marxist theory. These "Western Marxists" differed among themselves. Their ranks included neo-Hegelians like Georg Lukács (1885–1971) and Karl Korsch (1886–1961), theorists of culture like Antonio Gramsci (1891–1937) and the members of the Frankfurt School (Theodor Adorno (1903–1969), Max Horkheimer (1895–1973), Herbert Marcuse (1898–1979), and others), existentialist Marxists like Jean-Paul Sartre (1905–1980) and Maurice Merleau-Ponty (1908–1961), structuralist Marxists like Louis Althusser (1918–1990) and Etienne Balibar (b. 1941), and so on. For all their differences, though, there were, in retrospect, certain similarities. Western Marxism was distinguished more by grandiose, but obscure posturing than conceptual clarity or rigor. For all the many insights Western Marxists registered, and despite their invaluable role in keeping Marxism from degenerating into a justifying theory for Stalinism, Western Marxists never quite succeeded in restoring the classical Marxist synthesis. Neither did they connect with the working class or substantially advance understanding of the historical and economic issues that Marx himself addressed. Instead, they focused programmatically on grand reconstructions of Marxist theory, emphasizing aesthetic and cultural concerns.

Partly in response to the obscurantism of Western Marxism, some **analytically** trained academic philosophers and social scientists from the generation of 1968, mainly in Great Britain and the United States, set to work to apply the standards of their disciplines to Marxist topics – above all, to Marx's theory of history, and to the normative issues implicit in Marxist accounts of human emancipation. In consequence, central aspects of Marxist theory have been reconstructed and criticized according to exacting standards. As one would expect after intensive scrutiny, many of the old sureties have gone by the board. However, it has emerged that there are core Marxist insights that remain viable, and that some of them, especially those that cluster around Marx's theory of history, resist incorporation into any other discourse. But the vast majority of ideas that were once assumed to be Marxist, including key aspects of Marxist economic theory, have been effectively folded into the broad tent of mainstream social science and liberal political philosophy.

It is therefore less clear today than it has ever been what it means to be a Marxist. It is not far-fetched to say that there is nothing more to the designation than a historical connection to a past associated with the theory and practice of Marx and his followers. Evolutionary biologists today are "Darwinian" in a similar sense. They do not see Charles Darwin's (1809–1882) work as a repository of Truth, in the way that believers in the Abrahamic religions believe that all they need to know is contained in their sacred texts. But they do take Darwin's work as a point of departure for their own; recognizing their intellectual debt to the theoretical breakthroughs made by Darwin. Marxism, one hopes, will have a similar future. If only because so much historical baggage has become associated with the term, a self-identified Marxist Left may never reemerge. But the component parts of the old Marxist synthesis remain invaluable resources. There is much work to be done in ascertaining which of Marx's ideas remain viable and timely. There is good reason to expect that in the world that is emerging this necessary project can proceed with lucidity and without ideological illusions; and that Marx's thought and the thought of those who identified with it will come to function not as a new religion, but in just the way that Marx himself thought it should – as a contribution to an evolving scientific enterprise with profound political implications.

Further Reading

The English-language edition of the *Collected Work* of Karl Marx and Friedrich Engels (New York: International Publishers) runs to many volumes, but there are a host of manageable anthologies available. Robert Tucker, *The Marx–Engels Reader* (New York: Norton, 1978) is an example; another is Eugene Kamenka (ed.), *The Portable Karl Marx* (London: Penguin, 1984). I elaborate on the account of Marxism presented here in Erik Olin Wright, Andrew Levine, and Elliott Sober, *Reconstructing Marxism* (London: Verso, 1992), chapter 1; and in *A Future for Marxism? Althusser, the Analytical Turn, and the Revival of Socialist Theory* (London: Pluto, 2003). Aspects of "classical" Marxism are described in Leszek Kolakowski and P.S. Falla, *Main Currents of Marxism: The Founders, the Golden Age, the Breakdown* (New York: W.W. Norton, 2005). On "Western Marxism," see Perry Anderson, *Considerations on Western Marxism* (London: Verso, 1979). A comprehensive "analytical Marxist" reconstruction of Marxist theory is Jon Elster, *An Introduction to Karl Marx* (Cambridge: Cambridge University Press, 1987). An important recent investigation of what remains living in the Marxist tradition can be found in Philippe Van Parijs, *Marxism Recycled* (Cambridge: Cambridge University Press, 1993).

Militarism

See also: CAPITALISM, CLASS, COMMUNISM, CULTURE, FREEDOM/LIBERTY, HISTORICAL MATERIALISM, IDEOLOGY, INTERNATIONALISM, LABOR, LABOR MOVEMENT, LEFT/RIGHT/CENTER, LENINISM, LIBERALISM, REVOLUTION, SOCIALISM, STALINISM

Militarism

In militarized societies, the military is among the most important components of the state apparatus; *militarism* describes this state of affairs. The term also denotes justifying theories of militaristic regimes. These justifications are too limited to count as ideologies. But they do operate ideologically in more comprehensive theories – especially versions of nationalism and fascism. Modern states are susceptible to militarist temptations. This is hardly surprising inasmuch as the state is based ultimately on the use or threat of force – in other words, on what military power provides.

Except in very poor and desperate countries where **civil society** is weak and elite interests cannot be maintained otherwise, it is rare that militaries take direct control of the state. When they do, they establish an emergency government, nominally (and sometimes really) dedicated to restoring civilian authority when the emergency has passed. This fiction is maintained even in so-called "banana republics." In general, for militarism to take hold and flourish, there must be a perceived security threat that, according to common perception, the military is indispensable for countering. This threat can come from outside the boundaries of the political community, from internal "subversion" or both. To the degree that the militarization of a society is acknowledged and defended, it is on the grounds that the maintenance of security is the state's primary function.

In the strictest sense of the term, militarism is a creature of the modern era. However, similar phenomena preexist the emergence of the modern state system. Thus, there are societies in which a warrior class plays a preeminent role. Since the term has no very precise meaning, pre-modern societies can also be called *militaristic*. Ancient Sparta and **feudal** (pre-Meiji Restoration) Japan are examples. In pre-modern conditions, it is not "reasons of state" so much as conceptions of the good life and the virtues associated with it that propel militarism. Not so in our era. Even in the modern world, though, militarism can be motivated by conceptions of the good that esteem military virtues. Such views are more prevalent in some cultures than in others. Thus, some countries are more disposed towards militarism than others. The United States has been generally ill disposed, especially outside its southern states. However, thanks to its place in the world economy and to the conniving of economic and political elites, American society has increasingly taken a militarist turn.

Where the military rules directly, the societies they superintend become militarized almost automatically. Then the damage done to non-military institutions and to civil society generally can be difficult to rectify. Transitions to less militarized systems of governance – what common parlance misleadingly calls "democratization" – are difficult, and their outcomes are precarious. Countries that have experienced military *coup d'états* are more than usually susceptible to experiencing them again.

In most liberal democracies, even temporary recourses to martial law in emergency situations are prohibited. The United States is an example. Even so, as recent history shows, effective power can slip insidiously into the hands of the military, even if they do not seek it out. President Eisenhower in his farewell address (1961) warned of the encroachments of America's expanding "military industrial complex." Militarism in liberal democracies usually takes a more benign form than in traditional militaristic regimes. But the military domination of the social order is no less real. Nevertheless, explicitly militaristic public displays are rare in liberal democracies – including the United States. Despite the increasing militarization of American society, overt signs of militarism continue to offend popular sensibilities.

It is possible in principle to enlarge militaries significantly while retaining civilian control over them and keeping their societal influence at acceptable levels. Both liberal democratic and Communist states have attempted to do so – with at least partial success. To the degree militarism is warded off, it is almost always beneficial for the military, as well as for society at large. Unencumbered by political concerns, the armed forces are better able to discharge their mission in a "professional" way. Society at large is better off too for the simple reason that peace is better than war (even without overt combat). It is a virtuous circle because, knowing how devastating modern warfare is, professional soldiers nowadays are ill disposed to initiate wars. Even in highly militarized societies, military leaders are usually less bellicose than the civilian authorities. It is revealing that, in recent decades, the main political promoters of American militarism have been individuals with no personal experience of warfare.

For many on the Right, a propensity to war is part of human nature. For those who believe this, militarism is a "natural" temptation, whether or not it is something to celebrate. However, militarism is not confined to right-wing circles. Liberals and even socialists, caught up in nationalistic fervor or imperialist ventures, also endorse militaristic policies. They are militarists in practice, if not in theory. In principle, though, the Left opposes militarism – for its own sake, and for its connections to other anti-**progressive** political tendencies. In today's world, with the United States armed to the teeth, and with weapons of mass destruction proliferating, militarism, especially American militarism, is a grave menace. The struggle against it is central to the larger struggle for peace, and for a world order based on justice rather than open or barely concealed force.

Further Reading

Alfred Vagts, *A History of Militarism: Civilian and Military* (New York: Free Press, 1967) recounts the history of the idea from the inception of modern Europe to the time of the Cold War. Most studies of militarism focus on particular societies, both ancient and modern. In recent decades, particular attention has been paid to pre-World War II Germany and Japan – not surprisingly, since they lost the war. Recent American militarism is discussed in Ted Rall (ed.), *Masters of War: Militarism and Blowback in the Era of American Empire* (New York: Routledge, 2003) and Andrew Bacevich, *The New American Militarism: How Americans are Seduced by War* (Oxford: Oxford University Press, 2005).

See also: COMMUNISM, CULTURE, DEMOCRACY, FASCISM, IDEOLOGY, IMPERIALISM, JUSTICE, LEFT/RIGHT/CENTER, LIBERALISM, NATION/NATIONALISM, PROGRESS, SOCIALISM, STATE, WAR

Morality

For philosophers, *morality*, like rationality, is a **normative** standard for assessing actions and persons. In common parlance, the term is often used more loosely. Since the philosophical purchase on morality is cogent and insightful, while the colloquial usage is not, it is wise to defer to the former, even in ordinary speech.

The colloquial usage effectively joins morality, in something like the philosophical sense of the term, with religiously grounded notions of (mainly) sexual **mores**. The result is analytically unsound and politically dangerous. The danger is well illustrated by the way the religious Right in the United States has laid claim to the word. For them, morality pertains mainly to sexual conduct or, rather, to its repression; and to the defense of traditional mores connected, however tenuously, with sexuality. A *moral* person is sexually abstinent or, at least, monogamous and married (to someone of the opposite sex). Morality also requires the suppression of forms of expression offensive to the prudish, as well as opposition to abortion, homosexuality, and everything that smacks of sexual liberation. On this view, morality can only be "faith based." But since faith is a dubious guide, *morality*, in the colloquial sense, is often used to underwrite what one might suppose it would condemn – aggressive wars and brutal occupations, for example, and callousness towards the least well-off – so long as these ostensible offenses are committed in good faith by leaders "of faith." For the religious Right, relativism is a great enemy of morality, though they are not quite sure what that doctrine implies beyond a denial of so-called **absolutes**. So too is **atheism**. On their view, if God did not exist, morality would not exist either. It is therefore difficult, if not impossible, for them to explain how non-believers can be moral. Their position seems to be that, despite all evidence to the contrary, they are not. Needless to say, the majority of people who assume the colloquial usage have more reasonable and moderate views. But their thinking is of a piece with those who draw unreasonable and immoderate conclusions.

Even before G.W.F. Hegel (1770–1831) made an explicit distinction between **ethics** and *morality*, the philosophical sense of the term was well established. An ethic is a guide to what we ought to do or to how we should assess what we or other people do; morality is a kind of ethic – one that would have us act on universal principles. Inasmuch as principles are general, applying to all moral agents equally, morality assumes a point of view of generality, one that accords no special weight to how matters appear to particular actors, including oneself, but only to how they appear to actors in general. A clear, though primitive account of the moral point of view is implicit in the Golden Rule: "do unto others, as you would have others do unto you." What this dictum suggests is that, in deliberating about what to do, whatever distinguishes oneself from others should not be taken into account; what matters is what one has in common with everyone else. This is the idea that, two millennia later, Immanuel Kant (1724–1804) would formulate as a **categorical imperative**. So understood, moral theory was unknown to the ancient Greeks or to ethicists in Asian cultures. The idea was an invention of ancient Israel in the Prophetic age. By this route it helped to shape Jewish and Christian ethics and, later, the teachings of Mohammed. In time, as Christianity and Islam spread throughout the world, it became the dominant form of ethical thinking, especially in the modern period. But, despite its origins, moral theory has taken on an unrelentingly **secular** aspect. No significant moral theorist in centuries has maintained that morality must be based on religious convictions. Some religious thinkers – Søren Kierkegaard (1813–1855), for example – explicitly distinguish morality from faith. These positions are backed by unassailable arguments.

The consensus view on the nature of morality, that it involves acting on **agent-neutral** principles, holds only at a certain level of abstraction from actual moral theories. Utilitarians and **Kantians**, for example, advance moral theories, yet they have different views about what morality is. There are, in fact, a variety of distinct moral theories. But even at the level of abstraction at which there is a consensus on the nature of morality, there is no agreement on a related question – why be moral? Two kinds of answers are possible. **Externalists** suppose that the reason to be moral, whatever it may be, is distinct from the nature of morality itself. A crude moral externalism is implicit in the long superseded, but still widespread belief that the reason to be moral is that God commands it and backs the command with the promise of an eternity in heaven or hell. Externalist theories of moral motivation come in sophisticated versions too. In modern moral philosophy, externalists can and often do appeal to individuals' (enlightened) self-interest, not to rewards or punishments imposed by others. Following Kant's lead, most moral philosophers today are **internalists**. They believe that a proper grasp of the nature of the moral order itself suffices to motivate moral actions.

In the Western philosophical tradition, the most prominent non-moral ethical theories derive from Aristotle (384?–322? BC) and other ancient Greek ethicists. In modern times, the most important and original exponent of that approach to ethics, and also the most ardent critic of moral theory, was Friedrich Nietzsche (1844–1900). Ethical theories that are not moral theories typically appeal to individuals' **characters**, to their dispositions to act in certain ways, rather than to agent-neutral principles. They typically focus on **virtues** and **vices** – where virtues are dispositions to act appropriately and well in the circumstances one confronts, and vices are dispositions to act poorly. Nowadays, "virtue ethics" is a live topic. However, it is more often treated as a supplement to moral theory than a substitute for it. Since ethics took a moral turn several centuries ago, no one has offered compelling reasons to change course fundamentally.

Virtue ethics is often thought to be of political consequence. Since academic philosophizing is seldom directly politically engaged, it is usually misleading to ascribe deliberate political motivations to its practitioners. This case, however, is different. The revival of virtue ethics was, in the first instance, the work of right-leaning thinkers, like Nietzsche, opposed the universalist, and therefore implicitly democratic, drift of moral theory. Virtue ethics was a way of bringing aristocratic values back in. Oddly, in recent years, some feminist and anti-racist philosophers who believe that general principles are somehow oppressive to subordinate groups have also been drawn to virtue ethics. Although this conviction originates in a self-identified segment of the Left, it is at odds with the universalist aspirations of the historical Left. Its cogency is also problematic.

The revival of interest in Aristotle and other theoreticians of virtue, including Nietzsche, has nevertheless been a salutary phenomenon – if only because moral theory, for all its merits, has, to its detriment, sometimes veered away from the wisdom Aristotle and the others imparted. Efforts to fuse aspects of virtue ethics with moral theory are therefore welcome. But the easy conflation of morality and good character that resonates throughout the political culture – not just within the religious Right – should be exposed for the confusion it is.

Further Reading

A dated, but still useful discussion of the defining feature of moral theories is Kurt Baier, *The Moral Point of View: A Rational Basis of Ethics* (New York: Random House, 1966). A more recent and comprehensive account, organized around the distinction between internalist and externalist moral theories, is Stephen Darwall, *Philosophical Ethics* (Boulder, CO: Westview Press, 1998). Shelley Kagan's *Normative Ethics* (Boulder, CO: Westview Press, 1997) provides an instructive guide to the main types of moral theory. On the merits and shortcomings of virtue ethics, see Julia Driver, *Uneasy Virtue* (Cambridge: Cambridge University Press, 2001). Nietzsche's most telling briefs against moral theory – and for a different sort of ethics – can be found in Friedrich Nietzsche (Keith Ansell-Pearson and Carol Diethe, eds.), *"On The Genealogy of Morality" and Other Writings* (Cambridge: Cambridge University Press, 1994) and Friedrich Nietzsche (Walter Kaufmann, trans.), *Beyond Good and Evil: Prelude to a Philosophy of the* Future (New York: Vintage, 1989). For Aristotelian ethics, it is best to turn to Aristotle himself – see *The Ethics of Aristotle: the Nichomachean Ethics* (London: Penguin, 1974).

See also: DEMOCRACY, FEMINISM, FREEDOM OF EXPRESSION, LEFT/RIGHT/CENTER, RACE/RACISM, RELATIVISM, UTILITARIANISM, VALUES

Multiculturalism

Multiculturalism denotes a cluster of ideas and attitudes that have come to the fore in developed capitalist countries in recent decades. Its emergence is intertwined with the history of the capitalist world system. It is therefore best to reserve the term for this way of thinking. Superficially similar ideas in culturally divided countries outside the imperialist core have a different content and historical significance.

The reorganization of economic life along capitalist lines in early modern Europe gave rise to the state form of political organization which, in turn, helped foster the rise of nations – of peoples joined together by a common culture, language, and descent. Notwithstanding the fact that these linkages were more nearly willed into existence than discovered, once established, they are experienced as real – often to such an extent that nationalist identifications overwhelm other communal ties. During the nineteenth century, the nation-state came to be a fixture of Western political life, just as it would become everywhere else over the next century – sometimes, as in Japan, thanks to deliberate imitation, but, more often, in consequence of colonial policies that grouped indigenous populations together into administrative units, and the anti-colonial liberation struggles these subordinated populations subsequently waged. However, at no time have all nations had their own states, and few states, even in Europe, rule over all and only one nationality.

Imperial expansion has always been a feature of capitalist development. From the beginning of the state system, some of the more developed capitalist states brought peoples of very different **ethnicities**, cultures, and languages under their rule – either directly, by colonization, or indirectly, through political and economic domination. Spurred on by economic and political exigencies, almost all of Africa, Oceania, and, despite nominal independence, Latin America, as well as India, South East Asia, and parts of China, had become part of the imperialist system by the late nineteenth century. After the **Bolshevik** Revolution, and then, after World War II, with the Chinese Revolution and the extension of Soviet power in Eastern Europe, about a third of the world's peoples were removed, for a time, from the imperialist ambit. At the same time, the United States came to supplant Britain and France as the main imperialist power. But the colonial system constructed by the end of the nineteenth century did not disintegrate immediately. It was not until the beginning of the 1970s, with the collapse of Portuguese rule in Africa, that it became entirely undone. Throughout that period, the national homogeneity of the European imperial powers remained largely intact.

The United States – and, to a much lesser degree before the 1960s, the British dominions of Canada, Australia, New Zealand, and South Africa – never quite became nation-states in the way that the European imperial powers did.

Desperate for labor (or, in South Africa's case, for a counterweight to a black majority), they attracted immigrants of non-British (though, still, mainly European) origin. These states also ruled over indigenous peoples, though only in the South African case had significant numbers of these peoples survived the relentless European invasion of their homelands. In the United States too, there were large numbers of peoples of mixed colonial (Spanish) and indigenous ancestry whose lands in California, Texas, Arizona, and New Mexico, as well as Puerto Rico, were incorporated into the United States by force of arms. The United States and the others also imported Asian labor. And, of course, descendants of slaves brought from Africa have been American citizens – in theory, at least – since the Reconstruction period that followed the Civil War. With the arguable exception of Hispanic communities in the Southwest and small and scattered groups of native peoples, these Americans do not quite comprise distinct national groupings. Nevertheless, in the face of persistent legal and customary **oppression**, neither have they ever been fully integrated into the mainstream culture. Thus, the idea of a common nationality never quite applied in the United States – or, to a much lesser degree, in the far-flung settler states of the British Empire – in the way that it did in most of Europe.

Still, even in the American case, assimilation into the dominant (white Protestant) culture was, for a very long time, an almost universally held ideal, shared by immigrant and non-immigrant groups alike, and by members of the dominant culture. It even penetrated into the African-American community. The United States aimed to be, as the well-known slogan proclaimed, a "melting pot." Most immigrant groups did, in fact, assimilate rather thoroughly over the course of several generations, shedding their languages and all but a few, mainly culinary, tokens of their former cultures. Even the religions of the immigrants became acculturated. Racism made assimilation more difficult for non-immigrant populations – with the partial exception of some indigenous peoples who were absorbed into the majority community involuntarily and at great human cost. Even so, "American" never quite came to designate a nationality in the way that, for example, "French" or "Dutch" did. This state of affairs was widely thought to be yet another facet of American exceptionalism. Throughout the capitalist West, the nation-state remained the norm – in theory and, to a very large degree, in fact as well.

All this began to change in the 1960s, as technological advances in transport and communication made the world a smaller place, and as the mobility of **capital** and other facets of so-called **globalization** accelerated. At the same time, with the demise of the colonial system, imperialism came to rely more on economic than direct political control, along the lines the United States had pioneered in Latin America. Of arguably greater importance, in the United States and other imperialist centers, oppressed racial minorities began to assert themselves politically in unprecedented ways. The result was that barriers to immigration from the **Third World** into the nation-states of the imperial center began to crumble. These changes in immigration policies put strains on the assimilationist model at the same time that oppressed minority populations – both new and, like African-Americans in the United States, long established – became increasingly self-assertive. Thus, in many quarters, a call to "celebrate differences," not to melt them away into the dominant culture, became the watchword. Multiculturalism was born.

The assimilationist model was basically an extension of the older nation-building project. It was workable, so long as there were not too many people to assimilate, and so long as the people in question were easily assimilable because their cultures were similar to that of the dominant nationality. Formerly colonized peoples and "guest workers" imported into Europe from Asia and Africa – along with African-Americans and latinos in the United States – were more difficult to assimilate than the peoples who, long before, coalesced into distinct nationalities. Their ethnicities, languages, cultures, and even their religions were too different; also, as in the African-American case, racism was too pervasive. But, thanks to the intensifying inequalities between the imperial centers and the rest of the world, and in the face of capitalism's insatiable need for cheap labor, the numbers of ostensibly unassimilable people kept growing. In these circumstances, the assimilationist model was bound to prove unequal to the task at hand, at least in some instances. Multiculturalism makes a virtue of this necessity.

Defenses of multiculturalism tend to parallel and build upon standard liberal justifications for tolerance. In the aftermath of the Protestant Reformation and the ensuing wars of religion that devastated early modern Europe, the first liberals advocated tolerance not so much because they thought it desirable, but because the alternative was endless strife. In time, grudging acceptance gave way, in some circles, to enthusiastic endorsement. Thus, John Stuart Mill (1806–1873) argued, in *On Liberty* (1859), that free expression and experiments in living enhance overall well-being. Others argued that tolerance is indispensable for according persons the respect they are due. The idea emerged that diversity is something to celebrate; not just to accept for want of a better alternative. Classical liberalism encouraged diversity in the "marketplace of ideas" and in ways of living; not group differences based on accidents of birth. Celebrating differences over which individuals have little control is, if anything, inimical to its spirit. Still, it was natural for liberals and others in recent decades to extend traditional liberal rationales into this new domain. If disagreement and non-conformity makes outcomes better, why not diversities of peoples too? If support for the free expression of ideas and ways of life is essential for according humanity the respect it is due, why not also support for differences that, though unchosen, help to define persons' identities?

These questions may not answer themselves quite so easily as multiculturalists assume. It is far from obvious that the encouragement of heterogeneity within the citizenry enhances political life, especially when the differences multiculturalists encourage correlate with lingering racial and ethnic animosities. Indeed, the idea that heterogeneity makes **solidarities** based on common citizenship difficult is often invoked to explain, for example, the relative feebleness of American welfare state institutions in comparison with those of more homogeneous countries in Europe and Asia. Similarly, it is far from clear that respect for persons implies respect for differences that cannot be ascribed to what individuals freely do. It is worth recalling that in classical accounts of what respect for persons entails – Immanuel Kant's (1724–1804), for example – respect is based on what persons have in common, in Kant's case, on their capacity for acting **autonomously**, not on unchosen factors that differentiate them.

Although the conventional wisdom associates multiculturalism with the Left more than with any other political orientation – justifiably so, insofar as it focuses on the concerns of subordinated individuals and groups whose interests the Left has always championed – its rise and sustenance is problematic for all defenders of equality. Since many of the cultures multiculturalists would celebrate are illiberal and profoundly **patriarchal**, there is plainly a tension with feminism. There is also a more immediate problem to the extent that multiculturalism underwrites policies that encourage a demise of solidarities based on economic interests and, more generally, on class membership of the kind that that are central to Left accounts of social change. The tension between these different bases for social solidarity is an issue with which any revived Left will have to contend in the coming years. For better or worse, the issue will have to be resolved in a way compatible with the impulse that has given rise to multiculturalist thinking. Inasmuch as multiculturalism is a consequence of economic and demographic transformations that will continue to shape social and economic life for the foreseeable future, there is no alternative but to forge social solidarities based on this emerging reality; in other words, to join identity groups together on common bases of social solidarity.

Further Reading

Differences between contemporary multiculturalism and superficially similar phenomena in pre- or non-liberal societies are discussed in Michael Walzer, *On Toleration* (New Haven, CT: Yale University Press, 1999). Multiculturalism is debated in Charles Taylor et al. (Amy Gutmann, ed.), *Multiculturalism* (Princeton, NJ: Princeton University Press, 1994). A distinctively liberal purchase on multiculturalism is developed in Will Kymlicka, *Multicultural Citizenship: A Liberal Theory of Minority Rights* (Oxford: Oxford University Press, 1996). See also Seyla Benhabib, *The Claims of Culture: Equality and Diversity in the Global Era* (Princeton, NJ: Princeton University Press, 2002) for a rather different, but still generally liberal, account of the phenomenon. Tensions between feminism and multiculturalism are discussed in Susan M. Okin (Joshua Cohen, Matthew Howard, Martha C. Nussbaum, eds.), *Is Multiculturalism Bad for Women?* (Princeton, NJ: Princeton University Press, 1999). Aspects of multiculturalism are subjected to incisive criticism from a robustly liberal vantage-point in Brian Barry, *Culture and Equality: An Egalitarian Critique of Multiculturalism* (Cambridge, MA: Harvard University Press, 2002).

See also: CAPITALISM, CLASS, COMMUNITY, CULTURE EQUALITY/EGALITARIANISM, FEMINISM, FREEDOM OF EXPRESSION, FREEDOM/LIBERTY, IDENTITY POLITICS, IMPERIALISM, LEFT/RIGHT/CENTER, LIBERALISM, NATION/NATIONALISM, RACE/RACISM, REVOLUTION, STATE, WELFARE/WELFARE STATE

N

Nation/nationalism

Nation is sometimes used interchangeably with "country." Then *nationality* means "country of citizenship." In this sense, the United States of America is a nation, and "American" designates the nationality of citizens of the United States. What explains this usage is the widespread assumption that states are nation-states, ruling over distinct nations or nationalities. In this stricter sense of the term, a *nation* is a community of people, joined together by common descent and a common culture. Persons sharing a nationality usually also speak the same language, share a common history, and reside on a common territory.

These conditions do not comprise a strict definition. It is impossible to list a set of necessary and sufficient conditions for counting as a *nation* – first because the term is arbitrary in the sense that it denotes a **social construct**, not a pre-given social reality; and, second, because any list of conditions one might propose would seldom be satisfied even in paradigm cases, except in imperfect and imprecise ways. In a word, nations are made, not found. Their construction depends, as the French theorist Ernest Renan (1823–1892) remarked, on "forgetting a great deal," and also on imagining much more. Nations are willed into being, and maintained, deliberately or not, by ongoing institutional arrangements and ideological interventions. As Renan also said, nationality is a "daily plebiscite."

Even so, the bases and boundaries of nationalist identifications are never entirely arbitrary. Historical factors are decisive. Today's nationalities have come into being partly in consequence of migratory patterns and conquests that are centuries, even millennia, old. History determines why some people, and not others, share customs, languages, religions, and lands of residence to an extent sufficient for the imagination to project the idea that they constitute a national community. These long-established affinities served as bases, in recent centuries, for the political administrative units of the Austro-Hungarian, Russian and Ottoman empires, the seedbeds of many of today's nationalities. Somewhat more arbitrarily, they were also instrumental in establishing the administrative divisions of the colonial empires of Britain, France, Spain, and other European powers, and therefore of the legions of putative nation-states that were born in the process of decolonization. Nations are not concocted from plain air. For the idea to take hold, suitable background conditions must already exist. However, this requirement is easily satisfied. As has been shown in countless cases, in-group affinities and out-group animosities are eminently susceptible to taking a nationalist turn.

Typically, the social construction of nations and the process of state building are intertwined. In France and England – and, then, later, elsewhere in parts of Europe and in Latin America, Africa, the Middle East, and parts of eastern and south-eastern Asia – the state or, at least, the boundaries of the state came first. The French case is paradigmatic. As late as the French Revolution, after centuries of state building under the aegis of increasingly **absolutist** monarchs, French was not the first language of most citizens of France. Furthermore, most residents of the territory of the French Republic did not think of themselves as French first. It required the completion of the state-building process, under Napoleon, for the French nation to come fully into its own. In a few cases, though – Germany and Italy are examples – a sense of nationality, born in the aftermath of the French Revolution, preceded the formation of unitary states.

Nationalism, then, is a political ideology that privileges national identifications – usually, but not necessarily, at the expense of others. However, unlike most ideologies, it is sustained not so much by a coherent body of doctrine as by reflexive attitudes presented occasionally in a theoretical guise. It is important not to confuse nationalism with patriotism, though the two are often confounded in practice. In its modern form, patriotism, love of country, is shaped by the larger goals of the **Enlightenment**; nationalism was a creature of (mainly German) **Romanticism**. For some of its early proponents – Johann Gottfried von Herder (1744–1803), for example – it represented a reaction to core aspects of the Enlightenment project. Nevertheless, in recent decades, many on the Left have been sympathetic to "national liberation struggles" based, in part, on nationalistic aspirations. The idea has been to support the nationalism of subjugated peoples, but not the nationalism of **oppressor** states or nations. Thus, Left organizations have actively participated in some nationalist movements. But for all genuine internationalists, nationalism, even **progressive** nationalism, is something to be wary of – if only because the **solidarities** it privileges are ultimately at odds with genuinely cosmopolitan aspirations for universal human solidarity and justice.

Further Reading

An anthology of classical and contemporary writings on nationalism is John Hutchinson and Anthony D. Smith (eds.), *Nationalism* (Oxford: Oxford University Press, 1995). Outstanding studies of nationalism include E.J. Hobsbawm, *Nations and Nationalism Since 1780: Programme, Myth, Reality* (Cambridge: Cambridge University Press, 1990), Benedict Anderson, *Imagined Communities* (London: Verso, 1992), and Ernest Gellner, *Nations and Nationalism* (Ithaca, NY: Cornell University Press, 1983). An insightful and scholarly study of the history of the idea is Martin Thom, *Republics, Nations and Tribes* (London: Verso, 1995).

See also: COSMOPOLITANISM, CULTURE, FREEDOM/LIBERTY, IDEOLOGY, IMPERIALISM, INTERNATIONALISM, JUSTICE, LEFT/RIGHT/CENTER, MULTICULTURALISM, PATRIOTISM, STATE

Neo-conservatism

Neo-conservatism designates a political tendency within the American Right that began to emerge early in the 1970s – in reaction, on the one hand, to the **New Left**'s rejection of **Cold War** liberalism and, on the other, to the existence of cultural and ideological antipathies between future neo-conservatives ("neo-cons") and traditional ("paleo"-) conservatives. Surprisingly, neo- and paleo-conservatives have, for the most part, coexisted harmoniously. More remarkably, given the extent of their ideological disagreements, neo-conservatives have also made common cause with religious and social conservatives and with libertarians. On occasion, however, differences rise to the surface. This has been especially true in the aftermath of the 2003 invasion of Iraq. The Iraq War was largely a neo-conservative initiative. At the time, no significant strain of conservative opinion in the United States opposed the war outright. But some paleo- and libertarian conservatives were cool to the idea. Their wariness grew as it became increasingly clear, during the subsequent occupation, what a colossal blunder the neo-conservative adventure had been.

There are historical links between the neo-conservative movement and the most vehement anti-Communist elements in the Democratic Party in the post-World War II period. However, the alienation of future neo-cons from the Democrats was already underway by 1972, when liberals succeeded in nominating an anti-Vietnam War candidate, George McGovern, for president. Thereafter, neo-conservatives abandoned the Democratic and threw in their lot entirely with the Republican Party. They became a force to be reckoned with in the 1980s, when a number of top figures in the Reagan Administration were won over to their way of thinking. Neo-conservatives assumed an even greater importance in the administration of George W. Bush, thanks in part to the return of many Reaganite officials to positions of power. The neo-conservatives were, at first, ardent Cold Warriors. The movement persisted into the twenty-first century and thrived during the so-called "war on terror" because neo-conservative thinkers were adept at adjusting to the changed circumstances that followed the demise of the Soviet Union. They did so by remaining steadfast in their (vague but potent) vision of how the world should be. It should be a *pax Americana* – modeled more or less on Imperial Rome.

Because neo-conservatism is not an organized political movement, there are no clear markers indicating who is or is not a neo-conservative. But there is seldom controversy about the designation. It is less clear what the term is supposed to mean. Apparently, for some, what makes neo-conservatives new (*neo-*) is just the fact that they are newcomers to the American conservative movement. For others, the term implies a "new wave" in conservative thinking. But even those who believe that there is something novel in the positions neo-conservatives advance would have to concede that neo-conservatism is a provincial phenomenon, so tied to the American scene that there are few, if any, aspects of it that other political cultures could adapt.

Some neo-conservatives embrace the name. Others who are regarded as neo-cons reject it. Throughout the larger political culture, the term has a generally pejorative connotation. This is true even in right-wing circles. Paleo-conservatives often view neo-conservatives as parvenus. Conservatism is a family legacy for many paleos, especially those of Protestant ancestry, while the most conspicuous neo-conservatives are Jewish intellectuals with liberal or even socialist (often Trotskyist) backgrounds. For this reason too, there are many on the religious Right, both Catholics and evangelical Protestants, who are wary of neo-cons. In general, though, cultural and political differences pale in the marriage of convenience that the American Right has become.

Neo-cons reject *Realpolitik*, replacing it with an ostensibly moralistic stance on foreign policy questions. Their express aim is to spread what they call "freedom and democracy." But whatever they may believe, their foreign policy prescriptions are pretexts for consolidating American global domination and, not incidentally, for helping corporations tied to the Republican Party. In the minds of neo-conservatives, these objectives are of a piece with a dedication to refashion the Middle East along lines congenial to right-wing Zionist aspirations. Thus, there is a convergence between their foreign policy prescriptions and those of the Israeli government. Because Israel effectively operates as an offshore asset of American imperialism, it is difficult to tell whether it is American or Israeli interests that the neo-cons take most to heart. As neo-conservative initiatives in Iraq and elsewhere turn sour, one would expect that the question of dual loyalty would arise and, along with it, a resurgence of traditional **anti-Semitism**. However, the presence of so many Christian Zionists in influential right-wing circles in the United States, and the fact that the most powerful neo-conservatives in the Bush Administration are not themselves Jewish, makes this outcome unlikely, at least for now.

Neo-conservatives are more liberal socially than most American conservatives. They are, however, inclined to allow their social liberalism to fade into the background – in order to forge a common front with the religious Right on issues of mutual interest (including support for Israel). As the neo-cons moved into the Republican Party, they also distanced themselves from organized labor and from other traditionally Democratic constituencies. Thus, neo-conservatives favor **privatization** and corporate **globalization** more ardently than erstwhile **New Dealers** and proponents of the **Great Society** who still call themselves *liberals*. They evidently believe, as libertarians do, that political and economic liberties comprise a seamless web, and that free trade on a global level is indispensable for both. However, unlike libertarians, and in contrast to most other conservatives in the United States, their hostility to government regulation and to welfare state programs is mild. In this respect, neo-conservatism, so far from being *new*, resembles mainstream conservative thinking in continental Europe.

The Cold War liberal ancestors of today's neo-conservatives were, in fact, proponents of an American version of Social Democracy – partly in consequence of their aggressive anti-Communism. They saw in the welfare state a way of mitigating Communism's appeal. With the Soviet Union gone, opposition to political Islam has replaced Communism as the focal point of their concern. For the neo-conservatives, this was a natural transition – Communism and political Islam are alike, they believe, in being totalitarian ideologies. They conclude that political Islam, like Communism, should therefore be combatted by any means necessary. Because Muslim countries are far weaker than the (former) Soviet Union or China, neo-conservatives are more disposed to use military force against them than they were against the Communist superpowers. But, in contrast to the situation during the Cold War, there is no New Deal or Great Society that they are able to offer as an alternative to the system they oppose. It might seem otherwise. The neo-cons' express idea is to rebuild the regimes they overthrow on liberal democratic bases. But, on this score, they fool no one but themselves and the political elites who follow their lead. Everyone else sees only war-profiteering and the expropriation of indigenous resources for the benefit of American interests, sustained by puppet regimes. New Deal and Great Society alternatives to Communism genuinely did enhance social and economic security; they made peoples' lives better within the framework of the capitalist system. All the evidence suggests that neo-conservative policies make outcomes worse – in the United States, where social programs are depleted of resources, and abroad, where the purported beneficiaries of "nation building" suffer under the yoke of imperial domination.

Neo-conservative writing consists mainly of policy papers and articles for right-wing periodicals. There really is no developed neo-conservative political theory to speak of. However, because many of the prominent neo-conservatives involved in the buildup to the 2003 Iraq War had studied with the political philosopher Leo Strauss (1899–1973) at the University of Chicago decades earlier, it was widely reported that Strauss had somehow provided the intellectual inspiration for the movement. Apparently, this is also the view of some neo-cons. Even so, the claim is, at best, an exaggeration. To this day, there are academics in political science departments in the United States and Canada who identify with Strauss's idiosyncratic efforts to render Plato's political philosophy timely. Straussians agree with their master's critique of what he called relativism, and with his conviction that the landmark texts of Western political philosophy contain both an exoteric doctrine, intended for general consumption, and an esoteric doctrine, intended for the modern equivalent of Plato's "philosopher kings." Some neo-cons, taking these doctrines to heart, may indeed think of themselves as philosopher kings, unaccountable to democratic constituencies. But there is hardly a direct connection between Straussian political philosophy and neo-conservative machinations. Whatever neo-conservatives with philosophical interests may think, neo-conservatism is a strictly political phenomenon, un-associated with *any* philosophical project.

To struggle against neo-conservatism is therefore to wage a political, rather than a philosophical, battle. Central to any such undertaking is the relentless exposure of the dangers of empire. The self-serving idea that the United States does well for others by dominating them is chief among these dangers – because the policies this way of thinking encourage are bound to generate dangerous, perhaps catastrophic, "blowback." That the neo-cons and those whom they influence garb their deceits, and their self-deceptions, in the language of free-dom and democracy only makes the danger more insidious. Fortunately, however, the shallowness of the neo-conservatives' thinking makes it all the easier to reveal the perils inherent in the policies they advocate.

Further Reading

The major documents of the neo-conservative movement, such as they exist, are collected in Irwin Stelzer, *The Neocon Reader* (New York: Grove Press, 2004). A book-length account, authored by one of the founders of the movement, is Irving Kristol, *Neo-conservatism: The Autobiography of an Idea* (Chicago: Ivan R. Dee, 1999). Though only tangential to understanding neo-conservatism, the main contours of Strauss's political philosophy are evident in Leo Strauss, *The Rebirth of Classical Political Rationalism: An Introduction to the Thought of Leo Strauss* (Chicago: University of Chicago Press, 1989). An insightful, critical account of his political philosophy is Shadia B. Drury, *The Political Ideas of Leo Strauss* (New York and London: Palgrave Macmillan, 2005).

See also: CAPITALISM, COMMUNISM, CONSERVATISM, CULTURE, DEMOCRACY, FASCISM, FREEDOM/ LIBERTY, IDEOLOGY, IMPERIALISM, LABOR MOVEMENT, LEFT/RIGHT/CENTER, LIBERALISM, LIBERTARIAN-ISM, MORALITY, POLITICAL ISLAM, RELATIVISM, SOCIAL DEMOCRACY, SOCIALISM, TERROR/TERRORISM, TOTALITARIANISM, TROTSKYISM, WAR, WELFARE/WELFARE STATE, ZIONISM

P

Patriotism

Patriotism is standardly defined as "love of country." It would be more apt, however, to speak of *loyalty* to one's country. Affection usually does motivate patriotic dispositions to some degree. But patriotism can also be experienced as a duty, void of affect. There is no necessary connection between loyalty and love; and it is loyalty, not love, that motivates the patriot. Unlike nationalism, with which it is often confused, patriotism is neither a (partial) ideology nor a component of other ideologies. It is only a disposition on the part of individuals that helps to shape their thoughts and actions. A *patriot* is someone who thinks or acts in a patriotic way. *Patriotism* designates that quality in an abstract way.

Loyalty to one's country is not the same thing as loyalty to one's country's government. Nor is it loyalty to one's state. In the modern world, political communities assume the state form of political organization, and patriots are indeed loyal to the political communities to which they belong. But a patriot's loyalty need not be directed towards a state's constitutional arrangements or to any other elements of the regime in place. Revolutionaries, who aim to overthrow existing arrangements, can be – and often are – patriots. Typically, patriots evince affection for their country's traditions, customs, and **mores**; and even for its landscape. But it is not to these things either that patriots are loyal. Their loyalty is to something more abstract – to what might be called "the spirit" of their political community, understood as a unifying principle extending back in time and forward into an indefinite future.

This type of loyalty emerged, in its modern form, in Western Europe and North America in the seventeenth and eighteenth centuries. It reached self-awareness during the American and French Revolutions and in the emancipatory movements that identified with these historical events. In the seventeenth and eighteenth centuries, patriotism was a feature of republican political philosophy. It was in this form that the idea took root among the animators of the American and French Revolutions. Early in the nineteenth century, G.W.F. Hegel (1770–1831) and other thinkers associated with German **Romanticism** further developed the philosophical side of contemporary patriotism. It is to them that we owe the idea that political communities are manifestations of a common "spirit." Hegel's account is especially pertinent. It provides perhaps the fullest theoretical expression of this emergent reality.

In the twentieth and twenty-first centuries, patriotism has been an important element in anti-imperialist and resistance movements throughout the world. In the imperial centers, it is more often associated with the political Right. But, even in these quarters, it can still be compatible with the values that motivate the Left. So long as the world is divided into distinct political communities, each with its own "spirit," the goal of universal human emancipation can only be pursued on a country-by-country basis. Patriotism can and has motivated individuals and groups to engage in this project. It is therefore not to be despised. But patriotism is something to be wary of because it can, and often does, shade off into commitments that conflict with **progressive** ideals. The danger is especially acute in states that **oppress** other states or their own populations. Thus, it was that Samuel Johnson (1709–1784) famously and wisely proclaimed patriotism to be "the last refuge of a scoundrel." All too often, it is; and the more domineering a country is, the more likely it is that this will be the case.

Because the term carries a generally positive connotation, it is susceptible to misappropriation for **propagandistic** purposes. Political elites and the manufacturers of consent for their rule are wont to use the idea to characterize thoughts, deeds, and even persons that they favor; and to describe what they want to disparage as *unpatriotic*. When the historical moment has passed, the disingenuousness of propagandistic misuses of the term becomes clear to everyone – witness how the blatant misuses of *patriotism* and its opposite in the United States in the early days of the **Cold War** are now perceived. In the "war on terror," history is repeating itself, very nearly as transparently, and with distressingly similar effects.

Further Reading

On the genealogy of the idea and on its entailments, see Maurizio Viroli, *For Love of Country: An Essay on Patriotism and Nationalism* (Oxford: Oxford University Press, 1997). See also the discussions in Martha C. Nussbaum and Joshua Cohen (eds.), *For Love of Country? Debating the Limits of Patriotism* (Boston: Beacon Press, 1996). A theoretical account of the nature, form, and limits of "rational" patriotism is Margaret Levi, *Consent, Dissent and Patriotism: Political Economy of Institutions and Decisions* (Cambridge: Cambridge University Press, 1997). Contemporary misuses of the idea in the United States are exposed in David W. Orr, *The Last Refuge: Patriotism, Politics, and the Environment in an Age of Terror* (Washington, DC: Island Press, 2005).

See also: COMMUNITY/COMMUNITARIANISM, FREEDOM/LIBERTY, IDEOLOGY, IMPERIALISM, LEFT/RIGHT/CENTER, NATIONALISM, PROGRESS, REPUBLICANISM, REVOLUTION, STATE, TERROR/TERRORISM

Political Islam

Political Islam (*islamism* or "Islamic fundamentalism") designates a political tendency that emerged as a presence on the world scene during the Iranian Revolution of the middle and late 1970s. Thereafter, its influence in the Muslim world grew, as the influence of **secular** nationalist movements declined. Inasmuch as political Islam targets mainly the United States and Israel, it is ironic that the growth of islamist movements owes a great deal to American machinations in the waning days of the **Cold War**, when political Islam was viewed as a weapon in the struggle against the Soviet Union in Afghanistan and, on a more limited scale, to Israeli efforts to diminish the power and influence of the (secular) Palestine Liberation Organization (PLO) by encouraging theocratic rivals.

Political Islam's existence and Western reactions to it revive ancient animosities between Christians and Muslims. The problem is exacerbated by the fact that some islamists genuinely are terrorists, and by the fact that the movement as a whole condones terrorism as a legitimate form of struggle. Even if the victims of terror are few, terrorism strikes fear in domestic populations. With growing Muslim communities in many Western countries, this situation is dangerous – for everyone but, most of all, for the disempowered and vulnerable immigrant communities where political Islam is a pole of attraction. The hard-won practice of liberal tolerance is put in jeopardy.

Political Islam represents a challenge to the secular and **progressive** values of the **Enlightenment** tradition in both the Western and Muslim worlds. One would therefore expect that the liberal democratic West would undertake a serious effort to mitigate its appeal by offering progressive, secular alternatives. But that expectation would hold only if Western values were not deformed by the hypocrisy and incompetence of Western, and especially American, governments. Military repression has therefore become the countervailing instrument of choice, fueling an escalating cycle of violence. In addition, American predations in the Middle East and American support for the Israeli Right fuel the impulses that have generated and sustained the islamist movement.

The absence of a Soviet counterbalance to American power and, more generally, of a credible alternative to clerically driven resistance movements, is a major factor in political Islam's appeal. In this vacuum, political Islam has taken on the character of an anti-imperialist force. But it is an anti-imperialism of fools, because political Islam is a profoundly **reactionary** tendency. Islamists uphold Islamic law (*shari'a*) and traditional Islamic beliefs. They draw on ways of thinking and acting that extend back to the time of Mohammed (AD 570–630). Unlike Christianity, which emerged and developed as an otherworldly cult in the (still pagan) Roman Empire, Islam was, from its beginnings, a political movement seeking to extend the faith through conquest. Thus, Christianity's long-standing separation of temporal from ecclesiastical power had no analogue in the Muslim world. Nevertheless, it was not until the late nineteenth and early twentieth centuries, in the course of anti-colonial struggles in Muslim countries, that political Islam emerged as a distinct political current. For more than a century, it remained a marginal movement. In the 1930s and 1940s, as the Zionist colonization of Palestine unfolded with (sporadic and ambivalent but nevertheless real) British support, some islamists made common cause with Nazi Germany. They did so less out of shared anti-Jewish conviction than on the principle that "my enemy's enemy is my friend." Despite what is nowadays widely believed, Islam's attitude towards Jews has always been more benign than Christianity's. Thus, a very different historical consciousness survives even in islamist currents today, notwithstanding the animosity most Muslims feel towards Zionism, and towards Israel's treatment of Palestinians. In any case, it is only in the past two decades that the national movements of Muslim countries have taken on a clerical and theocratic flavor, or that a basically anti-secular and right-wing political ideology has had any significant appeal among the popular masses.

Partly because Muslim countries have been dominated for so long by imperial powers that profess secular and liberal values, liberal currents have been slow to mature within Islam itself. Therefore, in historically Muslim countries more than in historically Christian ones, it is difficult to be both religious and liberal. There are also aspects of Islam itself that make liberalization problematic. Of prime importance is the (comparative) lateness of the "revelation" on which the Islamic religion is based, and the nature of that revelation. These problems come to a head in the efforts of islamists to make Islamic law the law of the lands in which they live. The contrast with the other Abrahamic religions, Judaism and Christianity, is significant. Islam recognizes the **authority** of the revelations upon which those religions are based, while insisting that the revelation to the Prophet Mohammed supersedes them on all points where they conflict. Jewish law claims authority from the most ancient of these revelations. But the words passed down to Moses on Mount Sinai mainly concern the regulation of a temple cult. With the destruction of the second temple by the Romans in the first century AD and the demise of the priestly order it sustained, and then with the subsequent dispersal of the Jewish population of Palestine, everything had to be rethought. Jewish thinkers rose to the occasion. Every aspect of daily life was regulated to a remarkable and unprecedented degree. But the regulations the rabbis prescribed, then and in ensuing centuries, pertain to a people living under the jurisdiction of others. Jewish law therefore focuses mainly on matters that fall outside the usual scope of governance – what to eat, how to observe the Sabbath and the holy days, how to pray, and so on. Even today, with a Jewish state in existence, the rabbinate seeks only to control these aspects of daily life; following traditions forged over two millennia, they have little interest in the everyday conduct of the state itself. With its rampant legalism, rabbinic Judaism has always been relatively undemanding with respect to belief. What mattered was how observant one was, not what one thought. Christianity, in contrast, was concerned almost exclusively with beliefs. As it developed into the official religion of the Roman Empire, it could hardly sustain itself by enforcing uniform modes of living on the extremely diverse populations over which the Romans still ruled. But it could insist on doctrinal orthodoxy. From the beginning, official Christianity battled heretics and schismatics on this terrain. The Protestant Reformation and Catholic Counter-Reformation in Western Christianity fit this pattern exactly. Christianity has always emphasized right belief, rather than legalistic practice.

On both dimensions, Islam represents an intermediate position. It does demand belief in one God and in the prophesy of Mohammed. But finely honed doctrinal differences have played little role in its history. Even its main division, the one between the *Sunni* and the *Shi'a*, has more to do with (ancient) political conflicts and allegiances than with matters of belief. Like Judaism, and unlike Christianity, Islam insists on observance of a body of law. But these laws pertain as much to the actual governance of Islamic societies as to the regulation of daily life. With regard to individuals' conduct, they are generally less demanding than Jewish law. But, unlike Jewish law, they are little changed over the centuries. This is hardly surprising; until the modern era, very little in the social experience of Islamic peoples had changed in ways that would necessitate modifications in the laws that regulate their behaviors. For this reason, Islamic law, though not particularly demanding, is not very adaptable to modern circumstances. If the law requires, for example, that adulterous women should be stoned or that the hands of thieves should be cut off, there is no easy way around the injunction by reinterpreting it. To be sure, practical exigencies and the hypocrisy that is endemic in all religions can lead scholars and clergy to find ways to subvert the literal meaning of certain prohibitions, especially if they are obstacles to commerce. Already, subtle modifications of the rules regarding money lending and the collection of interest have been contrived that are acceptable to theocratic authorities. But the words of the Prophet are often too unequivocal to bear substantial reinterpretation. Thus, there remains a large and unbridgeable gap between *shari'a* and modernity.

Modern legal systems arrived in Muslim lands as part of an apparatus of imperial domination. Thus, their appeal is not always obvious to potential beneficiaries. Much the same is true of other achievements of modernity – tolerance, **gender** equality, democracy, and so on. There is good reason to think, even so, that these **progressive** (and still largely unrealized) elements of Western culture would be welcomed enthusiastically in historically Muslim countries. To this extent, the neo-conservatives are right. But it must be the genuine article; not the sham versions that neo-conservatives would impose by force. **Orwellian** uses of lofty terms by the architects of Western imperialism fool no one, except perhaps the imperialists themselves. Quite the contrary, the transparent hypocrisy of American efforts to establish friendly "democracies" in countries close by Israel and in areas where there is oil and other strategic resources to control discredits the values the imperialists claim to promote and at the same time fuels the islamist movement.

Ironically, political Islam has become the most important ideology fueling resistance to American and Israeli domination. It is also a cause identified, in the public mind, with persons from historically Muslim countries; that is, with people to whom **solidarity** is due. For these reasons, aggressive repudiations of political Islam can be problematic. But, as an IDEOLOGY, political Islam is a danger that progressives should oppose even as they stand in solidarity with persons of Muslim heritage.

Further Reading

For an account of the political bearing of islamism and its parallels with political trends in imperialist countries, see Tariq Ali, *The Clash of Fundamentalisms: Crusades, Jihads, and Modernity* (London: Verso, 2003). On the American role in conjuring political Islam into existence, see Robert Dreyfuss, *Devil's Game: How the United States Helped Unleash Fundamentalist Islam* (New York: Metropolitan Books, 2005). A scholarly and comprehensive study of political Islam is available in Mansoor Moaddel, *Islamic Modernism, Nationalism, and Fundamentalism: Episode and Discourse* (Chicago: University of Chicago Press, 2005).

See also: DEMOCRACY, EQUALITY/EGALITARIANISM, FEMINISM, FUNDAMENTALISM, IMPERIALISM, LEFT/RIGHT/CENTER, LEGITIMACY, LIBERALISM, NATION/NATIONALISM, NEO-CONSERVATISM, PROGRESS, TERROR/TERRORISM, THEOCRACY, VALUES, VIOLENCE/NON-VIOLENCE, ZIONISM

Populism

Although some nineteenth- and twentieth-century political parties adopted the name, and although some social movements embrace it, there is no fully articulated political ideology or set of ideologies that the term *populism* denotes. Instead, the word suggests any of an array of political currents that in one way or another side with "the people" against social, political, cultural, or economic elites. In recent years, especially in the United States, populism has become a matter of style more than substance. Often it consists in nothing more than rhetorical posturing. Thus, it is not uncommon for those who represent elite interests to assume a populist guise when, for electoral or other reasons, it suits their purpose – witness, for example, the sometimes folksy demeanor of George W. Bush.

Populist styles are common on both the Left and the Right. When leftists speak of right-wing populism, the term has a pejorative connotation, as it does when rightists speak of left-wing populism. Thus, *populism* is often used disparagingly. But it is also sometimes enthusiastically endorsed, especially on the Left. Some self-identified populists even use the term interchangeably with (small-d) *democrat*. Because its political bearing is so indeterminate, and because its meanings are so vague, the word is of little analytical use.

Marxists, especially Leninists, derided populism partly for historical reasons – because rival revolutionary groups in Russia identified with the description – and partly because a focus on an undifferentiated "people" denies the pertinence of class differences and the leading role of the working class. Most Left politics, however, exhibits a strongly populist inclination; it is even easy to find populist sentiments within the Leninist fold. Because genuine conservatism is elitist in principle, it is more difficult to recast with a populist inflection. But populist expressions are very much at home in the more **radical** fringes of the political Right, including some that call themselves *conservative*. Nationalistic and racist politics typically exhibit a populist coloration.

For the past century and a half, "the people" have been a fixture of political life everywhere. In consequence, populist politics has existed everywhere. Overtly populist political formations have been most successful, however, in Latin America. Juan Perón (1895–1974), president of Argentina from 1946 to 1955 and then again from 1973 until his death, was perhaps the most prominent political leader to whom the term is commonly applied. Perón was, in the main, a man of the Right. Today, left-leaning populist movements dominate South American politics. Prominent North American populists include William Jennings Bryan (1860–1925), Huey Long (1893–1935), and George Wallace (1919–1998). Recently, some left-wing figures in the United States like Jim Hightower (1943–) and Ralph Nader (1934–) have assumed the designation. In doing so, they identify with the traditions of the Populist Party of the late nineteenth century. Those Populists were agrarian radicals who initiated many of the reforms that **Progressives** and **New Deal** Democrats would later enact.

Ironically, in the United States today, conservatives accuse liberals of populism – intending by that charge to suggest that worker-friendly policies and support for welfare state institutions pit the poor against the rich. This, they insist, is a bad thing – an invitation to what they call "class warfare." In truth, liberals are even more intent than conservatives to quash class conflicts, and conservative anti-populists are themselves engaged in class warfare – on behalf of the ruling class. With these conservatives in power, and with Marxists, especially Leninists, all but gone from the scene, the most frequently heard disparaging uses of the term nowadays illustrate the all too common phenomenon of the pot calling the kettle black.

When *populism* is used approvingly on the Left, it is often because its users find it a benign way to identify positions that, were they more clearly

Power

articulated, would have a harder edge. Left activists today are inclined to muffle their radicalism precisely because the Right has been so successful in transforming the political culture. But in some cases, self-identified populists really just are what they claim to be. The Marxist reproach – that it is disabling to invoke support for an undifferentiated "people" – therefore applies to them. All but the most doctrinaire Marxists would agree, however, that the hearts of left-leaning populists are in the right place. What they and other socialists would insist upon, however, is the need to move beyond an inchoate "populist" politics to a more focused program for changing the world.

Further Reading

Inasmuch as contemporary uses of the term are largely bereft of analytical value, the literature in which the Right accuses the Left of *populism* or, less frequently, the Left accuses the Right, is seldom worth engaging. A partial exception, distinguished by its cantankerousness and hostility to liberalism, and interesting mainly as an example of the genre, is John Lukacs, *Democracy and Populism: Fear and Hatred* (New Haven, CT: Yale University Press, 2005). In marked contrast, the literature on self-identified nineteenth-century populist movements is a rich source to mine. On the American case, see Robert C. McMath, *American Populism: A Social History 1877–1898* (New York: Hill and Wang, 1990). On Russian populism, see the classic study of Franco Venturi, *The Roots of Revolution: A History of the Populist and Socialist Movements in 19th Century Russia* (London: Phoenix, 2001).

See also: CLASS, CONSERVATISM, CULTURE DEMOCRACY, IDEOLOGY, LEFT/RIGHT/CENTER, LENINISM, NATION/NATIONALISM, MARXISM, RACE/RACISM, REVOLUTION, SOCIALISM, WELFARE/WELFARE STATE

Power

In ordinary speech, parties, groups, or individuals who hold top government positions are said to be "in power." This usage can be misleading. In its most general sense, *power* is the ability to control outcomes. It is this sense of the term that is of philosophical interest – in political contexts and more generally. This is also the sense of *power* that bears the closest relation to non-political uses of the word. It is therefore appropriate to call *power* in this sense "real power." Being in power normally enhances real power. But it is neither necessary nor sufficient for it. If they are severely constrained by circumstances, incumbents of high offices can have very little control over outcomes; they can therefore be in power, but not have power (or not have very much of it). This is typically the case with parties of the Left, especially in recent years. Even when they are in power, outcomes seldom go the way that they or their constituencies want. Thus, they almost always disappoint – not so much because they betray the expectations of those they represent, although this is a chronic problem, but because they are obliged to accommodate to unfavorable conditions not of their making. This phenomenon has contributed importantly to the rightward drift of real world politics in recent years.

Being able to control outcomes is not as straightforward a notion as may appear. There are two major complications. First, it is not always clear, either to participants or observers, what it means for outcomes to go one way or another – unless we succumb to the mistake of identifying the control of outcomes with the realization of express desires. Thus, the concept of power raises problems of an **epistemological** nature that must be sorted out before the idea can be put to use in the analysis of actual situations. The second problem is that the notion is more subtle than may appear because causing decisions to go the way one wants is neither necessary nor sufficient for exercising real power. Controlling agendas is more important than prevailing in decision making. Ultimately, the framework within which agendas are formed is more important still for ascertaining where real power lies. That framework is usually beyond the ability of any individual or group to control directly. But it is, in the final analysis, nothing more than a background state of affairs constituted by the deliberate or unwitting activities of human beings. It is therefore susceptible to being altered or, in extreme cases, fundamentally transformed.

Epistemological problems arise in many guises. Marxists have popularized the notion of **false consciousness**, a condition in which workers and other **oppressed** people identify with the interests of their **exploiters** and oppressors. Then their actual desires contradict their true interests. In these circumstances, one could argue, as Marxists do, that political decisions are effectively concluded even before decision making takes place because the disempowerment of exploited and oppressed peoples is, so to speak, internalized. Competitive elections and a universal right to vote change nothing. Marxists believe that, unlike workers, (economic) elites know well enough where their interests lie. For this reason among others, they have the capacity to act on them. Everyone else is in some measure deceived and decapacitated – unless struggle itself clears the scales from their eyes.

The idea that elites know what they are doing while others do not has become a mainstay of much non-Marxist social and political theory too. It is not just Marxists, then, who believe that, in determining where power lies, what matters is not so much how decision making goes, but what is considered for decision making at all. If a municipality is debating, say, tenants' rights ordinances and the tenants' side prevails over the landlords' in some vote, it does not follow that tenants have power and landlords do not. Far more important to that question is what the issues in contention are, and therefore how far-reaching actual decision making can be. If fundamental questions about the ownership of **property** and tenancy remain beyond the power of elections to affect, then, win or lose on particular contests, the property-owning interests win on the deeper issue. The importance of agenda setting has become especially salient in recent years, as the constraints of corporate **globalization** increasingly intrude upon the capacities of states to determine the destinies of the populations they govern. It has become increasingly evident that (international) financial and corporate interests hold real power in the political arena, even when they do not participate directly in political affairs.

The idea that political power lies mainly in the political sphere is somewhat illusory. It becomes less so, however, when and insofar as economic and other constraints are loosened. Long-range structural tendencies, along with particular conjunctural circumstances, can facilitate this condition. Thus, the internal logic of capitalist accumulation can lead to crises in which new possibilities for change are opened up. Arguably, the world is on the threshold of such a period. If so, the immediate future is rife with both possibilities and dangers. In the final analysis, however, collective political action is an indispensable condition for any significant redistribution of political power. It could hardly be otherwise inasmuch as the institutional framework within which agendas are established is itself only a human contrivance – a consequence, intentional or not, of countless human activities. In principle, therefore, political action can always alter these circumstances or transform them altogether. But what is possible in principle is not always feasible in practice. Normal politics systematically conceals where power lies. It stabilizes existing arrangements. Only action outside the usual boundaries, enlightened by a clear understanding of power relationships and an awareness of the vulnerabilities of prevailing constraints, can change power relations fundamentally and for the better.

Further Reading

A classic and influential study of the exercise of political power in the modern period, emphasizing the role of elite interests, is Robert Michels, *Political Parties* (New York: Free Press, 1966). See also the classic study of Vilfredo Pareto, *The Rise and Fall of Elites: An Application of Theoretical Sociology* (New Brunswick, NJ: Transaction Publishers, 1991). An extremely useful anthology of late nineteenth- and twentieth-century writings on political power is Steven Lukes (ed.), *Power: Readings in Social and Political Theory* (New York: NYU Press, 1986). Robert A. Dahl's seminal *Who Governs? Democracy and Power in the American City* (New Haven, CT: Yale University Press, 1963) examines the exercise of political power (at the municipal level). The critique of it has focused attention on the importance of looking beyond actual decision making to agenda setting. An incisive account of the centrality of agenda setting is Steven Lukes, *Power: A Radical View*, 2nd edition (New York and London: Palgrave Macmillan 2005).

See also: CAPITALISM, CLASS, DEMOCRACY, LEFT/RIGHT/CENTER, LIBERALISM, MARXISM, REVOLUTION

Progress

To *progress* is to advance towards a goal; *progress* signifies movement towards a goal. Since the **Enlightenment**, the idea these words suggest has been central to the political project of the Left, both liberal and socialist, to such an extent that **progressive** is often used interchangeably with "liberal" or "socialist." The goal of the Left has always been, in the first instance, to implement the vision of society implicit in the French Revolutionary slogan "liberty, equality, **fraternity** (community)"; in more **radical** versions, it has been to realize a notion of human perfectibility arising out of these ideals. This understanding of progress has radiated throughout the entire political spectrum. Even modern conservative political movements assume it, though the connection is often strained. From its inception, the political sense of the term has been joined to notions of moral, technological, and cognitive progress. For most of the past two centuries, the consensus on these notions has been, if anything, even more secure across the political spectrum. Lately, though, progress in all its dimensions has become a controversial idea. Ironically, the challenge has come mainly from political forces that identify with the Left.

The idea that civilization today is more advanced morally than it used to be is very widely held. However, a clear understanding of the nature of moral progress is often lacking. If we use **ethics** to designate guides to individual conduct, then we can think of morality as a kind of ethic – one that adopts "the moral point of view," the perspective implicit in the Golden Rule according to which, in certain circumstances, one should deliberate about what to do, and evaluate the actions of oneself and others, from a universal or **agent-neutral** perspective. To "do unto others as you would have others do unto you" is to adopt a standpoint

173

according to which what matters is what one has in common with other moral agents, rather than what distinguishes particular agents from one other. Moral theory aims to give an account, at an appropriate level of abstraction, of the nature of agent-neutral deliberation and assessment. The **ethical** theories of the Greco-Roman world and the teachings of non-Western ethical traditions have very little to do with universally binding principles. Moral theories have, however, dominated Western ethical thought, especially in the modern era. The idea that moral progress is real therefore devolves into the contention that, at the societal level, more of what we do now passes muster from the moral point of view than in the past. A century and a half ago, the moral status of, say, **slavery** was controversial; it no longer is. This is a paradigm case of moral progress. Similar changes in attitudes towards **gender** equality provide another, less secure, example.

Moral progress should not be confused with progress in moral theory. That there can be progress in that philosophical enterprise is, of course, a belief shared by all its practitioners. But this conviction has little to do with real world politics. Where notions of moral progress are invoked, it is effectively assumed that whatever a correct philosophical account of morality might be, our understanding of what morality requires is generally sound. Moral progress has to do with the implementation of these settled convictions.

Impedances to moral progress have more to do with false beliefs about what is the case than with defective or inadequate moral theories. Often, the offending beliefs are unacknowledged. Moral progress occurs when these beliefs are exposed and rejected – in both theory and practice. It is, for example, a direct consequence of the moral point of view that, as Thomas Jefferson (1743–1826) declared in the *Declaration of Independence* (1776), "all men (sic) are created equal" – or, as we might say today (in terms that are arguably consistent with Jefferson's intention), that all human beings are equal in respects that matter to moral deliberation and assessment. For Jefferson though, and for the other founders of the American republic, this commitment was compatible with the enslavement of Africans and with denying full citizenship rights to women. There is no way Jefferson and the others, as moral thinkers, could countenance these practices unless they believed that, in relevant respects, persons of African descent and women are less than full-fledged moral agents. Today, we have become disabused of these false beliefs, though their consequences linger. However imperfectly, we have made moral progress. Perhaps future generations will look back on us, on how we treat ourselves and other living creatures, in much the same way that we now think of the attitudes towards slaves and women of Jefferson and his contemporaries.

The idea of moral progress is not a possession of any particular political tendency. But a view of how moral progress follows from technological and cognitive progress arguably is at odds with at least one important strain of conservative thought – the one that is heir of the Christian doctrine of Original Sin, of the idea that we human beings, thanks to our radical insufficiency (our "sinful" natures), are incapable of advancing our most fundamental concerns through our own efforts (without the benefit of "unmerited grace"). So far from advocating the free expression of human nature, conservatives of this type advocate **authoritarian** social and political structures to hold human nature at bay – to save us from the consequences of our Fallen condition. As a creature of the Enlightenment, the Left rejects this sensibility. It maintains that human beings can indeed advance their own fundamental interests, just as most non-Christian traditions in political thought, including those of ancient Greece and Rome, maintain. Left thinkers suppose that moral progress is both a cause and consequence of progress in liberty, equality, and fraternity.

The reality of technological progress, of advances in the (useful) arts and sciences, has been an undeniable feature of the lived experience of men and women in the West for more than half a millennium – and, more recently, as one of the very few beneficial consequences of Western imperialism, for everyone else. Armed with this idea, it is easy to find evidence of an irresistible impulse to progress in technology throughout all of human history – despite long periods of stagnation in Asia and elsewhere, and even regression, as in the so-called Dark Ages in Europe. From the Enlightenment on, the idea that technological progress leads to moral progress has become well established. In Marx's theory of history, historical materialism, the connection is direct and explicit. It is hardly less so in the thinking of many liberal social philosophers. Very generally, the thought is that technological progress is what moves human history along; and that, as G.W.F. Hegel (1770–1831) famously maintained, history culminates in the full-fledged emancipation of the human race. Marx incorporated a version of this idea in his notion of communism.

A goal of science has always been to provide a correct representation of what is the case. Since the rise of modern science in the seventeenth century, this task has been understood to consist mainly in discovering the causal structure of the real. To explain a phenomenon is to identify its causal determinations. Since physics is the science of **matter** at its most fundamental level, there is a sense in which a complete physics would provide a general theory of everything. In this sense, a true and complete physics would complete the scientific project. But inasmuch as matter organizes itself, so to speak, at different levels, even a complete physics would not explain everything. The problem is not just that, as we now know, causal indeterminacies exist at the atomic and sub-atomic level. Neither is the problem that causal accounts of all the fundamental units of matter involved in even very circumscribed events – the latest Iraq War, for example – would be impossible to assemble in real time, and impossible for anything less than the mind of an omniscient being to process and comprehend. Even if these intractable problems were somehow surmounted, a physical explanation of the Iraq War would not explain why, for example, the war occurred. To make sense of that, economic, social, political, and psychological causes, not just physical ones, would have to be invoked – not just because, as limited beings, a full physical explanation is unavailable to us, but in principle, because even a full physical explanation would not make sense of what we want to understand. Philosophers have pondered these issues extensively. Still, there is no settled view of how best to understand progress in science. There is no consensus either on whether there exist non- or extra-scientific ways of knowing. To the extent that there are, the growth of knowledge would involve more than just the progress of science. But, like questions about the nature of morality, these philosophical conundrums operate at a level of abstraction that is of no immediate political significance. What matters politically is just how progress in science or, if there is a difference, the growth of knowledge generally should be valued. The conviction that radiates throughout most of our political culture is that cognitive progress encourages moral progress and, along with it, progress in the advancement of liberty, equality, and fraternity.

Cognitive progress is, of course, essential to technological progress; and technological progress, in turn, facilitates the growth of knowledge. The two are joined in a "virtuous circle." The connection between progress in these domains and moral progress is more tenuous. As indicated, moral progress does generally require the undoing of false beliefs. But new scientific discoveries play little, if any, role in this process because whatever needs to be known to set matters right is almost always already sufficiently evident. The realization that persons of African descent and women are human beings – and therefore moral agents in just the way that white males are – does not depend on scientific discoveries unavailable until recently; these truths have been always been accessible. In this case, as in so many others, the problem is to overcome entrenched biases, grounded in ideological or psychological features of our condition.

In the end, what joins cognitive to moral progress is faith in the beneficent consequences of coming to see the world as it is. In eighteenth- and nineteenth-century Europe and North America, where Enlightenment ideas first took hold, the world was emerging from the thrall of theological illusions and clerical control. Science promised liberation from many, if not all, obstacles in the way of the development of moral capacities. But faith in the growth of knowledge is harder to maintain today – when, for example, weaponry, made possible by the growth of knowledge and technology, threatens the very existence of life on earth, and when ecological disasters that degrade human life follow, seemingly inexorably, from progress in these domains.

Belief in the beneficial consequences of the growth of knowledge is even harder to maintain when we realize the extent to which cognitive progress has come to depend on research that requires group efforts and massive funding, and that can therefore only come from governmental or corporate sources; in other words, where the agenda is set by factors external to the scientific community itself. Ideology and psychology have always blighted the forward movement of scientific discovery; economic and political pressures now magnify these distortions. But the problem is not science per se, but bad science. There is ample evidence that, in the long run, science corrects itself. Nevertheless, it does require a leap of faith to think that all obstacles to moral progress generated within scientific communities will in fact be overcome or that corrections can be made in a timely enough fashion to avert seriously deleterious, and perhaps even catastrophic, consequences.

To retain a dedication to cognitive progress today, more is therefore needed than the understandable, but implausible optimism of centuries past. In the end, the reason to retain this commitment has to do with the values inherent in the Left's Enlightenment roots. Immanuel Kant (1724–1804) famously wrote that Enlightenment is "humanity's emergence from its self-imposed nonage" (i.e. childhood); and went on to declare that its slogan is "dare to know." What this way of thinking prescribes is that we face reality squarely – without illusions born of wishful thinking. These values are honesty, authenticity, and, insofar as self-deception is a kind of pathology, mental health. They underlie the conviction that cognitive progress is a good, whether or not, in the long run, it benefits humankind.

Even if the optimism that motivated so many Enlightenment thinkers now appears naïve, a dedication to these Enlightenment values is hardly undone. What follows is just that "the Enlightenment project" must be pursued with a greater awareness of how its more utopian aspirations are probably unrealizable, thanks to limitations intrinsic in the human condition. This is not a new idea. It has been a motif of a dissident strain of Enlightenment writing from the time of Jean-Jacques Rousseau (1712–1778) to Sigmund Freud (1856–1939) and beyond.

Ironically, there are strains of contemporary **post-modern** thought, which identify with the Left, that reject "the Enlightenment project." They therefore eschew these and other notions of progress. On this view, *progress* is just a historically particular constituent of a "master narrative" that is, at best, only one story among others. The more common view, emanating from this quarter, is that notions of progress operate in "discourses" of **oppression**. Conceptual relativism underlies this conclusion; its rationale depends on the claim that truths are always only relative to particular discursive practices. Then narratives, being neither true nor false in themselves, are said to represent differential power relations only. The further claim is then made that somehow narratives that invoke notions of progress function to maintain existing elites in power. It is easy enough to demonstrate the shortcomings, and even the incoherence, of this rationale; it is harder to combat its effects in certain academic circles. But it is important to do so, lest those who might otherwise do service to genuinely progressive causes be misled. Defenders of the idea that progress is only a figment of defective master narratives represent themselves as heirs, at a theoretical level, of the historical Left because they claim to adopt the perspectives of "the wretched of the earth." Their posturing has merit to the extent that it enables many voices, some of them previously suppressed, to be heard. But adopting the vantage point of the victims of the system, even when it is more than a theoretical gesture, barely addresses concerns for liberty, equality, and fraternity. To that end, it is necessary to continue, not abandon, the Enlightenment project – its values, its ambitions, and, insofar as they give expression to both, its notions of progress.

Further Reading

A classic study of the history of the idea is J.B. Bury, *The Idea of Progress: An Inquiry Into Its Origin and Growth* (Honolulu, HA: University Press of the Pacific, 2004). Optimism about moral progress, from a liberal perspective, is evident in John Stuart Mill's *On Liberty* (London: Penguin, 1975). This was not, however, Mill's subject in that volume; his position must be teased out of accounts of free expression and experiments in living. An influential challenge to standard conceptions of progress in science is T.S. Kuhn, *The Structure of Scientific Revolutions*, 3rd edition (Chicago: University of Chicago Press, 1996). For Hegel's notion of progress, see G.W.F. Hegel, *The Philosophy of History* (Amherst, NY: Prometheus, 1990). A highly attenuated facsimile of Hegel's idea, according to which liberal democracy, rather than the realization of the Idea of Freedom, is "the end of history" is Francis Fukuyama, *The End of History and the Last Man* (New York: Harper, 1993). This idea is debated, in a larger context, in Arthur M. Melzer, Jerry Weinberger, and M. Richard Zinman (eds.), *History and the Idea of Progress* (Ithaca, NY: Cornell University Press, 1995). Rousseau was the first Enlightenment thinker to question Enlightenment optimism without putting the "Enlightenment project" itself in question; see his "Discourse on the Sciences and Arts (First Discourse)," in Jean-Jacques Rousseau, (Roger D. Masters, ed.), *The First and Second Discourses* (New York: St. Martin's Press, 1964). Freud's masterwork in the same genre is Sigmund Freud, *Civilization and Its Discontents* (New York: W.W. Norton and Co., 1989). Post-modernist thought owes much to Michel Foucault's efforts to construe truth as nothing more than an expression of power. See, for example, the writings collected in Paul Rabinow (ed.), *The Foucault Reader* (New York: Pantheon, 1984). There are many post-modern attacks on the idea of progress; none of them are especially lucid or illuminating, however. A historically influential tract that illustrates the tenor of this line of thought is Jean-François Lyotard, *The Postmodern Condition: A Report on Knowledge* (Minneapolis: University of Minnesota Press, 1984). An incisive critique of post-modernism from the Left can be found in Alex Callinicos, *Against Postmodernism: A Marxist Critique* (New York: St. Martin's Press, 1999).

See also: COMMUNISM, COMMUNITY/COMMUNITARIANISM, ENVIRONMENTALISM, EQUALITY/EGALITAR-IANISM, FREEDOM/LIBERTY, HISTORICAL MATERIALISM, IDEOLOGY, IMPERIALISM, LEFT/RIGHT/CENTER, LIBERALISM, MARXISM, MORALITY, RELATIVISM, SOCIALISM, TECHNOLOGY, VALUES

Public goods

Public good is sometimes used loosely to mean whatever is good for the public, where "good for" is left undefined. There is, however, a stricter sense of the term, derived from the modern theory of public finance, which is useful for understanding the key institutions of modern political life – especially the state and the market. Like other terms of art in economic theory, *public good* is susceptible to formal representation, but also encumbered with imprecisions and ambiguities that affect even its strictest applications. There are, however, a number of properties that typically cluster around the concept that are sometimes held, singly or in combination, to define it. These properties have to do with how the good is consumed, and with how it is produced.

Of the consumer-side properties, the most generally accepted holds that if the good is available to anyone in a group, it is available to everyone else at no additional cost to the beneficiaries. This property, called "jointness of supply," is closely related to another – that if any member of a group is enjoying a good, others cannot be prevented from doing so too, except at an inordinate cost. These properties differ insofar as other factors than high exclusion costs bear on jointness of supply. Related to these properties, but distinct from them, are these: that one person's consumption of the good does not diminish the amount for consumption available to anyone else; that one person's enjoyment of the good does not diminish the benefits available to anyone else from its enjoyment; that if anyone receives the good, no one else can avoid doing so without excessive cost; that if anyone receives the good, everyone receives the same amount; and that there can be more than one consumer of the good, and each consumes the total output. These are conceptually distinct properties. Not all public goods exhibit each of them. However, there is usually a considerable overlap.

In principle, a good satisfying some or all of these properties could be provided by a single individual. In practice, though, it is almost always the case that the provision of a public good requires the contributions of many. Even when it is physically possible for an individual or small group to produce the good, they would not do so, the argument goes, because the benefit accruing to the producers is generally less than the cost of production. Thus, **free rider** problems arise with respect to public goods; everyone wants the benefit, but no one is willing voluntarily to pay the cost. This is why there is a supply-side aspect to public goods provision as well as a consumption-side aspect. For a public good to exist, everyone (or some near approximation of everyone) in the population for which the good is public must contribute towards its production. This property is designated "jointness in production."

National defense or fire protection in congested areas are examples of public goods. It is impossible or inordinately expensive to protect only some parts of the national territory (the parts inhabited by people who have voluntarily paid for military protection) or some houses (those of homeowners who have subscribed to a fire protection service) and not others. This is because the benefits of these goods spill over to everyone regardless of contribution, because they require the contributions of many, and because some of the other properties usually associated with public goods apply to them.

Jointness in production along with jointness of supply and some or all of the other consumer-side properties that attach to the notion render markets incapable of providing public goods. There are no incentives for individuals to transact with one another voluntarily to produce the goods in question; everyone prefers instead to free ride on the contributions of others. But then, the good will not be produced, and everyone will be worse off than they might otherwise be. This is why, to obtain the public goods we want, we must, so to speak, bind ourselves by making ourselves unfree to free ride. We do so by making it impossible or inordinately costly to act on our free rider preferences. This, in turn, is why everyone who is not an anarchist assumes that states are necessary. Markets are incapable of providing public goods. If they are to be exist, contributions towards their production must therefore be **coerced**. This is what states do; states make individuals unfree to act on free rider preferences. This justifies their exist-ence. It also justifies the contention that one thing – and, in the view of some libertarians, the only thing – that states can rightfully do is supply public goods.

Strictly speaking, the need to solve free rider problems does not, by itself, mandate the state form of political organization, according to which all coer-cive institutions are concentrated into a single institutional nexus. That conclu-sion – that there should be a monopoly of the means of **de facto** legitimate violence – requires an independent argument. In the modern world, where the state form of political organization is assumed, that argument is seldom forthcoming. But the account Thomas Hobbes (1588–1679) provided in a few seminal chapters (13–16) of *Leviathan* (1651) gives theoretical expression to what everyone, except a handful of anarchists, believes. Hobbes's aim was to account for **sovereignty**, supreme authority over a given territory or population. He did so by making the institution of sovereignty a matter of individuals' rational choice – not natural or divine law. Thus, he modeled individuals' lives in their "natural condition" – that is, in the absence of a sovereign – as a "war of all against all." In these conditions, their interests, as Hobbes portrayed them, are poorly served. Given these interests, and given how thoroughly individuals' lives would be improved if only they could coordinate their behaviors, these individuals, because they are rational, want to leave this condition if they can. They would therefore be willing to "lay down" some or all of the rights they enjoy in their natural condition in order to obtain order or security. Needless to say, the concept of a public good, like the concept of a free rider, would not be developed until cen-turies later. But these ideas are implicit in Hobbes's account. Security, as Hobbes conceived it, is an unnatural contrivance that, as with other public goods, people generally want. For it to exist at all, it must be jointly produced; and, when it does exist, its benefits spill over to everyone, contributor and non-contributor alike. Thus, it satisfies the conditions of jointness in production and jointness of supply. It also satisfies most of the other conditions characteristic-ally associated with public goods.

Public goods

Because security has a public goods structure, everyone has an incentive to free ride on the contributions of others in bringing it about. In other words, what everyone wants most is for everyone else to act in an orderly fashion – by obeying publicly identifiable rules, such as those that a sovereign would proclaim – while themselves remaining free to do whatever they please. Everyone's first choice, then, is to remain outside the sovereign's power at the same time that everyone else follows his commands; in other words, everyone prefers lone disobedience to universal citizenship. And, because a war of all against all is contrary to their interests, everyone prefers universal citizenship to it. But, of course, it is logically impossible that everyone or nearly everyone be a lone disobedient; therefore, lone disobedience, though the most popular preference, cannot be a basis for general agreement. Indeed, were everyone to act on their lone disobedience preference, as they should if they are rational and self-interested, even each individual's second most preferred outcome, universal citizenship, would be unattainable. A collection of rational agents, seeking to realize their desires to be lone disobedients, would find themselves mired in a war of all against all, their least preferred outcome. Individuals therefore have an overriding interest in escaping this condition by forming a community ruled by a sovereign. Hobbes then went on to contrive a mechanism, a form of "covenant," that would allow self-interested rational agents to institute sovereignty without putting themselves at even greater risk than they already are in the war of all against all. The details need not concern us, except to say that, to the degree that Hobbes's solution works, individuals succeed in providing a public good for themselves. They do so by placing themselves under a sovereign's control; in other words, by creating a state that renders them unfree to act in ways that would result in a war of all against all. In this way, Hobbes's case for sovereignty anticipates the more general claim that states exist to supply public goods; strictly speaking, it is just a special case of it.

Needless to say, not all goods with public goods structures are generally desired. Security is an exception – because, as Hobbes modeled "the natural condition of mankind," it is, by hypothesis, in everyone's interest. But most public goods – railways, for example – benefit some individuals more than others. Though they have public goods structures, it is unclear how generally desirable they are, and therefore whether they ought to be provided by the state. This is a question for legitimate political institutions to determine. In democracies, it is a question for the people or their elected representatives to decide.

Further Reading

For a clear, philosophically perspicacious account of the nature of public goods and associated free rider problems, see Garett Cullity, "Moral Free Riding," *Philosophy and Public Affairs*, vol. 24 (1995), pp. 3–34. For Hobbes's argument, see Thomas Hobbes (C.B. Macpherson, ed.), *Leviathan* (Harmondsworth, UK: Penguin, 1980; originally published 1651), chapters 13–16. The structure of free rider problems and their relevance to justifying coercion is discussed in an illuminating way in David Lewis, *Convention: A Philosophical Study* (Malden, MA: Blackwell Publishers, 2002), chapter 3. On market incapacities, see Charles E. Lindblom, *The Market System: What It Is, How It Works, and What to Make of It* (New Haven, CT: Yale University Press, 2002), chaps. 9–12.

See also: ANARCHISM, DEMOCRACY, FREEDOM/LIBERTY, LEGITIMACY, LIBERTARIANISM, MARKETS, STATE, VIOLENCE/NON-VIOLENCE, WELFARE/WELFARE STATE

R

Race/racism

From time immemorial, human populations have differed from one another in complexion, facial characteristics, and the like. For the most part, these differences have not mattered socially or politically because contacts between peoples whose physical characteristics differ significantly were rare. In instances where contacts did occur, there were often consequences. Awareness of group differences helped to foster a sense of in-group **solidarity**. In some cases, this sensibility was benign; more often, it was invoked to justify the domination of some groups by others. In any case, stereotypical beliefs about alien groups, including beliefs about their superiority or inferiority, are not new. However, the modern concept of *race* is; it is a creation of eighteenth-, nineteenth- and twentieth-century (pseudo-)science. Thus, the **reification** of salient differences among human populations is a comparatively recent development. As this ostensibly scientific category seeped into political discourse, the social and political importance of the differences the concept designates increased enormously.

Institutional racism – the systematic **exploitation** of some peoples by others – therefore preceded the emergence of the concept of *race* and the development of *racialist* (or *racist*) ideology. Institutional racism has existed wherever distinct peoples have lived together as dominators and subordinates. It became a key structuring element in the lives of the peoples of Europe, Africa, and the

Americas after the European discovery of the New World and the rise of the African slave trade. The development of modern imperialism, with its global reach, has increased its importance in these continents. It has also added to or, more usually, superseded local institutional racisms in Asia, Australasia, and the Pacific Islands. But *racialism* or, as we more usually say (despite the potential confusion implicit in the usage), *racism* – ideological justifications for institutional racism that appeal to the purported inferiority of exploited races – did not appear until after the development of a world system based, in large part, on the exploitation of some peoples by others was already underway. It emerged in response to a situation in which a very long-standing, but nevertheless heterogeneous series of local phenomena, bearing only a family resemblance to each other, coalesced into global social divisions.

Race in its current sense developed out of earlier uses of the term. Some of these older meanings survive to this day. Like "stock" or "blood," *race* can signify a line of descent. It can also mean "species" of plants or animals or even the entire "human race." Or it can be used to indicate sub-species of various kinds. In some European languages, the term or its cognates is also used to designate stereotypical characteristics of, say, breeds of dogs or horses and, by extension, of exotic or at least unfamiliar human groupings. Used this way, it is more usually a term of praise than contempt. In French, for example, *racé* means "true to race". It is a complement to say of a particular animal or even of a human being that he or she is *racé*. Although the term had long been employed to identify sub-categories of human beings (for example, "the Scandinavian race"), it was not until the end of the eighteenth century that the term was used to indicate the broad categories of human beings (Negroid, Caucasian, Mongoloid, etc.) that it subsequently designated. That these categories exist was proclaimed a scientific discovery – based largely on observed systematic differences in skull features and, of course, skin color.

As racialist ideologies developed to justify institutional racism, a racial hierarchy came to register in the consciousness of both the exploited and their exploiters. It is based largely (but not entirely) on the amount of melanin in peoples' skin – whites were on top, followed by yellows, reds, and browns, and then by blacks. Within these groupings too, there were sub-hierarchies based, again, on lightness and darkness of skin color. This phenomenon is largely an effect of the racialist ideology of the dominant imperial culture. But there are parts of the world – for example, on the Indian subcontinent and in other parts of Asia – where it draws on indigenous beliefs as well.

What appeared to be biological and anthropological evidence for racial divisions was bolstered by research in comparative linguistics. Degrees of relatedness between languages were taken as evidence for relatedness between peoples. However, the linguistic evidence did not always mesh well with emerging racialist theories. It became clear, for example, that most European languages are descended from languages spoken in India, thereby linking dark Indians with white Europeans. It also became clear that many "Caucasians" spoke non-Indo-European languages – not just in the Middle East, where most languages were "Semitic," but also in Western, Eastern, and Northern Europe. Nevertheless, to this day, racial and linguistic categories are typically confounded. "Semitic," for example, designates a linguistic grouping (that includes Hebrew and Arabic), not a *race* in the modern sense. Nevertheless, because millennia ago some of the ancestors of modern Jews spoke Semitic languages, we use the word **anti-Semite** to mean "anti-Jewish" (as if "Jewish" somehow designated a racial or quasi-racial grouping). In short, the use of comparative linguistics by racialist ideologues has led to a morass of confusion. In this case, however, science ultimately corrected itself. The fact that linguistic evidence cohered poorly with racist claims was not what ultimately did in this line of thought. Its fate was sealed as it became increasingly evident that biological descent was only one factor bearing on the distribution of Eurasian, African, and Amerindian languages, and therefore that linguistic relatedness is, at best, a flawed indicator of anything that might be connected with racial affinities.

Social Darwinism, the idea that those on the top of social hierarchies must somehow be the "fittest," was also enlisted in efforts to provide scientific support for racialist ideologies. But Social Darwinism was, at best, a hodge-podge of misunderstandings. Among other things, its conception of "fitness" was not Darwin's. For Charles Darwin (1809–1882), "the fittest" organisms are those that are best able to reproduce in the environmental niche in which they find themselves; they are not, as the Social Darwinists believed, "the best" in any more general sense of the term. To infer from the fact that, in recent centuries, "the white race" and especially its "Nordic" components, has achieved political and economic dominance over other "races" does not entail that it is, in any biologically relevant sense, superior. For an extended tract of recent human history, whites came to dominate blacks – and browns and reds and yellows – for sociopolitical and economic reasons, not racial ones. To suggest otherwise is, at best, to mask a self-serving and deeply tendentious *post hoc, ergo propter hoc* explanation in Darwinian guise.

It is now beyond dispute that the science on which familiar racial categories rest is bogus. It is known, for instance, that there is more genetic variation within races than between them. Beyond differences in complexion and facial features there are very few biological properties that correlate with today's racial designations. This is not to say that all human populations are the same. Geneticists are able to establish lines of descent by focusing on the Y chromosome and the mitochondria of living persons. These comparatively small parts of the human genome do not divide in each generation and therefore do not change quickly. Consequently, they provide evidence of degrees of relatedness across human populations. By this means, it is now plain that all human beings are, so to speak, cousins, though some are only very distantly related to others. It is generally accepted that human beings first appeared in South Africa about 100,000 years ago. Thanks to migration, some human populations have been separated from others for many millennia. But there has not been nearly enough time for these scattered groupings to differentiate biologically, except with respect to superficial features. The only significant exceptions are a handful of characteristics of mainly medical interest. This is hardly surprising inasmuch as so-called racial (and sub-racial) groupings have, for a very long time, constituted distinct "breeding populations." Just as even recently established breeds of dogs or horses are more or less susceptible than others to certain illnesses, thanks to genetic traits that become lodged in their breeding stock, reproductively segregated human populations too can become unusually prone to particular ailments. As "interbreeding" increases, these differences are bound to diminish, along with the more salient, superficial differences that nineteenth- and twentieth-century pseudoscience reified.

By any rational standard, the differences that do exist at the present time ought to be of no political relevance. This would be the case even if somehow it could be established that there are differential levels of "intelligence" across racial groupings. That there are has been a long-standing claim of racialist ideologues. Were they right, it is far from clear what, if any, policy implications would follow. However, they are not right. The arguments they offer are unsupported by pertinent evidence; worse still, their ostensibly empirical findings are muddled. Even the concept of "intelligence," as they understand it, fails to pass muster.

For as long as distinct peoples have intermingled, there has been "interbreeding." Pseudo-science and its policy extensions have therefore had to refine criteria for membership in racial categories. Without exception, the process has been governed by political exigencies. The American case is exemplary. Because slave-masters sexually exploited their human chattel, and because most African-Americans today are descended from slaves, most African-Americans have some European ancestry. But, in the racial map of the American political culture as it existed for more than a century after the fall of the ante-bellum South, any-one with even one African great grandfather was deemed "black." The obses-sion with "white" racial purity helped to insure that the majority population would maintain its dominant position in the institutionally racist system. In more traditional colonial societies, including Apartheid South Africa, other mechan-isms were in place to keep white minority populations in control. In these circumstances, racial categories could be drawn more loosely, in ways that more accurately reflected the facts on the ground.

The most influential political movement ever to adopt an explicitly racialist ideology was German National Socialism (**Nazism**). Its historic defeat in World War II cast discredit on racialism in politics. Even so, vigilance is necessary to insure that this fortunate turn of events remains secure. Today, however, it is only on the fringes of the extreme Right that racialist ideologies flourish. Otherwise, anti-racism is the official policy across the political spectrum. More subtle ways of thinking that justify institutional racism survive, however. Tacit racism is, of course, less deadly than the overt racism that was once a pole of attraction in world politics. But it is more insidious. It is therefore more difficult to excise. Its elimination is an urgent task for all proponents of racial equality.

How independent this struggle should be from broader struggles for equality, especially economic equality, is a question that has been much debated in recent decades. There is no general formula; racist theory and practice is historically particular to distinct situations. In the American case, because slavery and its legacy loom so large, independent anti-racist struggles are almost certainly neces-sary. In other times and places, strategies can differ. But, in the final analysis, the struggle for racial equality is part of a larger struggle for equality gen-erally. Overcoming continuing institutional racism, along with its ideological supports, is a key component of that larger endeavor.

Further Reading

For a concise and accessible account of the history of modern racism and its purported background in the biological sciences, see George M. Frederickson, *Racism: A Short History* (Princeton, NJ:

Princeton University Press, 2003). On the misuse of science in this endeavor, Steven Jay Gould's *The Mismeasure of Man* (New York: W.W. Norton and Co. 1966) remains unsurpassed. The persistence of institutional racism and the continuing pertinence of racial distinctions in contemporary American social and political life are discussed in the articles collected in Steven Gregory and Roger Sanjek (eds.), *Race* (New Brunswick, NJ: Rutgers University Press, 1994) and in Eduardo Bonilla-Silva, *Racism Without Racists: Color-Blind Racism and the Persistence of Racial Inequality in the United States* (Lanham, MD: Rowman and Littlefield, 2003).

See also: CULTURE, EQUALITY/EGALITARIANISM, IDEOLOGY, IMPERIALISM, LEFT/RIGHT/CENTER, NATION/NATIONALISM

Relativism

In recent years, promoters of a "values-based politics" on the American Right, abetted by theocrats intent on enforcing their own conceptions of religious orthodoxy, have taken to inveighing against what they call *relativism*, a position they contrast with **absolutism**. Their misuse of these terms is abetted by **postmodernists** who think of themselves as defenders of relativism and therefore as exponents of all that the theocrats and their allies oppose. Philosophically, this all too common usage is confused; politically, it is tendentious. However, *relativism* does have reputable philosophical uses that warrant explanation. Their connection to the understandings that are rife in right-wing circles today is, at best, highly attenuated.

Sentences that genuinely make assertions express **propositions**, and propositions are either true or false. However, the truth values of some propositions depend upon how their terms are related to one another. For example, according to Albert Einstein's (1879–1955) special theory of relativity, space, time, and velocity are related in the sense that what is true or false of one or another of these concepts depends on its relation to the others. Einstein's discovery that this is the case was a major breakthrough for physics. But it in no way implied that physics is any less able than previously thought to assert true or false claims. What it changes is what is asserted to be true or false. Similarly, a moral relativist might deny, for example, that true or false claims about right and wrong actions can be made without relativizing them, say, to the identity of the agents involved or to their cultural setting or to any of a number of other possible candidates.

So understood, relativism should be distinguished from what, following Friedrich Nietzsche's (1844–1900) lead, we might call **nihilism**. A nihilist denies that a purported assertion is either true or false. This is tantamount to saying that it fails to express a proposition. Proponents of the verificationist theory of meaning, according to which a sentence is meaningful only if the proposition it expresses can in principle be verified **empirically**, would be nihilists with respect to such purported assertions as "God exists" or "killing is wrong." They would say that because these sentences are meaningless, they fail to express propositions and therefore have no truth values. The verificationist theory of meaning, favored by **logical positivists**, has long been abandoned along with logical positivism itself. Hardly anyone today thinks that "God exists" or "killing is wrong" are neither true nor false. However, there are some who do believe that "killing is wrong" is true or false relative to some conditions or circumstances. They would be moral relativists, and their position is plausible in the sense that good, though perhaps not compelling, arguments can be adduced in its defense. It is hard to imagine how anyone could be a relativist with respect to "God exists." Of course, there are people who would say (and think) that "God exists for one person but not for another." But then, appearance to the contrary, they are not making an **ontological** claim about God. If they are not uttering nonsense, they are just reporting on persons' beliefs about whether or not God exists.

One is a relativist or nihilist *with respect to* particular assertions or kinds of assertions. In Greek antiquity, a general or global relativism, relativism with respect to *all* assertions, was defended by some pre-Socratic philosophers – most famously, by Protagoras (481?–411? BC) who is supposed to have said "of all things, man is the measure; of the being of things that are, and of the not being of things that are not." However, for the past 2,500 years, it has been understood that the very idea of a global relativism is incoherent. How, after all, should we regard the claim that "global relativism is true." Nevertheless, a semblance of Protagorean relativism has been revived recently in post-modernist circles, ostensibly on Nietzsche's authority. Because their position radically deflates the idea of truth, what these post-modernists have in mind is best described as global nihilism, not global relativism, though it is almost never represented in those terms. Post-modernist nihilism (or relativism) draws on Michel Foucault's (1926–1984) development of Nietzsche's doctrine of "the will to power" – according to which any and all claims about what is the case articulate power relations between persons, not correspondence relations between linguistic utterances and matters of fact. Foucault's position is, in all likelihood, as incoherent as Protagoras' and for much the same reason – because, if true, it would refute itself. It is also plain that, despite post-modernists' misinterpretations,

Nietzsche was no global nihilist. He did fault pretensions of objectivity, and he was an opponent of the moral point of view. Nietzsche's view of **ethics** could therefore be construed as a kind of moral relativism (according to which what is right or wrong for agents depends on whom they are). But Nietzsche hardly dispensed with the notion of truth in the way that post-modernists do. The post-modernist position is philosophically untenable. Global nihilism (or relativism) is indeed an incoherent doctrine. Worse, it is grist for those who reproach modern modes of thought for being *relativistic*.

Relativism and nihilism are claims about what is the case. They are not directly claims about what we can know. They should therefore not be confused with **skepticism**. To be a skeptic with respect to some (or all) issues is not to claim that some assertion is only true or false relative to something else, and neither is it to deny that there is a fact of the matter at all. The skeptic would only insist that we cannot (or do not) know what that fact is, and that we ought therefore to withhold judgment. An **agnostic** is a skeptic with respect to the existence of God. Unlike a nihilist, an agnostic believes that "God exists" is either true or false. What the agnostic claims is just that we cannot (or do not) know which. Because we can only know what is the case, there is a sense in which nihilism, but not relativism, implies skepticism. But skepticism implies neither nihilism nor relativism. These terms denote distinct ideas.

Neither should *relativism* be confused with tolerance, as some post-modernist and otherwise leftish thinkers are wont to do. Attitudes and institutions are tolerant or intolerant, according to how accepting they are of differences. Individuals can be tolerant grudgingly or enthusiastically. Public institutions can promote or inhibit tolerance. Liberalism is a philosophy of tolerance. Thus, religious toleration is a long-standing liberal principle. But, as this example illustrates, tolerant attitudes and institutions are compatible with strong religious convictions; indeed, religious tolerance only becomes an important political issue when persons are seriously committed to different religious views. To be a liberal is not *ipso facto* to be uncommitted. Even liberalism itself can be and typically is supported by commitments to moral philosophical doctrines that are believed to be true by their proponents. To identify tolerance with relativism is to confound categories. Relativism and nihilism are metaphysical doctrines; skepticism is an **epistemological** position. Tolerance is a political **virtue**.

Arguably, one could use the word "absolutism" to contrast with *relativism*. Then a moral absolutist would be someone who believes that what is right or wrong is so relative to nothing. Similarly, pre-Einsteinian physicists who thought of space non-relationally are said to have upheld a concept of "absolute space." However, nowadays philosophers and scientists seldom use "absolutism" this way. If the term is used at all, it is in reference to the metaphysical beliefs of late-nineteenth-century **idealist** philosophers in Britain and elsewhere. For the most part, these philosophers were not relativists. But they were not absolutists on this account. They were absolutists because they adhered to a philosophical doctrine that maintained that, in the final analysis, all is One, and that that one real thing is what G.W.F. Hegel (1770–1831) called "the Absolute."

It is well not to abet the post-modernists' unwitting endorsement of the religious Right's confused and misleading depiction of a momentous political struggle between relativists and absolutists. *Relativism* is best reserved for the variety of serious, but politically inert positions that contemporary philosophers debate under that rubric. "Absolutism" is best used to refer to the long-departed philosophical tendency it used to name. There is a lively and important philosophical discussion to be had about relativism, especially moral relativism. But its political import is hardly what theocrats and right-wing ideologues would have us believe.

Further Reading

A concise, philosophical history of the concept that is, at once, sympathetic and critical is Maria Baghramian, *Relativism* (Abingdon, UK: Routledge, 2004). Moral relativism is debated in the papers collected in Paul K. Moser and Thomas L. Carson (eds.), *Moral Relativism: A Reader* (Oxford: Oxford University Press, 2000). See also Gilbert Harman and Judith Jarvis Thompson, *Moral Relativism and Moral Objectivity* (Malden, MA: Blackwell Publishers, 1996). Nietzsche's (not always adhered to) commitment to a version of relativism – according to which truth and falsity (and also right and wrong) is relative to particular "perspectives" – and its connections to nihilism is, at once, a source of insight but also, in post-modernist hands, of confusion. A clearheaded account of what Nietzsche's views actually were is set out in Steven D. Hales and Rex Welshon, *Nietzsche's Perspectivism* (Champaign, IL: University of Illinois Press, 2000).

See also: IDEOLOGY, LEFT/RIGHT/CENTER, LIBERALISM, MORALITY, THEOCRACY, VALUES

Republicanism

In the United States, *republican* usually refers to the Republican Party, the right-most of the two semi-established political parties. When it does, the name has no particular philosophical significance. But it was not always so. When the Republican Party was established in the 1850s, its main rival had already taken over the term *democrat*; hence the need for a contrast. *Republican* was apt because the Republicans were an anti-**slavery** party. Opposition to slavery was not, at that time, a majority position, even in the North. The name made the point that the United States was a republic, not a democracy, and therefore that popular attitudes towards slavery, though relevant, ought not to be decisive. That the United States was conceived as a republic was beyond dispute. As such, the Republicans maintained, it is governed by principles that make slavery unacceptable. They described these principles as *republican* largely to assert continuity with the thinking of the founders of the state. Of course, the founders, many of whom were, in fact, slave owners, had a different view of slavery than the Republicans of the Civil War and Reconstruction era. There is a point, even so, to Republican claims for continuity; arguably, those founders who accepted the existence of slavery and even those who owned slaves were committed, albeit ambivalently, to principles at odds with the institution. But, in historical fact, their use of *republic* had less to do with principled convictions than with a then – standard understanding of the term. For them, *republic* contrasted with *monarchy*; a *republic* was a country without a king. This usage persists. Fighters for Irish independence called themselves *republicans* because they sought independence from the British monarchy. So too do those who today favor the abolition of the monarchy in England, Scotland, and Wales.

   In the political theory of the early modern period, *republican* also had a rather different meaning that coexisted with the standard understanding. In the sense in question, even a monarchy could have a republican character. The term referred to contemporaneous understandings of the Roman republic. (Small-r) republicans took republican Rome – along with Sparta and other examples from classical antiquity – as models to emulate. Their focus, however, was not exactly on the political institutions of these ancient polities, but rather on the **virtues** of their citizens and the background conditions that encouraged their development. They maintained that, in republican Rome, citizens were concerned, above all, with advancing the interests of the political communities they comprised, even at the expense of their own private interests. Republican philosophers were intent on replicating these virtues under modern conditions. Thus they focused on **mores**, and on the construction of economic, social, and political institutions conducive to the formation of virtuous dispositions. In their view, as the Roman republic was transformed into an empire, virtue declined, and was replaced by the corruptions of luxury for the wealthy few and the corruptions of abject poverty for the vast majority. Republican philosophers saw their own world poised at a similarly critical juncture. Medieval forms of ecclesiastical control were no longer sustainable, nor were they any longer thought desirable. But the emerging **civil society**, based on untrammeled commerce, seemed, if anything, even worse than the world of the Dark Ages. Republican philosophers were intent on reviving the ancient precedents – as a sound **secular** basis for a reorganized social and political order.

(Small-r) republicanism celebrated the self-sufficient yeoman farmer and artisan. It advocated the dominance of the countryside over the cities. Above all, it praised simplicity in private life and selfless dedication to the common good in the public sphere. The republican account of a past Golden Age was **illusory**. It was based on nostalgia for a lost world that never was and certainly cannot now be. Republicanism was therefore a **utopian** theory with **reactionary** overtones. It opposed modern industry and, in consequence, the development of **productive forces**, the basis for moral progress. But the values republicans endorsed were estimable in their own right and implicitly anti-capitalist. In short, seventeenth- and eighteenth-century republicanism has a paradoxical character. It represented, in part, a reactionary longing for a mythical and unrealizable past. But it was also centuries ahead of its rivals in advancing reasons for transcending the capitalist order.

As industrialization and commercialization proceeded, republicanism's influence waned in both the United States and Europe. For nearly two centuries, it was of interest only to historians of political thought. In recent years, however, political philosophers have rediscovered republicanism. What they find attractive is not its jeremiads against the corruptions of modern life or its glorification of simplicity and self-sufficiency. What appeals instead is the idea that an individual or polity is free to the extent that others do not dominate it. The republicans' commitment to freedom as non-domination resonates today, especially among those who are not won over by the liberal and libertarian notion of negative liberty, but who also associate more positive conceptions of freedom with totalitarianism. In addition, the republicans' emphasis on political virtue connects with recent efforts of moral philosophers to reconstitute **ethical** theories based on notions of private virtue. These developments aside, the fact that the great seventeenth- and eighteenth-century revolutionary thinkers of Europe and the Americas were, on the whole, moved by republican aspirations is reason enough to suppose that critical scrutiny of this episode in political theory's past holds promise for its future.

Further Reading

On the Roman republic, see Michael Crawford, *The Roman Republic*, 2nd edition (Cambridge, MA: Harvard University Press, 1993). On early modern conceptions of freedom, including republican conceptions, see Quentin Skinner, *Liberty Before Liberalism* (Cambridge: Cambridge University Press, 1997). Republican attitudes are evident in the thinking of many of the authors of the US Constitution. See, for example, James Madison, Alexander Hamilton and John Jay (Isaac Kramnik, ed.), *The Federalist Papers* (Harmondsworth, UK: Penguin, 1987). An example of contemporary efforts to revive republican political philosophy is Philip Pettit, *Republicanism: A Theory of Freedom and Government* (Oxford: Oxford University Press, 2000).

See also: CAPITALISM, DEMOCRACY, FREEDOM/LIBERTY, LEFT/RIGHT/CENTER, LIBERALISM, LIBERTARIANISM, MORALITY, PROGRESS, STATE, TOTALITARIANISM

Revolution

In its original meaning, *revolution* signifies movement around a circle, as when a planet completes its orbit. More generally, it denotes any turning or spinning motion around an axis of rotation. In ordinary speech, *revolution* is used, and overused, to denote fundamental, usually abrupt, change. The term's political meaning draws on these images and understandings. A political revolution is a thoroughgoing and dramatic change of regime in which, speaking metaphorically, institutions are transformed "full circle." Plato (427?–347? BC) and Aristotle (384?–322? BC) anticipated this usage, but it was not until the seventeenth century in Europe, as fundamental changes in political institutions developed in the Netherlands and later in England, that the term, in this sense, came into widespread use. By the end of the eighteenth century, it was natural to call the American War of Independence a revolution. But it was not until the French Revolution that the term finally assumed the meaning it has today. The French Revolution, according to contemporaneous understandings and in the judgment of history, brought about a profound transformation not just at the political level, but in social and economic life too. Earlier revolutionary moments involved the seizure of state power and perhaps a transformation of fundamental constitutional arrangements. The French Revolution did all this and more. It was more **radical** than any of its predecessors, because it spilled over into non-political aspects of collective life – above all, into the economic sphere. Ever since, *revolution* has carried this implication.

Revolution

Even if we confine attention to the political realm, not all regime changes count as revolutions. **Secession** movements are revolutionary only to the extent that they involve fundamental changes in the form in which **authority** is exercised. Thus, a case could be made that the American Revolution was not, strictly speaking, a revolution at all, but an independence struggle with revolutionary aspects. Similarly, dynastic civil wars – for example, the War of the Roses – are not revolutions because they don't involve the construction of new institutional forms of governance. Neither are *coups d'états*. Like revolutions, they replace one set of elites with another. But coups seldom change fundamental institutions, and neither are they preceded by a breakdown of state power, as in the French Revolutionary model or in the twentieth century's paradigm cases – the Russian, Chinese, Cuban, and Vietnamese revolutions. After World War II, when the Red Army established Soviet-style regimes throughout Eastern and Central Europe, there was talk of "revolution from above." In retrospect, it is plain that this characterization was only part of a program, undertaken by Communists, evidently in vain, to confer a sense of legitimacy on Soviet-installed rulers.

Among socialists, especially Marxists, *revolution* contrasts with **reform**. The supposition is that reforms are less radical than revolutions in their consequences. However, this understanding can be misleading. In principle, reforms can be as far-reaching as changes instituted by revolutionary regimes. Indeed, revolutionary changes are simply reforms of fundamental institutional arrangements. However, in practice, revolutionary socialists are almost always more radical in their ambitions than reformist socialists are. But they need not be so. The main difference between reform and revolution is that revolutions are precipitated by fundamental crises of legitimacy within old regimes. When they succeed, new elites, vested with revolutionary legitimacy, take the place of the old. Reforms are instituted and maintained by existing elites. Revolutionaries deny that there is a reformist road to fundamental political, social, and economic change. But, if they are right, it would be for politically contingent reasons alone. The aggregate effect of deep, structural reforms can be as far-reaching as any directly revolutionary transformation.

It is widely assumed that political revolutions involve violence – on the part of insurgent forces seeking state power and by the state in its efforts at repressing insurgents. Historical evidence supports this contention. But, in this case too, the connection is contingent, not necessary. Ruling elites are almost always intent on maintaining their power by any means necessary; and, even if they are willing to cede power individually, they typically remain loyal to the regime in place – and will do almost anything to maintain it. Nevertheless, the possibility exists, at least in (somewhat) democratic polities, that constitutional means can be used for introducing changes as deep and dramatic as in paradigmatically revolutionary upheavals. However unlikely the prospect, non-violent revolution is a theoretical possibility.

Revolutionary times elicit extraordinary levels of **solidaristic** behavior. But experience has shown that golden ages of revolutionary generosity cannot be sustained indefinitely. Thus, nearly all theories of revolution suppose that, in time, as revolutionary regimes consolidate their power, revolutionary fervor gives way to ways of thinking and acting inherited from the old regime. In the French case, according to canonical interpretations, this happened on the ninth day of the month of Thermidor of the Year II of the revolutionary calendar (July 9, 1794). In his *History of the Russian Revolution* (1932), Leon Trotsky (1879–1940) described Joseph Stalin's (1879–1953) assumption of power in the Soviet Union as a Russian Thermidor. The Thermidor phenomenon, Trotsky implied, suggests the existence of a tendency for revolutionary ideals to be betrayed, and for revolutionary institutions to become "deformed." It was, in large part, to counter this tendency that Trotsky proposed that revolutionary **vanguards** embark on a course of **permanent revolution**. Communists, of course, rejected Trotsky's diagnoses and his proposals. They emphasized instead the need to combat counter-revolution – a point Trotsky and his co-thinkers also acknowledged. Counter-revolutions occur when former elites or their successors reassume power, undoing some or all of the institutional changes initiated by the revolution.

In the late 1960s and early 1970s, there was a widespread assumption in the **Third World** and even in the West that revolution was on the agenda again. The conventional wisdom nowadays is that this belief was a fanciful and romantic last gasp; that the revolutionary period that began in the seventeenth century in Western Europe and that eventually flowed over into Asia, Africa, and Latin America came to a definitive end with the collapse of Communism in 1989 and the dissolution of the Soviet Union in 1991. It is too soon to tell if this assessment is sound. But it is plain that, in the wake of the dashed hopes of twentieth-century revolutionary endeavors, the revolutionary impulse is, at the very least, in eclipse nearly everywhere.

Further Reading

Historical studies of particular revolutions, both failed and successful, abound. One that is more than usually comparative in its perspective is, as remarked above, Leon Trotsky's *History of the Russian*

Revolution (New York: Pathfinder Press, 1980). Marx's thoughts on the subject are presented in Hal Draper and E. Haberkern, *Karl Marx's Theory of Revolution: War and Revolution* (Alameda, CA: Center for Socialist History, 2005). A classical Marxist brief on the necessity of revolution is Rosa Luxemburg, *Reform or Revolution?* (New York: Pathfinder Press, 1973). An influential statement of the case against revolution is Alexis de Tocqueville (Stuart Gilbert, trans.), *The Old Regime and the French Revolution* (Garden City, NY: Doubleday Anchor, 1955). For a scholarly, comparative account of the major revolutionary ventures of the past, see Theda Skocpol, *States and Social Revolutions: A Comparative Analysis of France, Russia and China* (Cambridge: Cambridge University Press, 1979).

See also: COMMUNISM, DEMOCRACY, LEGITIMACY, LIBERALISM, MARXISM, POWER, SOCIALISM, STALINISM, STATE, TROTSKYISM, VIOLENCE/NON-VIOLENCE

Rights

We say colloquially that, for example, chess players have *rights* to move their pieces one way or another according to the rules of chess. This usage, like modern philosophical uses of the term, derives from Roman law and from contemporary analogues, where the rules of the game are specified by legal systems. Laws accord particular rights to individuals or more rarely to groups. By the seventeenth century in England, the concept began to be used to articulate extra-legal political demands and, more generally, visions of what rules *ought* to be. The term has proven so useful for this purpose that it has become a fixture of our political discourse. Rights talk is used everywhere, almost reflexively, to indicate both what is and what ought to be the case.

In the United States, the distinction between legal and extra-legal rights is blurred because the Bill of Rights of the US Constitution is a legal document, albeit one that is of little use without extensive judicial interpretation; and because, to a degree that is unusual in liberal democracies, policy decisions often fall to the courts to make. Political questions are therefore sometimes posed as questions about what is constitutional. Legal theorists can argue about the extent to which appeals to the Constitution are only devices for articulating non- or extra-legal demands. Nevertheless, it is plain that, in the United States more than elsewhere, claims about rights are treated as questions of constitutional interpretation. In less litigious political cultures, the extra-legal dimension of many rights claims would be more transparent.

Rights claims are addressed to others, imploring or commanding them to do or not to do certain things according to legal or extra-legal rules. The claimants are usually, though not necessarily, individuals. Therefore individuals outside society, like the fictional Robinson Crusoe of the Daniel Defoe (1660–1731) novel, can have no rights – for they have no one to whom rights claims can be made. Legal scholars have long maintained that rights impose "correlative obligations" on the part of others. For example, if there is a right to free speech, then others (especially the state) have a negative obligation – not to interfere with speech. If a right to health care is demanded, the idea is that others (presumably, in this case, only the state) have a positive obligation to provide it.

Human rights are rights that human beings have in virtue of being human – that is, apart from the rights they enjoy as citizens of particular states. They are addressed to all other individuals and social groups and, of course, to governments. But because there is no world **sovereign** and because existing states, the United States above all, have undermined efforts to establish a functional equivalent through the United Nations and other international organizations, there is no reliable human rights enforcement mechanism. Therefore, at this point, human rights have, at best, only a quasi-legal status. Also, because there is no global equivalent of a Supreme Court, there is no definitive method for adjudicating what particular human rights there are or what the policy implications of accepted human rights claims might be. Even so, where human rights are asserted, the presumption is that there is an obligation on the part of others – mainly, but not only, governments – to do or to forbear from doing certain things. As human rights talk has evolved and become pervasive, this understanding has come under strain. Thus in the United Nations' *Universal Declaration of Human Rights* (1948), rights are claimed – to a decent standard of living, for example – that seem to assert goals or standards of achievement rather than obligations. It is not clear whether this usage represents a political compromise, an acquiescence to the fact that there is no general and reliable way to enforce human rights claims internationally, especially when they assert obligations to do things that governments normally do not do, or whether, in recent years, the traditional concept has taken on a new significance. When, for example, it is claimed that there is a universal human right to adequate nutrition, it is apparently not implied that there is a quasi-legal (as distinct from a moral) obligation on the part of anyone (the international community, governments, private citizens) to supply food to the hungry. But perhaps someday this will be the general understanding. Then human rights will become more like other rights, and what now seems little more than a proclamation of an objective will be seen as an unequivocal assertion of a correlative obligation.

Rights

Rights talk is ubiquitous nowadays not only in political discourse, but in political theory too. In philosophical contexts, the main divide is between those who take rights to be morally primary and those who take them to derive from more fundamental moral principles. Neo-Lockean libertarians, exponents of moral philosophical theories derived from the work of John Locke (1632–1704), fall into the former category. For them, certain property rights are fundamental and inalienable; institutional arrangements must therefore accommodate to them. Where other concerns — for instance, the idea that outcomes should be as welfare-enhancing as possible — conflict with these rights, rights prevail. On the other hand, utilitarians, because they are dedicated to maximizing overall well-being, derive rights from this more fundamental concern. Should they conclude that the **property** rights neo-Lockeans uphold actually are utility maximizing and therefore justified, they too might express this conclusion in rights talk. But, for them, property rights would be, so to speak, theorems derived from utilitarian axioms, rather than axioms themselves. For neo-Lockeans, rights are axioms.

The first utilitarians were scornful of rights talk. Jeremy Bentham (1748–1832) famously described it as "nonsense on stilts." However, utilitarians, finding the concept useful, have made peace with the notion — in its non-axiomatic sense. In the not too distant past, there were some on the Left who disparaged rights talk for its tendentiously legalistic and individualistic character. However, it has become plain, after the experience of Communism, that states without robust conceptions of rights, including human rights, degenerate into **tyrannies**, even when they are officially dedicated to the values the historical Left espoused. Thus, Left criticism of rights talk has largely disappeared. Perhaps in some remote future, a less individualistic, less forensic term will supersede *rights* in its current descriptive and **normative** uses. However, for now and for as long as one can foresee, the concept that has proven so useful for so long is likely to remain a key part of our political life. Contestation will continue to occur over particular rights claims, but probably not over the viability of the concept itself.

(Small-r) rights should not be confused with the concept of (capital-R) Right. That notion is a fixture of continental European social and political theory. In English-speaking philosophy, it has, so to speak, a resident alien status. Even the word *Right* is, at best, a not very illuminating translation of *Recht, Droit, Diritto* and equivalent terms in other European languages. A better translation would be "public law," where "public" contrasts with "private." Very generally, *Right* designates moral principles in their institutional embodiments. Thus, the *Rechtsstaat* that G.W.F. Hegel (1770–1831) theorized in his *Philosophy of Right* (1821) – and that Karl Marx (1818–1883) investigated and found wanting in his 1843 *Critique of Hegel's "Philosophy of Right"* – is a set of institutional practices and arrangements based on universal (**Kantian**) principles of equal citizenship. Principles of Right can be and typically are expressed in (small-r) rights talk. But the concepts are distinct.

Further Reading

The source of the now-standard view of the connection between rights and correlative obligations is Wesley Hohfeld (Walter Wheeler Cook, ed.), *Fundamental Legal Conceptions: As Applied in Judicial Reasoning* (Clark, NJ: Lawbook Exchange, Ltd., 2001). On the history of rights talk and anticipations of the concept of universal human rights, see Micheline R. Ishay, *The History of Human Rights: From Ancient Times to the Globalization Era* (Berkeley and Los Angeles, CA: University of California Press, 2004). Political uses of the concept are discussed in Jack Donnelly, *Universal Human Rights in Theory and Practice* (Ithaca, NY: Cornell University Press, 2002). On the role of the United States and Great Britain in forging a system of international law, and then of the American role in weakening it, see Philippe Sands, *Lawless World: America and the Making and Breaking of Global Rules from FDR's Atlantic Charter to George W. Bush's Illegal War* (New York: Viking, 2005). The most influential libertarian tract that views rights claims as morally primary is Robert Nozick, *Anarchy, State, and Utopia* (New York: Basic Books, 1977). The distinction between (small-r) rights and the concept of Right is lucidly explained in Steven Lukes, *Marxism and Morality* (Oxford: Oxford University Press, 1985), chapter 3. I elaborate further on some of the themes set forth here in *Arguing for Socialism: Theoretical Considerations*, 2nd edition (London: Verso, 1988), chapter 4; and in *Engaging Political Philosophy: From Hobbes to Rawls* (Malden, MA: Blackwell Publishers, 2002), chapter 3.

See also: COMMUNISM, CULTURE, DEMOCRACY, LEFT/RIGHT/CENTER, LIBERALISM, LIBERTARIANISM, MORALITY, STATE, UTILITARIANISM, WELFARE/WELFARE STATE

S

Social democracy

Until the formation of the Third (Communist) International in 1919, two years after the **Bolshevik** Revolution, all member parties of the Second International (1881–), including the Russian party out of which Bolshevism sprang, called themselves *social democrats*. In the aftermath of World War I, with Communist groupings split off, Social Democrats joined the governments of several European states. From that time on, Social Democratic parties in liberal democracies have operated within the constitutional frameworks of their respective countries. From that time on too, Social Democrats and Communists have been at odds. With the onset of the Cold War, this mutual hostility intensified.

In some countries, social democrats call themselves simply *socialists*. Therefore, the term *social democrat* and *socialist* are sometimes interchangeable. This usage is usually harmless, but it can be misleading – because there are socialist currents that have little or no historical connection with Social Democracy. The name is sometimes eagerly assumed; sometimes avoided. But the theory and practice of social democracy have long enjoyed an appeal beyond the formal boundaries of the Second International. Labor parties have always been social democratic in their political orientation. In the United States, where large segments of the population were receptive to social democratic ideas, but where socialism was sometimes viewed as an unwelcome European immigrant, a functionally similar, though less far-reaching, politics emerged in the Populist and **Progressive** movements and later within the framework of **New Deal** and **Great Society** liberalism.

The name *social democracy* suggests a certain view of historical progress that social democrats endorse. It implies that, in the aftermath of the French Revolution, liberals and others succeeded in establishing democracy at the political level in some countries – albeit more in theory than in practice, even in the most democratic of them. From the beginning, social democrats were committed to consolidating these gains and to extending political democracy throughout the world. But their main concern was to move on to the next stage – to extend democracy throughout the entire social order. At first, social democrats maintained that, to do so, a break with capitalism is necessary. In later years, some Social Democratic parties repudiated this conviction explicitly; many did not. But social democrats everywhere repudiated it in practice, turning their movement's legacy of anti-capitalist creeds and programs into formal expressions, trotted out from time to time to energize elements of their electoral base that remained loyal to socialist ideals. By the second half of the twentieth century, if not earlier in most cases, Social Democratic parties had become integrated into the governing system of capitalist states.

With Communists to their left according to the conventional wisdom, Social Democrats advocated what were commonly perceived to be **moderate** socialist policies. They favored public – typically, state – ownership of major industries, but within the framework of "mixed economies" that also allowed for private ownership. Social democrats advocated **reform**, rather than revolution. Of course, they could be profoundly oppositional and even revolutionary in countries with illiberal and **oppressive** political regimes. But in liberal democratic countries, social democrats were anti-revolutionary – not just in practice (as the Communists were), but in theory too (as the Communists were not). Social democratic groupings have always had left and right wings. Left social democrats could sometimes be as far-reaching in their vision of institutional transformations, especially in the economic sphere, as Communists were. Outside the Soviet and Chinese spheres of influence, where Communist Parties controlled everything, Social Democratic parties were, in any case, more successful than Communists in moving societies in the direction they both officially desired.

After the split with Communism, it emerged that the main social democratic **strategy** for transcending capitalism was social spending aimed at diminishing the economic importance of capitalist markets, without directly abolishing them. The idea was that a policy of progressive **decommodification**, focused mainly on the provision of social necessities (housing, food, transport, healthcare), would eventually transform capitalism into socialism. More **moderate** social democrats, who effectively abandoned socialism as an ideal, were nevertheless also intent on providing financial security and social inclusion on an egalitarian basis. Thus, social democrats seized upon the welfare state, wresting its theory and practice away from the conservatives who had contributed so much to its early development. Left-wing social democracy saw the welfare state as a major component of a fundamentally new social system; center and right-wing social democrats saw it as a means for forging a more humane capitalism. Social democrats of all stripes also wrested the idea of **corporatism** away from the (fascist) Right. Especially in Northern Europe, Social Democratic parties effectively reorganized the state and **civil society** on the basis of institutionally entrenched mechanisms of governance grounded in principles of cooperation between capital and labor.

Even more than was the case with the Communists, the main constituency of social democrats everywhere has always been the organized labor movement. Social democracy's vitality and strength depends upon the vitality and strength of trade unions. With considerable plausibility, Social Democratic parties represent themselves as political representatives of the working class. Where working-class identifications are discouraged, and where "catch-all" parties, like the Democratic Party in the United States, funded mainly by business interests, represent workers politically, social democratic impulses are effectively suppressed. This is why social democratic programs never took hold in the United States to the degree that they did in countries with stronger labor movements and more open political systems.

In the twentieth century, the social democratic movement accomplished miracles – above all, in Scandinavia, where, for the first time in human history, poverty was effectively eliminated. Today, social democracy is on the defensive everywhere, along with many of its progressive achievements. Blame for this unhappy state of affairs is often cast on **globalization**. The claim is that the increasingly global reach of capital diminishes the power of states to organize social and economic life for the benefit of their own citizens. It is also said that globalization accelerates the movement of impoverished peoples into prosperous social democratic countries – straining welfare state institutions, and reinstituting poverty and the social ills that follow in its wake. There is some truth in these contentions, though it is far from clear that a revitalized Social Democratic movement could not adapt to twenty-first-century conditions by strengthening its long-standing internationalist commitments. Much the same is true of the labor movement upon which Social Democratic parties depend – not just for votes, but for ideas as well.

What is less well appreciated is how detrimental the end of Communism has been for Social Democracy. In the absence of any significant political force threatening their power, ruling elites have no incentive to compromise or to adapt to popular demands in ways that advance the objectives of the historical Left. Without a serious challenge to the old regime, beneficial reforms become all but unattainable. Unlike Communism, Social Democracy is not defunct. Institutionally, it remains intact. But, for the time being, the social democratic impulse appears to have run its course. Social Democratic parties today are more likely to wage defensive struggles to retain what earlier generations of Social Democrats won than to move forward in the way that earlier generations of Social Democrats did. If the movement is to resume its role in forging a more progressive future along socialist lines – or even if its role is only to help in developing and implementing Left alternatives within capitalism – it is in urgent need of revitalization.

Further Reading

An excellent history of European socialism that sets the social democratic project in its proper context is Donald Sassoon, *One Hundred Years of Socialism: The West European Left in the Twentieth Century* (New York: New Press, 1997). The recent travails of social democracy in both Europe and the United States are recounted in Norman Birnbaum, *After Progress: American Social Reform and European Socialism in the Twentieth Century* (Oxford: Oxford University Press, 2002). A classic statement of the view of progress implicit in social democratic theory and practice is R.H. Tawney, *Equality* (Lanham, MD: Rowman and Littlefield, 1964). An insightful and influential study of connections between social democracy and the welfare state is Gosta Esping-Andersen, *The Three Worlds of Welfare Capitalism* (Princeton, NJ: Princeton University Press, 1990). Esping-Andersen's analysis is criticized sympathetically and developed further, with ample empirical documentation, in Robert E. Goodin, Bruce Headey, Ruud Muffels, and Henk-Jan Dirven, *The Real Worlds of Welfare Capitalism* (Cambridge: Cambridge University Press, 1999). Connections between social democracy and corporatist theory and practice are explored in Herbert Kitschelt, *The Transformation of European Social Democracy* (Cambridge: Cambridge University Press, 1994). There are many recent discussions of the consequences of globalization for social democracy. A representative sample, focused on the Scandinavian countries, can be found in Robert Geyer, Christine Ingebritsen and Jonathan W. Moses (eds.), *Globalization, Europeanization and the End of Scandinavian Social Democracy?* (London and New York: Palgrave Macmillan, 2000).

Socialism

See also: COMMUNISM, CONSERVATISM, DEMOCRACY, EQUALITY/EGALITARIANISM, FASCISM, INTER-NATIONALISM, LABOR MOVEMENT, LEFT/RIGHT/CENTER, LIBERALISM, POPULISM, PROGRESS, REVOLU-TION, SOCIALISM, STATE, WELFARE/WELFARE STATE

Socialism

Socialism emerged in the aftermath of the French Revolution. It gave expression to the idea that the revolution was only partly successful because it was insufficiently **radical** in its efforts to reorganize society. In the nineteenth century, socialism became an influential ideology in the nascent labor movement. However, there have always been socialists not connected to organized labor; and, from the beginning, many, perhaps most, labor militants were not socialists. Today, throughout the world, the link between the labor movement and socialism has grown tenuous. Never strong in the United States, it has become even weaker now. Before World War I, the Socialist Party in the United States scored impressive electoral gains, and its influence exceeded its electoral appeal. Thereafter, along with other socialist groupings, the Socialist Party failed to thrive. For most of the twentieth century, the United States was exceptional among developed capitalist countries in not having a significant socialist presence. In recent decades, and especially after the fall of Communism in 1989, socialist theory and practice has been in eclipse everywhere.

From its inception, the socialist movement has had complex and often-troubled relations with liberals and others on the Left. However, in recent years, the differences between socialism and liberalism have blurred. It is now clear that liberals can be as egalitarian in their fundamental **normative** commitments as socialists, and that socialists and liberals can be equally dedicated to installing and maintaining basic freedoms. It is plain, though, that socialists envision a less **atomized**, more communal, social order than liberals do. Liberals are typically pro-capitalist, and capitalism, socialists believe, tends to fragment group **solidarities**. But socialists have never agreed on what their communal vision implies. For much of socialism's history, socialists were especially critical of the way that capitalism, with its reliance on market relations, joins people together through self-interest. However, by the late twentieth century, even this verity had become problematic, as prominent socialist thinkers became increasingly won over to **market socialism**. Socialists also agree that transformations of the economic and social spheres, not just changes at the political level, are indispensable for achieving the objectives of the Left. However, on the nature and scope of these changes, they have never been of one mind. Inasmuch as the socialist movement has always had **reformist** and revolutionary wings, socialists have also never agreed on how best to implement the social, political and economic transformations they envision.

The most cogent account of what socialism is derives from Karl Marx's (1818–1883) theory of history, historical materialism. Oddly, in view of Marx's enormous influence among socialists, his position has never been well understood, even among self-identified Marxists. But it does provide a sound basis on which to reflect on alternatives to capitalism. Historical materialism divides human history into epochal periods – culminating in communism. Capitalism precedes communism, creating the conditions for its possibility, and also making it necessary. On this view, socialism is not an epochal form in its own right; it is communism's "first stage." Its indispensable (and generally protracted) role is to transform an economy and society, developed but deformed under capitalism's aegis, in ways that are congenial to the construction of a communist order. The epochal divisions Marx identified are distinguished by the forms of **property** that constitute them or, what comes to the same thing, by successive episodes of **deprivatization** of revenue and control rights over productive resources. In precapitalist societies, there is private ownership of other persons and also of non-human things. Under capitalism, ownership of other persons ceases, but external things remain privately owned. Under socialism (communism's first stage), private ownership of external things is superseded too; productive resources are henceforth owned socially. Eventually, under full-fledged communism, property rights "wither away" in importance, as goods and services are distributed "from each according to ability, to each according to need."

Over the past several centuries, what capitalist property is has become well understood, even as the forms it takes have evolved. These understandings are represented in the laws of capitalist countries, which specify the forms and limits of revenue and control rights over productive resources. They are also reflected in mainstream economic, social, and political theory. In contrast, neither Marx nor any other socialist thinker produced comparable accounts of social ownership. A lack of pertinent historical experience only partly accounts for this deficit. Socialist thinkers have always been quick to assume that the future will somehow take care of itself. Marx even made this assumption a matter of principle. Even so, from the nineteenth to the late twentieth century, there was at least a tacit understanding, according to which social ownership was

Socialism

identified with state ownership. On this point, socialists of all varieties (including social democrats) and Communists agreed, and so did anti-socialists (pro-capitalists) in the mainstream political culture.

State ownership has long existed in capitalist economies too. But there are usually differences between pro-capitalist and pro-socialist rationales for it. Very rarely do pro-capitalists propose state ownership in order to accord governments control over "the commanding heights" of the economy, the better to move public policies in equality- and freedom-enhancing ways, or to promote community. More typically, the pro-capitalist's aim is only to administer what used to be thought of as "natural monopolies" – usually, but not only, in the provision of human necessities, energy resources, transport, and communication. Until recently, especially outside the United States, it was thought to be more **equitable** and more **efficient** for the state to run these services directly than for it just to regulate them. Nowadays, with the political Right in the ascendant and with **neo-liberal** economic policies the order of the day, both public ownership and significant regulation are everywhere in retreat. Before this turn in the political culture, many governments of capitalist countries took over failing enterprises, running them at a loss if need be, in accord with perceived national interests. Today, this seldom happens. In the aftermath of World War II, socialists endorsed **nationalizations** of capitalist enterprises almost without regard for the proposed rationale. They viewed nationalized enterprises as embryonic socialist forms – developing, as it were, in the womb of the old regime, much as capitalism itself emerged in feudal societies. As the hope of replacing capitalism receded, they became advocates of "mixed economies," for want of a better alternative. The idea was that, for the sake of both equity and efficiency, the state would control those sectors that work best under its direction, leaving the rest to the private sector. In this way, at least some of the benefits of genuine socialism would be retrieved. By the 1980s, though, as the socialist movement fell into crisis, and as Japan, Korea, and other East Asian economies scored success after success, erstwhile socialists who continued to favor strong state involvement in the economy came to endorse industrial policies and, in the case of France, "indicative planning" over outright state control. More doctrinaire socialists – and all Communists – remained faithful to the idea of state ownership. They were buoyed by the fact that, outside the capitalist ambit, state ownership continued in full force. Thus, in the Soviet Union and China and wherever else the Soviet and Chinese examples were followed, all productive assets were state owned. They were also state administered – not according to market criteria, but through

208

central planning. According to the consensus view, the Soviet model was of a piece with traditional socialist thinking; it was just several degrees more extreme. When the Soviet Union imploded and China embarked unabashedly on "the capitalist road," the entire structure of thought that these states appeared to implement fell with them.

Despite the conventional wisdom of decades past, state ownership is, at best, only one form of social ownership. Other forms of "social property," where revenue and control rights are held by collective entities of various kinds and where decisions are made democratically, are also conceivable. Indeed, since the inception of the socialist movement, small-scale attempts at non-statist forms of social ownership have been attempted, never in congenial circumstances, but often with encouraging results. These experiments deserve attention; there is much that can be learned from them.

Nevertheless, socialists should take care not to substitute notions of desirable socialism for the definition of *socialism* itself. Capitalist societies run the gamut from liberal democracies to fascist **dictatorships**, and sustain correspondingly wide variations in capitalist property relations. There is every reason to think that socialism admits of a similar variety – whether or not one or another form of it is rightly seen as the "first stage" of a vastly more far-reaching process of social transformation. For clarity's sake, it is well to acknowledge this fact definitionally – by identifying *socialism* with "post-capitalism" in the historical materialist sense. To reserve the term just for regimes that seem desirable, as many socialists do, only invites confusion.

Orthodox historical materialists apart, socialists argue for socialism by appealing to moral values like equality, justice, and freedom; to political values like democracy; and to economic values like efficiency. In periods when socialism is or seems to be on the political agenda, debates on these topics rage throughout the political culture and in academic circles. When the socialist project is in eclipse, as in the present period, the debate wanes. But its timeliness and urgency continues unabated. Classical Marxists, putting their faith in history's underlying dynamic, derided discussions of this sort – castigating those who would appeal to moral or extra-moral values in defense of socialism as **utopian socialists**. Today, however, as the merits and shortcomings of historical materialism have become better understood, it seems that only utopian socialism has survived. Socialism can no longer plausibly be defended by appeal to inexorable historical laws. Its defense requires arguments that are ultimately **normative** in character.

Further Reading

A useful study of American exceptionalism is Seymour Martin Lipset and Gary Marks, *It Didn't Happen Here: Why Socialism Failed in the United States* (New York: W.W. Norton and Co., 2001). On the history of socialism in Europe from the late nineteenth to the late twentieth century, see Donald Sassoon, *One Hundred Years of Socialism: The West European Left in the Twentieth Century* (New York: New Press, 1997). An accessible and insightful account of socialism's past and future is Immanuel Wallerstein, *Utopistics* (New York: New Press, 1998). A witty defense of socialist ideas, from a decidedly non-Marxist perspective, can be found in the recently reissued George Bernard Shaw, *The Intelligent Woman's Guide to Socialism and Capitalism* (Whitefish, MT: Kessinger Publishing, 2005). On market socialism, see John E. Roemer, *A Future for Socialism* (Cambridge, MA: Harvard University Press, 1994). Feasible socialism is defended – in theory and in reference to significant efforts to approximate socialist economic relations (for example, in the Mondragon cooperatives in Spain) – in David Schweickart, *After Capitalism* (Lanham, MD: Rowman and Littlefield, 2002). On how utopian socialism fares today from a still generally Marxian point of view, see G.A. Cohen, *If You're an Egalitarian, How Come You're So Rich?* (Cambridge, MA: Harvard University Press, 2001), chapter 3. My own views on the capitalism/socialism debate are elaborated in *Arguing for Socialism: Theoretical Considerations*, 2nd edition (London: Verso, 1988).

See also: CAPITALISM, COMMUNISM, COMMUNITY/COMMUNITARIANISM, DEMOCRACY, EQUALITY/ EGALITARIANISM, FASCISM, FREEDOM/LIBERTY, HISTORICAL MATERIALISM, IDEOLOGY, JUSTICE, LABOR MOVEMENT, LEFT/RIGHT/CENTER, LIBERALISM, MARKETS, MARXISM, MORALITY, REVOLUTION, RIGHTS, SOCIAL DEMOCRACY, STATE

Stalinism

Stalinism refers, in the first instance, to the institutional arrangements and style of governance of the Soviet Union from the late 1920s, when Joseph Stalin (1879–1953) assumed control of the Communist Party apparatus and the Soviet state, until his death. However, since the 1930s, when Trotskyists began to use the word, the understanding has been that Stalinism is a political phenomenon in its own right, and that Stalin himself was neither necessary nor sufficient for its existence. Today, the term does not so much denote a particular historical period in Russian history as a constellation of political practices, attitudes, and styles. Stalinism in this sense was most starkly manifest in the Soviet Union in the mid- and late-1930s, during the show trials of Nikolai Bukharin (1888–1938) and other **Bolshevik** leaders, and then again in Eastern Europe and Soviet Russia in the early years of the **Cold War** (from roughly 1948 until 1953). To a greater or lesser degree, it is a feature of all post-Leninist communist societies and of political tendencies that, in some cases, have little or nothing to do with Communism.

Although the term is widely used, there is only a vague consensus about the distinguishing features of Stalinism. Among its most salient characteristics is a permanent institutionalization of revolutionary terror designed to suppress political opposition and to control the general population through fear. In Stalin's time, terror was deployed directly against **peasants** and, sometimes, even workers. But its most conspicuous victims were incumbents of high offices – in the party apparatus, the state, the "commanding heights" of the economy and, as the Soviet Union prepared to enter World War II, the military. Stalinists out of power utilize similar techniques, though usually in more benign and selective ways, as their circumstances require. As self-identified revolutionaries, their goal is to discipline their own ranks and to assure the compliance or acquiescence of **fellow travelers**. Inasmuch as Stalin abruptly changed the general line of Soviet foreign and domestic policy several times, Stalinists were conspicuous for the sharp turns in their political orientation. In the late 1920s and early 1930s, they veered from right to left and back again; later they opposed fascism in the **Popular Front** period, supported Stalin's non-aggression pact with Adolph Hitler (1889–1945) in 1939, and then dedicated themselves wholeheartedly to waging war against **Nazi** Germany after Germany invaded the Soviet Union in 1941. Stalinists unconnected to Stalin or to Communism evince similar dispositions. They are unflinchingly loyal to the party (or its functional equivalent) and disposed to accept whatever such loyalty entails—even, if need be, at the expense of personal integrity or moral principle.

Another salient feature of Stalinism, in its narrower sense, is its reliance on bureaucratic forms of governance, organized more through the Communist Party apparatus than directly through state institutions (though leading positions in the state were effectively monopolized by Party members). In the period of classical Stalinism, the general line was established in the Party – indeed, in the highest echelons of the Party. Party cadre then implemented it unflinchingly. Everything was controlled from the center, and there was virtually no accountability except to Stalin himself. This system could achieve remarkable successes, as it did in the industrialization programs of the 1930s and then in World War II. But it was also a recipe for stagnation, especially as credible threats of subversion and foreign conquest subsided. There is little doubt that economic, political, and cultural stagnation, legacies of the Stalin period, contributed mightily to the demise in 1991 of the Soviet Union itself.

Stalinism

In opposition to Leon Trotsky (1879–1940) and V.I. Lenin (1870–1924), and indeed all classical Marxists, Stalin championed the idea of "socialism in one country" and, therefore, the subordination of social and political struggles everywhere to the national interests of the Soviet Union. Even after World War II, with the Soviet Union dominating Central and Eastern Europe, and with the Chinese Communist Party's victorious revolution, the doctrine of socialism in one country survived in its pre-war form. This commitment gave rise to other characteristics of Stalinist practice, especially in the West. It helps to explain why Stalinists evinced indifference, even contempt, for principles, especially moral principles; and why they turned themselves into instruments of Soviet *Realpolitik*. In the strictest sense, a Stalinist was someone who faithfully executed the orders of a political party controled, at least indirectly, by the Soviet state. Thoughtful Stalinists became Stalinists because they believed that, in their time and place, the Soviet Union's interests were tantamount to the long-term interests of the international working class. To this end, Stalinists were prepared to sacrifice the immediate interests of workers and **oppressed** peoples in their own countries and abroad. As classical Stalinism vanished from the scene, this aspect of Stalinism faded. The (implicit) meaning of the term changed accordingly. Nowadays, *Stalinist* is used to describe anyone who acts as Stalinists did on behalf of any interests – usually, but not necessarily, the interest of a state – for whatever reason, someone who slavishly follows a party line.

When Communism was still a reference point on the political landscape, the question of the relation between Stalinism and classical (Leninist) Bolshevism was much debated. Cold War anti-Communists emphasized continuities. They wanted to tarnish Lenin with Stalin's crimes. Trotskyists and other dissident Leninists maintained that, in one way or another, Stalin deviated from Lenin's path and, in doing so, betrayed the revolution. Following Nikita Khrushchev's (1894–1971) secret denunciation of Stalin before the Twentieth Party Congress of the Communist Party of the Soviet Union in 1956, the Communists themselves settled into a policy of "de-Stalinization." Khrushchev depicted Stalinism as a "personality cult." Thereafter, for official Communists, to de-Stalinize was to replace the vestiges of that cult, along with other traces of charismatic leadership styles, with bureaucratic forms of governance. Khrushchev's **reforms** improved the condition of the Soviet people, if only by reducing the role of institutionalized terror. From the mid-1950s on, only dissidents faced unremitting repression, not ordinary people or potential rivals within the ruling elite. But Khrushchev and his successors kept intact the political and economic system forged during the Stalin period. In this respect, their efforts at de-Stalinization were superficial. As the Communist movement became less monolithic, dissident Communists offered more nuanced diagnoses of Stalinism – typically emphasizing Stalin's obsession with industrial development at any cost. But they too were inclined to leave the system Stalin shaped undisturbed. Even the Chinese Communists continued to adhere to the Soviet model. Nevertheless, the Maoist insistence on putting "politics in command" suggested a more radical kind of de-Stalinization than anything proposed in the Soviet sphere. Ironically, though, the Maoists never quite acknowledged a break with Communism's Stalinist period. Their enemy's enemy remained their friend. Claiming to be the heirs of the revolutionary tradition that Lenin began and that Khrushchev, the enemy of the moment, ended, they continued to identify with Stalin, at least rhetorically. When the **Cultural Revolution** erupted, ostensibly to put politics in command, the chaos that ensued insured a return to forms of bureaucratic governance similar to those in place in the Soviet Union. But, in time, the Chinese Communists came to repudiate Communism itself, in all but name. As this situation developed, Chinese Communists effectively stopped invoking Stalin's memory. However, they never officially repudiated him. With the partial exception of the Chinese, and the full-fledged exception of North Korea and a few other now-defunct Communist regimes, all Marxist political formations, from the mid-1950s on, sought to distance themselves, in theory if not in practice, from the taint of Stalinism. They could hardly do otherwise. In the larger political culture, Stalin had come to be regarded as a historical villain, very nearly on a par with Hitler, his archenemy and the greatest villain of all.

With the demise of the Soviet system, one might expect that the Stalinist mentality would wither away. However, this would be an **illusory** hope. Stalinism gave expression to a sensibility that predates the conditions that gave rise to Stalin's rise to power, and that will doubtless remain a pole of attraction for some time to come. It is a sensibility that, in different circumstances, sustains religious orthodoxy, with its demands for doctrinal conformity and its visceral conviction that heresy is the greatest of all human transgressions. Stalinism was a **secular** phenomenon, but it is instructive to reflect on its affinities with the long and brutal history of ecclesiastical repression and intolerance. Nevertheless, it is important not to lose sight of the fact that classical Stalinism vested their faith in a particular state. Given their pretensions of universality, there is nothing comparable in the bloody histories of Christianity or Islam; and, thanks to the nearly two-millennia-long dispersion and subordination of the Jewish people, there is nothing in Jewish history either that offers any parallels – until the emergence of political Zionism a century ago. Today, with the Soviet Union gone and China's Communist leaders plunging their country headlong back into the world capitalist system, it is in the Zionist movement that the Stalinist mentality remains most evident – not so much in Israel itself as among its diaspora supporters, especially in the United States.

In our time, Stalinism, in its most general sense, appears to be a permanent temptation. History has shown that even people committed to universal humanist values can succumb to it. The temptation exists across the political spectrum. But it is a disorder to which the Left is especially vulnerable. However, the Stalinist style is hardly inevitable in efforts to exceed the horizons of mainstream liberalism. Its emergence is only a possibility. On the Left as elsewhere, Stalinism can be resisted successfully and, with proper vigilance, overcome.

Further Reading

The best political biography of Stalin remains Isaac Deutscher's *Stalin: A Political Biography* (Oxford: Oxford University Press, 1949). A recent and more hostile biography that benefits from new evidence and the advantage of hindsight is Robert Service, *Stalin: A Biography* (Cambridge, MA: Belknap Press, 2005). Representative historical assessments are available in David L. Hoffman (ed.), *Stalinism: The Essential Readings* (Malden, MA: Blackwell Publishers, 2003). Trotsky's assessment of the politics of his rival is still of great interest – see Leon Trotsky, *The Revolution Betrayed* (Mineola, NY: Dover Publications, 2004). Nikita Khrushchev's 1956 "Secret Speech" on Stalin's "personality cult" that launched the official Communist program of "de-Stalinization" is most easily found nowadays on the Internet or in the *Congressional Record: Proceedings and Debates of the 84th Congress, 2nd Session* (May 22, 1956–June 11, 1956), C11, Part 7 (June 4, 1956), pp. 9389–9403.

See also: COMMUNISM, CULTURE, FASCISM, INTERNATIONALISM, LEFT/RIGHT/CENTER, LENINISM, LIBERALISM, MAOISM, MORALITY, NATION/NATIONALISM, REVOLUTION, SOCIALISM, STATE, TERROR/TERRORISM, THEOCRACY, TROTSKYISM, ZIONISM

State

State is sometimes used to mean "political regime." Strictly speaking, though, the term designates only regimes that invest supreme **authority** over particular territories or populations in a unified set of (ultimately) **coercive** institutions. So conceived, the state emerged in the West, where it came to supersede the more diffuse political structures of European **feudalism**. Looking at the rest of the world and at past historical periods through this lens, it is possible to find intimations of the state form of political organization in other times and places. Calling these regimes *states* is usually harmless. But for clarity's sake, the term is better used in its stricter sense.

For those who reflect on political life, the state, in the strict sense of the term, has been Topic A from the time of its inception – in, roughly, the mid-seventeenth century. From their beginning, philosophies of the state reflected a long-standing division within Western political thought between those who, like the early Christians, see the political as a burden cast upon humankind, as one of the wages of Sin; and those who, like Aristotle and other classical thinkers, see politics as an indispensable component of the good life. For the former, states are necessary evils, concocted to ward off situations that, in their absence, would be even worse. For the latter, the state is (potentially) an instrument for advancing the good or otherwise making human societies better. Among the giants of modern political philosophy, Thomas Hobbes (1588–1679) and John Locke (1632–1704) were proponents of the former, "negative state" view, while Jean-Jacques Rousseau (1712–1778) and Karl Marx (1818–1883) defended more "affirmative" conceptions of the state. In the larger political culture, the contrast is less stark because reflections on political life are generally eclectic or confused.

Liberalism is partial to negative states. Throughout most of its history, it has depicted the state's sole legitimate role to be to safeguard and superintend a non-political **civil society**. For liberals, it is in civil society, not the state, that human beings can flourish. But the liberal tent is broad enough to include affirmative conceptions of the state too – as liberals did, for example, in the **New Deal** and the **Great Society**. Perhaps the most affirmative state of recent political theory is the one envisioned by V.I. Lenin (1870–1924) in *The State and Revolution* (1917), the (misleadingly named) "**dictatorship** of the **proletariat**." The express mission of this state is to oversee the transition from capitalism to (stateless) communism by systematically transforming the material and cultural conditions that make states in pre-communist societies necessary. Lenin agreed with the anarchists on the ultimate desirability of uncoerced, and therefore stateless, **cooperation**. The anarchists, however, believed that this end could be achieved directly, through the state's immediate abolition, along with other revolutionary transformations of existing social and economic institutions. In opposing the anarchist view, Lenin argued for the necessity of a protracted period of social

215

and economic transformation, superintended by a **radically** democratized but powerfully intrusive state. Only such a state, he argued, could render communism feasible. Lenin's position is extreme, but it is less out of line with mainstream thinking than might be thought. Libertarians excepted, everyone nowadays assumes some notion of an affirmative state. Certainly liberals who would resume and expand the New Deal–Great Society consensus and their social democratic counterparts do. So too do conservatives who would use state power to implement particular conceptions of the good.

Because states have overwhelming force at their disposal, they can, in principle, intrude massively into the lives of the populations they govern. They are restrained from doing so in practice only by custom and law. These constraints are sustained, in turn, by theoretical accounts of what states can rightfully do. The least controversial view is that states rightfully provide public goods. This is a position that even the most austere proponents of the idea of a negative state accept because, in their view, states exist to maintain order – by saving us from the free expression of our natures – and order is a public good. Somewhat more controversially, states can also rightfully help to advance justice. Insofar as considerations of justice (fairness) are distinct from questions about the nature of the good society, this too is a position that can be embraced by liberals and others who are inclined to view the state as a necessary evil. It is more controversial, and arguably illiberal, to hold that states can rightfully instill **virtue** or otherwise implement conceptions of the good (in contrast to the just) society.

It is widely assumed that individuals, outside of small groups held together by ties of affect, cannot coordinate their behaviors solely through cooperation. This is why coercion, exercised through states, is almost universally deemed indispensable for establishing order. Thomas Hobbes was the first to make this argument. It is implicit in a few chapters of his massive *Leviathan* (1651). Shorn of its anachronistic and idiosyncratic aspects, Hobbes's account of the institution of sovereignty by self-interested individuals in a **state of nature**, a world in which coercive institutions are (imaginatively) abstracted away, underlies all subsequent statist (non-anarchist) views. In brief, for Hobbes and his successors, the state is a unique "solution" to what is, in effect, a generalized **Prisoners' Dilemma** problem, a situation in which the unintended consequence of individuals doing what is best for themselves is that everyone becomes worse off than need be. Hobbes reasoned that, given human nature and the human condition, a state of nature would be a devastating "war of all against all." This is why everyone in its grip desires order or peace, above all. But, in the absence of a "common power to hold . . . [individuals] in awe," and lacking any basis for trusting that individuals will comply with (mutually advantageous) agreements to coordinate their behaviors, no one has an incentive to do what is necessary to end the condition of universal war. The only way out of that untenable situation, Hobbes maintained, is to concoct a **sovereign**, a supreme **authority**, capable of instituting order by the use or threat of force.

Marxists, like Lenin, implicitly make two emendations of the Hobbesian case for states. The first, an implication of historical materialism, is that in class-divided (that is, pre-communist) societies, the problem states solve is not exactly to insure order for undifferentiated individuals, but rather to organize the ruling classes' domination of subordinate classes – in other words, to establish a particular order based on class **exploitation**. To this end, the state solves an intra-ruling class Prisoners' Dilemma problem – not, as Hobbes and his successors believe, an inter-individual problem. The second emendation of the Hobbesian case emerged from reflections on the rise and subsequent defeat in 1871 of the short-lived Paris Commune. It is that each kind of class society (feudal, capitalist, socialist) gives rise to its own distinctive form of the state – in other words, to distinctive repressive and perhaps also cultural institutions. It was this idea that Lenin developed in *The State and Revolution*; what distinguishes the dictatorship of the proletariat from bourgeois "class dictatorships" (including liberal democracies with representative governments) are the distinctive institutional forms of these epochally distinct regimes. These emendations of Hobbes's argument are seldom taken into account, even by professed Marxists. They are no less pertinent, however, for being ignored or unknown.

Further Reading

All modern political philosophy and, in the larger sense, all political philosophy since Plato, focuses on the state – from the particular vantage points of the authors in question. I elaborate on the pivotal Hobbesian and Marxian arguments sketched above in *Engaging Political Philosophy: Hobbes to Rawls* (Malden, MA: Blackwell Publishers, 2002), chapters 1 and 6; and, with special attention to Marx and Lenin, in *The End of the State* (London: Verso, 1987), chapters 7–8.

See also: ANARCHISM, CAPITALISM, CLASS, COMMUNISM, CONSERVATISM, CULTURE, DEMOCRACY, HISTORICAL MATERIALISM, JUSTICE, LEGITIMACY, LIBERALISM, LIBERTARIANISM, MARXISM, PUBLIC GOODS, REVOLUTION, SOCIAL DEMOCRACY, SOCIALISM

T

Technology

In ordinary speech, *technology* designates new technologies that depend on computer science, electrical engineering, and related fields. In its proper application, however, the term designates any and all ways human beings contrive to adapt means to ends — whether by making implements (tools, machines, etc.), organizing production processes (for example, by instituting particular divisions of labor), or by deploying knowledge of physical, psychological, and social phenomena in productive activities. In this larger sense, human beings have always utilized technology. Technological change has been a fact of human life since before the dawn of civilization.

Human beings everywhere and for all time have also had some form of social existence, the nature of which is shaped, at least in part, by available technologies. All social theories recognize this fact in one way or another. Some, like historical materialism, accord it preeminent attention. Historical materialism is a technological determinist theory: it holds that what explains the nature of societies at their most fundamental level of organization is the degree of development of the productive technologies at their disposal. Rival theories, with different explanatory objectives, are typically less focused on technology and technological change. But none of them disregard technology's importance to human life.

Theories of human progress of a post-**Enlightenment** vintage are generally committed to the view that technological advances improve human life. At comparatively low levels of technological development, this is certainly the case. But for levels of development attained during the twentieth century, if not before, the situation is less clear. While few today would doubt that advances in technology can improve the human condition, we now know that they cannot be assumed to do so automatically. The problem is not just that advances in military technology are capable of wreaking destruction to an unprecedented extent, putting the very existence of human life on earth in jeopardy, or that new technologies can put other living things at equally grave risk. The deeper problem is that technological innovation, motivated as it is by the needs of the prevailing economic structure – specifically, by the exigencies of capitalist development – has become disassociated from its original purpose, the satisfaction of human needs. Thus, many people work ever longer hours, at ever more onerous jobs, without becoming in any meaningful way better off (except perhaps in their ability to consume more things). This fact has helped to give rise to political tendencies that oppose technological development – even to the point of promoting **illusory** visions of a pre-industrial golden age. Nostalgia of this sort helped to mobilize support for fascism. But elements of the political Left have taken this idea to heart as well, particularly, in recent years, in the environmental movement. In practice, though, nearly all **progressive** social theories can be modified to accommodate recent concerns about technology, and nearly all critics of modern technology have nuanced positions on technological change. This is why, nowadays, even the most ardent believers in their potential benefits seldom give an unqualified welcome to technological advances.

What has come increasingly into question over the past century is not exactly the value of technological progress, but the nature and value of particular technologies – both in themselves and in the context of the economic and social order in which they operate. This is a salutary development that is bound to improve the cogency and relevance of economic, social, and political theory – in line with twenty-first-, not nineteenth-century conditions.

Further Reading

An accessible and comprehensive history of technology is James E. McClellan and Harold Dorn, *Science and Technology in World History: An Introduction* (Baltimore, MD: Johns Hopkins University Press, 1998). On the disconnect between technological advances and human well-being in late capitalist conditions, see Juliet B. Schor, *The Overworked American: The Unexpected Decline of Leisure* (New York: Basic Books, 1993).

Terror/terrorism

See also: CAPITALISM, ENVIRONMENTALISM, FASCISM, HISTORICAL MATERIALISM, LEFT/RIGHT/ CENTER, MARXISM, PROGRESS, SOCIALISM

Terror/terrorism

Terrorism is a **tactic** deployed by governments at war with other countries or peoples, by governmental or other authorities against the individuals they rule, and by insurgent individuals or groups against other individuals, groups, or governments. In all cases, it consists in the use or threat of violence against civilian populations – with a view to instilling a generalized and pervasive fear (terror). In principle, this tactic, like any other, is deployed for particular political objectives. However, in the heat of conflict or in circumstances that drive individuals or governments to despair or even out of (depraved) habit, terrorism can take on a purely expressive purpose, independent of any plausible political goal. By definition, terrorism is directed against non-combatants, not at military or quasi-military forces (including police). Deviations from this usage, though commonplace in mainstream political discourse, are misguided or disingenuous or both.

The histories of terrorism and warfare are thoroughly intertwined. From time immemorial, the slaughter or worse of civilian populations, along with the terror that inevitably follows, has been a consequence of war. In many times and places, terror was employed **strategically** as well. In recent centuries, as European conquerors settled the New World and plundered Africa, Asia and Oceania, they endeavored to instill terror in native populations, the better to assure their subordination. But it required twentieth-century advances in technology for terrorism to become a widespread **tactic** in war. The bombing of anti-fascist civilians by the **Nazis** in the Spanish Civil War, and then the widespread use of saturation bombing by all sides during World War II, made the terrorization of civilian populations a pervasive feature of modern warfare. That this strategy is terroristic is seldom recognized in common parlance. This is how it was possible for the Bush Administration, at the outset of its 2003 invasion of Iraq, to speak without irony of a "shock and awe" bombing campaign in the context of a "war on terror." Nevertheless, the kind of wholesale terrorism that the American government unleashed against Iraq fits the strictest definition of the term. Terrorism, so understood, is a tactic of the strong, not the weak; and of governments, not insurgents. It is plain that, throughout the twentieth century and in the first years of the twenty-first, the major imperial powers, especially the United States, have been its main purveyors.

The use of terror in governance has an equally long and gruesome lineage. In Western Europe, for many centuries, it was mainly the Roman Catholic Church, and then some of the Protestant churches that revolted against it, that wielded this weapon. Elsewhere too, terror was widely employed in the service of ecclesiastical hierarchies. **Secular authorities**, insofar as they can be distinguished from clerical ones, also used terror from time to time. But it was not until the French Revolution, during the so-called Reign of Terror, that terrorism came to be adopted as a matter of explicit policy. When they assumed state power, the French Jacobins, the most **radical** of the revolutionary groupings, used terror ostensibly to save the revolution from internal betrayal and machinations organized from abroad. It was in this context that the term entered the political lexicon. The Jacobins and their sympathizers endorsed its practice, at least in emergency circumstances; British conservatives (for example, Edmund Burke (1729–1797) in *Reflections on the Revolution in France* (1790)) invoked opposition to terror as an argument against revolutionary change. A similar thought was advanced by G.W.F. Hegel (1770–1831) in the chapter on "Absolute Terror" in *The Phenomenology of Spirit* (1807) and by others in the German **Romantic** tradition. Until quite recently, revolutionaries and counter-revolutionaries agreed that terror is an instrument revolutionary states often find it expedient to deploy in order to consolidate gains and to thwart counter-revolutionary forces. The **Bolsheviks** and their co-thinkers adopted this understanding. However, in contrast to late-nineteenth- and early-twentieth-century anarchism and populism, Bolshevism out of power was unambivalently hostile towards strategies intended to instill fear in civilian populations. But, following the Jacobin precedent, the Bolsheviks had no problem using terror in defense of the revolutionary state they established. At first, they did so reluctantly. Then, during the Stalin years, a more or less permanent use of terror became a pervasive feature of state policy. Fascist states also relied on terror to consolidate their rule. This fact helped to shatter the impression, implicit since the French Revolution, that terrorism was a creature of the Left. But it reinforced the idea that it is joined inextricably with revolutionary politics. This thought is basic to theories of totalitarianism. When states use terror against their own populations, it is to assure a measure of social cohesion through the inculcation of fear. Viewed in this light, liberal democratic regimes are not averse to kinder, gentler uses of terrorism. American history offers many examples – most recently, during the **Cold War** and, again in the Bush government's "war on terror."

Nowadays, it is retail terrorism–terrorism perpetrated by individuals or groups out of power, not by governments – that dominates public discourse. Indeed, the term is often used to designate only this phenomenon. This usage can be consistent with the strict definition of the term. Retail terrorism almost always involves violence on a comparatively small scale, unlike its wholesale counterpart. But it can have far-reaching consequences. Ironically, the fact that it can attests to the general democratization of the political culture. Retail terrorism can be effective because, in the modern world, governments require popular support for the implementation of their policies and, ultimately, for their legitimacy. In some circumstances, a generalized and pervasive anxiety can undermine that legitimacy. Given prevailing balances of power, it is extremely unlikely that retail terrorism, by itself, can lead insurgent movements to victory. Terrorism of this sort, in contrast to the kind governments perpetrate, is almost always a recourse of the weak. It is seldom able to modify the balance of power significantly. However, retail terrorism is potent enough to erode liberties and deform institutions. Thus, terrorists can inflict grave harm on their enemies. But they are seldom able to benefit those in whose behalf they fight. Typically, terrorist acts harm the communities from which terrorists come – not just in a moral sense, but in consequence of the retributions their terrorism incites. In many cases, though, retail terrorism does benefit the rulers of targeted countries; it strengthens their capacity to control their populations through fear. This fact, well understood by the political classes of all countries, helps to explain why rulers encourage the identification of retail terrorism with terrorism per se. In the United States, the Reagan government launched a concerted effort to that end in the 1980s. Because the threats they conjured up lacked substance, they failed ultimately in their effort to throw the country into a full-fledged "war on terror." But they did succeed in debasing political discourse and eroding Americans' liberties. Exploiting the genuine terror unleashed on September 11, 2001, the government headed by George W. Bush took up where the Reaganites failed. They succeeded too; at least for a while.

It is fair to say that the consequences of retail terrorism are almost always bad for everyone, though of course not to the extent that the terrorism perpetrated by states is. However, its bad consequences only partly explain why terrorism is morally indefensible. Terrorism generally fails the test of any **consequentialist** morality because it makes outcomes worse. More importantly, it fails utterly to accord with peoples' settled moral convictions – and the non-consequentialist (**deontological**) moral theories that give these intuitions expression. The problem with terrorism, reduced to its core, is that terrorists unfairly use people as means; that they treat persons like things, to be utilized or destroyed as need be – not as beings worthy of unconditional respect. Retail terrorists acknowledge the force of this conviction implicitly, when they argue, as the nineteenth-century French anarchist, Emile Henri famously proclaimed at his 1894 trial for terrorist acts that resulted in civilian deaths: "there are no innocents." Henri's intent was to collapse the distinction between combatants and non-combatants – to depict his murders as legitimate acts of war. There is no way such a thought can pass muster. But the fact that he believed it did and that his counterparts today do too speaks to a pervasive concern. From a moral point of view, terrorism is always and everywhere wrong. Terrorists must therefore resign themselves to the charge of immorality. They can do so consistently if they believe that the requirements of morality are overridden for transcendent reasons – because God wills it, for example, or because they are the agents of History. But they cannot do so for reasons that those who do not share their (contestable) convictions will find plausible.

Because there is a tendency to focus only on retail terrorism, and because the charge of immorality so clearly attaches to this notion, it is not surprising that the term is often wrested away from its strict meaning and applied, especially by governments and their **propagandists** in the mass media, to any political violence they disfavor, including violence directed against combatants in war situations. It is even commonplace that political opponents who don't engage in violence at all are deemed *terrorists*. Thus, the observation that one person's "freedom fighters" are another's *terrorists* rings true. But uses that trade on the sense of opprobrium the term connotes, in disregard of the facts, ought always to be avoided. After all, *terrorism* does have a clear meaning. To invoke the term recklessly in order to exploit its rhetorical force is to cast moral and intellectual clarity aside for the sake of some (usually nefarious) political purpose.

It is also plain that terrorism, because it is only a tactic, is not the sort of thing against which a war can be waged. Thus, the "war on terror" (or "terrorism"), launched by the Bush administration, is an incoherent notion. Interpreted charitably, the expression is a confused but expedient way to designate a war against those who would use terror against the United States. In practice, this amounts to a war, if not on Islam itself, on an increasingly important component of Islamic society – a component US foreign policy has formerly done much to foster. But, for both geopolitical and pecuniary reasons, this is a point that the American political class, dependent as it is on corrupt rulers of Islamic states, is reluctant to concede. Their reluctance is hypocritical. In view of the United States' role in purveying wholesale terror around the world, and its support for other states that do the same, and in view of the fact that Islamic (retail) terrorism is essentially blowback from earlier Cold War and imperial ventures, it is, to put it mildly, disingenuous for America's leaders to declare themselves at war with a tactic they have done so much to promote.

Further Reading

An informative account of modern terrorism is Walter Lacqueur, *Origins of Terrorism: Psychologies, Ideologies, Theologies, States of Mind* (Washington, DC: Woodrow Wilson Center, 1998). Since the 1980s, when the Reagan Administration first tried to launch a "war on terror," lucid analyses of the phenomenon have been swamped by politically motivated accounts of terrorist threats. However, there is useful information in some of the more scholarly work in this genre. See, for example, Bruce Hoffman, *Inside Terrorism* (New York: Columbia University Press, 1999). The fatuity of political uses of the threat of terror has been well documented for as long as political elites have floated so-called wars against it. See, for example, Edward S. Herman, *The Real Terror Network: Terrorism in Fact and Propaganda* (Boston: South End Press, 1982), and Noam Chomsky, *The Culture of Terrorism* (Boston: South End Press, 1988).

See also: ANARCHISM, CLASS, CONSERVATISM, DEMOCRACY, FASCISM, FREEDOM/LIBERTY, IMPERIALISM, LEFT/RIGHT/CENTER, LEGITIMACY, LIBERALISM, MORALITY, POLITICAL ISLAM, POPULISM, POWER, REVOLUTION, STALINISM, STATE, TECHNOLOGY, THEOCRACY, TOTALITARIANISM, VIOLENCE/NON-VIOLENCE, WAR

Theocracy

In a *theocracy*, priests or other clerics rule, ostensibly in behalf of the "higher power(s)" they represent. The term is also used to designate political formations in which priests or clerics exercise significant political influence, even if they do not directly occupy government posts. In countries like the United States, with a long-standing tradition of **secularism**, and in societies that have emerged out of struggles against clerical forces, the term is used disparagingly across the political spectrum.

It is a tenet of liberalism, and therefore of the dominant political culture of the West, that religion, once the main cement of society, ought to be solely a matter of private conscience. All **secular** political tendencies agree with liberals in this regard; they all aver that religious identifications ought to be of no political significance. It is not an accident that this conviction emerged in cultures shaped by Christianity. Thanks to its early history – first, as a messianic sect in Jewish Palestine, then as one of many religious tendencies within the Roman Empire – the first Christians eschewed political power, preferring "to render unto Caesar the things that are Caesar's." From the beginning, mainstream Christian doctrine recognized a distinction between temporal and clerical **authority**. Needless to say, Christian churches are not immune from theocratic temptations. Throughout their histories, many of them, including all the most important ones, have succumbed repeatedly. But historically Christian countries have never come close to becoming full-fledged theocracies, except for brief periods. In this respect, Christian culture stands apart from cultures shaped by other so-called world religions – not just Islam, but also Hinduism, Buddhism, and Shintoism. Judaism is another exception. It is worth noting, though, that theocratic sentiments have also emerged recently in some Jewish quarters. This is ironic. Because Jews were a besieged minority in the Christian world, they became wedded to secularist politics from the moment that the French Revolution opened up the possibility of equal citizenship regardless of creed. Even the state of Israel, though a confessional state, was founded on secular principles. Jewish nationalism took the place of the Jewish religion. But since the Jewish people comprised a religious, not a national or proto-national grouping for more than 2,000 years, it was probably inevitable that the Zionist movement would develop a theocratic wing, and that Israeli politics would in time take a theocratic turn. Today, Israel remains a secular state, but its institutions are increasingly under siege from theocratic forces.

Before castigating institutions or practices as theocratic, care should be taken not to confuse form and substance. Christian symbols and nominally Christian institutions dot the political landscape of decidedly post-Christian European countries. Similar phenomena exist in secular Japan and other countries with non-Christian religious traditions. For many of the citizens of these countries, however, religious symbols and institutions function more like repositories of national culture than as elements of a genuinely **theistic** faith. They are constituents of a fundamentally secular civil religion. In contrast, in the United States, the separation of church and state is constitutionally mandated and, for the most part, enforced. But the American political culture is less secular than that of other developed countries, and the United States is prone to fall prey from time to time to the wiles of barely disguised theocrats – not least at present. It could be argued that, where generally liberal conditions obtain, the separation of church and state works to the advantage of the churches, in part because they then avoid the hostility that the state inevitably draws to itself. No doubt, other factors weigh in too. But it is telling that, for more Americans than Europeans or Japanese, the churches are a refuge from the vicissitudes of life in an increasingly harsh and anomic capitalist society. The situation in officially atheist Communist countries was very similar, as has become clear since the fall of Communism. At least since the **Enlightenment**, it has been plain that there are sounder, more authentic ways to confront a heartless world. But this understanding has yet to reach large numbers of people in countries that are conspicuously secular in their institutional forms.

Further Reading

There is an enormous literature on past and present theocratic politics around the world and the struggles between proponents of theocracy and secularism. An informative historical account, focused on the Christian and Muslim worlds, is Talal Asad, *Formations of the Secular: Christianity, Islam, Modernity* (Stanford, CA: Stanford University Press, 2003). See also Pippa Norris and Ronald Inglehart, *Sacred and Secular: Religion and Politics Worldwide* (Cambridge: Cambridge University Press, 2004). Two pertinent studies of theocratic tendencies in recent American politics are Frederick Clarkson, *Eternal Hostility: The Struggle Between Theocracy and Democracy* (Monroe, ME: Common Courage Press, 1997) and Esther Kaplan, *With God on Their Side: How Christian Fundamentalists Trampled Science, Policy, and Democracy in George W. Bush's White House* (New York: New Press, 2004).

See also: CAPITALISM, CIVIL RELIGION, COMMUNISM, CULTURE, LEFT/RIGHT/CENTER, LIBERALISM, NATION/NATIONALISM, POWER, STATE, ZIONISM

Totalitarianism

In the 1920s, Italian fascists introduced the term *totalitarian* to describe the regime they created. *Totalitarianism* therefore had a positive connotation to those who first used the word. In the ensuing years, the term's meaning has remained roughly the same. A totalitarian state is one that mobilizes the entire population it governs in pursuit of a common, ostensibly redemptive aim (such as the realization of the spirit of a nation). To this end, it collapses the liberal distinction between the state and **civil society**, extending the scope of the state's **coercive** apparatus into what liberals would consider the private sphere. Thus, it is pervasive or *total*. Until the end of World War II, the term was used mainly to designate fascist regimes in Europe (including Nazi Germany), and political movements aimed at establishing fascist regimes elsewhere. It was used approvingly by the fascists themselves; disapprovingly by liberal democrats and socialists of all types (including Communists).

With the onset of the **Cold War**, anti-Communist **intellectuals** expanded the term's reference to include Communist regimes. Their point was that illiberal states of both the Left and Right share common features – especially a reliance on untrammeled police measures, periodic popular mobilizations, and **dictatorial** forms of governance sustained, in part, by a personality cult focused on a Leader. Totalitarian states of both the Left and the Right control ostensibly independent institutions like trade unions and churches, and regulate the daily lives of their citizens extensively. It was even suggested that Communist regimes were more totalitarian than fascist ones because, unlike the latter, they control the economic sphere along with everything else. Fascist states allowed capitalists to retain a measure of economic power and therefore independence. Hannah Arendt (1906–1975) was one of the first political thinkers to use the concept this way. Her book *The Origins of Totalitarianism* (1951) remains a point of reference. However, Arendt's account of totalitarianism was considerably more nuanced than the anti-Communist literature that followed. In the 1950s and 1960s, with fascism, especially **Nazism**, discredited and therefore no longer a threat, and with powerful Communist parties operating in many countries in the American sphere of influence, political thinkers in the West mounted a deliberate effort to turn the anti-fascist consensus into an anti-Communist one. The concept of totalitarianism was serviceable for this purpose.

In the final two decades of the Cold War, as the historical memory of Nazism receded, talk of totalitarianism also subsided. Correspondingly, the concept all but vanished from academic political theory. In Europe, especially France, some erstwhile Left philosophers recycled the old Cold War arguments, mobilizing them against the vestiges of Marxist politics in their own countries. But their views were unoriginal and never traveled well. With the demise of Communism, this attempt to revive the concept passed from the scene as well. Nevertheless, talk of totalitarianism never entirely disappeared. Indeed, there now appears to be yet another effort underway to reinsert the concept into mainstream political discourse. Today, however, the reference of the term is not what it was decades ago. *Totalitarianism* is still invoked to discredit so-called fundamentalist Communist regimes like the ones in North Korea and (for reasons that have mainly to do with domestic politics in the United States) Cuba. Capitalist-friendly Communist countries like China or Vietnam are seldom reproached on this account. But, with the demise of the Soviet Union, Communists are no longer the main targets. Instead, from the moment the United States declared a "war on terror," the term was deployed to discredit theocratic regimes in the Muslim world. This is an unfortunate turn of events. As the term's reference has expanded, its analytical usefulness, never very great, has diminished. The variety of regimes that fall under its scope have little in common – except that their political structures are not limited in the ways that those of liberal states characteristically are. To call them *totalitarian* explains nothing.

In the 1950s and 1960s, when the term was in wide use, some political theorists depoliticized its content, using it to describe the "totalizing" aspect of the modern state form of political organization – its concentration of political **authority** into a single institutional nexus. However, the insights conveyed under this rubric could have been less misleadingly represented in other terms. In any case, this usage has now all but disappeared too.

It was once conventional wisdom on the Left that, because of their totalitarian nature, fascist states would never evolve into benign liberal regimes. It was believed that fascism could only be overthrown by revolutions from within or by external force. When the term *totalitarian* was taken up by Cold Warriors and applied to Communist states, this idea was taken on board. It was said that totalitarian regimes would remain permanently in place unless they are overthrown. That contention was fundamental to the neo-conservative claim, promoted in the 1970s and 1980s, that, notwithstanding the commonalities in institutional structures, there is a distinction between **authoritarian** and totalitarian regimes. Authoritarianism was supposedly a transitional condition for states on the road to democracy; totalitarianism was a permanent cul-de-sac. This contention was popularized by Jeanne Kirkpatrick (1926–), Ronald Reagan's ambassador to the United Nations; she is widely believed to have been its inventor. What was obvious from the beginning, though, was that the real basis for the distinction was not what was claimed, but the fact that authoritarian regimes were friendly to the United States and useful to it, while totalitarian states, falling outside the American sphere of influence, were not. In any case, the vaunted distinction between totalitarianism and authoritarianism faded into oblivion just a few years after it was promulgated – as the Soviet Union imploded, and as ostensibly totalitarian regimes the world over evolved into states congenial to capitalists' interests and, not coincidentally, neo-conservative tastes. Somehow, though, the idea that regimes designated *totalitarian* cannot reform themselves survives. Neo-conservatives are especially disposed to press this view, as they pursue their vision of a Middle East congenial to American and Israeli interests.

It is clear why neo-conservatives and others won't abandon *totalitarianism*. Because it retains its pejorative connotations, the term is a weapon to wield against opponents. Moreover, there is just enough merit in the claim that all non-liberal regimes are alike that it cannot be immediately dismissed. But it has never been of much analytical use. This is even truer now that the term has migrated so far from the understandings of thoughtful early 1950s intellectuals like Hannah Arendt. Political Islam is a very different phenomenon from fascism and certainly from Communism. Polemical uses apart, there is no good reason to confound them all with the *same* description.

For genuine defenders of democracy, there is an additional reason to eschew the concept. For as long as Communism has fallen under the totalitarian rubric, some political theorists have maintained that **radical** democracy, because it is **utopian**, is the root cause of the totalitarian temptation. Democracy, the argument goes, must be tempered – by the institutions of representative government and by legally recognized liberal constraints. This position too cannot be easily dismissed. However, proponents of self-rule need not be deterred by it. Recent theories of deliberative and participatory democracy provide reasons for thinking that radical democratization need not culminate in totalitarian usurpations of democracy. To focus on totalitarianism in the way that Cold War political philosophers did is to set democratic theory on an unnecessary and unproductive course.

To be sure, utopianism is a danger and there is plainly a battle to be waged for liberal protections – in states where liberal protections are already, to some degree, established, and in historically illiberal ones. But it only clouds the stakes in these struggles to invoke a concept that is so thoroughly tainted by its Cold War past, and so vague as to be nearly useless. One might have thought that, with the Soviet model defunct, the term would disappear. That would have continued a trend that began in the waning decades of the Cold War, and that was nearly complete as the twenty-first century dawned. Now, however, the "war on terror" has brought *totalitarianism* back into public **consciousness**. Perhaps this is only a temporary detour in an otherwise inexorable trajectory. One would hope so. However important it may be to mobilize opposition to theocratic politics, Islamist and otherwise, it is well to resist the reintroduction of a flawed and tendentious concept in the service of a so-called war waged to mask an imperialist project.

Further Reading

Among efforts to depict both fascism and Communism as totalitarian movements, Hannah Arendt's *The Origins of Totalitarianism* (San Diego, CA: Harvest Books, 1973) is of continuing interest. A more recent account of totalitarian politics and its links to the history of political thought is Michael Halberstam, *Totalitarianism and the Modern Conception of Politics* (New Haven, CT: Yale University Press, 2000). A depoliticized version of the concept is evident in Sheldon S. Wolin, *Politics and Vision* (Princeton, NJ: Princeton University Press, 1960). Interestingly, the 2004 reissue of a much-expanded version of this magisterial and extremely worthwhile work deemphasizes the earlier usage. The now-lapsed but once-commonplace distinction between authoritarian and totalitarian regimes never quite rose to the level of political theory, though it was implicit in right-wing policy documents of the 1980s, and continues to resonate in neo-conservative circles. The most interesting uses of the distinction can be found in contemporary analyses of Chinese post-communist communism. See, for example, Suijan Guo, *Post-Mao China: From Totalitarianism to Authoritarianism?* (Westport, CT: Praeger, 2000). Perhaps the most cogent attempt to join totalitarianism to (radical) democracy is Jacob Talmon, *Origins of Totalitarian Democracy* (New York: W.W. Norton and Co., 1970). The two volumes of Karl Popper's *The Open Society and Its Enemies*, vol. 1 (Plato), vol. 2 (Hegel and Marx) (Princeton, NJ: Princeton University Press, 1971) famously impute the origins of modern totalitarianism to elements of the Western philosophical tradition. The French *nouveau philosophes* of the 1970s and 1980s made careers out of pursuing a similar line of thought, though with much less originality and cogency. An example is André Glucksmann, *Master Thinkers* (New York: Harper Collins, 1980).

See also: CAPITALISM, COMMUNISM, DEMOCRACY, FASCISM, FUNDAMENTALISM, IMPERIALISM, LEFT/RIGHT/CENTER, LIBERALISM, MARXISM, NATION/NATIONALISM, NEO-CONSERVATISM, POLITICAL ISLAM, SOCIALISM, STATE, TERROR/TERRORISM, THEOCRACY, WAR

Trotskyism

Leon Trotsky (1879–1940) was, after V.I. Lenin (1870–1924), the principal architect of the October Revolution (1917) in Russia. In the ensuing civil war, he was the founder and leader of the Red Army. But, then, as Joseph Stalin (1879–1953) came increasingly to control the Communist Party apparatus, Trotsky's power waned. In 1929, after a series of intra-party struggles that Trotsky lost, Stalin sent him into exile. Eventually, Trotsky took up residence in Mexico City where, in 1940, Stalin had him assassinated. The term *Trotskyist* was first used in the 1920s to designate Trotsky's political allies in the Soviet Union and in Communist parties abroad. But it was not until the 1930s that Trotsky's followers around the world began to think of Trotskyism as a full-fledged alternative to Stalinism. Intent on belittling their opponents, Stalinists customarily referred to Trotskyists as *Trotskyites*, the connotation being that they comprised a small, though dangerous, sect, not a significant political tendency. This usage persists in the mainstream political culture, where the term *Trotskyite* still predominates. Trotskyists were never very numerous and, unlike Stalinists and Maoists, they never controlled a state. Ironically, though, Trotskyism survived on the political landscape long after Stalinism – the name, if not the reality – was universally rejected. It is unclear, however, what Trotskyism means in the absence of its historical antagonist. This is one reason why the movement has dwindled in recent years.

In the mainstream political culture, the conventional wisdom is that Stalinism and Trotskyism are branches of the same tree, and that their differences seem large only to partisans on one or the other side. This is like saying that Catholicism and Protestantism are basically the same phenomenon. From a great enough distance, this contention is true. But to focus on their differences at that level is to overlook some of the most important controversies of recent political history. Trotskyists see themselves as genuine Leninists. Since Lenin was nothing if not **strategically** flexible, and since the circumstances Lenin (and Trotsky) confronted at the time the **Bolsheviks** seized power in Russia differed considerably from those that Communists there and elsewhere faced from the 1920s on, it is impossible to evaluate this contention definitively. It is fair to say, though, that it is plausible.

Trotsky never questioned the basic institutional structure of the Soviet state under Stalin's rule, and he thought it imperative to maintain the Soviet system even after Stalin had taken control of it. By the mid-1930s, however, some of Trotsky's dissident followers did offer critiques of the Soviet model – still in the name of Leninist orthodoxy. During the **Cold War**, these self-identified Trotskyists became **third campers** – resolutely anti-capitalist, but anti-Soviet too. Orthodox Trotskyists, following Trotsky's lead, maintained a more ambivalent attitude towards the Soviet Union. But Trotsky's analyses of the Soviet experience were sufficiently complex that even third campers could plausibly claim not to have broken from the spirit of Trotsky's thought.

Trotskyism

Stalinists were committed to the doctrine of socialism in one country – the idea that, even in the absence of a world revolution, it is possible – and, indeed, necessary, if the world **proletariat** is to advance – to build socialism in the Soviet Union alone. Despite his dedication to maintaining the regime the Bolsheviks established in the absence of the world revolution all Bolsheviks expected, Trotsky insisted, as any classical Marxist would, on the impossibility of building socialism in a single, underdeveloped country. Thus, Trotskyists were proponents of world revolution – not as a distant and increasingly remote goal, but as an essential component of their immediate political practice. By their own lights, they were the ones who kept the revolutionary flame alive after Stalin turned the Communist movement into a conservative political force. In his magisterial *History of the Russian Revolution* (1930), Trotsky likened the ascension of Stalin to the French Thermidor – a reference to the *coup d'état* of 9 Thermidor (July 27, 1794) that marked the downfall of Robespierre and Jacobin rule in revolutionary France. From this point on, with the popular masses (or rather their ostensible representatives) out of power, the French Revolution veered to the right. But just as revolutionaries continued to support the Directory and later the **dictatorship** of Napoleon Bonaparte (1769–1821) in opposition to a counter-revolutionary restoration, Trotsky urged continuing support for the Soviet regime, even after it "degenerated" into its Thermidor phase. He was equally insistent, though, on the need for a **radical** change of course.

Trotsky ventured that a Thermidorian moment is an inevitable feature of the revolutionary dynamic. What is crucial, therefore, if revolutions are not to be stalled or turned around, are deliberate political initiatives arising out of a popular base. Thus, in opposition to the doctrine of socialism in one country, Trotsky, following some suggestions of Marx's, formulated a doctrine of **permanent revolution**. Exactly what he had in mind was never entirely clear. For many decades, Trotskyists read their own ideas into his proposals. In retrospect, permanent revolution appears to amount to much the same as the Maoist notion of **cultural revolution**. No Maoist would concede this description, inasmuch as the Chinese Communists, for their own reasons, insisted, at least nominally, on identifying with Stalin against Trotsky. Neither would any Trotskyist press the point. For them, Maoism is a continuation of Stalinism, and therefore a force to oppose. In any case, the kind of cultural revolution Trotsky's doctrine might be said to have anticipated is of a very different order from the one that actually occurred in China from the mid-1960s to the mid-1970s. That chain of events was a nearly unmitigated disaster. It is understandable, therefore, that contemporary Trotskyists would not want to draw attention to the similarities between Trotsky's and Mao's thinking.

Stalinist literature and art was notoriously crude, reflecting the cultural level of the dictator himself. In the 1930s and 1940s, many **intellectuals**, eager to make common cause with the world proletariat, effectively acceded to Stalinist cultural norms. But it was never an easy alliance, despite the arguments that were mustered in defense of a "socialist realism" accessible to workers and peasants. Trotsky, however, was an intellectual in the grand tradition. Small wonder, then, that Trotskyism attracted intellectuals and artists into its fold. Despite its **workerist** pretensions, Trotskyism has always been more a movement of intellectuals than of workers. In this respect too, it differs from its Stalinist rival. Trotskyism's appeal to intellectuals was strengthened by the fact that its claim to legitimacy within the larger Communist movement consisted in its purported fidelity to Leninist orthodoxy. Where Stalinists could point to the ostensible successes of Five Year Plans and the might of the Red Army, Trotskyists had only textual exegesis to offer in rebuttal. This situation rendered the Trotskyist movement attractive to persons with a taste for disputation over texts. In conjunction with unrelenting Stalinist **propaganda**, it also helped to render it odious to many workers who might otherwise have been inclined to follow a Trotskyist line.

The effect of sending Trotsky into exile and then definitively reading him out of the Communist movement was analogous to a Church schism. Trotskyists became the Protestants of the Communist world. Hostile to the authority of Church hierarchies, the Protestants had only their own consciences to guide their interpretations of sacred texts. The result was perpetual splintering, as interpretations differed. Where the one "true" Church had enforced unity, a multitude of ever-smaller sects developed. Despite Trotsky's best efforts, something similar happened within the Trotskyist movement. Trotsky sought to maintain unity by establishing a Fourth International. He argued reluctantly but trenchantly that the Communist Third International had become hopelessly deformed. But once the bond of orthodoxy had been broken, there was no turning back. Trotskyists succumbed to sectarian temptations similar to those that led Protestant Churches to multiply. Trotskyist groups proliferated, even as the Trotskyist movement itself grew slowly or not at all.

A point of doctrinal difference among Trotskyists, and between Trotskyists and Maoists, centered on their respective views of the Soviet Union. For Trotsky himself, and for his orthodox followers, the Soviet Union remained a

Trotskyism

"workers' state," albeit a deformed or degenerated one. More radical Trotskyists and third campers denied that the Soviet Union was socialist at all. Ironically, Maoists came to the same conclusion – castigating the Soviet Union as "state capitalist," a term introduced by third campers. Nowadays, with the Soviet Union gone, this debate has an anachronistic aspect. But there is still much that can be learned from it. Even so, a political orientation that takes that defunct state as its point of reference is bound to wither away as an express political tendency. This process is already underway. It would be a great loss, however, if the theoretical insights and moral imperatives the Trotskyist movement generated in over a half century of sustained political and theoretical work were to become forgotten.

Further Reading

The best account of Trotsky's life and thought is still the three volumes of Isaac Deutscher's biography, *The Prophet Armed: Trotsky 1879–1921*; *The Prophet Unarmed: Trotsky 1921–1929*; and *The Prophet Outcast: Trotsky 1929–1940* (London: Verso, 2003). Among Trotsky's own writings, of special pertinence are *The Revolution Betrayed* (New York: Dover, 2004) and *Literature and Revolution* (Chicago: Haymarket Books, 2005). A useful analytical account of Trotskyism in theory and practice is Alex Callinicos, *Trotskyism* (Minneapolis: University of Minnesota Press, 1990). On American Trotskyism, see James P. Cannon, *The History of American Trotskyism, 1928–38: Report of a Participant* (Atlanta, GA: Pathfinder Press, 2002).

See also: CAPITALISM, COMMUNISM, CULTURE, INTERNATIONALISM, LEFT/RIGHT/CENTER, LEGITIMACY, LENINISM, MAOISM, MARXISM, REVOLUTION, SOCIALISM, STALINISM, STATE, WAR

U

Utilitarianism

In ordinary speech, *utilitarian* means "useful." Though it is seldom the case, what is described as utilitarian may also be aesthetically pleasing or otherwise remarkable. But, when the term is used in its colloquial sense, the idea is to call attention just to its usefulness. In the philosophical traditions that shape our political culture, *utilitarian* has a different meaning. There the term refers to an **ethical** theory, an account of how individuals ought to act, and to a public philosophy, an account of how social practices and institutional arrangements should be organized. In both cases, the guiding idea is the same: what is right – and therefore what ought to be – is what maximizes overall goodness. Thus, for philosophers, it is the good, not the useful, to which the term *utility* refers. That we should seek to maximize utility in this sense is utilitarianism's fundamental claim. In retrospect, one can find intimations of this doctrine in ancient Greek and Roman thought. But *utilitarianism*, as we now understand it, was an invention of British moral philosophers in the late eighteenth and early nineteenth centuries.

Utilitarians are committed to the view that, ultimately, there is one supreme good, and that all other goods – or at least all other goods that matter for ethical deliberations or for deliberations about public policies and institutional arrangements – are only means for increasing how much there is of the one supreme good. For utilitarians, the good that should be maximized is welfare or well-being. Welfare is susceptible to a variety of interpretations. But it is not a mere place-holder term, void of all content. All the standard interpretations converge on the idea that welfare, however understood, is a good for individuals. If we suppose, then, that we can identify feasible alternatives well enough to deliberate about their consequences, utilitarianism tells us to choose the one that brings about the greatest amount of welfare – in other words, the one that makes individuals as well off as they can be in the circumstances. Utilitarians typically do but, strictly speaking, need not claim that the supreme good is the only good there is. They could maintain, for example, that there are aesthetic goods that are not means for maximizing welfare. They could even hold that there are many incommensurable goods. But they must deny that maximizing or even maintaining these goods has any relevance in deliberations about what to do.

Philosophers standardly distinguish **consequentialist** from **deontological** moral theories. For consequentialists, the only thing that matters in **normative** deliberations and assessments are consequences. For deontologists, consequences matter too, but not exclusively. John Locke's (1632–1704) notion of inviolable, morally primary rights that trump all other considerations in normative deliberations is a deontological theory. **Kantian** moral philosophy provides another, more plausible, example. Utilitarianism is a consequentialist theory. But utilitarians are not concerned with all consequences, just consequences for individuals' well-being or, what comes to the same thing, utility consequences.

Utility measures value. Since utilitarians believe that, for deliberative purposes, there is only one intrinsic value, and since they characteristically identify that end-in-itself with welfare, we can say that utility measures welfare. The first generation of utilitarian philosophers, Jeremy Bentham (1748–1832), James Mill (1773–1836) and others, identified welfare with pleasure or, if they believed there is a difference, as James' son, John Stuart Mill (1806–1873) did a generation later, with happiness. Today, the idea that welfare designates a conscious state (like pleasure or happiness) coexists with the alternative idea that welfare should be identified with desire satisfaction; in other words, that individuals are well off to the degree that their desires (or, sometimes, their preferences) are satisfied. There are also interpretations of welfare that have nothing to do with individuals' desires – that instead identify the good with certain, ideal-regarding states of affairs. The influential British philosopher G.E. Moore (1873–1958) even produced a version of utilitarianism that identified the good with a unique, directly intuited property that, unlike other interpretations of welfare, is not part of nature, where "nature" designates whatever is **empirically** accessible.

However variously welfare is understood, utilitarians agree that it is measurable at least in principle, and that *utility* is its measure. There are, in fact, two types of welfare measurement that utilitarianism assumes. There is, first of all, intrapersonal utility measurement. There must be a way to assign (cardinal) numbers – 1, 2, 3 . . . and so on – to the conscious states like pleasure or happiness or to the satisfied desires of each individual in a theoretically meaningful (nonarbitrary) way. Once an appropriate scale is established, these numbers would convey pertinent information about how individuals rank the alternatives in contention, and also about the comparative intensity of their pleasures or desires within these rankings. Then it must be possible in principle to measure utility interpersonally – to compare the utility levels of different persons. For utilities to be compared, they must be expressible in a common unit. Needless to say, no one knows how to do this except in crude, intuitive ways. Nevertheless, utilitarian economists have contrived ingenious means for making interpersonal comparisons in stylized cases.

Utilitarianism hardly stands or falls on the practical feasibility of making precise utility measurements. But it would be in jeopardy if the very idea of welfare measurement were somehow incoherent. In the early part of the twentieth century, some economists and social theorists believed that utilitarianism does fall on this account. They were concerned that interpersonal utility comparisons assumes access to the contents of minds other than our own – a notion that has been out of favor from the time that René Descartes (1596–1650), the most influential philosopher of the early modern period, deemed such knowledge impossible. It was, in part, this consideration that led them to substitute the idea of **efficiency** (construed as **Pareto optimality**) for the utilitarian maximum. A state of affairs is Pareto optimal when any change would make at least one individual worse off in a welfarist sense.

Utilitarian theories are, above all, moral theories; theories that prescribe deliberation from an **agent-neutral** point of view. However, their purchase on morality is distinctive. Utilitarians believe that, for each individual, there is, in principle, a well-defined "utility function" – a way of representing individuals' welfare levels in interpersonally comparable cardinal numbers. To seek to maximize one's own utility is to deliberate in an egoistic (and therefore non-moral) way. To seek to maximize the sum of all individuals' utilitities is, however, to deliberate in an agent-neutral and therefore moral way. If we think of U_s as a (numerical) representation of overall utility, for individuals 1 through n, and if we represent their respective utility functions as $U_1, U_2, \ldots U_n$, then $U_s = U_1 +$

$U_2 + \ldots U_n$. In the utilitarian view, morality requires that we maximize the value of U_s. However, it does not require that we always deliberate with that end in mind. Utilitarians could concede that, in some circumstances, the best way to maximize overall welfare, U_s, may be for each individual 1 through n to deliberate in an egoistic way. Although he was not strictly a utilitarian, and although his claim lends itself to non-utilitarian construals of social welfare too, this was essentially the thought advanced by Adam Smith (1723–1790) in *The Wealth of Nations* (1776) when he asserted that private greed in market transactions produces the best possible public outcomes, as if by the workings of an "invisible hand."

Utilitarianism is **individualistic** not just because its conception of the good, welfare (however interpreted), is an individualistic notion, but also because the quantity it seeks to maximize is the sum of individuals' utilities. It is also egalitarian in the sense that it treats individuals equally as bearers of utility. In sum, utilitarianism is a consequentialist, welfarist, individualistic, and egalitarian moral theory.

It is also a theory of great plasticity. It has proven capable, over the years, of surviving many ostensibly withering rebuttals. There are, as noted, problems clustering around the notion of utility that led economists and others to abandon it, while attempting to retrieve as much as they could of utilitarianism's basic ideas. Others fault utilitarianism for its passivity; for the way it treats persons as bearers of utility rather than as doers who flourish through the exercise of their capabilities. Still others maintain that, because it is a consequentialist theory, utilitarianism cannot adequately account for defensible intuitions we have about particular institutions – for example, punishment. Utilitarians can only look to the future; thus, they can only justify punishment for its deterrent effects – not for its role in rectifying or expiating past wrongs. The list goes on. The most telling, and probably the most pervasive case against utilitarianism comes from **Kantians** who fault it for its apparent inability to accord to moral personality the unconditional respect that it is due. In treating individuals as bearers of utility, utilitarians can find themselves advocating sacrificing the welfare of some in order to maximize welfare levels overall. This, Kantians maintain, constitutes a fundamental offense to justice. These and other objections may ultimately be correct. But utilitarianism is sufficiently malleable to sustain modifications that have enabled it to withstand the challenges that have come its way, at least to the satisfaction of its many continuing adherents.

That so much effort has been expended defending utilitarianism is not surprising. Its core doctrinal commitment articulates a sound intuition – that in acting and in organizing social and political life, what matters is the impact of what we do on affected individuals. Utilitarianism expresses this position in an intuitively appealing, commonsensical way: by treating individuals as equals, and then adding up the measures of their respective welfares. To the extent that this program can be made to work, one very simple principle would govern all practical deliberations. As the first generation of utilitarian philosophers boasted, this would amount to a breakthrough in the "moral sciences" even more remarkable than Sir Isaac Newton's (1643–1727) formulation of earthly and celestial mechanics in three (not just one!) laws of motion constituted a breakthrough in the physical sciences.

On the Left, especially the Marxist Left, utilitarianism has generally been disparaged; at least in part because of the way it reduces normative deliberations to calculations of costs and benefits. Utilitarians, it is said, are glorified bookkeepers. Historically, though, utilitarianism has been associated more with the Left than with the Right. As some nineteenth- and twentieth-century British socialists made clear, it has strongly egalitarian implications, at least when joined with assumptions common in the economic theory of the time. Consider, for example, income distribution. Utilitarianism favors that distribution which maximizes utility overall. If we suppose that there is diminishing **marginal utility** for income – in other words, that the more income one has, the less utility one derives from an additional increment – and if we stipulate (probably harmlessly, though plainly contrary to fact) that all individuals process income into utility at the same rate, then it follows that the best distribution is an equal distribution. Suppose, for example, that all individuals earn $50,000 per year, except Jones who earns $60,000 and Smith who earns $40,000. Given our assumptions, the utility loss to Smith by redistributing $10,000 of his income to Jones would be more than offset by the utility gain to Jones. The distribution that would maximize welfare overall would therefore be the one that distributes income equally.

Environmentalists sometimes find utilitarianism objectionable because of its claim that the only thing that matters in practical deliberations are effects on persons. Environmental degradation might be something utilitarianism could recommend against, but only if there are individuals who would be made worse off in some pertinent sense by it. A sound environmental philosophy, some might think, should take the interests of non-human things more directly into account. No doubt, there is merit to this complaint. But its consequences are mitigated somewhat if we realize that the usual utilitarian understandings of welfare – as pleasure (or happiness) or desire satisfaction – are states of all sentient beings, not just human beings. Thus, it could be argued that taking only human beings into account in making utilitarian calculations is indefensible, and that the interests of at least some other parts of nature should be considered too. It should be noted, though, that if the problem of interpersonal utility comparisons seems intractable, how much more so would be the problem of interspecies comparisons! How can we compare our own pain or pleasure with that, say, of a giraffe? And even if we could find a common unit of measurement, should we weigh the giraffe's desires or conscious states (if any) equally with our own? That these questions can only be answered in arbitrary ways suggests the futility of trying to extend utilitarianism's moral compass beyond the confines of its founders' horizons.

In short, utilitarianism is a moral philosophy beset with grave, possibly insurmountable, difficulties. But it is a way of thinking about what we ought to do and how our institutions should be constructed that is eminently worth engaging with. Properly elaborated and refined, it is, at the very least, a plausible and appealing theory. Utilitarianism is therefore likely to remain a pole of attraction, and a point of contention, for a long time to come.

Further Reading

Among the classics of the utilitarian tradition are John Stuart Mill, *Utilitarianism* (Indianapolis, IN: Hackett, 2002) and Henry Sidgwick, *Methods of Ethics* (Indianapolis, IN: Hackett, 1981). A more recent work that is arguably of comparable importance is Derek Parfit, *Reasons and Persons* (Oxford: Oxford University Press, 1986), chapters 1–9. For G.E. Moore's idiosyncratic account of welfare, see G.E. Moore, *Principia Ethica* (Cambridge: Cambridge University Press, 1993). Though somewhat dated, a sense of the merits and shortcomings of utilitarianism can be gleaned from the debate between J.J.C. Smart and Bernard Williams in *Utilitarianism: For and Against* (Cambridge: Cambridge University Press, 1973). A sympathetic and useful account of utilitarianism and its differences from rival views is also available in Shelly Kagan, *Normative Ethics* (Boulder, CO: Westview Press, 1997). On utilitarian justifications for institutional arrangements, see Robert Goodin, *Utilitarianism as a Public Philosophy* (Cambridge: Cambridge University Press, 1995).

See also: CULTURE, ENVIRONMENTALISM, EQUALITY/EGALITARIANISM, JUSTICE, LEFT/RIGHT/CENTER, MARKETS, MARXISM, MORALITY, RIGHTS, SOCIALISM, VALUES, WELFARE/WELFARE STATE

V

Values

Value has many colloquial and quasi-technical meanings, most of which have little political import. For the "classical economists" of the early nineteenth century, it was a fundamental concept – values determine prices. Because Karl Marx (1818–1883) cast his account of "the laws of motion" of capitalist economies as a **critique** of classical political economy, the economic concept has, from time to time, taken on a political significance. But the sense of the term that matters for political life today has no connection with these economic debates or with most other meanings that the term can assume. It does, however, have a tenuous – and misleading – connection to a venerable philosophical debate about the relation between *values* and facts.

How best to conceive this relation is a still unsettled question. The **positivist** tradition, following the lead of the British **empiricist** philosopher David Hume (1711–1776), has always insisted on a rigorous separation. Nineteenth- and twentieth-century intellectual currents that owe a similar debt to G.W.F. Hegel (1770–1831) propose more nuanced connections. There are other even less settled and arguably deeper questions about values: among them, how to conceive their nature, how to understand the difference between values that have implications for what we do, as in **ethical** theory, and those that do not, as in aesthetic judgments, and how ultimately to grasp the nature of **normativity** itself. For reasons that were always obscure but that have something to do with Marxism's

Values

Hegelian roots, some Marxists believed that identifications with positivism were to be avoided at all costs. They were therefore inclined to suppose that an answer to at least the first of these questions mattered politically. But they never succeeded in making a defensible case in support of this supposition, and it is difficult to see how anyone could. Answers to philosophical questions about values can be of great importance for any number of purposes. But they have no immediate political implications. How values are understood philosophically and what one thinks and does politically are different matters.

Nevertheless, the American political scene in recent years has become rife with talk of *values*. Part of the explanation for this turn of events has to do with the efforts of churches and other religious organizations to influence and, where possible, to control political life. This has been, in the main, a project of the Right, though some left-leaning religious individuals and groups are not beyond attempting the same thing – albeit more defensively than aggressively. Part of the explanation also has to do with a popular revulsion towards the amoral character of modern politics, where reasons of state typically take precedence over the moral constraints that govern private lives. But what those who advocate for values seem to have in mind hardly addresses what is at stake in this complaint. In fact, political entrepreneurs who appeal to values often do so less out of conviction than in order to manipulate popular sentiments to their own advantage. Thus, they are a part of the problem they inveigh against. In any case, these explanations tell only part of the story. The main problem is just what it has always been since the dawn of **enlightened**, **secular** politics: ignorance and confusion on the part of those who are susceptible to being useful to entrenched elites.

According to the conventional wisdom, the 2004 Presidential election in the United States that retained the Bush Administration in power, despite its manifest unworthiness to rule, was settled by "values voters." What values could they have had in mind? Evidently not any that are offended by lying the country into war, unleashing murder and mayhem, condoning and even encouraging torture, hastening environmental catastrophes, and stealing from the poor to give to the rich. Rather, George W. Bush was favored by values voters because he conspicuously endorsed a **patriarchal** sexual ethic that opposes abortion and same-sex marriage, and because he is inclined to treat questions of sexual conduct that have public health consequences as matters of theological concern. In the fantasy world the Right cultivates and exploits, values contrast not with facts, but with reasonableness itself – in other words, with the modern, scientific worldview and the cast of mind it promotes. In these circumstances, even transparent hypocrisies can and do become the norm.

It is Protestant evangelicals in the United States who comprise the shock troops of the values movement. Lately, however, they have been joined by fundamentalist Jews and Muslims, and by conservative Catholics. Thanks to Catholicism's long-standing support for so-called rational theology, the inclusion of Catholics in this unholy alliance inevitably introduces a measure of philosophical sophistication into what would otherwise amount to little more than a **reactionary** reflex. Thus, some so-called values concerns – those having to do with abortion, contraception and euthanasia, for example – are sustained by a theology that promotes "reverence for human life." Ironically, in view of their historical opposition to the Roman Catholic Church, some of the more thoughtful Protestant evangelicals have taken up this Catholic line. For the Catholic hierarchy, however, reverence for life also entails opposition to capital punishment and to wars of the kind that American governments routinely wage. Most evangelicals, along with most rank-and-file Catholics, reject these implications of their adopted rationale. But even if its thinking is more consistent, the Catholic hierarchy exhibits a similar cast of mind. For them as much as for the others, it is still the maintenance of a patriarchal order based on sexual repression that matters most. Thus, during the 2004 Presidential election, Catholic bishops went so far as to suggest that Catholic politicians who support abortion rights, like Bush's opponent, John Kerry, should be denied communion. The support of all Republicans and most Democrats, including Kerry, for the death penalty and for Bush's war in Iraq elicited no comparable threat.

In exposing the shallow and reactionary nature of values-based politics, philosophy can be therapeutic. Were standard understandings better known, the ignorance and confusion that sustains this morass would diminish. In the final analysis, though, philosophical disputes about the nature of value have as little to do with the promotion of justice and **virtue** as, say, philosophical disputes about the nature of numbers have to do with the practice of mathematics. If only for this reason, it is probably best not to join the Right's values debate, except to debunk it. To advance the values enlightened people everywhere have always upheld, the wiser course would be to change the conversation – back to where the struggle for liberty, equality and **fraternity** can more effectively resume.

243

Further Reading

On economic uses of the term, see Maurice Dobb, *Theories of Value and Distribution Since Adam Smith: Ideology and Economic Theory* (Cambridge: Cambridge University Press, 1973). Sophisticated discussions of the relation between facts and values (in the pertinent philosophical sense) can be found in Peter Railton, *Facts, Values, and Norms: Essays Toward a Morality of Consequence* (Cambridge: Cambridge University Press, 2003). Historically important conceptions of value are discussed in Stephen Darwall, *Philosophical Ethics* (Boulder, CO: Westview Press, 1998). Recent philosophical treatments of issues clustering around notions of value and associated accounts of normativity include Christine M. Korsgaard, *The Sources of Normativity* (Cambridge: Cambridge University Press, 1996), and T.M. Scanlon, *What We Owe Each Other* (Cambridge, MA: Belknap Press, 2000). See also Ernest Sosa, *Normativity: Philosophical Issues* (Malden, MA: Blackwell Publishers, 2006). On contemporary uses of the term in American politics, see John Kenneth White, *Values Divide: American Politics and Culture in Transition* (London: Chatham House, 2002).

See also: COMMUNITY, CONSERVATISM, EQUALITY/EGALITARIANISM, FEMINISM, FREEDOM/LIBERTY, FUNDAMENTALISM, JUSTICE, LEFT/RIGHT/CENTER, LIBERALISM, MARXISM, MORALITY, STATE, THEOCRACY

Violence/non-violence

The paradigmatic *violent* act is an assault – an aggressive infliction of physical force on people by people. However, in both political and extra-political contexts, the term is often used more loosely. Because the term implies moral condemnation, it lends itself to self-serving applications. Thus, it is sometimes used to refer to any use of force that the speaker or writer wishes to condemn. There are other, even vaguer uses that also carry negative connotations. *Violence* can denote unruly or non-decorous behavior. *Violent* sometimes even contrasts with "calm." In political theory, the term can also be used in a more neutral way – as a synonym for (**coercive**) force. It was this meaning that Max Weber (1864–1920) had in mind when he said of the state that it exercises a monopoly of the (legitimate) means of violence. Violence can also be used to bring about consequences that do not directly involve the coercion of particular individuals. Thus, terrorism is violent; it demoralizes public opinion by establishing a generalized sense of anxiety.

In the first instance, it is actions that are violent. But the term can also be used to describe representations of actions – violent television shows or movies, for example – and non-representational works of art like abstract paintings or music. The term is sometimes even applied to states of affairs or to the way they are experienced. Thus, we speak of "violent situations," understanding the expression to refer to more than just the violent acts taking place at the time. Because so much imprecision surrounds the term, its senses are often confounded. It is fair to say, therefore, that the word is more useful for its rhetorical effects than for the analytical clarity it provides. But, for all its flaws, the term is probably indispensable. The vagueness and ambiguities that attach to *violence* are generally harmless, and there are enough similarities linking its various senses to warrant a common description.

The usual understanding is that violence is a means to an end. For those who believe that, in some or all cases, only ends are appropriate objects of moral (or extra-moral **normative**) assessment, it then follows that the only standard for justifying or condemning violence in particular instances is its efficacy for bringing about the objective(s) for which it is deployed. It is this position that people have in mind when they ask whether "the end justifies the means." (Clearly, this is a misleading formulation. What else, besides ends, could "justify" means?) It is doubtful, though, whether anyone has ever actually held the view that *only* ends, never means, matter from a moral point of view. The (near) consensus view is that morality (or perhaps other normative considerations instead of or in addition to morality) constrains the choice of means, including those for which the (imprecise and ambiguous) description *violent* is apt. But even if there really were no normative constraints on means, the fact that most people believe that there are must be taken into account in assessing the efficacy of violent means in particular circumstances. This fact alone often diminishes the effectiveness of violent means, especially when disempowered groups or individuals, unable to influence the terms of debate, are its perpetrators.

As Weber's definition suggests, violence is intrinsic to the exercise of political **authority** – not just in warfare, but also in the ordinary operation of the state. The retail violence of opponents of established regimes pales in comparison with the wholesale violence of **de facto** legitimate governments. In both cases, though, advocates of violence typically assume a "surgical" model – according to which a judicious and skillful use of violent means facilitates the realization of desired ends without, in the long run, affecting outcomes in unpredictable or untoward ways. This assumption is often problematic. The means used to bring about outcomes typically do affect outcomes in unexpected and detrimental ways. Thus, in addition to moral constraints, those who advocate violence must consider whether the means they would deploy will adversely affect the ends they seek to realize.

There have been political thinkers who maintained that violence is justifiable for reasons that have nothing to do with the realization of particular goals – that it is, or can be, redemptive or empowering, or that it is conducive to instilling **virtues** like courage, bravery, and boldness. This view has roots in many cultures. It is especially prominent in so-called "warrior societies." Though their bloody practice belies the hesitations they profess, the Abrahamic religions, and especially Christianity, have not been well disposed towards this position. Nevertheless, glorifications of violence have emerged from time to time in Christian (and Jewish and Islamic) contexts and, in the modern period, in **secular** contexts as well. On the Left, proponents of violence include revolutionary Jacobins and other revolutionaries throughout the nineteenth and twentieth centuries. On the Right are the fascists and the political theories they drew on for inspiration. Even some **Third Worldists** advance violence-friendly views – arguing that it alone can liberate oppressed peoples psychologically.

This has always been a minority position, however. The near-consensus view has been that an ideal world would be a non-violent one, and therefore that there is a presumption in favor of non-violence. Whoever would exercise violent means shoulders the burden of justifying their use. But it is also very nearly the consensus view that this presumption is easily overcome – that violence is often justified in our imperfect, violent world. Indeed, the vast majority of people nowadays, as in the past, appear to believe that, at least in some circumstances, to abstain from violence is to be complicitous in its perpetuation. For most people, therefore, the pertinent question is: to what degree should people living in the actual non-ideal world, where violence is a fact of daily existence, act as they would in ideal conditions? Or, equivalently, when are recourses to violence, with their attendant dangers, justified?

Proponents of *non-violence* believe that the answer to this last question is Never. Almost without exception, their reasons are moral – they conclude that morality precludes all (or nearly all) recourses to violence. For some, though, instrumental considerations also militate against violent means. They believe that, even with the best of "surgical" intentions, violence is generally not effective in the ways its defenders assume, and that, therefore, it is never (or almost never) wise to resort to it. No doubt, most contemporary defenders of nonviolence believe this, even if it is not their main reason for being non-violent. Otherwise, they would find themselves in the uncomfortable position of maintaining

246

that, for moral reasons, they are obliged to help make outcomes worse than need be.

While agreeing that an ideal world would be a non-violent one, those who believe that the presumption in favor of non-violence can be and often is overcome deny that there are **categorical** moral constraints on recourses to violence. This is the view of the vast majority today. Now, as in ages past, most people believe that, for the sake of its consequences, violence is sometimes justified – in both war and peace. This view does not imply that non-violence can never be effective or that, contrary to what its promoters intend, it is part of the problem, not part of the solution. It is only to maintain that, in the world as it is, non-violent **strategies** cannot be relied upon *exclusively* for making the world better or even for simply making it less violent.

As a strategic doctrine, *non-violence* carries with it many of the imprecisions that attach to *violence*. Thus, it is impossible to say precisely what non-violent political action involves. At one extreme, any form of political activity – voting, demonstrating, petitioning, attending meetings – that is not violent (in some plausible sense of the term) is non-violent. This is the everyday meaning of *non-violence*. For some political activists, however, non-violence implies forms of struggle involving **civil disobedience** and passive resistance – along the lines advocated by Mahatma Gandhi (1869–1948) in his campaign to overthrow British rule in India. In the face of warfare, **pacifists** had long deployed similar techniques, but Gandhi was the first to employ them in order to free a people from colonial domination. Gandhi's strategy and tactics have been subsequently adopted by others. Following his lead, from roughly the late 1950s until the middle of the 1960s, the Civil Rights movement in the United States was committed to non-violence in this sense.

With respect to non-violence, the Left has generally been of one mind with the mainstream political culture – holding that an ideal society would be non-violent, that there is therefore a presumption in favor of non-violence, but that a judicious use of violence sometimes is necessary in our imperfect world. To deny this conclusion, one would have to defend the claim that nothing can override the presumption for non-violence – a claim that is implausible on its face for both moral and instrumental reasons. Thus, the general attitude on the Left towards proponents of non-violence has been much like its secular component's attitude towards religious **progressives** – to welcome their dedication, to admire their courage, to make common cause with them whenever possible, but not to endorse their core beliefs or to accept their comradeship uncritically.

Violence/non-violence

Further Reading

A useful, though dated, historically focused reflection on the concept is available in Hannah Arendt, *On Violence* (San Diego, CA: Harvest Books, 1970). Among those who propose redemptive uses of violence are Georges Sorel, *Reflections on Violence* (Cambridge: Cambridge University Press, 1999) and, from a Third World perspective, Frantz Fanon, *The Wretched of the Earth* (New York: Grove Press, 1965). A more nuanced view is implicit in almost any work of Friedrich Nietzsche, but nowhere more so than in *Thus Spoke Zarathustra* (Mineola, NY: Dover, 1999). On non-violence, see the writings collected in Mahatma Gandhi, *Gandhi on Non-Violence* (New York: New Directions, 1965). Weber's account of the state's foundation in violence and its implications for political morality can be found in Max Weber (Hans Gerth and C. Wright Mills, eds.), *From Max Weber: Essays in Sociology* (Oxford: Oxford University Press, 1958).

See also: CIVIL RIGHTS/CIVIL LIBERTIES, CULTURE, FASCISM, LEFT/RIGHT/CENTER, LEGITIMACY, MORALITY, POWER, REVOLUTION, STATE, TERROR/TERRORISM, WAR

W

War

Wars are organized, violent conflicts that persist for extended periods of time. They are typically comprised of battles, but are not reducible to them. As Thomas Hobbes (1588–1679) made clear in *Leviathan* (1651), a state of war consists not in overt combat, but "in a known disposition thereto." Hobbes's understanding is standard. Nevertheless, Hobbes used *war* in an idiosyncratic way. He called the generalized antagonism he found in the **state of nature**, "where every man is enemy to every man," a "*war* of all against all." The usual view, even for political philosophers influenced by Hobbes, is that wars are waged by political entities, not individuals. For as long as the state system has been in place, the assumption has been that wars are waged by states. The exception is that where other forms of political **authority** exist – for example, in tribes or clans or where territories are ruled by so-called "war lords" outside the state system – these non-state forces can also fight wars among themselves or against genuine states.

War contrasts with *peace*. Few, if any, human societies have been uniformly and consistently peaceful for extended periods; war has been a fact of human life since before the dawn of civilization. But since all **ethical** codes restrict violence, and since murder and mayhem are everywhere proscribed, justifications for war have always been problematic. So pervasive is the phenomenon, though, that purported justifications abound. Few ethical codes prohibit war altogether. Indeed, in nearly all cultures, conceptions of **virtue** characteristically include the virtues of warriors. In many cultures, they are especially recognized and celebrated.

There have been as many variations in forms of war as there are variations in human societies. In some times and places, warfare was a highly ritualized activity. Elsewhere, it has been conceived and practiced on an "anything goes" basis. Reasons for fighting can be similarly various. In the modern world, wars are characteristically waged for reasons of state. As the German theoretician of warfare Karl von Clausewitz (1780–1831) famously maintained, war is an extension of diplomacy. As such, it has a self-limiting aspect. In the twentieth century, this understanding partially gave way as wars of (total) annihilation unfolded – for example, during World War II, in the **Nazi** campaign against the Soviet Union, and in the American war against Japan. Wars of annihilation are hardly new in human history. What is new are the means of waging them. When the United States used nuclear weapons against Japan in 1945, the prospect of a thoroughly annihilating war – devastating the entire planet and destroying human civilization – entered into the **consciousness** of humankind. Not surprisingly, ensuing wars have been more limited in scope and means than was the case during the world wars that preceded them.

There exists a body of theory that addresses the question of when, if ever, wars are *just*, and the distinct question of *justice in wars* – that is, of what morality requires in the waging of wars. Much of this theory derives from the work of Catholic theologians, some of it centuries old. Thus, it is almost universally maintained that wars of aggression are not just. Indeed, it is sometimes held that the only just wars are those that are fought in self-defense to resist aggression. It is also widely agreed that it is never just to attack civilian populations deliberately. Wars are fought between official (and identifiable) combatants, organized into militaries. Even in the Middle Ages, however, it was difficult to reconcile this conviction with the practice of warfare. Thus, Catholic thinkers developed the doctrine of **double effect**, according to which it is permissible to do something wrong in the course of doing something that is justifiable, so long as the wrong is not intended (even if it is foreseen). Thus, civilians can rightfully be harmed or even killed during warfare, so long as killing them is not the combatants' express intention. The doctrine of double effect has been employed by Catholic and other casuists outside the theory of warfare. For example, in the Catholic view, abortion is always impermissible; not even saving the life of the mother countervails the prohibition against it. But radiation treatments for cancer are permissible upon pregnant women, even if they have the foreseeable consequence of aborting the fetus she is carrying. Because it is obviously susceptible to abuse, Catholic casuists were disposed to apply the doctrine of double effect cautiously. The contemporary notion of "collateral damage" to which American and other military planners appeal is a morally sloppy descendant of it. Its transparently hypocritical aspects exemplify what more scrupulous theorists of warfare sought to guard against.

From time immemorial, occupied and **oppressed** peoples have fought back against their oppressors. Thus, irregular warfare, both organized and spontaneous, has long existed. In the twentieth century, during the Chinese Revolution and then in anti-colonial and anti-imperialist struggles in Asia, Africa, and Latin America, guerilla warfare – the most common form of irregular warfare in **peasant** societies – took on new forms and a more central importance. This phenomenon coincided with the emergence of the nuclear threat, and therefore with a renewed dedication to limited war. So long as the bipolar post-World War II order existed, the two superpowers found it in their mutual interests to limit the devastation they each could level against insurgents in their respective spheres of influence and in the **Third World.** However, with the demise of the Soviet Union, the United States was no longer held back by this constraint. Nevertheless, the fact remains – it is difficult and often impossible to repress genuinely popular insurgencies or to enforce occupations for protracted periods of time.

War has always wreaked havoc on the civilian population of countries at war as well as on active combatants. It is sometimes difficult even to distinguish these harms because, throughout history, wars have been fought mainly by soldiers taken out of the general population and forced into service. During the French Revolution, in the heat of revolutionary fervor, there was the first mass mobilization (the *levée en masse*). There have been others subsequently, especially in the twentieth century. To some extent, the world wars democratized warfare. But the norm is still for wars to be fought by professional soldiers – with an officer class drawn from elite social strata and the mass of soldiers drawn from desperate populations at the lower rungs of the social order.

The American people have generally been wary of the martial life. Thus, the United States has always had difficulty raising armies. To this end, American political elites have usually preferred the carrot to the stick in recruiting armed forces. But the carrot is not always enough. Conscription was employed during the Civil War and then in World War I. However, it was not until World War II that it was widely supported; no doubt because the war itself was. This support did not last long. Opposition surfaced during the Korean War, though the institution survived for two more decades. When conscription helped to turn popular sentiment in the United States against the Vietnam War, it was ended summarily. Subsequent US wars have been fought by volunteers, rather than conscripts; though there is little doubt that most volunteers are actually economic conscripts who enlist for want of better alternatives. There is no surprise in this. Outside those cultures that are exceptionally militaristic, citizen soldiers do not do well in imperialist wars. For ordinary people to kill or be killed, to maim or be maimed, they need reasons they can accept. Imperialist rationales seldom satisfy this requirement.

With the aid of servile media, governments can sometimes succeed for a while in gaining acquiescence and even support for imperialist ventures. This has been the rule in the United States at least since the end of World War II. Nevertheless, the memory, real or imagined, of a country drawn together by a common existential need to fight in a "good war" persists. So too does the idea of mass mobilization. It is these associations that political leaders draw on when they speak of wars on real or imagined societal evils, as they have done frequently in recent decades. This use of the term was pioneered during the Johnson Administration for "the war on poverty." It was carried over, with dimishing plausibility, to "wars" against cancer and inflation in the administrations of Nixon and Ford. A so-called "war on drugs" was launched during the Reagan years. It continues to this day without genuine or lasting successes. Recently, under George W. Bush, a "war on terror" (or "terrorism") has been unleashed. Obviously, it makes no sense to wage war on a **tactic** or on an abstract noun. Almost as obviously, the war on terror (or terrorism) is a cover for imperialist wars abroad and for assaults on liberties at home. That this usage could be accepted so widely attests to the fact that our political vocabulary, along with our general political culture, has become extraordinarily debased.

Given existing and foreseeable military technologies, for humankind to flourish or even survive it is urgent that war be eliminated altogether. To that end, it is necessary to think clearly about war and therefore useful to struggle against unwarranted extensions of the concept. The "war on terror" is an especially egregious instance of the problem. Plainly the best way to combat terrorism is to attack its causes – not to exacerbate them, with potentially devastating consequences, under the pretext of waging war against them. The very idea of a war on terror (or terrorism) is cynical or confused or both – and therefore extremely dangerous.

Further Reading

Geoffrey Parker (ed.), *The Cambridge Illustrated History of Warfare* (Cambridge: Cambridge University Press, 2000) provides a richly informative account of Western styles of warfare from the time of the ancient Greeks to the present. A more theoretical account of the role of warfare in shaping the nature and course of human history is Michael Mann, *The Sources of Social Power: Volume 1, A History of Power from the Beginning to AD 1760* (Cambridge: Cambridge University Press, 1986), and *The Sources of Social Power: Volume 2, A History of Power from 1760–1914* (Cambridge: Cambridge University Press, 1993). On Hobbes's account of "the state of war" as "the natural condition of mankind," see Thomas Hobbes (C.B. Macpherson, ed.), *Leviathan* (Harmondsworth, UK: Penguin, 1980), chapters 13–14. I discuss Hobbes's position in *Engaging Political Philosophy: From Hobbes to Rawls* (Malden, MA: Blackwell Publishers, 2002), chapter 1. For Clausewitz's account of war as an extension of diplomacy, see Carl von Clausewitz, *On War* (London: Penguin, 1982). Throughout history, the best accounts of war have been literary (or, more recently, journalistic). Perhaps the greatest masterpiece of this genre is Leo Tolstoy (Rosemary Edmonds, trans.), *War and Peace* (London: Penguin, 1982).

See also: CULTURE, DEMOCRACY, FREEDOM/LIBERTY, IMPERIALISM, JUSTICE, MILITARISM, MORALITY, REVOLUTION, STATE, TECHNOLOGY, TERROR/TERRORISM, VIOLENCE/NON-VIOLENCE

Welfare/welfare state

Philosophers and economists use *welfare* and *well-being* interchangeably. The idea, in colloquial terms, is that one's welfare or well-being is enhanced the better off one is. *Welfare* is a placeholder term, susceptible to various interpretations. But it is not void of content: *welfare* designates a particular kind of good – specifically, a good for individuals. In the British moral philosophical tradition in which this usage developed, that good is usually understood as desire satisfaction or, more traditionally, as pleasure or happiness. Individuals' welfares are enhanced the more their desires are satisfied or, alternatively, the more they experience pleasure or happiness. Less subjective notions of welfare also occur. Thus, it can be said that individuals are well off to the degree that certain objective conditions obtain. Utilitarianism is a welfarist theory because it holds that, in deliberating about what to do, what matters is how much welfare there is. It is for this reason too that economists use "welfare economics" to designate **normative** economic theory.

Because it is widely believed that public policies should enhance welfare, the term came to be used in connection with institutional arrangements concocted for that purpose. Hence the term *welfare state*. Welfare state institutions are mainly publicly organized insurance programs intended to keep individuals socially and economically secure in the face of the inevitable vicissitudes of human life and the particular insecurities capitalist economies generate. Welfare state institutions also provide relief from poverty – by providing cash or in-kind assistance to the poor. In popular political discourse in the United States, *welfare* is often used only in this sense.

Because it has come to be associated with socially stigmatized and politically disempowered poor people, *welfare* has become a term of opprobrium in the United States, where class prejudice has been successfully exploited by the political class, Republican and Democrat, to mobilize opposition to comparatively feeble welfare state institutions. At risk are not just measures aimed at the relief of poverty, but also the social insurance programs that comprise the bulk of even the American welfare state. In Northern Europe, where poverty has been largely eliminated, thanks as much to powerful labor movements as to welfare state programs themselves, social insurance remains enormously popular. It is popular too in the United States. This is why, although the American welfare state, such as it is, has been under attack since the early 1980s when Ronald Reagan became president, it is still largely intact. However, with a political class that has careened sharply to the right in recent years, its survival is more precarious than it has ever been.

What moves the attack on the welfare state in the United States and elsewhere is not so much a clear perception of self-interest on the part of the well-off as the ideologically driven conviction that individuals have entitlements to their **market**-generated holdings. Adherents of this libertarian view find transfer payments problematic because they seem to violate these entitlements. Evidently, libertarian ways of thinking about distributive justice have seeped into the body politic. To be sure, everyone, beneficiaries and victims alike, would be better off if they could individually avoid paying taxes for welfare state transfer payments. They would be better off still if they could avoid taxes altogether. In recent years, political entrepreneurs in the Republican Party have exploited this preference shamefully, and Democrats have gone along with this. Everyone agrees, however, that taxation is indispensable because states need the revenues they provide to supply public goods. It is an open question how the welfare state fares in light of this fact. It could even be argued that what welfare states do is provide public goods which everyone, well-off or not, has an interest in having supplied. After all, no one benefits from social and economic insecurity.

254

If anything, the self-interest of the rich, even more than of the poor, favors stability. Thus, the rich should be willing to pay for social and economic security, if that is the only way it can be obtained. This is the conclusion that economic elites in other countries have reached. Because economic elites in the United States are unusually enamored of libertarian self-justifications, they are more likely to oppose welfare state measures – partly from conviction, partly because they misconstrue their own interests.

The traditional, conservative case against the welfare state is an extension of nineteenth-century arguments against the "moral economy" of pre-capitalist times. These arguments take many forms. Some appeal to notions of individual responsibility. Thus, it is maintained that individuals ought to be held accountable for their own economic well-being, and that no one else, including the state, has any responsibility for it. Any of a variety of underlying moral philosophical justifying theories, including utilitarianism, can be invoked in support of this view, though, in nearly all cases, it would be more natural to draw contrary conclusions. Or it could be argued that it promotes or even exemplifies **virtue** to go it alone, as it were, in market economies, and therefore that welfare state measures militate against virtue. These arguments raise complex issues. But the welfare state's defenders have little to fear from any of them. Appeals to individual responsibility run aground on the realization that market-generated shares are not in fact the exclusive results of individuals' own efforts. Their nature and size are affected to a far greater extent by a panoply of social practices and institutional arrangements, past and present – including the state's legal system, its **monetary** policies and, of course, its **fiscal** system, including its tax policies. The virtue-based argument fails too insofar as it depends, as do all arguments appealing to virtue, on a vision of the good society. Perhaps some fictional Dickensian characters or contemporary followers of Ayn Rand (1905–1982) would defend such a vision. Hardly anyone else would. A society in which no one helps anyone else is unappealing even to doctrinaire conservatives.

During the 1980s, as the assault on the welfare state unfolded in the English-speaking world, the Right's argument took a slightly different turn. The idea was not so much that welfare state goals offend notions of moral responsibility or virtue, but that welfare state means are self-defeating. So far from helping to advance welfare, the argument went, the welfare state creates social pathologies, giving rise to a permanent "underclass." On this view, the ostensible beneficiaries of welfare state programs are, in fact, made worse off by them. What they need is not assistance in the form of cash or in-kind services, but "tough love" to force them into paid employment. Needless to say, the vast majority of the beneficiaries of poor relief are victims of circumstances beyond their control, including an absence of employment opportunities; "workfare" programs do little to rectify this situation. This argument is therefore a non-starter. Moreover, it only pertains to programs that aim to relieve poverty; social insurance programs, the mainstays of the welfare state, are unaffected by it. Nevertheless, the case for tough love drifted over into where it had no plausible application. Programs like workman's compensation turned up guilty by association. In retrospect, this way of thinking appears to have been motivated more by political exigencies than philosophically or empirically compelling arguments. At a time when welfare state institutions still enjoyed considerable support, it was easier to attack their efficacy than their goals. Now that the pendulum has moved farther to the right, it is safe, again, to attack the objectives too. Thus, efficacy arguments against the welfare state are now heard less frequently, while the old moralistic case is enjoying a resurgence.

The development of welfare state institutions was perhaps the signal achievement of the twentieth century in developed capitalist countries, and a triumph for the Left. However, the welfare state was not entirely a creature of the Left. To be sure, some of its proponents, especially in the Scandinavian countries, saw it as a way to advance the socialist (or social democratic) project of moving beyond capitalism by **decommodifying** key aspects of social life. But this was seldom the principal objective of the welfare state's founders or defenders. Especially in the English-speaking world, welfare state measures were advanced by liberals seeking only to mitigate capitalism's more unsavory aspects. There were also proponents of welfare state institutions, especially in continental Europe, who were motivated by conservative convictions. They realized that capitalism upsets traditional forms of life; their goal therefore was to counteract its effects. By instituting health and unemployment insurance, for example, and even by pursuing high-wage policies, they endeavored, in the face of inexorable economic forces, to retain a family structure in which the man of the house is the breadwinner and the wife stays at home, rearing children and attending to domestic concerns. Today, these various and conflicting motivations have melded together to the point that they barely register at the level of institutional design. In today's world, the welfare state is unequivocally the main bulwark against the vicissitudes of life in capitalist societies.

Because welfare state programs target particular categories of individuals, they can be stigmatizing in ways that are detrimental to self-esteem and social inclusion. This danger is greatest with programs that aim at poverty relief. But all welfare state programs are potentially **paternalistic** in ways that can diminish freedom. In offering assistance to targeted populations, they promote views about how individuals ought to live. Inevitably, these views are those that predominate in the general culture. In this way, the welfare state can still function as a conservative force.

In principle, the welfare state could be reengineered with a view to minimizing its conservative aspects. It is an open question, though, whether this is the best approach to follow. One could argue, as some now do, that public provision should take a different form altogether. This thought underlies proposals for unconditional basic income grants or other unconditional transfers of wealth. In today's world, proposals of this kind are more nearly philosophers' fantasies than feasible political programs. This has more to do with the political climate than with the merits of the proposals themselves. But it is nevertheless a fact that cannot be wished away. This is why, for now, even as we envision qualitatively new and better ways to address the problems the welfare state was devised to confront, the main battle is to defend and improve what we already have.

Further Reading

A comprehensive account of the nature of the welfare state and of traditional and recent arguments for and against it can be found in Robert Goodin, *Reasons for Welfare: The Political Theory of the Welfare State* (Princeton, NJ: Princeton University Press, 1998). See also Brian Barry, "The Welfare State Versus the Relief of Poverty," *Ethics*, vol. 100 (1990), pp. 503–29; reprinted in Robert Goodin and Allen Ware (eds.), *Needs and Welfare* (London: Sage, 1990). The emergence of welfare state institutions is discussed in Gosta Esping-Andersen, *The Three Worlds of Welfare Capitalism* (Princeton, NJ: Princeton University Press, 1990). Esping-Andersen's analysis is criticized sympathetically and developed further, with ample empirical documentation, in Robert E. Goodin, Bruce Headey, Ruud Muffels, and Henk-Jan Dirven, *The Real Worlds of Welfare Capitalism* (Cambridge: Cambridge University Press, 1999). On the American case, see Theda Skocpol, *Social Policy in the United States* (Princeton, NJ: Princeton University Press, 1995). Unconditional basic income grants, as an alternative to traditional welfare state forms of public assistance and social insurance, are debated in Philippe Van Parijs, *Arguing for Basic Income: Ethical Foundations for a Radical Reform* (London: Verso, 1992). An alternative form of wealth redistribution is proposed in Bruce

Welfare/welfare state

Ackerman and Anne Alstott, *The Stakeholder Society* (New Haven, CT: Yale University Press, 1999). The merits and shortcomings of their proposal in comparison with basic income are debated in Bruce Ackerman, Anne Alstott, and Philippe Van Parijs, *Redesigning Distribution: Basic Income and Stakeholder Grants as Cornerstones for an Egalitarian Capitalism* (London: Verso, 2006).

See also: CAPITALISM, CLASS, CONSERVATISM, CULTURE, FEMINISM, FREEDOM/LIBERTY, JUSTICE, LABOR MOVEMENT, LEFT/RIGHT/CENTER, LIBERALISM, LIBERTARIANISM, MARKETS, MORALITY, PUBLIC GOODS, SOCIAL DEMOCRACY, SOCIALISM, STATE, UTILITARIANISM

Z

Zionism

For some, *Zionism* is the national liberation movement of the Jewish people; for others, it is a form of racism. In fact, Zionism is a form of nationalism that embodies distinctive tensions and contradictions. At least since the 1967 Six Day War between Israel and its Arab neighbors, geopolitical factors have rendered it an especially prominent and potentially dangerous presence on the world scene.

Zionism differs from other nationalisms in several respects. First, even if all nations are "imagined" into existence, the Jewish people lack many of the usual raw ingredients that go into the **social construction** of nationalist identifications. Divided into distinct regional groupings and scattered in many countries, the Jews were without a common territory and language for nearly two millennia. Though (usually) prohibited by prevailing **authorities** and by Jewish law and custom from marrying non-Jews or even from interacting socially with them, there was in fact considerable "intercourse." Thus, Jews became, in time, more like their neighbors in physiognomy and culture than like their co-religionists in distant Jewish communities. All nationalists strain to maintain claims of common descent; Jewish nationalists have an especially difficult time of it. The idea that, after nearly 2,000 years, Jews share a common history is strained too. Jewish communities everywhere were persecuted and segregated. Otherwise, those that were separated from one another by vast distances had little in common apart from Judaism itself. Circumstances did conspire to keep expressions of Jewish religiosity more or less similar everywhere. What has joined Jews together, then, is, in the main, a shared religious heritage. In this respect, Jewish nationalism is unique. It is also unique in having arisen in a liberal and **secular** milieu, but in reaction to a rising tide of persecution that was more a backlash to liberalization than a regression to long-standing theologically based animosities. From its inception, Zionism simultaneously expressed the universalist aspirations of the historical Left but also a sense of its failure. In this respect, Zionists and **anti-Semites** have always agreed that, in the end, Jews cannot coexist with non-Jews; that "the Jewish problem" can only be solved by separating Jews from other populations.

Like other nationalisms, Zionism did not spring whole cloth out of nothing. From the time of the Roman destruction of the Jewish state in Palestine in AD 70, a longing to return to "the promised land" had become a fixed conviction of the dispersed Jewish population. But this longing was expressed in a religious form; it had no political significance. To be sure, in certain periods, a few scholars and zealots took up residence in Palestine, but it was an article of faith that the return of the Jews to Zion would be the work of a Messiah who would appear at the end of time. In the aftermath of the American and French Revolutions, assimilation became possible for Jews in North America and Western Europe. Assimilation was almost never complete and, in any case, only a few were tempted. However, a far-reaching cultural assimilation did occur as secular and **enlightened** values took hold in Jewish communities. This phenomenon affected the meaning of the idea of a return to Zion. What had once been a tenet of an otherworldly faith became, for some Jews, a call for cultural identification, consistent with the spirit of the age. Palestine remained a pole of attraction. But, for emancipated Jews, its theological significance gave way to more secular understandings. The idea was that it should become a center of a Jewish cultural renaissance in which distinctively Jewish, but still secular, values would flourish. This de-theologized version of cultural Zionism attracted some Jewish intellectuals. It had little or no mass following.

The Zionist movement was therefore marginal and basically apolitical until Theodor Herzl began to organize for the formation of a Jewish national state as a solution to the problem of anti-Semitism. In the wake of the Dreyfus Affair in France and lethal anti-Semitic pogroms in Russia and Eastern Europe, he convened the first World Zionist Congress at Basel in 1897. Thereafter, Zionist groups were established in countries with significant Jewish populations. Still, Zionism remained a fringe movement. It was, at first, divided on the question of Palestine. For those early Zionists whose main concern was the security of Jewish populations, Palestine was not essential. But, from the beginning, most political Zionists thought otherwise. Thus, a majority of the delegates to the 1905 Zionist World Congress rejected a British offer of a homeland in Uganda, preferring to seek concessions from Palestine's Ottoman rulers. In 1917, with the British at war with Turkey and, by then, in effective control of most of the Ottoman Middle East, Britain issued the Balfour Declaration, establishing a national homeland for the Jewish people in Palestine. When World War I concluded, the League of Nations gave Great Britain a mandate to rule Palestine. Jewish immigration then proceeded in fits and starts, subject to the vagaries of British imperial policy. As could only be expected, the indigenous Arab population resisted the invasion of their land. Because they did, and in light of the discovery of oil in the Middle East, the main objective of the British came to be to maintain control of its subject Arab populations. To this end, they restricted Jewish immigration and endeavored to keep the settler population from igniting overt hostilities. This set the Jewish settlers on a collision course with the British. Influential Jews in Britain, France, and the United States kept the British from clamping down too hard. Nevertheless, on the eve of World War II, tensions were rife.

In the 1930s, the Zionist movement was still not supported by a majority of diaspora Jews, religious or secular. Most Left political movements, with their large Jewish memberships, were also hostile, seeing Jewish nationalism as an obstacle in the way of the universalist vision they upheld. It therefore required a confluence of events during and after World War II – including, above all, reaction to the Nazi genocide, but also a very dire refugee problem in Europe and an interest, on the part of both the Soviet Union and the United States, in undoing British rule in the Middle East – to lead to the formation of the state of Israel in 1948. In very short order, the vast majority of Jews worldwide came to support the Israeli state. Very few, however, chose to live there, at least so long as they had other choices.

With the establishment of the state of Israel, the meaning of Zionism became radically transformed. Cultural Zionism faded from the scene; today, hardly a remnant survives. So too did proposals for bi-national solutions to the problem of Jewish and Arab coexistence. Zionism became, in effect, an ideological extension of the Israeli state. Zionists might take any of a variety of views towards Israeli governments, but no Zionist questions the legitimacy of the regime itself.

With the state in place, religious Jews made peace with it. There are, to this day, ultra-orthodox Jews who reject the very idea of an Israeli state. But the vast majority of believers have become, if anything, even more ardent Zionists than were the founding generations of the movement. For secular Jews, the idea of a "promised land" had always been an embarrassment. By contrast, religious Zionists unquestioningly accept this notion and its theological presuppositions. However, even secular Jews never entirely separated Zionism from Judaism. How could they? There was no other bond uniting all Jews. The extent to which the first Zionists could be anti-clerical was therefore circumscribed. Zionists might endorse the universalistic principles of the American and French Revolutions. But, in practice, they were willing to make concessions. This is why, from its inception to this day, the orthodox rabbinate controls important aspects of Israeli civil society – including decisions about who, in the end, is a Jew and therefore who is entitled to full citizenship rights in the Jewish state.

The state of Israel is widely lauded in the United States and elsewhere as a democracy, the only one in the Middle East. If *democracy* denotes a parliamentary system of government, then indeed it is. But as a "state of the Jewish people" with a large Arab population it has never been and can never be a state of its citizens, as all genuine democracies are. Zionists, before and after statehood, struggled with this problem. But there is no way to square the circle. In the pre-state period and in the first several decades of Israel's existence, this stubborn fact could be and often was overlooked. But, in the shadow of a four-decade-long occupation of Palestinian territories, and with the Arab population in Israel itself growing, denial is no longer an option. It has become increasingly clear to thinking people everywhere that the Israeli state can be Jewish or it can be democratic, but it cannot be both.

For some decades after its founding, Israel was also lauded, in Left circles, as a bastion of socialism. The Israeli economy did indeed have a large public sector, where the state and other Zionist institutions, left over from the pre-state period, controlled the "commanding heights" of the economy. And, of course, Israel's collective agricultural enterprises, its *kibbutzim*, inspired the world. In recent decades, however, many of the more progressive components of Israel's economic and social system have declined in importance. The Israeli economy today is unequivocally a capitalist economy. Contemporary Zionist ideology reflects this reality.

The main contours of the Israeli political scene, its division into left and right wings, were established before independence. For the first quarter century of the state's existence, the Left ruled continuously. Since the mid-1970s, the Right has mainly been in charge. Inasmuch as Zionist ideology has become subordinate to the interests of the Israeli state, this is reflected in the rightward turn in Israeli politics. Unlike the Zionists of a generation or more ago, the majority of contemporary Zionists are in thrall of the Israeli Right.

Until the mid-1960s, American policy towards Israel was friendly but restrained. Like the British before them, American policy makers were wary of siding too blatantly with Israel, lest their favoritism jeopardize their control of the oil-rich Middle East. They were especially wary of pushing Middle Eastern states into the Soviet camp. Also, before the 1956 Suez War, in which Israel made common cause with Great Britain and France against Egypt, American dominance of the region was not yet total. But in the aftermath of Suez, as the United States replaced British and French influence in the region, Israeli policy makers staked everything on close relations with the United States. Then the stunning Israeli victory in the Six Day War demonstrated, for all to see, that Israeli military superiority in the Middle East could be deployed in the service of American interests. Since that time, Israel has become, in effect, an offshore asset of American imperialism.

It is often observed that, while Israel is dependent on American diplomatic and financial support, Israel's influence over American policies in the Middle East is considerable; in other words, that the tail wags the dog. It is impossible to say which matters more – Israel's usefulness to American interests or the influence of the Zionist lobby in the United States. Both are important; they reinforce each other. It should be emphasized, though, that the Zionist lobby is not exactly a Jewish lobby. Many Jews disagree with the policies of the Israeli government; some oppose Zionist ideology altogether. And there are Zionists who are not Jews. In recent years especially, some Christian fundamentalists have conspicuously adopted the Zionist cause; their influence resonates in Republican Party circles. Their interest stems from their belief that Jewish control of the Biblical Holy Land is a precursor to the prophesied conversion of the Jews, the Apocalypse and the Final Judgment. Needless to say, Christian and Jewish Zionists make strange bedfellows. The fundamentalists' beliefs are bizarre, even by the standards of orthodox Jews. Worse still: they harken back to the darkest moments of Christian anti-Semitism, demeaning both Jews and Judaism. Still, the Israeli state and its defenders abroad enthusiastically welcome the support of Christian Zionists, and go to great lengths to cultivate it.

The warm reception the Zionist establishment accords fundamentalist supporters of Israel, along with its ruthlessness in dealing with Jews and others who oppose it in any way, has a distinctly Stalinist flavor. The Stalinists too were disposed to sacrifice everything – including principles and self-respect – for the sake of a national cause, and they were notoriously merciless towards their opponents. To its (dubious) credit, genuine Stalinism operated under the cover of a more worthy, or at least more secular and universalistic, justifying theory. Zionism, like other nationalist ideologies, makes no similar pretense.

Christian Zionism is a form of anti-Semitism. This fact makes plain a simple distinction that is often overlooked in the mainstream political culture: that anti-Semitism and anti-Zionism are different phenomena. The Israeli government and its Zionist defenders have pressed the contrary view assiduously. They shamelessly draw on memories of the Nazi genocide to tarnish opponents of Israel and Israeli policies with the taint of Hitler. In the United States especially, this strategy has proven successful. But it is dangerous, not least to Jews themselves. The danger is that justifiable opposition to Israeli (and American) policies will indeed take an anti-Semitic turn; in other words, that the Zionists' identification of anti-Zionism with anti-Semitism, though false on its face, will turn into a self-fulfilling prophesy. So far, this has not happened. Of course, Zionists are quick to point to a rise in anti-Semitic incidents, especially in Europe. But, almost without exception, these are the work of desperate people of Middle Eastern origin, who side with the victims of Israeli and American domination, and who see Jews as their representatives, if not their aiders and abettors. The historical consciousness of these perpetrators of anti-Jewish violence has almost nothing to do with European anti-Semitism. But there is always the danger that age-old animosities will reignite; there is certainly no assurance that it cannot happen again. Needless to say, atrocities perpetrated against Jews or any other population must be thoroughly and rigorously denounced. But they should not be misinterpreted in ways that fuel Zionist objectives. In an earlier epoch, the great German Social Democratic leader August Bebel (1840–1913) called anti-Semitism "the anti-capitalism of fools." In present-day circumstances – as the Israeli state continues its brutal occupation of the fraction of mandate Palestine that remains Palestinian in the eyes of the world, committing atrocities against Arab peoples with American acquiescence and sometimes, no doubt, at America's behest – it is crucial to prevent anti-Semitism from becoming an anti-imperialism of fools.

For Americans, especially American Jews, the first priority must be to force the government of the United States to require their Israeli clients to end the occupation of what the world now recognizes as Palestine, and to make peace with the Palestinians and neighboring states. So dependent is Israel on the United

States that the American government could do this, if it chose. Perhaps, as this bitter conflict recedes into historical memory, it will become possible to learn positive lessons from the history of the Zionist movement. Zionist institutions did, after all, once harbor idealistic militants imbued with socialist values. In part for this reason, Israeli society has always sustained a courageous and genuinely internationalist Left. Unfortunately, the transformation of Zionism into a tool of the Israeli state and therefore, ultimately, a weapon in the arsenal of American imperialism means that today it is difficult to learn positive lessons from Israel's past and present. For the sake of everyone committed to progress – Israelis and Palestinians above all – it is urgent that this should change.

Further Reading

On the early history of Zionism, see Walter Laqueur, *A History of Zionism: From the French Revolution to the Establishment of the State of Israel* (New York: Schocken, 2003). Arthur Hertzberg, *The Zionist Idea: A Historical Analysis and Reader* (Philadelphia: Jewish Publication Society, 1997; originally published 1960) collects and analyses key Zionist writings from the period before the Six Day War, when Zionist politics and American imperialist strategies effectively fused. A recent book that is useful mainly for presenting nearly all the warmed-over mainstream and right-wing rationales for Israeli policies is Alan Dershowitz, *The Case for Israel* (Hoboken, NJ: John Wiley and Sons, 2003). For an incisive rebuttal, see Norman G. Finkelstein, *Beyond Chutzpah: On the Misuse of Anti-Semitism and the Abuse of History* (Berkeley and Los Angeles: University of California Press, 2005). A good antidote to pro-Zionist propaganda is Michael Neumann, *The Case Against Israel* (Oakland, CA: AK Press, 2006). As Neumann's example illustrates, Jews have been among the most trenchant critics of the Zionist project. Some landmark examples are collected in Adam Shatz (ed.), *Prophets Outcast: A Century of Dissident Jewish Writing About Zionism and Israel* (New York: Nation Books, 2004). Israeli historians have led the way in disputing some of the fabrications that surround the idea that the state of Israel differed morally from other settler states – specifically, that it did not, as a matter of deliberate policy, engage in "ethnic cleansing" of the indigenous population in order to provide land for Jewish settlers. A seminal example is Benny Morris, *Righteous Victims: A History of the Zionist–Arab Conflict, 1881–2001* (New York: Vintage, 2001). For a more comprehensive and synthetic account of Israel's origins, see Zeev Sternhell (David Maisel, trans.), *The Founding Myths of Israel* (Princeton, NJ: Princeton University Press, 1999). On the exploitation of the Nazi massacre of European Jews by Israeli and Zionist propagandists, see Tom Segev, *The Seventh Million: The Israelis and the Holocaust* (New York: Owl Books, 2000). On American uses, see Peter Novick, *The Holocaust in American Life* (New York: Mariner Books, 2000). The general phenomenon is discussed in Norman Finkelstein, *The Holocaust Industry: Reflections on the Exploitation of Jewish Suffering* (London: Verso, 2003). On the geopolitical implications of the Israel–Palestine conflict, and Israel's connections with American imperialism, see Noam Chomsky, *The Fateful Triangle: The United States, Israel and the Palestinians* (Boston: South End Press,

1999), and Norman G. Finkelstein, *Image and Reality of the Israel–Palestine Conflict* (New York: W.W. Norton and Co., 2003). A forceful case for the view that it is the pro-Israel lobby, more than geopolitical considerations, that accounts for the American–Israeli "special relationship" is made in John Mearsheimer and Steven Walt, "The Israel Lobby," *London Review of Books*, vol. 28, no. 6 (March 23, 2006). The viciously hostile reception of this carefully argued analysis in the United States – in marked contrast to its reception in Israel itself – provides evidence in support of its central thesis and of the claims made above for the Stalinist character of contemporary American Zionism.

See also: CAPITALISM, CULTURE, DEMOCRACY, FREEDOM/LIBERTY, FUNDAMENTALISM, IDEOLOGY, IMPERIALISM, INTERNATIONALISM, LEFT/RIGHT/CENTER, LEGITIMACY, LIBERALISM, NATION/NATIONALISM, PROGRESS, RACE/RACISM, REVOLUTION, RIGHTS, SOCIAL DEMOCRACY, SOCIALISM, STALINISM, STATE

Glossary

absolutism: misleadingly contrasts with MORAL RELATIVISM. The idea, apparently, is that *absolutists* uphold moral laws while relativists believe that "anything goes." This usage is confused and should be avoided. The term also has a very different, more cogent meaning. An *absolutist* maintains that political **authority** is unrestricted (*absolute*) in principle. In this sense, *absolutism* contrasts with LIBERALISM. In the early modern period, *absolutist* IDEOLOGY played an important role in STATE building.

abundance: contrasts with "scarcity." A good or resource is *abundant* when individuals can have all of it they want at no cost to others. For example, normally, air is *abundant*. In colloquial speech, *abundance* is also used to indicate the presence of ample quantities of goods or resources, even when their acquisition is not strictly costless.

agent-neutrality: a deliberative stance, from which doers (*agents*) deliberate from a perspective according to which it is of no moment whom the agent is. "Egoists" deliberate from an agent-specific standpoint (their own); so do "altruists" who deliberate from the point of view of others. When an agent deliberates from a neutral point of view, he or she takes his own position into account as much as any other agent's, but accords it no special weight. *Agent-neutrality* defines the MORAL point of view.

agnostic: see **theism/atheism/agnosticism**

analytical Marxism: a style of MARXIST theorizing, launched in the 1970s, that endeavors to reconstruct and, where possible, defend Karl Marx's (1818–1883) ideas utilizing the methods and standards of analytical philosophy, mathematical economics, and empirical social science. Among its key practitioners are G.A. Cohen (1941–), John Roemer (1945–), Jon Elster (1940–) and Erik Olin Wright (1947–). There are also many philosophers and social scientists working on Marx who are effectively *analytical Marxists*, but who do not identify themselves in these terms. In recent years, as interest in Marxism generally has waned, many erstwhile, self-identified *analytical Marxists* have ceased working directly on Marxist topics.

analytical philosophy: a name applied, in retrospect, to a philosophical tradition launched around the beginning of the twentieth century by such figures as Gottlob Frege (1848–1925), Bertrand Russell (1872–1970), G.E. Moore (1873–1958) and, later, Ludwig Wittgenstein (1889–1951). One feature of this tradition, that helps explain the name, is a focus on conceptual analysis; another is an emphasis on logical reconstructions of philosophical positions. This tendency continues to influence academic philosophy decisively, especially in the English-speaking world. As such, it contrasts with "continental philosophy" – a diverse collection of philosophical tendencies, including phenomenology, existentialism, and various neo-Hegelian philosophical currents. Nowadays, the term is also used in a more general sense to designate any kind of philosophical practice that resembles classical *analytical philosophy* in its goals, standards, and styles of argument. It is far from clear that the analytical/continental divide is as great as is sometimes supposed.

anthropocentrism: a tendency to see the non-human world in human terms. *Anthropocentrism* is universally recognized as mistaken. However, it is notoriously difficult to expunge.

anti-Semitism: institutional and/or attitudinal hostility towards Jews. The term is a misnomer, inasmuch as *Semitic* designates a category of historically related languages that includes Hebrew. Nineteenth-century pseudo-science RACIALIZED this linguistic category. Even so, hostility towards, say, Arabs (who also speak a *Semitic* language) never counted as *anti-Semitic*. Modern *anti-Semitism* derives from Christian anti-Judaism, and from nineteenth-century racialism. In the Islamic world, Jews along with other non-Muslims suffered social and political disabilities, but modern *anti-Semitism* does not derive from this source. *Anti-Semitism* in the Islamic world today is largely a consequence of the influence of Western IDEOLOGIES. It is exacerbated by the ZIONIST colonization of Palestine, and sustained by Israeli domination of the Palestinians. *Anti-Semitism* elsewhere in the world, to the extent it exists, is also, in the main, a Western import of recent vintage, without indigenous roots.

aristocracy: in an *aristocracy*, a privileged elite (etymologically, "the best") rule. There are few historical examples. But in the CLASS structure of nearly all pre-CAPITALIST societies, there are *aristocrats*, landowners who live off the labor of subjugated **peasants** or serfs. In almost all cases, they exercise considerable political influence, even if they do not directly govern. In general, membership in this class is inherited. To be an *aristocrat* is to enjoy high social status and, usually, considerable wealth. *Aristocrats* typically do not work, though they may take part in managing their estates. The term is also used to designate the top strata of any economically significant group. Thus, LENINISTS call skilled workers in IMPERIALIST countries "labor *aristocrats*."

Aristotelianism: Aristotle's (384?–322?BC) philosophy or, more commonly, ideas and positions characteristic of it. Of particular importance to modern politics is the **normative** preeminence Aristotle accorded to self-realization. Of great importance too is Aristotle's emphasis on public and private **virtue**.

atom/atomization: in some ancient metaphysical doctrines, *atoms* were the fundamental constituents of **matter**. As the etymology of the word implies, *atoms* are indivisible. *Atoms* are also independent of one another in the sense that they are what they are apart from their relations to other *atoms*. The emergence of MARKET relations in European **feudal** society can be depicted metaphorically as a process of *atomization* – inasmuch as traditional social **solidarities** were fragmented in ways that severed individuals from the bonds that joined them together, turning them into radically independent fundamental constituents of the social order.

authoritarianism: attitudes or practices that encourage obedience to **authority**, in contrast to FREEDOM of action or judgment, are *authoritarian*. In recent decades, NEO-CONSERVATIVES used the word to contrast with TOTALITARIAN. COMMUNIST regimes were totalitarian; equally repressive governments friendly to the United States were *authoritarian*. This usage suggested that the friendly regimes were somehow less bad, and also that they were evolving into DEMOCRACIES on the Western model. With the end of the **Cold War**, the contrast has passed into desuetude. But the description *authoritarian* remains intact.

Glossary

authority: the right to command, take action, or make final decisions. In political contexts, the term's use generally implies a right to compel compliance through force.

autonomy: a conception of FREEDOM, according to which one is free to the extent that one is self-directing or self-governing or, metaphorically, that one is the author of one's own actions. For Jean-Jacques Rousseau (1712–1778) and Immanuel Kant (1724–1804), whose accounts of *autonomy* helped shape current understandings, to be *autonomous* was, as the etymology of the word implies, to be subject to laws one has legislated for oneself. So understood, *autonomy* contrasts with **heteronomy**. In some instances, *autonomy* is also used more or less interchangeably with "independence."

Bolshevism: In 1903, the Russian SOCIAL DEMOCRATIC Party split into majority (*Bolshevik*) and minority (*Menshevik*) factions. It was the Bolsheviks, under V.I. Lenin (1870–1924), who led the 1917 October REVOLUTION, establishing the Soviet STATE. *Bolshevism* designates political practices of the kind Lenin and his fellow *Bolsheviks* deployed. Key to *Bolshevik* practice is a hierarchically structured **vanguard** party, comprised of professional revolutionaries, dedicated to introducing "revolutionary **consciousness**" among workers and other oppressed groups, and to directing political affairs.

bourgeoisie: the term originally designated freemen in European medieval towns. Later, it was used to refer to the "middle classes" – where **aristocrats** were on top of the social hierarchy, and serfs and **peasants** beneath. By the nineteenth century, the term was used to designate the ruling CLASS under CAPITALISM – the idea being that capitalists, whose power is based on the ownership of the productive assets of industrial or industrializing societies, had superseded aristocrats, whose power was based on ownership of land. In yet more recent times, especially among Asian COMMUNISTS, the term is used to designate any supposed class enemy.

capital: the term is often used to designate wealth in any form owned or used by persons or corporations, whether accumulated or used for business purposes. In MARXIST theory, the term designates the fundamental **social relations** (of ownership and control) that define CAPITALIST economic systems and the social orders they sustain.

Castroism: REVOLUTIONARY **strategies** based on the model of the 1959 Cuban Revolution, led by Fidel Castro (1926–), involving mobile guerilla tactics sustained by support from **oppressed** peoples in the countryside, and culminating in direct military assaults on weakened and delegitimated colonial or semi-colonial governments.

categorical/categorical imperative: in standard logic, *categorical* means "absolute" or "without qualification." It was this sense of the term that Immanuel Kant (1724–1804) had in mind when he formulated the idea of a *categorical imperative*, a command of (pure) reason to do or forbear from doing something, irrespective of any particular (contingent) end. The most well-known formulation of the *categorical imperative* holds that agents should act in such a way that the maxim (principle) that determines their action be a universal law – in other words, that it be a principle binding on all rational agents.

central planning: an economic system in which fundamental decisions about the allocation of resources, production targets, and the like are made by hierarchically structured bureaucracies, in contrast to individual economic agents joined together through MARKET relations.

character: a disposition to act in certain ways. Individuals who are disposed to act well have good *characters*; otherwise bad.

civil disobedience: forms of protest that deliberately involve violations of laws perceived to be UNJUST. The term can also be used to denote violations of (normally) just laws – for example, laws forbidding trespass – for the sake of calling attention to an injustice. *Civil disobedience* is not in itself an act of **rebellion** because it does not challenge **authority** per se, but only laws or policies existing authorities advance. In seeking out punishment, *civil disobedients* implicitly acknowledge the authorities' RIGHT to punish them and therefore their LEGITIMACY.

civil society: the term is used in different ways by different authors, but the general idea is that the non-STATE institutions of societies with states comprise its *civil society*. This could include the family, the economy, the churches, and the like. In some early modern political theory, the term is also used to indicate any social order superintended by a state.

clerical fascism: in its original meaning, the term referred to regimes in which the Roman Catholic (or Orthodox) Church hierarchy collaborated with FASCISTS. It has come to be used to refer to any clerisy seeking or exercising political influence that is disposed to implement policies similar to those instituted by classical fascists. Many so-called **authoritarian** regimes exhibit clerical fascist tendencies. The term is also sometimes used to refer to the political practice of ISLAMISTS and THEOCRATS generally. These extensions of the term have rhetorical force, but they are ahistorical and misleading.

coercion: to *coerce* is to force or compel. In the first instance, *coercive* force is physical force. However, there is also what John Stuart Mill (1806–1873) called "the moral *coercion* of public opinion." In addition, as Karl Marx (1818–1883) and other critics of CAPITALISM maintained, circumstances can be *coercive*. A worker who is offered the choice of exchanging LABOR power for a wage, where the alternative is starvation, is effectively *coerced* into accepting this ostensibly voluntary transaction.

Cold War: the condition that obtained between the United States and its allies, on the one hand, and the Soviet Union and its allies, on the other – from shortly after the end of World War II until the collapse of the Soviet Union in 1991. More generally, *cold war* can refer to any generalized state of mutual antagonism, where there is no overt combat. The contrast is with (hot) fighting WARS.

commodity/commodification/decommodification: a *commodity* is any good or service that is subject to exchange. To *commodify* is to render something susceptible to being bought or sold. Thus, prostitution *commodifies* sex and the sale of broadcast licenses commodifies broadcast communication. When something that had been bought or sold is made available in other ways – for instance, when the public provision of health care replaces market mechanisms – that service is *decommodified*. In CAPITALIST societies, there is a powerful tendency to *commodify* everything. SOCIALISTS seek to *decommodify* as much as possible.

consciousness, class consciousness, social consciousness, consciousness raising: For social theorists, *consciousness* means awareness of social and political conditions. Individuals who are *class conscious* are especially aware of their CLASS position, and are disposed to act in behalf of the interests of their class. In the 1930s and 1940s, *social consciousness* was used to indicate a concern with alleviating dire social conditions. This usage has largely disappeared. *Consciousness raising* refers to efforts to enhance *consciousness* (and *social consciousness*) with a view to advancing social change. The expression entered the political lexicon during the CIVIL RIGHTS movement in the United States. It was then taken up and vigorously promoted by second wave FEMINISTS.

consequentialism: an **ethical** theory is *consequentialist* if, like UTILITARIANISM, it ascribes the rightness or wrongness of actions solely to their consequences.

contractarianism: a form of political argument evident in the work of some seventeenth- and eighteenth-century political philosophers and revived in the twentieth century, according to which institutional arrangements are justified if and only if suitably characterized individuals, living without them in a **state of nature**, would choose them – either through bargaining or in consequence of a more impartial, but still self-regarding deliberation.

cooperation: the term is sometimes used to refer to any way of coordinating individuals' behaviors, whenever coordination requires that one or more individuals be deterred from doing what they most want to do . Strictly speaking, though, *cooperative* methods contrast with political (**coercive**) methods for coordinating behaviors. *Cooperation* occurs when one or more individuals voluntarily defer from doing what they most want to do – for the sake of realizing a collective goal.

corporatism: the term refers to any of a variety of governing **strategies** based on organized **cooperation** between ostensibly competing interests, especially CAPITAL and the LABOR MOVEMENT. Classical FASCISM was *corporatist;* so are some SOCIAL DEMOCRATIC regimes. For *corporatist* governance to be feasible, the interests involved must be internally organized to a degree that they can speak with one voice in dealings with their partners.

coup d'état: a sudden overthrow of a government. *Coups d'état* are not social REVOLUTIONS because they do not result in changes of regimes. They are extra-legal events that change incumbents of governing positions within regimes.

Critical Theory: a kind of social theory, developed in the so-called Frankfurt School in the 1930s and subsequently. *Critical Theory* is a version of MARXIST and Freudian theory. It is self-consciously emancipatory in intent: it aims to advance understanding (to interpret social phenomena) in order to change the world. Its leading practitioners included Max Horkheimer (1895–1973), Theodor Adorno (1903–1969), Herbert Marcuse (1898–1979), and, more peripherally, Walter Benjamin (1892–1940). In addition, many leading intellectuals of the period, like Franz Neumann (1900–1954) and Erich Fromm (1900–1980), were closely associated with *Critical Theory*. Thanks to Marcuse, **New Left** theorists identified with the *Critical Theory* tradition. Many prominent theoreticians today – Jürgen Habermas (1929–), for example – owe a substantial debt to this tradition as well.

criticism: Colloquially, to *criticize* is to find fault with. The term is also used to indicate reflective assessments, as in "art *criticism*." In the **Kantian** tradition, however, a *critique* is an account of the conditions for the possibility of some phenomenon or condition. It is this sense of the term that Karl Marx (1818–1883) adopted in his early writings, along with his **Young Hegelian** co-thinkers, when they spoke of their own theoretical and political program as *critical*. It is also this sense of the term that, a century later, Frankfurt School theorists would make their own.

Cultural revolution: The name entered the political lexicon when the MAOISTS in China unleashed the Great Proletarian *Cultural Revolution* in 1966, a period of intense social upheaval that waxed and waned for about a decade. More generally, the term refers to any sustained effort to transform societies at the CULTURAL, not just the political or economic, level.

de facto: actual, in fact.

de jure: in right.

deontology: MORAL theories that, unlike **consequentialist** theories, accord priority to the right over the good, are *deontological*. Conceptually and historically, **Kantian** moral philosophy is the most prominent example.

deprivatization: see **privatization**

despotism: see **tyranny/despotism**

dialectic: from Plato's (427?–347?BC) time on, philosophers have employed *dialectical* methods in which claims (theses) are countered by opposing or contradictory claims (antitheses), and then joined together in a synthesis that incorporates elements of both, thereby transcending the earlier opposition. For G.W.F. Hegel (1770–1831) and many of his followers, knowledge – or, rather, **consciousness** – has a dialectical structure. So too, in their view, does the reality that comes to be known as consciousness unfolds.

dialectical materialism: Second International MARXISTS and then official COMMUNISTS used this term to describe Marxist philosophy. In the STALIN era and thereafter, Communists endeavored to fix its key doctrines. However, thanks to dissident Marxists, *dialectical materialism* never quite degenerated into sheer dogma. *Dialectical materialists* employ what they take to be G.W.F. Hegel's

(1770–1831) **dialectical** method. **Analytical Marxists** oppose this understanding, insisting that there is no distinctively Marxist method.

dictatorship: in ancient Rome, a *dictator* was a magistrate, appointed during emergencies, and vested with supreme **authority**. In modern times, *dictators* are individuals who rule for indefinite periods, exercising absolute, or nearly absolute, power. *Dictators* rule **tyrannically** – in ways that are unrestricted by law. In the MARXIST and especially LENINIST traditions, each **mode of production** is thought to sustain a particular form of the STATE – each of which is a CLASS *dictatorship* in the sense that the power of the economically dominant class is exercised in ways that are unrestricted (even when legal systems regulate governing institutions). On this view, representative government, ostensibly the antithesis of *dictatorship*, would be a form of **bourgeois** class *dictatorship*.

double effect: a doctrine developed by Catholic theologians in the late Middle Ages according to which actions that have MORALLY impermissible consequences can be done – in WAR and, by extension, in other aspects of life – so long as the impermissible consequences are unintended (though perhaps foreseeable) by-products of actions done for MORALLY LEGITIMATE purposes.

due process: a course of legal proceedings established to protect individuals' RIGHTS and LIBERTIES. In the American legal system, and in many others too, due process rights are constitutionally mandated.

dystopianism: see **utopianism**

economism: in the MARXIST tradition, the term is used to denote political **strategies** or ways of thinking that accord preeminence to economic, as opposed to political or CULTURAL, changes. LENINISTS and other REVOLUTIONARY Marxists disparage *economism*.

effective demand: in economic analyses that focus on the economy as a whole (macro- as distinct from micro-economics), the expression is used to denote *demands* for goods and services that are backed by the capacity and will to pay.

efficiency: colloquially, whatever works well or without waste (of time or resources) is *efficient*. In economic theory, *efficiency* means **Pareto optimality**. An allocation of goods or resources is *efficient* if any change would make someone worse off.

Glossary

empiricism: an **epistemological** doctrine according to which all knowledge comes directly or indirectly from sense experience (perception). The term *empirical* designates whatever is in principle perceivable. The only evidence *empiricists* count as supporting or infirming claims is *empirical* evidence. However, one can value and even rely exclusively on *empirical* evidence in the sciences without being an *empiricist*.

endogenous: contrasts with **exogenous**. A factor is *endogenous* to a system or process if it arises within it.

Enlightenment: an eighteenth-century philosophical movement dedicated, above all, to upholding rational standards for belief acceptance and freedom from clerical domination and **theistic** belief. Most *Enlightenment* thinkers also upheld a notion of human perfectability. Enlightenment thought is politically **progressive**. The best-known Enlightenment thinkers were French. But there were distinct Enlightenments in Scotland, England, and throughout continental Europe. Immanuel Kant (1724–1804) famously proclaimed that the motto of *enlightenment* thought is "dare to know."

epiphenomenon: in **metaphysics**, a phenomenon that is itself caused but that has no causal efficacy of its own.

epistemology: the theory (*logos* in Greek) of knowledge (*episteme* in Greek) – specifically, of its forms and limits. Any issue pertaining to knowability can be viewed as *epistemological*. In some non-English-speaking philosophical traditions – in France, for example – *epistemology* is sometimes used interchangeably with "philosophy of science."

equity: often used interchangeably with JUSTICE. In social policy debates, *equity* considerations are widely assumed to conflict with **efficiency** considerations, requiring trade-offs, since both are desirable. In legal contexts, *equity* considerations sometimes supplement existing legal rules, when they are deemed inadequate for capturing the sense of fairness. In economics, *equity* is also used to mean assets minus liabilities – in other words, net worth.

essence: in **metaphysics**, the *essence* of an entity is given by its necessary and sufficient conditions. For example, if, as Aristotle (384?–322?BC) maintained, man (*sic*) is *essentially* a rational animal, then nothing could count as a man that was not a rational animal (rationality and being an animal are necessary for being a man) and anything that is a rational animal would be a man (rationality and being an animal are sufficient for counting as a man). It is always an open question whether all the entities designated by a particular term or expression have a common *essence* or whether the usage, insofar as it is not arbitrary, is based on the existence of certain "family resemblances."

ethics: any **normative** account of individual conduct. MORAL theories, that adopt the deliberative vantage point of **agent-neutrality**, are *ethical* theories, but not all *ethical* theories are moral theories. Accounts of individual conduct can proceed from conceptions of **virtue**, from religious doctrines, from codes of honor or shame or from any of a variety of other sources. The term is also used to designate codes of conduct appropriate to particular offices or positions – as, for example, in "legal" or "business *ethics*." This usage is imprecise, however, inasmuch as violations of, say, business *ethics* can and typically do involve breaking moral rules, not just professional codes of conduct.

ethnicity: characteristics of persons that join them together into social groups. *Ethnic* similarities and differences derive, among other things, from real or imagined commonalities of descent, language, history, customs, place of residence, individual characteristics, and religion.

exogenous: contrasts with **endogenous**. A factor is *exogenous* to a system or process if it arises outside it.

exploitation: to *exploit* a person or group is to take unfair advantage of it; this is the only sense of the term with an expressly **normative** significance. When FEMINISTS say that men *exploit* women, or when ENVIRONMENTALISTS decry the *exploitation* of nature, it is usually this sense of the term that they assume. However, one can also say that to *exploit* a resource is to put it to productive use. In MARXIST economic theory, *exploitation* has an officially non-MORALIZED sense, close to the latter usage. Workers are *exploited* inasmuch as their LABOR power produces more **value** than is required for its reproduction, the surplus going to the CAPITALISTS who own the **means of production** with which the workers toil.

external relations: contrasts with **internal relations**. As Gottfried Leibniz (1646–1716) developed the notion, *a* and *b* are *externally related* when the identity conditions for *a* and *b* are independent of any relational properties that may obtain between them. Entities that are *externally related* – **atoms**, for example – are radically independent of one another.

externalism: contrasts with **internalism**. MORAL theories are *externalist* if their account of the reasons to be moral are independent of their account of what morality requires. For example, a moral theory that holds, as Thomas Hobbes's (1588–1679) did, that morality consists in acting on agent-neutral principles, and that the reason to adopt this deliberative stance is **prudential** is *externalist*.

externality: a cost or benefit that MARKETS cannot tally because it falls on parties who are not directly implicated in the exchanges that generate it. For example, if A sells B sulfur to burn in a factory, and C, living next door, incurs costs from the foul and dangerous odor, those costs are not counted by the price system – they don't figure in the market price. They are "negative *externalities*." On the other hand, if a storekeeper benefits from the presence nearby of a restaurant with which he has no direct involvement, he reaps benefits without paying the costs for their production. This would be a "positive *externality*." *Externalities* detract from **efficiency** (**Pareto optimality**).

false consciousness: in MARXIST theory and more generally in the sociology of knowledge, those who misapprehend their own condition to the point of acting in ways that are detrimental to their own interests suffer from *false consciousness*.

fellow travelers: persons who are not actual members of LENINIST (typically COMMUNIST) parties who, out of sympathy with their goals, act in ways consonant with Party programs.

feudalism: any economic structure, based on agricultural production, in which owners of land (lords, **aristocrats**), the principal productive resource, have control and revenue RIGHTS (in other words, **property**) in the direct producers (**peasants** or serfs). *Feudalism* is normally distinguished from **modes of production** based on **slavery** – in other words, from economic systems in which the direct producers are owned outright – but it is not clear whether, from a HISTORICAL MATERIALIST point of view, this is a theoretically significant distinction. *Feudalism* has existed throughout the world. CAPITALISM developed out of European *feudalism*.

fiscal: the term covers all economic policy matters, including tax policies, that involve public revenues or that are otherwise in the dominion of STATE treasuries.

fraternity: one of the three words (along with LIBERTY and EQUALITY) that comprise the slogan of the French REVOLUTIONARIES. The term is roughly synonymous with COMMUNITY, though, unlike some senses of the latter term, it implies the existence of affective ties similar to those that exist between brothers.

free rider: anyone who benefits from a good or service without bearing a fair share of the cost of its production is said to *free ride* on the contributions of others. *Free riding* violates widespread intuitions of fairness. It is therefore MORALLY reprehensible. Because persons are generally averse to letting others *free ride* on their contributions, it can also be an obstacle in the way of organizing collective endeavors.

functional explanation: *functional explanations* are causal explanations in which the *function* of what is explained plays a crucial explanatory role. Imagine, for example, a room heated by a furnace regulated by a thermostat. The ambient temperature causes the furnace to go off and on, and the furnace's operation causes the room to heat and cool. Each causally affects the other. But the *function* of the furnace is to heat the room; the *function* of the room temperature is not to cause the furnace to go off and on. Where this kind of causal symmetry and explanatory asymmetry co-exist, we have a genuine *functional explanation*. *Functional explanations* are common in biology thanks to the foundational role of Darwinian theory. Genuine *functional explanations* are more rare in the social sciences than is commonly supposed because social scientists often confound *functionality* with providing benefits. If X is *functional* for Y, X does benefit Y. But the converse is not always the case.

gender: a term introduced into the political lexicon by second wave FEMINISTS to refer to specifically social aspects of sexual differentiation. The intended contrast is with "sex," a biological category. Nowadays, "sex" and *gender* are often used interchangeably.

globalization: the process through which economic and CULTURAL phenomena that had previously been mainly NATIONAL in scope become increasingly INTERNATIONALIZED. This process has accelerated in recent decades under the aegis of multinational corporations based in the United States and other IMPERIALIST centers. At an IDEOLOGICAL level, corporate globalization is bolstered by **neoliberal** arguments about the merits of "free trade." In recent years, through the World Social Forum and in other venues, SOCIALISTS and other **progressives** have begun to develop alternative forms of economic, social and cultural globalization that are substantively anti-imperialist and that accord with LEFT concerns.

Glossary

Great Society: the name given in the 1964 Presidential election in the United States to the social programs proposed by the Johnson campaign and introduced in the early years of the Johnson Administration. *Great Society* LIBERALISM aimed at completing the **New Deal** by eradicating poverty and incorporating African-Americans and other oppressed minorities into the so-called "American Dream." As spending for the Vietnam War increased, *Great Society* programs suffered. Some of them nevertheless survived for many years – continuing to benefit the poorly-off. From the 1980s on, under both Democratic and Republican administrations, surviving *Great Society* programs were further weakened or undone.

heteronomy: in **Kantian** moral philosophy, *heteronomy* contrasts with **autonomy**, the distinctively Kantian conception of FREEDOM. An agent's will is *heteronomously* determined when that agent's actions are determined by another (*heteros* in Greek), where the agent's passions and interests, and indeed everything other than the agent's own rational self, counts as "another."

human capital: wealth of an intangible sort that cannot be separated from those who hold it. The term refers to knowledge, skills, health and, more generally, to developed or realized human capacities. To invest in education or health care is to invest in *human capital*.

human rights: RIGHTS ascribed to human beings just in virtue of their being human – regardless of the legal systems under which they live or any other special circumstances. Exactly what rights should count as human rights is controversial. The point of departure for addressing this question is the *Universal Declaration of Human Rights* issued by the United Nations in 1948.

idealism: in **metaphysics**, *idealism* is the view that everything that is is ultimately *ideal* or mental in nature. *Idealism* contrasts with **materialism**. *Idealist* positions in modern, Western philosophy derive from René Descartes' (1596–1650) **metaphysical** dualism, according to which there are only two substances – mind and matter. *Idealists* maintain that what Descartes regarded as material is, in fact, a form of existence of mind. In the eighteenth and nineteenth centuries, *idealism* was associated with **theism** and political CONSERVATISM. This sense of the term should not be confused with colloquial understandings according to which *idealists* are dedicated to high-minded *ideals* and/or have little concern for material things.

illusion: Colloquially, and in some philosophical contexts, *illusions* are false perceptions. In Freudian psychology, they are beliefs held in consequence of unconscious desires (in contrast to evidence). In this sense, it is the aetiology, not the truth value, of the belief that is crucial for determining whether or not it is an *illusion*. Though usually false, *illusions* in this sense can also be true.

individualism: social or political theories are *individualistic* if they regard *individuals* and their interests (in contrast to social groups and their interests) as fundamental concerns in **normative** and/or descriptive accounts of social and political practices and institutions. The term can also be used to indicate self-reliance or perhaps even idiosyncratic (as distinct from conformist) ways of being and acting.

intellectual: in the nineteenth century, the term was used to refer to members of the *intelligentsia* – the class of educated and enlightened persons. To be an *intellectual*, it was usual, but not necessary, to take a lively interest in public affairs and to be engaged in political life. In the twentieth century, as educational levels rose, public involvement increasingly became the distinguishing mark of *intellectuals*. *Intellectuals* nowadays are "public *intellectuals*." Thus, most academics, scientists, engineers, and other professional people would not fall under this description. In the past half century in Europe and elsewhere, most *intellectuals* have been associated with the LEFT. But there are and can be CENTRIST and RIGHT-wing intellectuals too. In the United States, from the 1970s on, right-wing foundations have actively recruited and developed intellectuals of the Right.

interest group: in political theory, *interest groups* are collections of individuals joined together by common interests. They usually hold these interests in consequence of their situation or other ascriptive properties. Thus, the LABOR MOVEMENT can function politically as an *interest group*, as can RACIAL or **ethnic** minorities. In theory, however, *interest groups* can form for any reason. In political theories that construe political processes as efforts by competing interest groups to gain advantages, CAPITALISTS and other beneficiaries of the system in place also constitute *interest groups*. But in mainsteam political discourse, this is not usually acknowledged. Instead, their interests are effectively identified with the interests of the whole community, which is then depicted as being besieged by "special interests."

internal relations: contrasts with **external relations** As Gottfried Leibniz (1646–1716) developed the notion, *a* and *b* are *internally* related when the identity conditions for *a* and *b* depend upon the relations that obtain between them.

internalism: contrasts with **externalism.** MORAL theories are *internalist* if their account of the reasons to be moral are ultimately identical to their account of what morality requires. **Kantian** moral philosophy is a paradigm case.

jingoism: a *jingoist* is a chauvinist who is boastful, ostentatiously patriotic, and in favor of an aggressive foreign policy. The term derives from a British music-hall song of the late nineteenth century.

Kantianism: The philosophy of Immanuel Kant (1724–1804) or ideas and positions characteristic of it. Of particular importance to modern politics is Kant's account of the MORAL point of view (**agent-neutrality**) and related notions of universalizability, as formulated in the **categorical imperative.** Kantian moral philosophy is **internalist** in that, on his account, apprehension of the moral order motivates agents to act morally. However, as Kant and his many followers recognized, other factors pull human beings in opposite directions. Kantians regard **essential** humanity ("dignity") as priceless. Thus they reject **consequentialist** moral theories, like UTILITARIANISM, that, in their view, treat persons as means only, rather than as "ends-in-themselves." Kantian moral theory is therefore **deontological.**

laissez-faire: in economics, the policy of letting CAPITALISTS themselves fix the terms of trade and the conditions of labor without government regulation or control. Early LIBERALS advocated *laissez-faire* in opposition to prevailing **mercantilist** policies. Sometimes the term is also used to denote any policy or practice of letting people do as they please, without state or societal interference.

logical positivism: a philosophical movement that revolved around the idea that statements are meaningful if and only if they can either be established using logical methods or, more usually, verified by sense experience. *Logical positivists* therefore considered most **metaphysics, ethics,** aesthetics, and political philosophy to be literally meaningless. *Logical positivism* (or "logical empiricism," as it is sometimes called) was developed in the late 1920s in the Vienna Circle under the leadership of Moritz Schlick (1882–1936). It took its inspiration from Ludwig Wittgenstein's (1889–1951) *Tractatus Logico-Philosophicus* (1922) and from developments in mathematical logic and modern physics. The leading exponent of logical positivist ideas in the English-speaking world was A.J. Ayer (1910–1989). As a distinct philosophical tendency, *logical positivism* effectively expired by the 1960s, along with the verificationist theory of meaning. However, its influence continues in the social sciences; and it remains a point of reference for **analytical philosophers.**

marginal utility: the utility derivable from an additional increment of a utility-producing good or service. The "law of diminishing *marginal utility*" maintains that, the more of any good or service one already has, the less utility one derives from an additional increment. This law is plausible only at a very high level of abstraction. In practice, it is plainly susceptible to counterexamples.

market socialism: the term denotes any SOCIALIST theory or practice that accords a substantial or determining role to MARKET mechanisms in the determination of prices. Nineteenth-century socialists were opposed to markets. However, in time, the **efficiency** advantages of relying on markets instead of **central planning** encouraged some socialist thinkers to propose their introduction into socialist economies. The term is also misleadingly used to describe economies, such as China's, where capitalist enterprises coexist with state-run enterprises.

materialism: in **metaphysics**, the view that everything that is is ultimately *material* in nature. *Materialism* contrasts with **idealism.** *Materialist* positions in modern, Western philosophy derive from René Descartes' (1596–1650) metaphysical dualism, according to which there are only two substances – mind and *matter*. *Materialists* maintain that what Descartes regarded as mental is, in fact, a form of existence of matter. In the eighteenth and nineteenth centuries, materialism was associated with **atheism** and anti-clericalism and with **progressive** and even REVOLUTIONARY politics. This sense of the term should not be confused with the colloquial understanding according to which *materialists* are concerned with consuming "material things," and generally indifferent to ideals.

matriarchy: the rule of women or, more usually, ideas and attitudes associated with social orders in which women dominate society. *Matriarchy* contrasts with **patriarchy.** *Matriarchies* are extremely rare in historical times. Arguably, they have never existed outside the imagination of a few FEMINIST writers.

means of production: tools and other TECHNOLOGICAL instruments used in production processes. The term plays a prominent role in MARXIST accounts of class structure and class struggle.

Glossary

mercantilism: in economics, the policy of protecting home industries through government regulation of trade, aggressive promotion of export industries, and the accumulation of bullion (monetized metals). The doctrine arose in early modern Europe with the demise of **feudalism**. It played an important role in nation building. It contrasts with **laissez-faire**.

metaphysics: for philosophers influenced by Aristotle (384?–322? BC), *metaphysics* is comprised of **epistemology** and **ontology**. More commonly, it includes just ontology, broadly construed. *Metaphysics* aims to give an account of what is the case at a more general level than the sciences. The etymology of the word is instructive. If physics is the science of **matter** at its most fundamental level of organization, then *meta* (beyond)-*physics* is about the most general properties of the world physics describes.

mode of production: for MARXISTS, a *mode of production* (or "economic structure") is a discrete set of **production relations**. In the HISTORICAL MATERIALIST view, there are only a small number of possible *modes of production*. An **endogenous** dynamic moves humanity along from one to another until COMMUNISM, the end of the process, is reached.

moderate: contrasts with "extreme." In current political discourse, however, *moderate* is often used to identify soft RIGHT or CENTER-right political positions (as in "*moderate* Republican") or to suggest friendliness towards the government of the United States (as when Middle Eastern governments that collaborate with American IMPERIALISM are called *moderate*).

monetary: having to do with money. *Monetary* policy is that part of **fiscal** policy that regulates the money supply.

monopoly: *monopolies* have exclusive (or at least inordinate) control over particular commodities or services. **Mercantile** regimes deliberately create *monopolies*. In CAPITALIST MARKET economies, *monopoly* formation is a constant danger. But, according to mainstream, neo-classical economic theory, their existence threatens **efficiency**. This is why, nowadays, even proponents of **laissez-faire** believe – in theory, at least – that states should actively undo monopoly concentrations in order to bolster competition between economic agents.

mores: the term is used to refer to prevailing ways of acting and being, and especially to social customs and manners. *Mores* are the bases for laws. They also shape individuals' mentalities and therefore, at the collective level, peoples' consciousness of themselves and others, and their beliefs and desires insofar as they bear on public matters.

nationalization: contrasts with privatization. To *nationalize* an industry is to transfer property RIGHTS over all or part of it from private hands to the government.

Nazism: the version of FASCIST IDEOLOGY and practice developed by "the National Socialist German Workers' Party," founded in 1919 and abolished in 1945 after Germany's defeat in World War II. Under the leadership of Adolf Hitler, the *Nazis* installed a TOTALITARIAN regime that actively pursued RACIST (especially anti-Semitic), NATIONALIST and aggressive policies. Extreme RIGHT-wing fascist groups today sometimes describe themselves as "neo-*Nazis*." In the larger political CULTURE, the term is used, often ahistorically, as a term of extreme reproach.

neo-liberalism: the name used throughout the world, though seldom in the United States, to describe the political-economic policies constituting the so-called "Washington Consensus" of recent decades. Though hypocritically implemented, *neo-liberal* IDEOLOGY favors FREEDOM from government intervention in domestic economies, along with active government encouragement of free trade at the global level. *Neo-liberals*, like the nineteenth-century LIBERALS whose ideas they have revived, vest their faith in MARKETS, supposing that somehow market mechanisms can, in time, cure social ills. Thus *neo-liberals* oppose bureaucratic regulation and other forms of STATE interference in NATIONAL economies, at the same time that they actively favor (corporate) globalization. *Neo-liberals* also support privatization and the extension of private property RIGHTS.

New Deal: the name given to the social programs undertaken in the United States by the Roosevelt Administration in the 1930s, in the context of the great economic Depression of that decade. *New Deal* programs aimed to provide relief from economic insecurity and poverty. Thus, *New Deal* LIBERALISM supports affirmative uses of STATE POWER to address social problems.

New Left: a form of LEFT political theory and practice that emerged in developed CAPITALIST countries during the Cold War, at a time when traditional left (especially COMMUNIST) political parties were suffering from intellectual and moral exhaustion or, as in the American case, severe repression. The *New Left* emerged at a time when capitalist economies were expanding rapidly and when – in consequence of New Deal and Great Society policies in the United States, and their SOCIALIST and SOCIAL DEMOCRATIC counterparts abroad – the conditions of most working people were improving. *New Left* politics was partly a generational phenomenon inasmuch as its main protagonists were relatively well-off students and youth. *New Leftists* emphasized CULTURAL rebellion and RACIAL EQUALITY. They had little affinity for or contact with the LABOR MOVEMENT or workers generally.

nihilism: the term can refer to any political strategy that accords primacy to annihilating or destroying existing institutions. Or it can be used to mark a distinction among positions sometimes designated as RELATIVIST. In this case, a *nihilist* with respect to some **proposition** denies that it is either true or false. For example, for a **logical positivist** proponent of the verificationist theory of meaning, the statement "God exists" is neither true nor false, because it is literally meaningless. Logical positivists would therefore be *nihilists* with respect to "God exists." A relativist, on the other hand, would hold that its truth value is relative to some situation or circumstance.

norm: a **socially constructed** rule that is internalized. *Norms* are typically enforced – sometimes only internally (psychologically), often by the external imposition of legal or customary sanctions.

normative: *Normative* accounts provide standards for assessment and/or tell what ought to be the case or what ought to be done. The term contrasts with "descriptive" or "positive," though the nature of the distinction is controversial. **Positivists** and those influenced by them believe the distinction should be rigorously maintained; Hegelians and those influenced by them would disagree.

ontology: an account (*logos* in Greek) of what is or, more generally, of "being" (*ontos* in Greek). Ontological issues arise in both **metaphysics** and science. **Idealism** and **materialism** are *ontological* positions in metaphysics. When physicists claim, for example, that there are quarks, they are making an *ontological* claim within physics, as distinct from a metaphysical claim. In general, it is wise to distinguish carefully between *ontological* claims and **epistemological** ones.

oppression: the condition of being "kept down" by UNJUST and usually cruel uses of POWER. *Oppression* is always bad and therefore always to be resisted. But because the term has no direct analytical meaning, it should be distinguished from the related notion of **exploitation**, which sometimes is utilized in illuminating ways.

Orwellian: a term used to describe uses of language similar to those depicted by George Orwell (1903–1950) in his 1948 **dystopian** novel, *1984*. *Orwellian* speech is manipulated for political ends. The paradigm case is when words are used in ways that denote the opposite of what they mean – as when "defense" is used to mean "aggressive WAR."

pacifism: opposition to WAR and, more generally, to the use of force under any circumstances. Most people believe that ideal societies would be *pacific* or non-VIOLENT. *Pacifists* believe that, even in a violent world, persons should act as if the ideal already obtained. They may consider recourses to violence MORALLY impermissible in all circumstances or they may just think that *pacifistic* **strategies** are more efficacious than non-*pacifistic* strategies for obtaining desired ends.

Pareto optimality/optimum: named for Vilfredo Pareto (1848–1923) who introduced the concept, a situation or outcome is *Pareto optimal* if any change would make someone worse off. Pareto's concern was to retrieve the core intuition underlying UTILITARIANISM – that there should be as much WELFARE (well-being) as possible. He endeavored to retain this idea without having to make welfare comparisons between persons. He reasoned that even if all we can know are individuals' rankings of alternatives in contention, we can still conclude that one alternative is better than another in a welfarist sense ("Pareto superior") if it is unanimously preferred (in the sense that it stands higher in each individual's ranking). Each Pareto-superior outcome is *optimal* in the sense that a welfare improvement for anyone will result in a welfare loss for someone else. There is, therefore, no unique Pareto optimum in the way that there is a unique utilitarian maximum. To *optimize*, then, is not exactly to "maximize." It is to maximize subject to the constraint that everyone be as well-off as can be in the situation in question. In formal economic models, **efficiency** is construed as *Pareto optimality*. In some political contexts, as in colloquial speech, *optimal* can also mean "as good as possible, given prevailing constraints."

paternalism: *paternalistic* interferences with adult individuals' lives and behaviors are made to prevent them from harming themselves and/or to make them better off. The model is a parent's or more specifically, a father's (*pater*) interferences with the behaviors of his minor children. LIBERALS generally oppose STATE or societal interventions for these purposes. In general, *paternalism* has a negative connotation, though many believe it justifiable in some circumstances.

patriarchy: the rule of men or, more usually, ideas and attitudes associated with male dominance of society. *Patriarchy* contrasts with **matriarchy.** Nearly all human societies are *patriarchal* to some extent, and *patriarchal* attitudes are very widespread.

peasant: throughout history, most people living in settled agricultural societies have been *peasants* – independent, subsistence, agricultural producers. *Peasants* are not farmers, who produce mainly for MARKETS rather than their own consumption; they are less fully integrated into CAPITALIST economies. Neither are they **slaves**, inasmuch as they are not owned outright. However, in some **feudal** societies, *peasants*, like serfs (near slaves), do owe some labor or some of the product of their labor to feudal lords. Perhaps the greatest social transformation in the developed world in the twentieth century was the effective disappearance of the *peasantry* as a class – the majority of former *peasants* or their children moving off the land, the rest becoming farmers. In the United States, because there is no history of feudalism, there never was a *peasant* CLASS in the strict sense, though tenant farmers or "sharecroppers" in the South lived under similar social relations.

peoples' democracy: a designation assumed by COMMUNIST regimes after World War II. Unlike DEMOCRACIES in the West, *peoples' democracies* were one-party states without competitive elections. The ostensible rationale for their appropriation of the term *democratic* was that in states of this type, the people (*demos* in Greek) rule through the medium of Communist parties that direct the STATE and other major societal and economic institutions. Needless to say, this rationale rings hollow. The term is now used only in Asia, where officially Communist regimes remain in power.

permanent revolution: Marx's notion, that became a TROTSKYIST core doctrine, formulated in opposition to the STALINIST doctrine of "socialism in one country." *Permanent revolution* implies active support for REVOLUTIONARY movements throughout the world, not their subordination to NATIONAL interests. It also suggests that, even when CAPITALIST regimes are successfully overthrown, workers and their allies must struggle against the ossification of STATE institutions and the decline of revolutionary spirit if they are to attain a genuinely COMMUNIST future.

philosophical anthropology: philosophical accounts of what is distinctively human. *Philosophical anthropologies* are typically, but not necessarily, **essentialist** – supposing that their task is to reveal the nature of the human essence. However, some *philosophical anthropologies* effectively shade off into naturalistic theories of human nature. *Philosophical anthropology* should not be confused with the academic discipline "anthropology"; the two have almost nothing to do with one another beyond a very general concern with identifying distinctively human universals.

political correctness: a term used disparagingly, across the political spectrum, to designate **coercively** internalized or enforced attitudes or ways of speaking and acting that are non-disparaging of individuals or groups who suffer from social disabilities or prejudice. The expression has been in general currency since the 1980s. It derives from the COMMUNIST movement, where it had been used non-disparagingly to denote positions that accord with the Party's political line. Occasionally, the term is turned on its head to designate views that are unofficially suppressed because they fail to support power.

Popular front: In the mid- to late 1930s, COMMUNIST parties in Europe formed broad alliances, *popular fronts*, with anti-FASCISTS. The policy carried over to other parts of the world, where Communist parties, following Moscow's instructions, would soften their REVOLUTIONARY line in order to join forces with non-Communists. Subsequently, the term has been used to denote any broad coalitions of LEFT (especially Communist) parties and CENTER-left or centrist groupings. *Popular fronts* are typically formed in opposition to fascist or **authoritarian** threats. TROTSKYISTS historically opposed popular front strategies, advocating "united front" programs (alliances of "workers' parties" only) instead.

positivism: a philosophical tendency, launched and named by August Comte (1798–1857) early in the nineteenth century and continued into the present in various forms. *Positivists* regard scientific knowing as the only path to knowledge and endorse the distinction between facts and VALUES. They are also "anti-holists" in the sense that they suppose that knowledge of particular facts or of discrete sorts of phenomena does not logically depend on knowledge of "totalities." In these and other respects, *positivists* oppose Hegelian positions that endorse extra-scientific (dialectical) ways of knowing, integral connections between what is and what ought to be, and holism.

postcolonial: the term can be used to refer to societies that were, in their recent past, colonized by IMPERIAL powers. More commonly, it refers to their literature and art.

post-modern: the term is used to refer to any of a variety of positions in literary criticism, philosophy, or the arts that is viewed as emerging from or in **reaction** to modernism. The term can also refer to societies generally, the implication being that they have somehow moved beyond the modern period. Post-modern thought denies that there are foundations for knowledge or true narrative accounts of history's structure and direction. More generally, post-modernists advance a general conceptual RELATIVISM, according to which there are no "objective" truths at all. Post-modern writings are often obscure to the point of incoherence. For **analytical philosophers**, therefore, the term has a pejorative connotation.

pragmatism: a philosophical movement that began in the late nineteenth century in the United States. Leading pragmatist thinkers include Charles Sanders Pierce (1839–1914), William James (1842–1910) and John Dewey (1859–1952). More recent philosophers influenced by *pragmatist* thought include W.V.O. Quine (1908–2000), Hilary Putnam (1926–) and Richard Rorty (1931–). Pragmatists reject foundationalism in philosophy and regard usefulness as an important criterion of meaning and truth. In colloquial speech and in contemporary political discourse, *pragmatic* sometimes contrasts with IDEOLOGICAL. In this usage, *pragmatists* typically have no knowledge of or interest in philosophical *pragmatism*. To count as *pragmatists*, they need only be concerned more with results than with steadfast adherence to beliefs or principles.

praxis: in its **Aristotelian** sense, *praxis* denotes actions that are performed for the sake of an ideal. All higher animals are capable of purposive action, but *praxis* presupposes rational capacities unique to human beings. It requires that agents have "second-order" purposes – purposes about their purposes.

primary goods: in John Rawls's (1921–2002) theory of JUSTICE, *primary goods* are goods that are generally useful for realizing any individual's particular conception of the good. According to Rawls, justice is concerned, in the main, with the distribution of *primary goods*. They include basic RIGHTS and LIBERTIES, POWERS, and offices, the bases of self-respect and, in some accounts, leisure.

prisoners' dilemma: a "game" in which the equilibrium solution that results when all players play their best strategy is sub-**Pareto optimal**. *Prisoners' dilemma* situations are states of affairs that can be modeled using *prisoners' dilemma* games. They arise whenever individuals most prefer that others abide by some convention or rule while they themselves do not. Exchange relations have a *prisoners' dilemma* structure, as do **states of nature** in **contractarian** political philosophy.

privatization/deprivatization: the obverse of **nationalization**. To *privatize* an industry or service is to transfer ownership RIGHTS from public (usually STATE) to private hands. To *deprivatize* is to take what was formerly privately owned and to terminate **property** rights in it altogether. Thus, in the HISTORICAL MATERIALIST view, the transition from pre-CAPITALIST to capitalist economic systems, terminates private property rights in other persons.

production relations/social relations of production: in HISTORICAL MATERIALISM, real (as distinct from juridical or legal) **property** relations – that is, relations of ownership and control of productive resources.

productive forces/forces of material production: in HISTORICAL MATERIALISM, the means through which raw materials are transformed into socially useful objects of LABOR. *Productive forces* include **means of production**, the organization of production processes, and knowledge insofar as it is employed in productive economic activities.

progressive: in the most usual sense of the term, whatever is conducive to PROGRESS is *progressive*. However, on the LEFT, the term has sometimes been used as a euphemism for words that have fallen into disfavor. When American COMMUNISTS were the victims of repression, they called themselves and their **fellow travelers** *progressives*. Today, with **New Deal** and **Great Society** LIBERALISM in retreat, many liberals prefer to be identified as *progressives*. A variety of political movements and parties have also assumed the name. In economics, a tax is said to be *progressive*, in contrast to *regressive*, if it enhances income or wealth EQUALITY.

proletariat: in ancient Rome, *proletarians* were persons with no wealth other than their offspring (*proles*). Karl Marx (1818–1883) used the term to refer to **propertyless** workers. In classical MARXIST thought, the *proletariat* is more or less coextensive with the class of industrial workers. There can, however, also be an agricultural *proletariat*. Marxists use the term "lumpen*proletariat*" pejoratively to designate propertyless persons who are not workers and therefore not integral to the capitalist mode of production.

propaganda: any sort of communication aimed at influencing public opinion, in contrast to providing information impartially. The term has a negative connotation, though it need not. It is used most commonly in political contexts, though one can also call advertisements "commercial *propaganda*." Political *propaganda* is usually, but not necessarily, produced by governments. It can include significant and deliberate falsehoods, and typically omits pertinent truths. But a message does not have to be untrue to count as *propaganda*. What matters is its intended function.

property: in social and political theory, it is often useful to think of *property* as a set of RIGHTS – to control (control rights) and/or benefit from (revenue rights) productive assets. These assets may be tangible, like **means of production**, or intangible, like talents. Where *property* rights assign significant POWERS to individuals or collections of individuals, there is "private *property*." Where they assign significant powers to public entities, there is "social" or "public *property*." "Personal *property*" designates items owned by individuals that are not, in the main, productive assets.

proposition: in philosophy and logic, a *proposition* is an assertion that is either true or false. Declarative sentences that make assertions express *propositions*.

prudence: enlightened self-interest. Individuals act *prudently* when they seek to realize what they would desire, given full knowledge and adequate reflection. They act *imprudently* when the actual desires that motivate their actions fall short on these accounts or when they exhibit what Aristotle (384?–322? BC) called "weakness of will" – that is, when they fail to do what they know to be best.

radicalism: *radical* is often used to mean "extreme." Some LEFT currents in the United States used the term, throughout the nineteenth and twentieth centuries, to designate any generally **progressive** movement that sought fundamental institutional change. It was in this sense that **New Left** militants referred to themselves as *radicals*. In Europe and Latin America, the term more commonly designates political parties of a **moderate** or even CONSERVATIVE but generally anti-clerical cast.

rationalism: colloquially, *rationalists* are dedicated to regarding reason alone as authoritative in determining opinions or courses of action. In **epistemology**, however, the term designates the principal rival to **empiricism**. *Rationalists* do not deny the importance of empirical evidence in science. But they do deny that all scientific knowledge comes directly or indirectly from sense experience. Anyone who holds that there are "innate ideas" or, in more contemporary terms, that some knowledge is, as it were, "hard wired" into our brains and is therefore not learned, is a *rationalist*.

reactionary: the term can be used loosely to refer to any extreme CONSERVATIVE position. Strictly speaking, though, *reactionaries* are not conservatives. What they advocate is not exactly gradual change, but a return to a lost or, more often, imagined past. *Reactionaries* do not so much oppose change as *react* against it.

Realpolitik: power politics, implemented by governments, motivated by what is regarded as NATIONAL self-interest, in contrast to IDEOLOGICALLY or MORALLY grounded principles.

rebellion: armed resistance to one's government, with or more usually without deliberate REVOLUTIONARY intentions. *Rebel* can also be used to designate individuals who evince attitudes of defiance or opposition to prevailing *authorities* of any sort.

reification: in philosophy, the mistake of treating as a thing (*res* in Latin) something that is not a thing. Some twentieth-century MARXISTS, including **Critical Theorists**, made extensive use of this concept in their efforts to understand ways of thinking that sustain CAPITALISM.

reformism: the term designates any of a variety of political strategies that aim to institute LIBERAL or SOCIALIST objectives through piece-meal reforms. Among socialists, *reform* normally contrasts with REVOLUTION, though the difference can be obscured when fundamental "structural *reforms*" are proposed.

Romanticism: in addition to its many non-political meanings, the term refers to an artistic and intellectual movement that began in the late eighteenth century in Europe and continued to develop for several decades thereafter that had important implications for political thought. In partial opposition to **Enlightenment** thinking, *Romantics* emphasized feeling and, more generally, the affective side of experience and also the importance of nature and "spirit." They also placed a particular significance on the achievements of heroic individuals. G.W.F. Hegel (1770–1831) was perhaps the most influential and penetrating thinker whose work falls broadly under this description.

secession: the act of formally withdrawing from a settled political entity. Prior to the US Civil War (1861–1865), southern states *seceded* from the United States. Quebecers who seek independence from Canada are also *secessionists*. There are many *secessionist* movements in the world today.

Glossary

secularism: *secular* contrasts with "theological" or "religious." *Secularism*, accordingly, is the belief that ecclesiastical institutions and their concerns should not impinge upon governance and, more generally, on institutional arrangements and modes of thought. *Secular* is also used in economic theory to describe processes that last for extended periods of time.

separatism: the idea that particular social or political groups (women, members of oppressed racial minorities, members of religious sects) should voluntarily *separate* themselves as much as possible from the institutional arrangements of the dominant CULTURE and, wherever possible, forge their own institutional forms.

skepticism: an **epistemological** stance taken up with respect to some claim or category of claims or to knowledge generally, according to which one should withhold assent from positions that cannot be established according to (usually rather stringent) standards for belief acceptance.

slavery: *slaves* are **property**; slave societies therefore accord property RIGHTS in persons. *Slavery* has existed in many societies throughout history. An extreme version was the system of "chattel *slavery*" that obtained in the American South before the Civil War (1861–1865), where slaves had virtually no rights against their owners. In many societies, the vast majority of direct producers were *slaves*.

social construction: social phenomena, including attitudes, institutional arrangements, and structures, that emerge as unintended consequences of the activities of individuals or groups are *socially constructed*. How important *social construction* is in the formation of social facts is always an open question. Those who use the term are inclined to suppose that it is overwhelmingly or perhaps even uniquely important. For example, when RACE is said to be *socially constructed*, the implication is that there are no extra-social (presumably biological) factors that importantly affect the formation of racial categories.

social contract: in **contractarian** political philosophy, a *social contract* is a (usually hypothetical) agreement that forms the basis for the establishment of a political regime or for the relation between a people and its government. The term is also used to indicate any (implicit) understanding underlying prevailing social or political practices.

solidarity: unity of purpose and affect. Relations between individuals based on social bonds, rather than explicit or hypothetical agreements, can be described as social *solidarities*. To act in *solidarity* with an individual or group is to support their endeavors either symbolically or at some personal or collective cost or both.

sovereignty: supreme **authority** over a given territory or population.

state of nature: in **contractarian** political philosophy, an imagined state of affairs in which what is to be accounted for by a **social contract** is abstracted away. If, for example, the aim is to account for the establishment of **de jure** political **authority**, the *state of nature* would be a condition in which political authority and all its actual or imaginable consequences are absent.

strategy: contrasts with **tactics**, though the distinction is vague and the terms are sometimes used interchangeably. *Strategies* in military operations and, by extension, in other endeavors involve large-scale or long-range planning with a view to realizing particular objectives. To think *strategically* is to adopt a long-range vision. *Strategic* action can involve (temporary) retreats undertaken in order ultimately to advance towards one's goals.

structuralism: an intellectual tendency begun in the late nineteenth century by linguists and psychologists that became influential in the social sciences and in literary and artistic criticism from roughly the 1950s through the 1970s. *Structuralism* explores relations between ostensibly universal formal elements of social or psychological phenomena upon which particular *structures* are built, and through which meanings are constituted. Influential *structuralist* thinkers included the linguist Ferdinand de Saussure (1857–1913) and the anthropologist Claude Lévi-Strauss (1908–). Louis Althusser (1918–1990) is widely regarded as a "*structuralist* Marxist," and Jacques Lacan (1901–1981) sought to recast psychoanalytic theory according to *structuralist* principles. *Structuralism* also had important implications for literary criticism. Many **postmodernist** ventures in the social sciences and in literary and artistic criticism represent themselves as *post-structuralist*, the implication being that they grow out of the *structuralist* tradition, but reject or otherwise **react** against many of its tenets.

superstructure: in HISTORICAL MATERIALISM, legal and political phenomena are considered *superstructural* insofar as they are **functionally explained** by the economic base – that is, the set of **production relations** or **mode of production** in place.

surplus value: in the "classical" political economy of the late eighteenth and early nineteenth centuries and therefore in MARXIST economic theory, VALUES determine prices. In Marxist theory, workers' wages are normally equal to the value of their LABOR power. But labor power produces value in excess of its own value. That extra or *surplus value* is appropriated by capitalists, who supply workers with the **means of production** without which they would be unable to expend their labor power.

tactics: contrasts with **strategy**, though the distinction is vague and the terms are sometimes used interchangeably. *Tactics* in military operations and, by extension, elsewhere are means employed for realizing strategic objectives.

theism/atheism/agnosticism: positions on the existence of God (conceived as an omnipotent, omniscient, perfectly good Being with whom individuals can have personal relationships). *Theists* believe that God exists; *atheists* deny that God exists; and *agnostics* believe that either God does or does not exist but that we don't (or can't) know which. *Agnostics* are **skeptics** with respect to the existence of God. *Theism* contrasts with "deism," a position held by some **Enlightenment** thinkers and by many of the founders of the American republic. Deists believe in a supreme power, but they deny that it plays any role in human affairs or that individuals can have a personal relationship with it.

third camp: during the **Cold War**, *third campers* were SOCIALISTS, usually TROTSKYISTS, who, unlike orthodox Trotskyists, opposed the American and Soviet systems equally.

third way: a term invoked, with no clear meaning, by former SOCIALISTS, SOCIAL DEMOCRATS, and LIBERALS in the 1990s to designate political **strategies** that aim at achieving traditional LEFT objectives, while somehow transcending the old divisions between the Left and the Right. The term has largely passed into much deserved desuetude.

Third World: A name used to describe the countries of Asia, Africa, and Latin America, their peoples, and sometimes also persons of *Third World* origin living in the West ("the First World"). The term came into general currency following the 1955 Bandung Conference of "non-aligned" NATIONS, countries not formally allies of either the United States or the Soviet Union ("the Second World") in the **Cold War**. The name self-consciously invokes "the Third Estate" of old regime France, the "commoners" who waged and won the

French REVOLUTION. *Third World* countries were, from the beginning, too dissimilar in history, CULTURE, and levels of development to constitute a genuine bloc in world politics, despite the efforts of many to forge the requisite **solidarities**. Many, but not all, **New Leftists** were *Third Worldists*, engaged in solidarity work with *Third World* liberation struggles. Many New Left militants believed that the Third World had effectively superseded the working classes of developed countries as the principal agent of revolutionary change. With the end of the Cold War, *Third World* identifications and *Third Worldist* politics have been in decline. The decline has been exacerbated by the increasingly evident shortcomings of many *Third World* governments and political movements.

Transcendentalism: An early nineteenth-century American literary, political, and philosophical movement, based, in part, on ideas derived from post-Hegelian German **Romanticism**. Leading *Transcendentalists* included Ralph Waldo Emerson (1803–1882) and Henry David Thoreau (1817–1862). In **Kantian** philosophy, *Transcendental* arguments provide an account of the conditions for the possibility of some form of experience, regardless of **skeptical** doubts about its reality.

tyranny/despotism: a *tyranny* is an UNJUST and generally lawless regime. In modern times, the term implies censure. However, in ancient Greece, a *tyrant* was just a usurper of rightful (LEGITIMATE) power. Inasmuch as tyrants sometimes overturned the governments of city-states with popular support, being a *tyrant* had no necessary negative connotation. Not so in modern times. In contemporary usage, the term is sometimes interchangeable with *despot*. In ancient Greece, *despots* were absolute rulers – **dictators**, in modern terms – who were not subject to the rule of law. *Despots* often ruled *tyrannically* (in the modern sense of the term). But "benevolent *despotism*" was and still is a theoretical possibility. In contrast, *tyranny*, in modern usage, can never be benevolent. Both terms are sometimes used loosely, outside expressly political contexts.

utopianism/dystopianism: a term used, almost always with a negative connotation, to refer to social programs that aim at bettering or perfecting the human condition, but that are, for one reason or another, impossible to implement. It is widely believed that *utopian* ventures lead to disastrous consequences. The term was coined by Sir Thomas More (1478–1535). In 1516, he used it as the title for a book about a perfect world. It is a neologism formed of Greek words meaning "no place." A *dystopia*, such as George Orwell's *1984*, is a negative *utopia*.

Glossary

utopian socialism: a disparaging name, given by Karl Marx (1818–1883), to the theories of his SOCIALIST predecessors. According to Marx, *utopian socialists* went astray when they supposed that socialism could be brought into being by appealing to moral principles, in contrast to the **endogenous** causal dynamic HISTORICAL MATERIALISM identifies. Nowadays, the term is used to describe anyone who argues for socialism by appealing to its **normative** superiority over CAPITALISM.

vanguard/avant-garde: the term is of military origin – a *vanguard* (advanced guard) goes ahead of the main military force. This is the sense of the term implicit in discussion of *avant-garde* art, and it is sometimes used in this sense in political discourse as well. In LENINIST theory, a *vanguard* is a REVOLUTIONARY political party that introduces "revolutionary **consciousness**" to the working masses, directing their struggle against CAPITALISM and for COMMUNISM.

vice: contrasts with **virtue** in **Aristotelian** philosophy. In colloquial speech, *vice* is often used loosely to denote any bad habit or **character** trait.

virtue: for Plato (427?–347? BC), a *virtue* is what makes an object perform its function well. Thus, the *virtue* of a runner is speed. Aristotle (384?–322? BC) incorporated this notion into a general account of human flourishing. In **Aristotelian** philosophy, the *virtues* are character traits conducive to the realization of **essential** human capacities. The REPUBLICAN tradition in political theory emphasized specifically civic *virtues* – character traits that are conducive to the flourishing of political COMMUNITIES. "*Virtue* **ethics**" refers to ethical theories that, following Aristotle's lead, identify acting well with exhibiting *virtuous* behavior, downplaying or rejecting specifically MORAL notions of acting on **agent-neutral** principles.

workerism: in SOCIALIST theory, a term used to describe political **strategies** that focus mainly or exclusively on the LABOR MOVEMENT or, more generally, the working CLASS.

Young Hegelianism: The *Young* – or, as they are sometimes called, LEFT – *Hegelians* were a group of **radical** students and young professors at the University of Berlin in the (late) 1830s and (early) 1840s. They sought to derive REVOLUTIONARY conclusions from Hegelian philosophy. Unlike their rival RIGHT Hegelians, many of whom held prominent university and government posts, and unlike G.W.F. Hegel (1770–1831) himself, the *Young Hegelians* were materialists, not **idealists**; and also **atheists**. The leading figure of the group was Ludwig Feuerbach (1804–1872). Other prominent *Young Hegelians* included David Strauss (1808–1874), Bruno Bauer (1809–1882), and Karl Marx (1818–1883). Marx broke with Feuerbach and the other *Young Hegelians* while he was still in his early twenties. By the end of the 1840s, the movement had effectively ceased to exist. *Young Hegelian* thinking was revived by mid-twentieth-century "MARXIST humanists" intent on recovering the letter and spirit of Marx's early work.